Windows 98 Multimedia: Lights! Camera! Action!

Adam Vujic, et al.

201 West 103rd Street
Indianapolis, IN 46290

Windows 98 Multimedia: Lights! Camera! Action!

Copyright © 1999 by Que Corporation

International Standard Book Number: 0-7897-1857-x

Library of Congress Catalog Card Number: 98-86956

Printed in the United States of America

First Printing: January 1999

01   00   99   4   3   2   1

Trademarks

Warning and Disclaimer

Executive Editor
Grace Buechlein

Acquisitions Editor
Tracy M. Williams

Development Editor
Gregory Harris

Managing Editor
Brice Gosnell

Project Editor
Kevin Laseau

Copy Editor
Pamela Woolf

Indexers
Heather Goens
Mary Gammons

Proofreader
Benjamin Berg

Technical Editor
Kyle Bryant
Eric Richardson

Software Development Specialist
Jack Belbot

Interior Design
Gary Adair

Cover Design
Dan Armstrong

Layout Technicians
Ayanna Lacey
Heather Hiatt Miller
Amy Parker

Contents at a Glance

Contents

About the Authors

Adam Vujic is a Microsoft MVP (most valuable professional) who specializes in providing technical support for the Windows 95 and Windows 98 operating systems. Adam strives to provide assistance to Windows users in the simplest and most direct way possible. He has many months of hands-on experience with the latest Microsoft operating system. He was also one of a handful chosen to assist users in the Windows 98 Consumer Preview Program, of which there were 100,000 participants. Today, you can find Adam on the Microsoft public newsgroups, where he devotes much of his time to answering technical questions about Windows multimedia. He can be reached at `avujic@entelchile.net`.

Phil Callihan is the MIS manager at the National Center for Manufacturing Sciences (NCMS), a research and development consortium based in Ann Arbor, Michigan. Phil has seven years of experience with Windows, UNIX, and Macintosh systems and holds both the MSCE and MCT certifications from Microsoft. In addition to his employment at NCMS, he works as consultant and performs training in Microsoft NT BackOffice products relating to Internet collaborative technologies. He is a 1993 graduate of the University of Michigan. Phil lives in Ann Arbor, Michigan, with his wife Lisa, their daughter Emma, and the family dog Tribble. He was a contributing author on Que's *Platinum Edition Using Windows 98* and *Special Edition Using Windows 98* books. Phil can be reached on the Internet at `philc@ncms.org` and on his home page `http://mis.ncms.org/philc/phil.htm`.

Robert DeStefano, a technical support specialist for Sony Electronics Inc., Microsoft MVP, and computer consultant, has been working with computers for over a decade. Robert started using a computer when the Commodore 64 was introduced. He completed two years of consumer electronic product service training in 1991. Posting in the Microsoft newsgroups for end user software support, he has achieved the MVP award (most valued professional) two years in a row. Robert lives in Cape Coral, Florida, with his wife Melissa and their cocker spaniel Sidney.

Scott Downie wonders if you know somebody who surveyed fallout shelters in central Kansas; received a B.S. in electrical engineering; analyzed Sidewinder air-to-air missile data; worked as a full-time sound man; received a B.F.A. in music theory; tuned and rebuilt pianos and harpsichords; taught electronics at a junior college (while playing keyboards and bassoon in various ensembles); received an M.A. in the history of science (while teaching the same); worked as the senior music editor and technical director for a player-piano company; worked as an engineer/sound designer at a company that made MIDI equipment and sound cards; generated printed and online documentation for Macintosh and Windows consumer software; got accepted to law school; changed his mind about law school; worked as a quality engineer at Intel; and then wrote some more software documentation? You do? When did you meet him?

Bruce A. Hallberg has been in the computer industry since 1980. He has consulted nationally on accounting, distribution, and manufacturing system implementations for small, medium, and large companies. He is currently director of IS and corporate services for a public biotechnology company located in the Silicon Valley area of California. Since 1992, he has authored over 20 books on a variety of computing topics, including best-sellers on subjects such as Windows 98, Windows NT, and Microsoft Office.

Michael E. Porter is a systems consultant for the Triad SS company in Dayton, Ohio. Mike earned a bachelor of science degree from Miami University in Oxford, Ohio, and a master of business administration with a concentration in MIS from the University of Dayton. Mike is also a senior instructor with Learning Tree International focusing on Microsoft operating systems, TCP/IP, and systems security. He has a background as a NetWare systems administrator, NT administrator, and programmer in C++. Mike currently holds an MCSE and is in the process of completing the CISSP designation. He and his wife Lisa live in Oakwood, Ohio, with their basset hound Hank.

Dave Adams Saltz is a Microsoft Certified Systems Engineer (MCSE) and has been named a Microsoft most valuable professional (MVP) for the past three years. Dave is a network specialist and a self-avowed technology junkie, as well as president of GenesisPC, a consulting firm focusing on Windows NT networking, planning, and implementation. He lives in Shrewsbury, Massachusetts, with his very understanding wife Vicki and his golden retriever Riley.

Serdar Yegulalp is associate technology editor for *Windows* magazine and has contributed to other Que publications in the past, such as *Platinum Edition Using Windows NT Server 4* and *Windows NT 4.0 Installation and Configuration*. When not up to his elbows writing about or working with Windows 98 and NT, he composes music and writes many other things (such as fiction) which haven't been published yet. Email him at syegul@winmag.com.

Tell Us What You Think!

As the reader of this book, *you* are our most important critic and commentator. We value your opinion and want to know what we're doing right, what we could do better, what areas you'd like to see us publish in, and any other words of wisdom you're willing to pass our way.

As the executive editor for the operating systems team at Macmillan Computer Publishing, I welcome your comments. You can fax, email, or write me directly to let me know what you did or didn't like about this book—as well as what we can do to make our books stronger.

Please note that I cannot help you with technical problems related to the topic of this book, and that due to the high volume of mail I receive, I might not be able to reply to every message.

When you write, please be sure to include this book's title and authors as well as your name and phone or fax number. I will carefully review your comments and share them with the authors and editors who worked on the book.

Fax: 317-581-4663
Email: opsys@mcp.com

Mail: Executive Editor
          Operating Systems
          Macmillan Computer Publishing
          201 West 103rd Street
          Indianapolis, IN 46290 USA

Introduction

Welcome to the wonderful world of Windows 98 multimedia! Prepare yourself to explore all the exciting capabilities of your computer, entertain yourself with music and graphics, and learn about the nitty-gritty operation of your system. In a way, multimedia has been a part of personal computing since the very beginning, in the form of the tiny speakers that produced the familiar beep on bootup. True PC multimedia arose in the early 1990s as one of the strong potentials offered by Windows 3.x. Unfortunately, the technology, still in its infancy, was often a little too obscure for the everyday user. Configuring sounds card interrupts (IRQs) and other settings—often in DOS-based programs—was infrequently an intuitive process. And, even if you got everything properly configured, the available hardware—16-bit sound cards, early CD-ROM drives, 256-color video cards, 9600 baud modems, and processors that are molasses-slow by today's standards—lacked the juice to provide a full multimedia experience. As a result, the initial buzz about multimedia subsided to a low hum.

But Windows 95, along with concurrent hardware improvements—changed the multimedia picture and the process has continued with Windows 98. Advances in technology have led to much more powerful, entertaining, and easy-to-use applications for enjoying graphics, video, music, digitized sound, and more. Hardware, from fast processors, huge hard drives, 16-speed CD-ROM drives, 3D video cards, and 32-bit sound cards, is much improved. At the same time, Windows 98 provides a standardized interface for configuring these various resources in a similar manner—greatly simplifying the task for the user. (And that's when Windows 98 doesn't go ahead and configure the devices for you!) Moreover, Windows 98 comes with built-in support for a wide variety of multimedia formats, and you can download a variety of other viewers and editors from the Internet. You'll be amazed at the variety of file types you can access with a simple double-click—this is a far cry from the days of DOS when you needed to install and configure separate programs to access nearly every type of graphic or sound file. Windows 98 goes beyond support for basic multimedia offering more advanced hardware and software support, such as Universal Serial Bus (USB) devices, DVD, streaming video, 3D video and multiple monitor capability.

The Purpose of this Book

This book is designed both to give beginning Windows 98 users an introduction to the amazing capabilities of their computers and to give more Windows-savvy users a guide for installing and configuring a wide variety of multimedia devices. Along the way, we'll describe the inner workings of much of the multimedia technology.

- First you'll get started with a basic understanding of sound, video, and WebTV technology.

- You'll learn how to customize your Windows 98 interface with your favorite color scheme, system sounds, desktop wallpaper, and all-in-one themes.

- You'll take a tour of the alphabet soup of multimedia devices, from CD-ROM drives to MIDI. You'll see how they work and how to install and configure them.

- Next you'll get the lowdown on top multimedia applications that let you unlock the power of graphics editing, video playback, and more. You'll even see how to take advantage of the many multimedia capabilities of the Internet.

- In the last section, you'll cover advanced multimedia concepts from using multiple monitors to troubleshooting common problems to installing the enhancements of Microsoft Plus! 98.

Along the way, you'll be able to take advantage of a number of Internet sites where you can check out more detailed information, download the latest version of a program, or enjoy multimedia file samples. But you don't need Web access to enjoy the multimedia experience—the accompanying CD-ROM contains sample files, an online glossary, and other enhancements. Using the CD-ROM is as simple as popping it into your CD-ROM drive and following the onscreen prompts.

So why wait? Let's begin with the basics of multimedia. By the time you've finished, you'll have not only a greater knowledge of your system's capabilities but also a much greater enjoyment of Windows 98's entertainment potential.

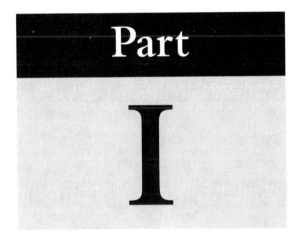

Part

I

Getting Started

Chapter

1

Getting Started with Sound

by Adam Vujic

Windows 98 offers a cornucopia of recorded, sampled, and synthesized sounds to entertain you, notify you of system events, and let you customize your Windows interface. In general, playing a sound is as simple as double-clicking its icon in the My Computer or Windows Explorer windows. Many sounds are available by default in Windows 98, and more can come through add-ons such as Microsoft Plus or by downloading them from the Internet. You can even record your own sound bites. As if all this digitized sound weren't enough, Windows 98 also lets you play any audio CD by dropping it into your CD-ROM drive.

In this chapter I'll introduce you to the process of playing and recording sounds and playing audio CDs. Before you begin, however, you should check the volume configuration of both Windows 98 and any external speakers.

Adjusting Volume Controls

Before playing any sound, it's a good idea to make sure all volumes are set at the correct levels. This includes your speakers, sound card, and Windows 98 itself.

1. If you have powered speakers, ensure that their volume controls are set to an appropriate level. One-quarter to halfway should be adequate.

2. Follow your speaker's cable to the back of your computer and see where it connects to your sound card. If you see a small dial in the surrounding area, adjust it to the halfway level. (This dial is not found on all sound cards.)

3. On your computer screen, locate the yellow Speaker icon next to the clock in the lower-right corner of the taskbar. Click the icon once and a volume slider appears (see Figure 1.1). Drag the slider to one-quarter or one-half of maximum volume.

That's all there is to it! Your computer is now ready to play sound.

WARNING	When in doubt, it's better to set a volume control lower rather than higher. This way there is less chance of an unusually loud sound causing damage to your speakers or ears.

Figure 1.1

The master volume control is accessible at all times by clicking the taskbar Speaker icon.

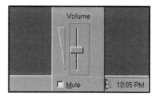

Showing/Hiding the Taskbar Volume Control Icon

In some cases, the yellow Speaker icon isn't there. There are a few possible causes for this problem:

- Your computer does not have a sound card installed. This possibility is not likely considering that you are reading a book about multimedia.

- Your sound driver is not set up correctly, or it is conflicting with another device in your computer. To see if the latter is true, do the following:

  1. Click Start, point to Settings, and then click Control Panel.

  2. Double-click the System icon. The System Properties dialog box appears.

  3. On the Device Manager tab, click the plus (+) next to sound, video and game controllers.

  4. Look at your sound card's entry. If there is a red cross or yellow exclamation mark next to it, your sound card is not working properly. Refer to Chapter 19, "Common Problems and Their Solutions," for some suggestions on how to resolve this problem.

- The third cause for a hidden Speaker icon is an option located in the Control Panel. You can configure this option by following these steps:

  1. Click Start, point to Settings, and then click Control Panel.

  2. Double-click the Multimedia icon. The Multimedia Properties dialog box appears (see Figure 1.2).

  3. Check Show volume control on the taskbar to show the taskbar Speaker icon. Uncheck it to hide the Speaker icon.

  4. Click OK to save changes.

Adjusting Individual Volume Controls

To satisfy power users' needs, Windows 98 divides sound into a number of different sources, each with its own volume control. The most common sources are Wave, MIDI, CD Audio, Line-In, and the Microphone.

> **NOTE** The exact number and type of sound sources vary among sound cards, so what you see on your screen might be slightly different than what is shown here. Chapter 6, "Knowing Your Multimedia Devices," provides a more detailed explanation for each of these sources.

Perform the following steps to adjust the volume of the sound source.

Figure 1.2

The option to configure the taskbar Speaker icon is hidden within the Control Panel.

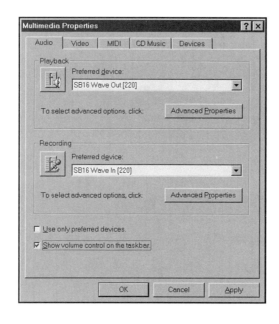

 1. Double-click the yellow Speaker icon in the lower-right corner of your screen and the Volume Control dialog box appears (see Figure 1.3).

Figure 1.3

A complete range of volume controls is accessible by double-clicking the taskbar Speaker icon.

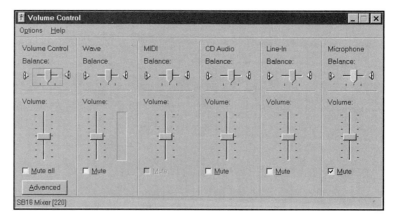

2. Drag the appropriate vertical slider to the desired level. For example, to set CD Audio to its maximum volume, drag the Volume slider under CD Audio up to the highest position.

3. To mute a source, click the appropriate Mute box. A check mark appears indicating that the mute is in effect. Click the box again to unmute the source.

> **NOTE** The MIDI Mute box might be grayed out on your Volume Control display, particularly if you have a recent sound card from the Sound Blaster® family. If you'd like to prevent MIDI sound from being heard, then reduce the Volume slider to its minimum level.

Adjusting Recording Volume Controls

You can often get by with only adjusting the volume controls. However, another set of controls exists that allows you to have greater control when recording sound.

For example, you might want to record yourself singing along to your favorite song, which is on an audio CD. Windows 98's recording controls enable you to select the CD Audio and Microphone sources, while ignoring all other sound coming through the Wave, MIDI, and Line-In sources.

Before you can select recording sources, you need to bring up the Recording Control display.

1. Double-click the speaker icon on the taskbar to open the Volume Control applet.

2. Click the Options menu and choose Properties. The Properties dialog box appears (see Figure 1.4).

Figure 1.4

Customize the Volume Control display to suit your individual needs.

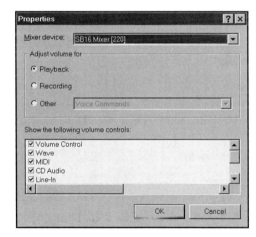

3. Under the heading Adjust volume for, select Recording.

4. Click OK and the Recording Control dialog box is displayed (see Figure 1.5).

Figure 1.5

*You can select
which sound
sources to record
from in the
Recording
Control dialog
box.*

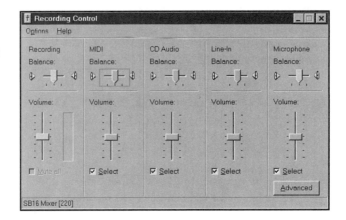

Figure 1.5

*You can select
which sound
sources to record
from in the
Recording
Control dialog
box.*

> **NOTE**   You might find that the Recording Volume slider is unavailable (refer
> to Figure 1.5). This omission is common with many sound drivers and
> can safely be ignored. If the Master Recording volume is grayed out on your system
> and you'd like to adjust it, then adjust the volumes of all individual sound sources.

Despite the Recording Controls title for this dialog box, the Volume sliders here
have exactly the same effect as the normal Volume Control sliders. In fact, if you
move a slider here and then return to the Volume Control display, you'll notice
that the respective volume slider has moved to the same position.

The primary difference in the Recording Control display is that Mute boxes have
been replaced with Select boxes. These boxes are used to select which sources you
would like to record from.

Building on the previous example, to record from both an audio CD and a
microphone, you need to make sure that the Select boxes are checked under the
Microphone and CD Audio headings. Then uncheck the remaining Select boxes
to ensure that all other sources are not included in the recording. If one of the
default Windows sounds happens to play while you're singing it will be ignored.

Configuring the Volume Control Display

As you might have noticed, not all of the volume controls (Wave, MIDI, CD
Audio) are regularly used. Fortunately Microsoft understands this and has given
you a way to remove the rarely used controls, and add the controls that you do
need.

> **NOTE**   The term *PC speaker* is very misleading. It does not refer to your
> computer's main speakers but to the tiny speaker located inside the
> system box. The PC speaker is a prehistoric component that has not changed much
> since the early 1980s. The only time you might hear output from this speaker is when
> your computer powers up. Beep!

Perform the following steps to add or remove volume controls.

1. Double-click the Speaker icon on the taskbar to bring up the Volume Control applet.

2. Click the Options menu and choose Properties. The Properties dialog box appears (refer to Figure 1.4).

3. Under the heading Show the following volume controls is a list of all available sound sources for your particular sound card (you might need to scroll down to see the full list). Uncheck a box and the respective sound source is removed from your Volume Control display. Check a box and the sound source is added to the display.

4. Click OK to save changes and return to the Volume Control applet.

Adjusting Individual Balance Controls

In addition to loudness, the *balance* of a sound source can also be controlled individually.

To shift the balance toward the left speaker, move the horizontal Balance slider to the left. Moving the same slider toward the right has the opposite effect.

> **NOTE** If the balance controls don't seem to work, check the balance dials on your speakers; they should be set to halfway.

Testing Your Speaker Setup

Believe it or not, the balance controls are a great way to test if your speakers are set up correctly (that is, left speaker on the left, right speaker on the right).

Follow these steps

1. Insert an audio CD into your CD or DVD drive. The first track should start playing in a few seconds.

2. Double-click the Speaker icon on the taskbar to open the Volume Control applet.

3. Under the heading CD Audio, drag the Balance slider all the way to the left.

   ■ If sound is heard only from the left speaker, your speakers are set up correctly.

   ■ If sound is heard only from the right speaker, swap your speakers. The left speaker should now be where the right speaker was and vice versa.

Getting Started with Sound

4. Drag the Balance slider back to its original position in the center.

> **NOTE** The Balance slider under the heading Microphone is grayed out because the majority of microphones are not stereo devices. That is, they only record input through a single channel.

Advanced Playback Volume Controls

Depending on the installed sound card and driver, you might have the ability to set some extra options in the Volume Control applet. The most common controls are bass and treble and simulated 3D effects.

To enable advance volume playback controls

1. Double-click the Speaker icon on the taskbar to bring up the Volume Control applet.

2. Click the Options menu.

3. Next, take a look at the Advanced Controls option.

   - If there is a check mark next to this option, it is already enabled. Click this option to remove the Advanced button from the Volume Control display.

   - If there is no check mark next to this option, it is disabled. Click this option to add the Advanced button to the Volume Control display.

   - If this option is grayed out, your sound card or driver does not support this feature.

Adjusting Advanced Playback Volume Controls

When Advanced Controls are enabled, an Advanced button appears on the Volume Control display. Click it to see which options are available for your sound card.

> **NOTE** The availability and range of effects on your system is determined by your sound card and sound driver. Most older sound cards support basic controls only (such as bass and treble) whereas many recent sound cards support 3D and reverberation effects. Updating your sound driver can sometimes add new options to the Advanced Controls dialog box.

As an example, Sound Blaster 16® owners might see Bass and Treble options only (see Figure 1.6). To decrease one of these effects, drag the appropriate slider toward the left. To increase an effect, drag the slider toward the right.

Figure 1.6
You might enjoy increasing the Bass control to maximum, but your neighbors sure won't.

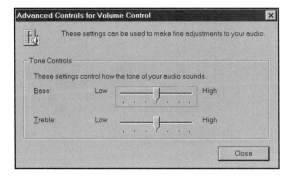

Three-dimensional and reverberation effects are also available on some sound cards. These can be enabled or disabled by clicking the appropriate check boxes.

With some early sound cards, 3D effects can adversely affect the overall sound quality. If you have one of these cards, it is preferable to disable any 3D audio settings. However, recent sound cards, such as Sound Blaster Live!®, are designed to take advantage of 3D and environment effects, and they provide a much better experience when these features are enabled. See Chapter 6.

Advanced Recording Volume Controls

Many sound cards include extra options for recording. Here, you will learn how to enable and disable these controls, as well as how to adjust them to suit your particular needs.

You'll need to bring up the Recording Volume Control before continuing (refer to the section "Adjusting Recording Volume Controls" earlier in this chapter for instructions).

To enable advanced recording volume controls

1. In the Recording Control display click the Options menu.

2. Next, take a look at the Advanced Controls option.

    ■ If there is a check mark next to this option, it is already enabled. Click this option to remove the Advanced button from the Recording Control display.

    ■ If there is no check mark next to this option, it is disabled. Click this option to add the Advanced button to the Recording Control display.

    ■ If this option is grayed out, your sound card or driver does not support this feature. Installing an updated sound driver might enable these features.

Adjusting Advanced Recording Volume Controls

When Advanced Controls are enabled, an Advanced button appears on the Recording Control display. Click it to see which options are available for your sound card.

> **NOTE**   Bass and Treble options are typically unavailable in the Advanced Controls for Microphone dialog box, so don't worry if they appear grayed out.

The most commonly available option in the Advanced Controls for Microphone dialog box controls how sound is heard through a microphone. It might be labeled Microphone Gain Control or Advanced Gain Control, depending on your system (see Figure 1.7). Typically sound recorded from a microphone is much clearer and more audible when this option is enabled. Unless you are having trouble with your microphone, I recommend turning on Microphone Gain Control. Click Close to save changes.

Figure 1.7

Enable the Microphone Gain Control option to increase the clarity of your sound recordings.

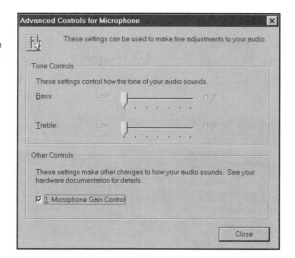

Choosing an Alternative Mixer Device

With a minority of sound drivers, there might be a choice of more than one mixer in the Volume Control applet.

Here's how to choose a different mixer.

1. Double-click the Speaker icon on the taskbar to bring up the Volume Control applet.

2. Click the Options menu and choose Properties.

3. Select a different mixer from the Mixer device drop-down list.

4. Click OK to save changes and return to the Volume Control display.

An entirely different set of controls is now displayed. While some sound sources might have the same labels, moving a slider will control a different sound device (for example, a secondary sound card) in your computer.

Playing Sound

There are three main ways to play a sound in Windows 98:

- Double-clicking a sound's icon in Explorer

- Starting a sound player and then opening the sound itself

- Dragging a sound's icon and dropping it onto a sound player

NOTE Believe it or not, there are even more ways to play a sound than are described here. Most of these methods involve previewing sound, which is covered later in Chapter 13, "Working with Multimedia Files."

Playing a Sound via Explorer

This method of playing a sound is the most common. All you need to do is find the sound you want to play then double-click it.

Sound files are represented by the following icons:

MIDI

Wave

AU, SND, and RealAudio

AIFF

NOTE As shown previously, Wave files are represented by a blank page with a small yellow speaker. Similarly, a small red speaker indicates an AIFF sound file, whereas a green speaker represents an AU, SND, or RealAudio file.

In the following example you play the Windows start-up sound:

1. Click Start and then Run.

2. Type the following and press Enter.

```
c:\windows\media
```

A folder appears containing all the sounds installed by Windows (see Figure 1.8).

Figure 1.8

The Microsoft sound is one of several multimedia files you'll find in the Media folder.

3. Double-click the icon labeled "The Microsoft Sound." An appropriate player (for example, ActiveMovie) opens and begins playing the sound. After the sound has finished, Windows automatically closes the player.

Opening a Sound via Explorer

Windows 98 also gives you the option of opening a sound without actually playing it. When a file is opened in this way, the sound will not play until you click the Play button.

In addition, when the sound has finished playing, the player will remain open. This action allows you to modify the sound or play it again if you want.

To open a sound rather than playing it, right-click a sound's icon, then choose Open from the menu that appears.

> **NOTE**   In addition to playing and opening a sound, a third option, Record, is available when you right-click a sound's icon. Choosing this option opens the sound in Sound Recorder without playing it. You might then add effects to the sound or modify its contents using the tools available to you.
>
> For more information on using Sound Recorder, see the "Recording Sound" section later in this chapter.

Playing a Sound via Drag and Drop

Windows 98 supports the drag-and-drop technique throughout the operating system, and multimedia is no exception.

If you already have a sound player open (such as Sound Recorder), drag a sound's icon onto the player to hear the sound.

Playing a Sound via a Sound Player

It is relatively easy to open a sound file from Explorer, but there are times when it is desirable to open a sound from within a sound player.

Sound Recorder is used in the following example, but you can apply the same procedure to almost any sound player.

1. Click Start, point to Programs, Accessories, and Entertainment, then click Sound Recorder.

2. Click File and choose Open. The Open dialog box appears (see Figure 1.9).

Figure 1.9

To open a sound for playing, double-click its icon in the Open dialog box.

3. Locate the sound file on your hard drive and select it.

4. Click Open.

Choosing the Best Sound Player

Microsoft has included a collection of three sound players in Windows 98, two of which have been superceded by the new version of Media Player (included in the Multimedia Update). Following is a description of each player; a summary of their properties is listed in Table 1.1.

- Sound Recorder   This was once the default sound player in Windows, but it has been replaced by ActiveMovie. As the name suggests, Sound Recorder is designed specifically to record sound from an external source (most commonly, a microphone). It can also be used to perform simple modifications to sound files, including adding echo and reverse effects.

- ActiveMovie   This is the default sound player in Windows 98. ActiveMovie is based on the latest sound standards and includes support for streaming audio over the Internet. It also has the capability to play more than one sound at a time.

- Media Player   In previous versions of Windows, Media Player was the primary player for CD Audio and MIDI files. However, due to its lack of support for streaming audio and recording/editing features, it now ranks a distant third behind ActiveMovie and Sound Recorder.

> **WARNING**   Sound Recorder is terrible at handling large sound files. It attempts to load the whole file into memory, regardless of its size. This action can cause your computer to temporarily hang or slow down. To avoid this problem you should play all multimegabyte sounds in ActiveMovie or Media Player.

You can find all of the preceding players on the Start menu, under Programs -> Accessories -> Entertainment.

> **NOTE**   Depending on the options selected when Windows 98 was installed, not all multimedia players might be available on your Start menu. In that case, you'll need to install them via the Add/Remove Programs icon in Control Panel. See Chapter 4, "Configuring Multimedia," for details.

Table 1.1   Summary of Windows 98 Sound Players

	Supported Sound Formats	*Okay For Playing Large Files*	*Records Sound*	*Edits Sound*	*Plays Multiple Sounds at Once*
Sound Recorder	Most formats except streaming audio	No	Yes	Yes	No

	Supported Sound Formats	Okay For Playing Large Files	Records Sound	Edits Sound	Plays Multiple Sounds at Once
ActiveMovie	All popular formats including streaming audio	Yes	No	No	Yes
Media Player	Most formats except streaming audio	No	Yes	No	No

The basic rule is this: If you want to play a sound, use ActiveMovie (or Media Player, if you have installed the Multimedia Update). If you want to record or edit a sound use Sound Recorder.

NOTE Windows 95's Media Player was superceded by ActiveMovie when Windows 98 was released but this didn't last for long. Microsoft decided that Media Player needed an upgrade and has made this available in the form of a Multimedia Update.

Viewing a Sound's Properties

Each sound file carries with it a lot more than just audio data. As with all other file types, Windows 98 can tell you when a sound was created, its exact size in bytes, and even the name of the author.

To view this data, right-click a sound's icon in Explorer and choose Properties. Click the Details tab for more specific information, including the length and quality of the sound (see Figure 1.10).

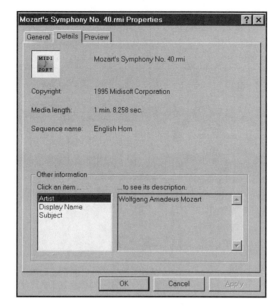

Figure 1.10

Depending on the sound file, you might see additional information such as the composer's name.

Playing an Audio CD

Playing an audio CD in Windows 98 is a easy. Insert the CD into your CD or DVD drive and the first track starts playing; this feature is called *AutoPlay*.

> **NOTE**   If you have installed Plus! 98, an enhanced CD player will open when you insert an audio CD. Information on the Deluxe CD Player can be found in Chapter 17, "Getting the Most Out Of Plus! 98" If you want, you can open the original CD player by clicking Start, pointing to Programs, Accessories, and Entertainment, then clicking CD Player.

Controlling CD Player

Many elements of the CD Player *interface* resemble their real-life counterparts, which helps to reduce the learning curve. See Figure 1.11 for a detailed look at the CD Player interface.

Figure 1.11

CD Player is perhaps the most intuitive application in Windows. Even novice users can begin listening to an audio CD in seconds.

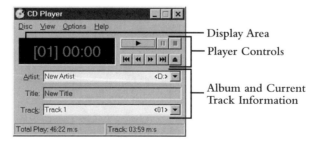

If you prefer to use toolbars rather than menus, CD Player can help. Click the View menu and choose Toolbar for shortcuts to the most common CD player features.

The toolbar buttons perform the following functions:

Edit Play List

Track Time Elapsed

Track Time Remaining

Disc Time Remaining

Random Track Order

Continuous Play

Intro Play

Each of these features is discussed in detail in the following sections.

Setting the Play Mode

Just like a standard CD player, the one in Windows 98 allows you to mix and match three different play modes.

Clicking the Options menu reveals the following play modes:

- Random Order—Selecting this option scrambles the original order of the audio tracks.

- Continuous Play—With this option enabled, your audio tracks loop continuously. CD Player starts over from track one when the final track has finished playing.

- Intro Play—To hear a sneak preview for your audio tracks choose this option. Each track plays for about ten seconds then skips over to the next track.

> **NOTE** If you are using Intro Play mode and want to adjust the delay between tracks, click Options and choose Preferences. Change the setting Intro Play length (seconds) accordingly.

Setting the Display Mode

The CD Player display (in the top-left corner) can show several different pieces of information. Click the View menu to see the available display modes:

- Track Time Elapsed—Shows how much time has gone by since the current track started playing. This is the default display mode.

- Track Time Remaining—This mode shows how much time is left for the current track.

- Disc Time Remaining—The Disc Time Remaining mode shows how much time is left for the entire CD.

> **NOTE** The display's font size can be set to small or large, according to your preference. To do so, click the Options menu and choose Preferences. The font size option is under the heading Display Font.

Entering CD Information

Here's one feature that you won't find on an ordinary CD player. Windows 98's CD Player enables you to enter information specific to each of your music CDs such as album title, artist names, and track names, (see Figure 1.12). Then the next time you insert the CD, all of this information is displayed.

To enter CD information in CD Player:

1. Insert a CD into your CD or DVD drive.

2. When the CD Player applet appears, click the Stop button.

3. Click the Disc menu and choose Edit Play List. The Disc Settings dialog box is displayed.

4. Type the artist's name and album title in the appropriate spaces (if applicable).

5. To enter the names of each audio track, start by clicking Track 1 under Available Tracks.

6. Type the name of the track in the Track # box, then click the Set Name button.

7. Repeat step 6 until all track names have been entered.

Your Disc Settings should now look similar to those in Figure 1.12. Of course, you probably have entered information from a different album. Don't forget to click OK to save the data.

Figure 1.12
Everything you type in the Disc Settings dialog box is saved. It will be there the next time you insert the CD.

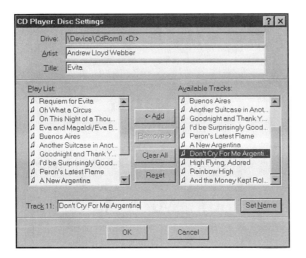

> **NOTE** If you own a large CD collection and want to store all the album information on your computer, you might come across a problem: There is a 64Kb limit on the amount of data that can be stored in CD Player. Data entered above this limit is ignored. A better option for CD collectors is the new Deluxe CD Player included with Plus! 98 (see Chapter 17 for more information).

Creating a Play List

One great feature of CD Player is that it can be programmed to play only your favorite tracks and in the order of your choice. This is known as a *play list*. Perform the following steps to create a play list.

1. Insert the CD into your CD or DVD drive.

2. When the CD Player applet appears, click the Stop button.

3. Click the Disc menu and choose Edit Play List.

4. Click the Clear All button so that Play List box contains no tracks.

5. Under Available Tracks, select a track to be played and click the <-Add button.

6. Repeat step 5 until all chosen tracks have been added to the Play List box. You might add the same track more than once if you want.

7. Click OK to save changes.

After you have created the play list, you might find that some of the tracks are in the wrong order. There's no need to start over—you can move an individual track by selecting it in the Play List box, then dragging it to the new position.

> **NOTE** All information entered into CD Player is stored in a file called
> `cdplayer.ini`. This file is located in your Windows folder. To back up
> your play lists, just copy `cdplayer.ini` to a floppy disk or other medium.

Recording Sound

Unless you own a third-party sound editor, all recording is done with the
Windows 98's Sound Recorder applet. You can open it by clicking Start, pointing
to Programs, Accessories and Entertainment then clicking Sound Recorder.

Recording from a Microphone

Before attempting to record from a microphone there are a few things you should
check:

- Ensure that your microphone is connected to the correct input jack on
  the sound card (usually labeled `mic`). Refer to your sound card's manual
  for details.

- Ensure that your microphone's volume is set to an appropriate level and
  that its Select box is checked. You might want to disable the other sound
  sources (such as Wave, MIDI, CD Audio, and Line-In) to minimize the
  chance of interference. Refer to the section "Adjusting Recording Volume
  Controls" earlier in this chapter for details.

- For best results, I recommend enabling Microphone Gain Control. The
  section "Adjusting Advanced Recording Volume Controls" earlier in this
  chapter has more information on this procedure.

> **NOTE** While a hand-held or karaoke microphone might be adequate, it does
> not always give the best results. Uni-directional models designed
> specifically for computer use produce the clearest and most accurate sound.

You are now ready to begin recording.

1. Click Start, point to Programs, Accessories and Entertainment, then click
   Sound Recorder.

2. When you are ready to record, click the Record button in Sound
   Recorder.

3. Speak into the microphone.

4. When you have finished recording, click the Stop button.

5. Click the Play button to review what you have just recorded.

> **NOTE**   When recording your voice, speak at least eight inches away from the microphone. Try not to hold the microphone too close to your computer's speakers because doing so generates unwanted feedback.

Recording from an Audio CD

In addition to recording from the microphone, Sound Recorder is useful for recording snippets from an audio CD track (no longer than 60 seconds).

Before recording, you need to make sure everything is set up correctly:

1. In the Recording Control applet, ensure that the CD Audio volume is set to an appropriate level and that its Select box is checked. It's a good idea to disable the other sound sources (such as Wave, MIDI, Line-In, and Microphone) to minimize the chance of interference. Refer to the section "Adjusting Recording Volume Controls" earlier in this chapter for details.

2. Insert the audio CD you want to record from. In a few seconds, the CD Player applet appears and begins playing the first track.

3. Click the Stop button shown in Figure 1.13 then select the desired track from the Track drop-down list. Use the Previous Track and Next Track buttons to locate the position of the sound you want to record.

Figure 1.13

Use the controls on the CD Player applet to find the track you want to sample.

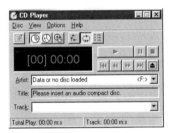

> **NOTE**   You cannot record for longer than 60 seconds; this restriction is a design limitation of the Sound Recorder program. For some suggestions on how to work around this problem, see the "Recording" section in Chapter 19.

You are now ready to begin recording.

1. Click Start, point to Programs, Accessories, and Entertainment, and then click Sound Recorder. Make sure that both Sound Recorder and CD Player are visible onscreen.

2. When you are ready to record, click the Record button in Sound Recorder.

3. Immediately click the Play button in CD Player.

4. When you want to stop recording, click the Stop button in both Sound Recorder and CD Player.

5. Click the Play button to review what you have just recorded.

There will likely be a period of silence at the beginning of the recording and some unwanted sound at the end. For information on how to remove these fragments see the section titled, "Editing Sound with Sound Recorder," in Chapter 12, "Working with Multimedia Applications."

Post-Recording with Sound Recorder

Now that you have recorded a sound, there are several things you can do:

■ Save the Sound to Disk—If you are satisfied with the sound and want to save it, click the File menu and choose Save. Then locate an appropriate folder, type a name for the file, and press Enter.

■ Discard the Sound and Start Over—If you want to try recording again without saving the original sound, click the File menu and choose New. You are now ready to record another sound.

■ Edit the Sound—Sound Recorder includes some basic editing features which you can use to modify the sound. See the section "Editing Sound with Sound Recorder" in Chapter 12 for information on how to do this.

■ Close Sound Recorder and Discard the Sound—If this was just a test and you'd rather not save the sound, click the File menu and choose Exit to close Sound Recorder. In the resulting dialog box, click No to discard the sound.

Chapter

2

Getting Started with Video

By Adam Vujic and Serdar Yegulalp

PC video technology—like its audio counterpart—has come a long way in recent years. At the beginning of the decade, it was considered remarkable to have a postage-stamp size movie playing on a computer screen—not to mention at a choppy 5fps (frames per second).

These days, thanks to improved compression techniques such as MPEG and faster CPUs such as the Pentium II, modern PCs can comfortably play back full-motion (30fps) video that fills the entire screen. Provided, of course, that your hard disk has the space to store the massive files that hold the video data.

That's where *DVD* comes in. Designed to be a natural extension of the popular CD technology, DVD allows up to 14GBs of data to be stored on a single disc. The result is interactive, digital quality, feature-length movies that can be viewed on your home PC.

Playing a Video

ActiveMovie is used to play videos in this section.

ActiveMovie is the default Windows multimedia player, which supports just about every popular format—including Apple® QuickTime®. In addition, it can be enhanced to support the latest video formats as they arise.

Playing a Video via Explorer

Playing a video in Windows 98 is as simple as locating the file in Explorer and double-clicking its icon.

> **NOTE**   AVI files are represented by a blank page with a gray video camera. Similarly, a blue video camera indicates an MPEG file, and a green camera represents a QuickTime file.

In the following example you will play an MPEG video from the Windows 98 CD-ROM:

Playing a video from the Windows 98 CD-ROM

1. Click Start then click Run.

2. Type the following and press Enter:

    `d:\cdsample\videos`

    where d is the letter name of your CD-ROM or DVD drive.

    A folder appears with some Microsoft® promotional videos (see Figure 2.1).

Figure 2.1

Watch promotional videos for all the Microsoft products you don't own yet.

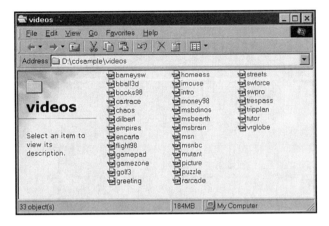

3. Double-click the icon labeled Intro. ActiveMovie opens and starts playing the video. When the video is finished, Windows automatically closes the player.

Opening a Video via Explorer

As with sound, it is also possible to open a video without actually playing it. When a video is opened, ActiveMovie appears and waits for you to click the Play button. If you stop the video playback, and then resume it, ActiveMovie will not close automatically. This allows you to watch the video again or edit ActiveMovie's options.

To open a video, use the right mouse button to click the video's icon then choose Open from the menu that appears.

> **NOTE**   With Windows 98's improved *multitasking* capabilities and 32-bit architecture, it is possible to play more than one video at once. To do so, double-click each video's icon in succession. Note that this operation puts considerable strain on your computer's processor and might slow down your system as a result.

Playing a Video via Drag and Drop

If ActiveMovie is already open, you can drag a video's icon onto the player and the video starts playing. The same procedure can be applied to just about any Windows video player.

Playing a Video via ActiveMovie

If you prefer, you can open ActiveMovie first, followed by the video. Here's how:

1. Click Start, point to Programs, Accessories, and Entertainment, and then click ActiveMovie Control.

Getting Started with Video

2. ActiveMovie's Open dialog box appears (see Figure 2.2).

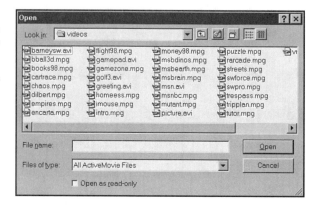

3. Locate the video file on your hard disk and double-click its icon.

4. Click the Play button.

Setting the Video Size

ActiveMovie can be configured to display a video at any size you want, including the entire screen. There are several ways to do this:

1. *Resizing via Properties*—Right-click anywhere inside the video window and choose Properties. The ActiveMovie Properties dialog box appears. Click the Movie Size tab, and then select the desired size from the drop-down list. Alternatively, check the Run Full Screen box if you'd like the video to fill the entire screen (see Figure 2.3).

> **NOTE** If your computer has a slower video card, performance might be less than satisfactory after resizing the video window. Setting the video to its original size or full screen double size usually gives the best results.

Figure 2.3
Enable the Run Full Screen option for a TV-like experience, albeit at low quality.

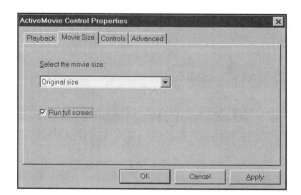

2. *Dynamically Resizing*—Move the cursor to a corner of the video window then click and drag. Depending on which direction you move the mouse, the video shrinks or grows. Resizing in this way might cause performance problems for older video cards.

3. *Maximize/Restore*—To have the video fill the desktop area (not the entire screen), click the Maximize button. Clicking this button again restores the video window to its original size. You might notice a reduction in performance after maximizing a video.

Unfortunately, enlarging the video window past its original size also reduces the quality of the video. If you must increase the video's size while keeping the quality at an acceptable level, choose the Double Original Size option.

If you find yourself changing the size of every video you watch, there is an option in the Control Panel that saves you some time.

To Set the Default Video Size

1. Click Start, point to Settings, click Control Panel. Double-click the Multimedia icon.

2. Click the Video tab and select the desired size under the heading Show Video In.

3. Click OK to for the changes to take effect.

Configuring ActiveMovie Playback Settings

To bring up the playback settings, right-click anywhere in the ActiveMovie window and choose Properties. The ActiveMovie Control Properties dialog box is displayed, as shown in Figure 2.4.

> **NOTE** With ActiveMovie, you can pause a video by double-clicking the video window. Double-clicking again will pick up the movie from where it left off.

The following options are available:

■ *Volume*—Move the vertical slider to adjust the volume of the video. The horizontal slider controls the balance of your speakers.

■ *Start and Stop*—These two settings control the video's starting and finishing positions. The time format is `hrs:mins:secs:1000s/secs`. For example, to play the last two minutes of a ten minute video, type `00:08:00:000` in the Start box. The Stop box can be left as is—it already shows the correct finish time.

Getting Started with Video

Figure 2.4

*Control how
ActiveMovie
plays your video
files via the
Playback tab.*

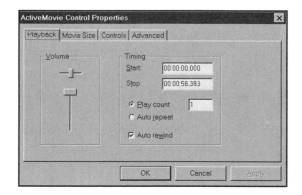

- *Play count*—This setting tells ActiveMovie how many times to repeat the video. For example, to play a video five times, click Play count and type 5 in the space provided.

- *Auto repeat*—Select this option if you want a video to loop continuously.

- *Auto rewind*—To have ActiveMovie rewind the video automatically when it has finished playing, place a check mark in the Auto rewind box. Thankfully, the process of rewinding is automatic and instantaneous in the digital world of computers.

Configuring the ActiveMovie Display

As with the playback settings, you can bring up ActiveMovie's display settings by right-clicking the video window and choosing Properties. Then click the Controls tab on the following dialog box (see Figure 2.5).

Figure 2.5

*Configure
ActiveMovie's
display, color
scheme, and more
via the Controls
tab.*

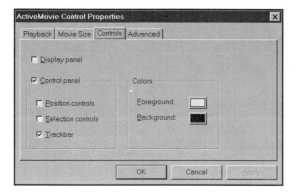

Here are the available options (see Figure 2.6 for the onscreen locations):

> **NOTE** To quickly show or hide the ActiveMovie Control Panel, right-click inside the video window and choose Controls. You can also choose Display to toggle the Display Panel on and off.

- *Display Panel*—Enables a display area, which provides numerical information such as the video's length and current position.

- *Control Panel*—Select this option to add playback controls to the ActiveMovie display. For example, you can toggle the AV Play and Stop buttons.

- *Position Controls*—Adds four buttons to the Control Panel, namely: Previous, Fast Forward, Rewind, and Next.

- *Selection Controls*—Adds two more buttons to the Control Panel, making it easier to select the video's Start (In) and Stop (Out) positions.

- *Trackbar*—Toggles the horizontal time slider at the base of the ActiveMovie display.

- *Colors*—You can even customize the colors of ActiveMovie's display panel. Select the foreground and background colors of your preference.

Figure 2.6

This is how ActiveMovie looks with all display options enabled.

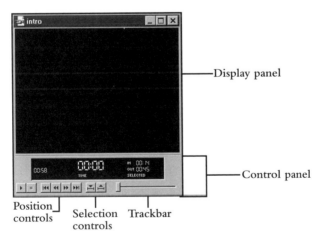

It's also possible to have information displayed using frames (rather than time) as the units of measurement. To do so, right-click in the video window and choose Frames. You can switch back by right-clicking again and choosing Time.

> **NOTE**   After you have selected Start and Stop (In and Out) positions on ActiveMovie's trackbar, you can use the Previous and Next buttons to jump between them. The concept is similar to the Next Track and Previous Track buttons on a CD player.

Viewing a Video's Properties

There are basically two ways to view the properties of a video. The first method provides information in a more user-friendly format, although both require a basic understanding of audio and video concepts.

1. Locate a video via My Computer. Right-click its icon and choose Properties. Click the Details tab to see information specific to video files such as resolution and frame rate (as in Figure 2.7).

2. Open a video in ActiveMovie. Next, right-click anywhere inside the video window and choose Properties. Click the Advanced tab for more information than you can poke a stick at.

Figure 2.7

The Details tab provides information on both the audio and video components of a file.

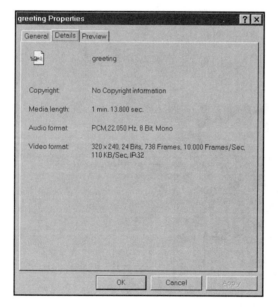

Playing a DVD Movie

One of the highlights of Windows 98 is its built-in support for DVD video. In the following section, you will learn how to take full advantage of DVD's exciting features using the DVD Player application.

> **NOTE** Only a limited number of DVD decoder boards are supported by Windows 98. If you do not own one of these cards, the DVD player will be unavailable, but you will be able to use the manufacturer's own player program. Contact the DVD manufacturer for more information.

Playing a DVD Movie with DVD Player

In this section you'll learn how to play back a DVD movie. Because very few DVD players are directly compatible with Windows 98, the example uses the Creative Labs PC-DVD Encore decoder, which uses its own player application. Your own player will probably vary slightly, depending on which manufacturer makes it, but the basic concepts are very much the same.

1. Insert a DVD disc into your DVD drive.

> **NOTE** DVD movie discs are often two-sided, with the contents of each side printed on the hub ring for the DVD disc. For instance, some movies are sold with different versions of the same film—widescreen versus full-screen—on different sides of the disc. Make sure you are inserting the disc with the correct side up.

2. If you have a board that works directly with Windows 98 then click Start, point to Programs, Accessories, and Entertainment, and then click DVD Player. Otherwise, follow the manufacturer's directions for launching the DVD player. In the case of the Creative Labs PC-DVD Encore, the program is found in Programs, PC-DVD Encore.

3. The DVD player application appears and the movie automatically begins to play. If the movie does not automatically begin to play, click the Play button on the application.

4. To stop the movie, either click Stop or press the Eject button on the DVD-ROM drive. You cannot damage a DVD by ejecting it while playing it back.

> **NOTE** Most discs are preprogrammed to display an international copyright notice and warning against copyright violation for several seconds when they first start playing. There's no real way to disable or get around this notice, and the player's controls might be disabled during this time.

Making Sense of DVD Regional Zones

Due to copyright restrictions, most DVD movies only function in certain areas of the world. There are several reasons for this.

First, different regions of the world use different television standards. North America, Japan, and most of the Far East use NTSC, but most European nations use PAL or SECAM.

Second, a title might have different copyright ownership in different parts of the world, and the regional zones help regulate purchases of those titles so that proper royalties can be paid to the owners. For instance, the mega-hit *Titanic* was distributed domestically by Paramount, but internationally through Twentieth-Century Fox.

Third, some material may not be legal in certain parts of the world. Adult movies from the United States are generally not legal for export to other countries, although adult movies from the Far East can be imported to the U.S. Region codes are one way of enforcing this.

There are six regional zones in total and their locations are as follows:

Region 1   North America
Region 2   Japan, Europe, Middle East, South Africa
Region 3   Southeast Asia (including Hong Kong)
Region 4   Australia, New Zealand, Central and South America
Region 5   Northwest Asia, North Africa
Region 6   People's Republic of China

It's a good idea to keep this in mind when purchasing a DVD disc over the Internet (especially if you live outside the U.S.). Otherwise, you might get a shock when a DVD is delivered to your door in perfect condition but your computer refuses to play it.

Some movies are not sold with a region code and can be played anywhere, which boosts sales. Many discs from Hong Kong are regionless. Specifying a region code is not required by law in most jurisdictions—it's just a voluntary practice adopted by the DVD manufacturers for their own benefit.

> **NOTE**   Some DVD drives (such as the Creative DXR2) can play discs from any region via a software switch. However, there are a limited number of times you can switch between regions. The only way to reset the switch is to reinstall Windows and the Creative software.

Controlling a DVD Movie

Like a CD player, a DVD player includes several buttons that control how the movie is played. Additional buttons, such as Next and Previous, can be used to quickly locate a scene in the movie.

Here is an overview of DVD player's controls, as featured in the PC-DVD Encore. Your own player might have slightly different controls.

- *Play*—This should be self-evident.

- *Stop*—Stops playback completely.

- *Fast Forward*—Skips ahead through the disc, and gives you visual feedback as to how far you've gone. Different programs will handle this function differently, so you might see things move at varying speeds depending on what player you're using.

- *Reverse*—Moves backward through the disc with visual feedback. Some players do not have this function because it requires some extra programming to work properly. (DVDs are really only designed to be played from beginning to end.)

- *Pause*—Halts playback with a freeze frame, but can be resumed by either clicking Pause again or Play.

- *Eject*—Pops the disc out of the drive (and stops playback, of course).

- *Next Scene*—Skips to the next indexed scene on the disc.

- *Previous Scene*—Goes back to the preceding indexed scene on the disc.

- *Slow Motion*—Moves forward a frame at a time, usually at 1/4th playback speed.

- *Full Screen/Window*—Changes the way the playback is displayed. Some players do not play back in full screen mode at all; some do play back but with a degraded image. Most players that use hardware to decode the picture, such as the Creative Labs player, can handle full-screen playback very well.

- *Menu*—This switches to the disc's main menu, from which you can access specific scenes or enable special features.

Working with Enhanced DVD Features

Although DVDs are great for watching movies, a special bonus is some extra content on the disc that you won't find anywhere else. Extra features can include movie trailers, alternative languages, behind-the-scenes footage, directory commentary, and wide-screen format. Every movie is different.

To find which options are available on your DVD disc, click the Menu button on your player. A menu appears, allowing you to configure DVD options or browse through additional information on the movie.

Getting Started with Video

Setting an Alternative Language

More often than not, DVD movies include multiple languages on the one disc. An alternative language can be in the form of an entire audio track or textual subtitles. For example, the DVD movie *The Sweet Hereafter* provides audio in both English and French on the same DVD. English, French, and Spanish subtitles are also included.

To select a different language (audio)

1. Click the Audio Menu icon on the player remote to produce the Audio menu.

2. Select the audio format you want to hear by clicking it (see Figure 2.8). Note that you can also choose the mix of the audio—mono, stereo, or stereo surround, as well.

Figure 2.8

On the Creative Labs PC-DVD player control, the Audio Menu icon contains a list of all available audio tracks.

To select a different language (subtitles)

1. Click the Subpicture Menu icon on the player remote to produce the Subpicture, or Subtitle menu.

2. Select the subtitle language you want to see by clicking it, as shown in Figure 2.9.

Another way to select a different language, either through audio or subtitles, is to choose the other language from the disc's own features menu. Every disc does this a little differently, and some discs do not support alternative languages or audio at all.

Figure 2.9

The Subpicture, or Subtitle menu, with a list of all available subtitles. Off turns subtitles off completely.

Recording Sound from a DVD Movie

Although it is not possible to record video from a DVD movie (due to copyright restrictions), it's relatively easy to sample sound from a DVD's audio track.

Before recording, you need to check that everything is set up correctly.

1. In the Recording Control applet, ensure that the CD Audio volume is set to an appropriate level and that its Select box is checked. It's a good idea to disable the other sound sources (for example, Wave, MIDI, Line-In, and Microphone) to minimize the chance of interference.

2. Insert the DVD you want to record from. Click Start, point to Programs, Accessories, and Entertainment, and then click DVD Player.

3. Click the Stop button then locate the position of the audio you'd like to record. You can use the Fast Forward and Rewind buttons to pinpoint the exact location.

To record the DVD audio track, follow these steps:

1. Click Start, point to Programs, Accessories, and Entertainment, and then click Sound Recorder. Make sure that both Sound Recorder and DVD player are visible on the screen.

2. When you are ready to record, click the Record button in Sound Recorder.

3. Immediately after, click the Play button in DVD Player.

4. When you want to stop recording, click the Stop button in both Sound Recorder and DVD player.

5. Click the Play button to review what you have just recorded.

You can use Sound Recorder's editing tools to remove the unwanted audio at the beginning and end of the recording.

Chapter 3

Getting Started with WebTV

Imagine this. In one part of the house, a young girl sits down at her PC to research a science project. She opens WebTV to watch a program about some recent developments in the area she's working on. She types notes in her word processor as she watches the show and even uses her Web browser to check out an Internet site mentioned in the program.

In another part of the house, the girl's mother checks her email and notices that a show of particular interest to one of her business clients is on in five minutes. She opens WebTV to watch the show, while at the same time she holds an Internet conference with that client to discuss the broadcast.

This is one type of scenario where using Windows 98's WebTV on your PC would be valuable. The PC is fast becoming the center of our information-related lives. It's a natural progression to use WebTV on your PC to more fully enhance and ease your daily tasks. In this chapter, you'll learn what WebTV is and how to set it up for the first time. You'll learn how to use its Program Guide and trouble-shoot WebTV. Finally, you'll see the potential that interactive WebTV offers.

NOTE	For more information on WebTV, browse to these Web sites, which provide good information and useful links.

```
http://www.webtv.com
http://www.microsoft.com/windows/WEBTV
```

What Is WebTV?

Windows 98 has built-in support for using your PC and TV Tuner Adapter card to watch television in an entirely new way. WebTV blends television with the interactivity of the World Wide Web, creating *interactive television* on your PC.

Some of the features of WebTV in Windows 98 include:

- An electronic Program Guide that lists programs based on your particular cable company's schedule, or by your broadcast region. This guide lets you have a customized listing of television shows that are on in your area and channels that are already familiar to you from your regular TV set. The Program Guide automatically updates itself via the Internet.

- The capability to watch interactive television programs that are enhanced during production to provide information about the show or to allow interactivity between you, the viewer, and the show itself.

- Watching TV on your monitor at the same time as you do other tasks on the PC.

- Receiving data such as Web pages, documents, and software updates over traditional broadcast airwaves, eliminating the need for a telephone line.

Interactive TV has many useful applications. One would be the capability of the viewer to retrieve up-to-the-minute statistics on a particular football player as a game is in progress. Another would be perhaps to buy merchandise seen on the TV with a single click of the mouse.

At this time, WebTV in Windows 98 supports the use of both cable and over-the-air broadcasting to receive signals. Support for satellite and other transmission types is planned for the future.

Setting Up WebTV for the First Time

The software required to run WebTV is not installed by default in Windows 98. You can opt to install the WebTV software during the initial Windows 98 setup, or you can add it after Windows is already installed on your system.

To install WebTV on a Windows 98 system:

- Make sure your system meets the minimum requirements (see the next section, "Hardware Required for Using WebTV") for installation.

- Open the Control Panel

- Double-click the Add/Remove Programs icon

- Select the Windows Setup tab

- In the Components window, place a check next to the Web TV for Windows option.

You'll notice that the check box you just clicked now has a black check mark in it with a gray background. This notation indicates that all the options for this component are not selected. To see what other options are available for WebTV, click the Details button.

After you click the Details button, you'll see that the option for WaveTop Data Broadcasting is not checked. If you want to install WaveTop, check this box and click OK. WaveTop is not necessary for WebTV to work.

NOTE	WaveTop enables features in WebTV that might not be available in your broadcast area.

Getting Started with WebTV

Click OK in the Add/Remove Program Properties box to begin the installation of WebTV. The installation of WebTV might ask you for the Windows 98 CD-ROM or for the location of the Windows 98 installation files. Reboot your machine when prompted.

Hardware Required for Using WebTV

Microsoft lists the following as a minimum configuration for using WebTV. It's also useful to know that while these minimum requirements might enable you to use WebTV, most people with real-world experience find these minimum requirements produce less than optimal performance.

- Intel Pentium or compatible 120MHz processor

- 16MB of RAM

- 1GB hard disk

- ATI All-in-Wonder or ATI All-in-Wonder Pro display adapter

- Cable or antenna connection attached to the PC through an ATI All-in-Wonder Adapter

- SVGA display capable of at least 800×600 resolution with 60Hz non-interlaced refresh rate

- Internet connection for full interactive functionality

- Pointing device with two buttons

Although the preceding list is the minimum requirements, Microsoft recommends you have the following components installed for best results with WebTV:

- Intel Pentium or compatible 200MHz processor

- 32MB RAM

- 2GB or larger hard disk with fast data transfer rate.

- 28,800 bps or faster internal fax modem

- Speakers

- Wireless battery-operated keyboard with built-in pointing device

- Wireless TV-style remote control

- Sound system expansion card with digital audio support, a MIDI port, a MIDI-controlled wavetable synthesizer, multiple analog and digital audio inputs, software-controllable low-noise audio mixer/preamplifier, and multiple-audio outputs.

- A built-in microphone or a front-mounted microphone jack suitable for teleconferencing, education, karaoke, and other programs that might require sound input.

Upgrades such as a faster processor, more RAM, and speakers are rather logical to have for running such advanced software as WebTV. Of course, you might find things such as a wireless remote control and digital audio a bit frivolous for just getting started with WebTV. Remember, as long as your system meets or exceeds the minimum requirements, you should be fine.

To watch TV via cable or over-the-air broadcast on your PC, you need to have a video card installed in the system that is capable of receiving these signals. Windows 98 ships with native WebTV support for the ATI technologies All-in-Wonder and the ATI All-in-Wonder Pro video cards. Microsoft recommends using one of these ATI cards at this time for WebTV. The Hauppauge TV video card, STB TV PCI card, and other TV-enabled video cards might also work using driver software supplied by their manufacturer; however, you will not be able to use WebTV in Windows 98 at this time.

> **TIP**   If you have an ATI All-in-Wonder video card installed in your machine, you might have to check your display settings and make a minor modification. The All-in-Wonder card is based on the ATI Mach64/Rage II+ video chipset. Windows 98, on some systems, detects the All-in-Wonder card as simply the ATI Rage II+. If this is the case, you'll need to change the video adapter software to the ATI All-in-Wonder driver for WebTV to work properly. See Chapter 7, "Installing and Configuring Multimedia Devices," for instructions on how to change your video driver.

Starting WebTV the First Time

After your machine has rebooted, start WebTV either by the new shortcut on the QuickLaunch toolbar, or by clicking Start, Programs, Accessories, and Entertainment. Then, click on WebTV. You'll see a splash screen, shown in Figure 3.1, for WebTV as the program starts up.

You'll be launched into WebTV configuration (or TV-C or TV CONFIG), which introduces you to WebTV with a short tutorial, as well as allowing you to customize your setup by asking you a few short questions. You will also enter your ZIP code and download current TV listings for your area based on that information.

Getting Started with WebTV

Scanning for Channels

The WebTV configuration attempts to scan for all available channels that are being broadcast, much in the same way as many newer TV sets or VCRs do. It will scan through the normal range of broadcast and cable channels, as shown in Figure 3.2, and will automatically add channels that it receives. Conversely, it will not add channels to your setup if the reception is poor, or if there is nothing being broadcast on a particular channel.

Downloading Gemstar G-Guide Program Listings

The TV configuration asks for your ZIP code so it knows which geographical broadcast region to download TV listings for. It will also know of any cable companies that operate in that ZIP code, and gives you the full listings for every channel your cable company offers.

After entering your ZIP code, WebTV configuration asks you which of two ways you want to download listings. Gemstar G-Guide (or G-Guide for short) listings can be gathered automatically from data that is contained on a local TV channel. This option takes several hours to finish, and should only really be used when there is no Internet connection available.

The preferred method of downloading G-Guide listings for most people is to click the hyperlink on the TV configuration Get TV Listings screen, shown in Figure 3.3, and go to the Gemstar G-Guide Web page and download the listings from there. This option takes only a few minutes.

Figure 3.2
WebTV can automatically scan for channels.

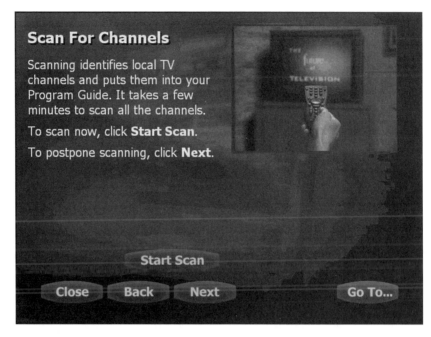

You can also skip getting the listings altogether by clicking the Next button.

Figure 3.3
The Get TV Listings screen gives you a choice of how to get program listings.

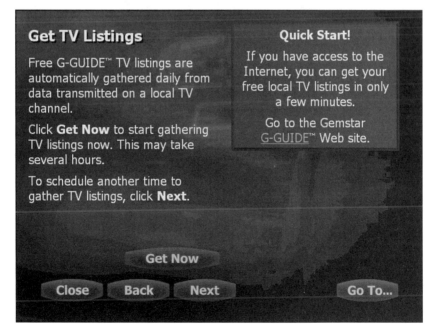

Scheduling Updates

The G–Guide downloads 24 hours worth of TV listings the first time you run it.
WebTV configuration, shown in Figure 3.4, allows you to schedule a time each
day when your machine automatically connects to the Gemstar Web site to
download the next 24 hours of listings. Most people pick a time when the
computer is on, but is not being used.

> **NOTE**   The time you indicate here is added as a task in the Windows 98 Task
> Manager, which is an applet that runs in your System Tray and
> executes prescheduled events at a predetermined time. The System Tray is the area on
> the right-hand side of the taskbar next to the clock.

Figure 3.4

*You can choose
what time of day
WebTV
downloads new
program listings.*

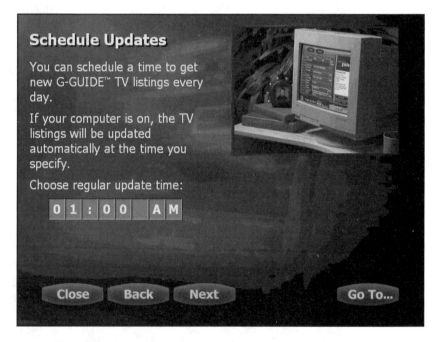

Assign Video Inputs

If you have a VCR or a video game player, these can also be attached to your PC,
via the TV video card installed in the system. TV Config allows you to assign
inputs to these devices by assigning them their own channel number, as shown in
Figure 3.5. For instance, if you don't have any programming being received on
channel 80, this channel would be a good one to assign to your VCR. Then, if
you wanted to use the VCR hooked to your computer, you would tune WebTV
to channel 80, and operate the VCR as normal.

Figure 3.5
You can connect other video devices to your system and use them in WebTV.

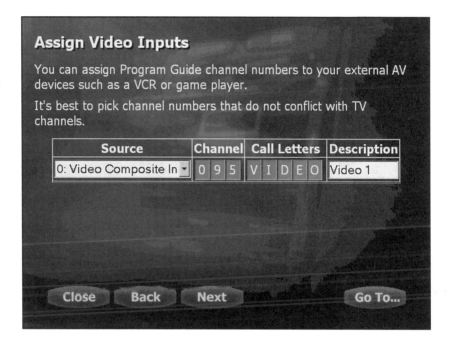

Assign Video Inputs

You can assign Program Guide channel numbers to your external AV devices such as a VCR or game player.

It's best to pick channel numbers that do not conflict with TV channels.

Source	Channel	Call Letters	Description
0: Video Composite In ▾	0 9 5	V I D E O	Video 1

Close   Back   Next   Go To...

Configuration Complete

When you have reached the Configuration Complete screen, shown in Figure 3.6, you're finished. Click the Finish button to display the Program Guide to begin watching TV on your PC.

> **NOTE**   If you ever need to go back to any of the steps in the TV configuration, double-click the TV configuration channel. By default it's Channel 96, denoted by the call letters TV C. Doing so reruns the whole configuration program for you, or allows you to jump to any one part that you would like.

Working with the Program Guide

The Program Guide you see in Figure 3.7 is the main interface of WebTV. You'll recognize the look and feel of it from the TV listings you might have in your local newspaper or from the cable listings channel that your cable company might provide.

The Program Guide gives you a comprehensive, up-to-date listing of the channels available to you and the programming they carry. The listings are displayed in one-half hour increments on each channel.

Figure 3.6

Click Finish to end the WebTV configuration.

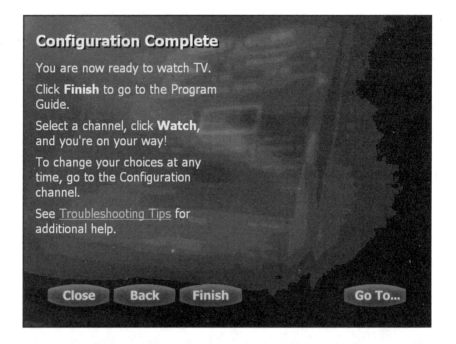

Configuration Complete

You are now ready to watch TV.

Click **Finish** to go to the Program Guide.

Select a channel, click **Watch**, and you're on your way!

To change your choices at any time, go to the Configuration channel.

See Troubleshooting Tips for additional help.

Close   Back   Finish   Go To...

Figure 3.7

The Program Guide is your main interface in WebTV.

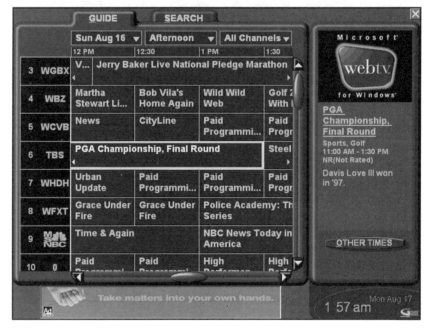

Additionally, along the upper-right hand of the Program Guide, you'll have a small-screen view of the channel you're currently watching, the name of the show, it's duration, any rating the program has been assigned, and a brief synopsis of the show.

You can search for a specific program from within the Program Guide. You can also look for other times that show might be on, and you can even set a reminder to alert you when something you want to watch in the future comes on. And as is the case with more and more software every day, you can set up *Favorites*—channels that you can return to with a quick mouse click.

Choosing a Channel

To watch a channel, select it with your mouse (or remote control) in the Program Guide. The small-screen display on the right-hand side of the Program Guide begins showing the program on that channel.

To watch the show in full-screen mode, either single-click the small-screen display or click the Watch button on the lower-right side of the Program Guide, as shown in Figure 3.8.

Figure 3.8
To change from the Program Guide to watching your show, click the Watch button.

NYPD Blue
Drama
1:35 AM - 2:35 AM
NR(Not Rated)

TV14 Schoolgirl is sexually assaulted by classmates.

WATCH

OTHER TIMES

Changing Channels

Changing channels can be done a few different ways. You can use the numbers on your keyboard to manually enter a channel number, use the TV banner, or pick a predefined Favorite channel you've set up, (see the next section, "Creating a Favorite"). If you have a remote control hooked to your PC, you can use it or you can go back to the Program Guide to pick a new channel.

Favorite Channels

With WebTV you can predefine up to four Favorites and add them to your TV toolbar for easy access.

Creating a Favorite

To create a Favorite on the TV toolbar, first switch to the channel that you want to create. If your TV toolbar is not visible, show it by pressing the F10 or Alt key. Then, click the Add button on the TV toolbar shown in Figure 3.9. You should see a new button appear on the TV toolbar with the call letters of the station and the channel number of your new Favorite.

Figure 3.9

Adding a Favorite channel to your TV toolbar is as easy as clicking the Add button...

Deleting a Favorite

To delete a Favorite you've created, show your TV toolbar by pressing the F10 or Alt key. Click the Favorite you want to delete then click the Remove button on the TV toolbar, shown in Figure 3.10.

Figure 3.10

...and to delete a Favorite, click the Remove button.

Looking at Listings for Different Days and Times

Your Program Guide has more listings than just those available for viewing right now. You can also look at listings for programs coming up later on in the day, sometime tonight, or even on a different day.

In the Program Guide, there are three drop-down tabs near the top of the screen, as you can see in Figure 3.11. These tabs are similar to drop-down lists you see elsewhere in Windows. These drop-down tabs show you what date you're looking at listings for, the time of day you're looking at (Afternoon, Evening, Night, and so on) and if you're looking at all the available channels or just your Favorites.

Looking Through Time by Scrolling

If you want to just check up to a couple hours ahead or behind of the current time, you can scroll back and forth to view listings. This gets a little cumbersome when the time frame you want to look at is a few hours away from the current time, or in another part of the day altogether.

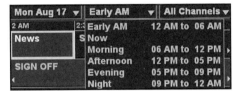

Looking at a Different Time of Day

You can show listings for a particular segment of the day as well. WebTV breaks the day down into five categories:

Early AM—12AM to 6AM
Morning—6AM to 12PM
Afternoon—12PM to 5PM
Evening—5PM to 9PM
Night—9PM to 12AM

To have the Program Guide display listings for a certain segment of the day, click the drop-down tab that is displaying a time, such as the ones shown in the list, and choose the time you'd like to see listings for.

Looking at a Different Day

There might be times when you want to take a look at what is going to be on tomorrow, for instance. Using the Program Guide to check another day's listings isn't difficult.

Using the drop-down tab that is displaying a date allows you to choose a different day at which to look.

Bringing the Program Guide Back to the Here and Now

After looking around at different times and days, you'll probably want to come back to the current day and time at some point. Again, this isn't difficult.

In the lower-right corner of the Program Guide, you'll see the current date and time displayed. Simply give a single-click on the current date and time, and the Program Guide automatically returns to the listings of what's on right now.

The TV Banner

The TV banner is the toolbar-like item that comes into view whenever you change a channel on WebTV. It also appears when you press the F10 or Alt button to bring up the TV toolbar. The TV banner shows you what you're watching, as well as allowing you to change channels, turn interactive TV on or off, and close WebTV via the X in the upper-right corner of the TV banner.

The TV Toolbar

The TV toolbar can be made to appear a few ways. You remember from earlier in this chapter that the F10 or Alt buttons on the keyboard bring the TV toolbar into view. But you can also make it appear by moving the mouse to the top of the screen (in full-screen mode), hitting the Menu button on the remote control (again, if your system has one attached), or by clicking the mouse anywhere in the TV picture. For the latter technique, you must be using WebTV in window mode, not full-screen mode. The TV toolbar has many uses.

Bringing Up the Program Guide

On the TV toolbar, you'll see the Guide button. Clicking it brings up the Program Guide, with the channel you were just watching as the current selection.

Change the Channel List

On the TV toolbar, the next button you have is the Settings button. Clicking this brings up a list of all current channels. You can selectively decide which channels you want to show up in the Program Guide by checking or unchecking them in the Settings box, as shown in Figure 3.12.

Additionally, you can also turn closed-captioning on and off in the Settings box.

Figure 3.12

You can customize which channels you see in the Program Guide in the Settings dialog box.

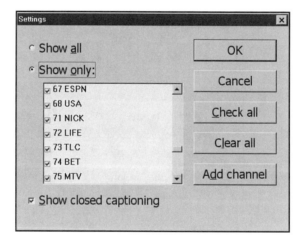

Need Help?

The third button on the TV toolbar is Help. As the name suggests, clicking this button brings up the Windows 98 help topics for WebTV.

Searching for Programs

One added feature of WebTV's Program Guide that you won't find in the newspaper or magazine TV listings is the capability to search for programming in a myriad of ways.

You can search for a specific program, for instance, when *The X-Files®* is on, any day, any channel. Because some cable channels show this popular program several times a day, this feature is especially useful. Or you can search by category, such as comedy shows. You can also search for shows starring a particular actor, or even movies according to the reviews given by critics.

To begin your search, bring up the Program Guide from the TV toolbar. Then, click Search near the top of the screen. The Search screen appears. Take a moment and get acquainted with the layout of the search screen. You'll notice similarities to the Program Guide in Figure 3.13.

Figure 3.13
The Search screen has similarities to the Program Guide.

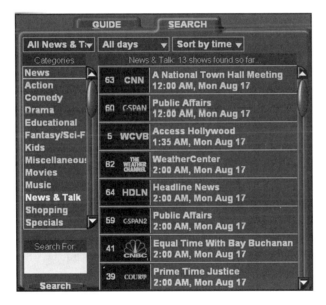

Now you need to select some search criteria. You can do a general search by selecting an entry in the Categories list on the left side of the screen. The categories range from sports to home shopping (refer to Figure 3.13).

Alternatively, you can enter text in the Search For box in the lower-left corner of the screen (refer to Figure 3.13).

This text can be anything you want to search for, from the name of a show to an actor's name to keywords that might bring up programs you're interested in. Type in your text and press Enter.

Getting Started with WebTV

Tips to Make Your Search Easier

Be aware that any text you enter or category you choose will be further narrowed down by other criteria on the Search screen. For instance, you can change the All Days drop-down tab to limit your search for a certain program.

If you aren't interested if the show is on two days from now, this would be a good restriction to set.

Also, assuming you know exactly how to spell the name of the show or other criteria you're searching for, you can place an equal sign (=) in front of the text you entered. (for example, =Football) This inclusion makes your search go faster, but be aware that you need to spell the item or items you're searching for exactly as they appear in the program listing. If in doubt, leave off the equal sign.

You can also search for movies that have a certain rating (on a four-star scale). To do this, you need to enter some special search text in the Search For box. First, as your search criteria, hit the Spacebar. Then, enter in the number of ratings stars (*) you want to search for by placing each star inside of square brackets ([*]). Lastly, place a closing parenthesis. So your search string should look like this *Spacebar*[*][*][*]) to search for all three-star movies.

Sorting Your Search

After your search criteria have returned some results, you can sort the list by time, or by title.

Click the Sort by Time drop-down tab to sort chronologically, or choose Sort by Title from the same tab to sort the results alphabetically.

Reminders

Sometimes, you might want to be alerted when a certain program comes on, whether it's every day, once a week, or even a one-time event, such as the Grammy Awards. Plus, if you want to have a reminder to record a program on your VCR, WebTV can put you at the right channel automatically when the show comes on.

Reminders can be set to alert you that your show is coming on from one to 30 minutes ahead of time, even if you're not watching TV at the time. Note that if your PC is in sleep mode at the time a reminder is set to go off, it will not wake unless the reminder was originally set for recording.

You can have a maximum of 50 reminders set up in WebTV. If you try to add more than 50 reminders, the oldest one you set is deleted so that the new one can be added. To avoid having this happen, you should keep tabs on your reminders, and delete old ones as needed.

Setting a Reminder

To set up a reminder, you should first look at either the Program Guide or the Search screen. Select the program you want to be reminded about then click the Remind button on the lower-right side of the screen, as shown in Figure 3.14.

Figure 3.14

The Remind button appears when you select a program in the future in the Program Guide.

A Remind dialog box appears (see Figure 3.15) in which you can set specifics for the reminder.

Figure 3.15

The Remind dialog box lets you customize your reminders.

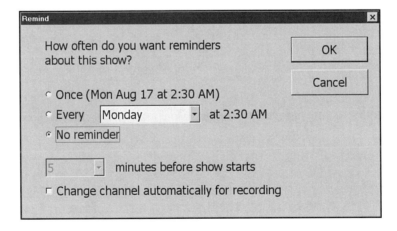

When the reminder triggers at the specified time, you see a dialog box similar to the one in Figure 3.16. Answer Yes or No to indicate whether you want to switch over to that channel or not.

Getting Started with WebTV

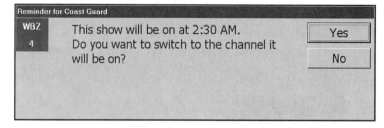

Forget Your Reminders?

If you need to check on the reminders you have already set up, go to the Search screen and select My Reminders from the Categories list on the left side of the screen. Any reminders that are set will show up here.

Cancel that Reminder

To cancel a reminder you have already set up, get the list of My Reminders as described in the preceding paragraph and select the program you want to cancel the reminder for. Next, select the Reminder button. In the dialog box that appears, select No Reminder and click OK. The reminder is deleted.

Keyboard Shortcut Commands for Use with WebTV

There are various keyboard shortcuts you can use that accomplish different tasks within WebTV for Windows 98.

Key combination	Function
F10 key	Shows the WebTV menu
F6 key	Toggles between a full screen or a window
0–9	Changes channels
Up or down arrow key	Scroll up or down
Windows logo key	Accesses the Windows 98 Start menu
Windows logo+Ctrl+Shift+Z	Accesses the Program Guide (grid view)
Windows logo+Ctrl+Z	Launches WebTV or toggles between a full screen or a window
Windows logo+Ctrl+V	Increases volume
Windows logo+Shift+V	Decreases volume

Key combination	Function
Windows logo+V	Toggles mute on or off
Windows logo+Ctrl+Alt+Z	Views the next channel
Windows logo+Ctrl+Alt+Shift+Z	Views the previous channel
Windows logo+Ctrl+Alt+Shift+F	Left arrow
Windows logo+Ctrl+Alt+Shift+P	Up arrow
Windows logo+Ctrl+Alt+F	Right arrow
Windows logo+Ctrl+Alt+Shift+G	Recall
Windows logo+Ctrl+Alt+P	Down arrow
Windows logo+Ctrl+Alt+G	Pause
Page up	Views the next channel
Page down	View the previous channel

Troubleshooting WebTV and the Program Guide

Sometimes things don't go as planned, and things don't work perfectly. I have been using WebTV for almost two years including during the Windows 98 technical beta test period, and I've seen many issues come up with fellow testers as well as with typical end users since Windows 98 was released. There are some common things that you might see when things don't seem to be working properly.

WebTV Cannot Find the Necessary Hardware

Often times this error happens because either you don't have the ATI All-in-Wonder or All-in-Wonder Pro card installed in the machine, or because Windows doesn't have the proper drivers installed for the card. Right now, the only TV tuner cards officially supported by Microsoft are the ATI models just mentioned. If you do have one of these cards physically installed in your machine, check the Device Manager to make sure the proper drivers are loaded. If not, you can install the correct drivers by running the Add New Hardware Wizard in the Control Panel.

> **NOTE** There are other TV cards on the market that enable you to use their software to watch TV on your PC. But because Windows 98 has built-in drivers made specially for the ATI All-in-Wonder cards, users of other TV cards will not be able to use WebTV for Windows 98 at this time.

Getting Started with WebTV

Uh, Is This Thing On?

Some users have started up WebTV only to have nothing happen. Sometimes an error occurs, and sometimes it seems to just hang there forever. I've found that many times this happened because the user was running a beta version of Windows 98, and then installed the final, released version directly on top of that beta. With over 200,000 copies of the Beta 3 release of Windows 98 distributed by Microsoft, this problem was common.

Unfortunately, if you are one of these people, the only way to ensure full WebTV functionality is to essentially wipe the hard drive clean to rid it of any leftovers from the Windows 98 beta version, and then reinstall the retail version of Windows 98 from scratch. Let's hope this isn't the case for you.

Another reason for this type of problem occurs when, for whatever reason, all the different components of the ATI video card didn't install properly. The proper components for the ATI card are located in the Device Manager, under Sound, Video and Game controllers and are as follows:

> ATI TuneP, WDM TV Tuner
> ATIXBar, ATI WDM Video Audio Crossbar
> Bt829, WDM Video Capture
> Closed Caption Decoder
> NABTS/FEC VBI Codec

If these items do not appear in the Device Manager, you should run the Add New Hardware Wizard in the Control Panel to add them in.

Cannot Connect to the Gemstar Guide to Download Listings

Sometimes the security settings in Internet Explorer 4 prevent you from successfully downloading the Program Guide listings. To fix this, click the View menu and choose Internet Options. Then go to the Security tab and click the Zone drop-down list. Choose Trusted sites zone. Click the Add Sites button and type in http://*.microsoft.com. Click the Add button. If there is a check mark in the box for Require Server Verification (https: for all sites in this zone), deselect it. Click OK, and then choose Low as the security for this type of site. Click OK.

ATI All-in-Wonder Users Who Upgraded to Windows 98

If you do have either the ATI All-in-Wonder, or the All-in-Wonder Pro installed on your machine and you upgraded your previous operating system directly to Windows 98 with this card installed, you might have to install updated drivers to ensure proper operation of WebTV. The easiest way to do this is to go into the Device Manager and find your display adapter in the list. Double-click your display adapter, and then go to the Driver tab. Click Update Driver and click Next. Then choose Display a List of All the Drivers in a Specific Location, so You Can Select the Driver You Want, as shown in Figure 3.17. Insert your Windows 98 CD-ROM and click Next. Then choose your card from the list (either the ATI All-in-Wonder or All-in-Wonder Pro) and click Next again. After the installation is complete, click Finish and you are prompted to restart your computer. After restarting, your ATI TV card drivers are updated, and you are set to watch WebTV.

Figure 3.17
Updating ATI All-in-Wonder drivers.

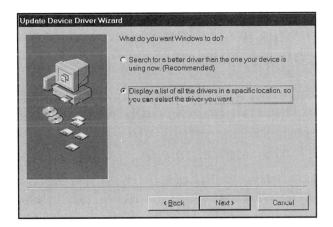

Manually Adding a Channel to the Channel List

Sometimes, after scanning for channels, you notice in the Program Guide that a channel is missing that shouldn't be. For instance, if you know that channel 4 is available to you, but it doesn't appear in the channel list, you can add it manually. Click the Settings button on the TV toolbar, and then click Add Channel in the box that appears. Choose a number for the channel that you want to add (assuming the number is not used yet), and then click OK.

Possible Issues with Interactive TV

Some things you'll encounter with interactive TV require feedback that is provided by you. This data is sent over the Internet, and thus requires you to be logged in to your Internet service provider (ISP) in order for it to work properly. If you don't have a way of connecting to the Internet, you might not be able to use certain features of interactive TV.

Getting Started with WebTV

Switching to Windowed Mode Shows Only WebTV Title Bar

Another common issue end users have encountered is that when switching WebTV into windowed mode by pressing the F6 key, only the title bar of the window can be seen. This occurs when WebTV was minimized the last time it was closed.

To remedy this problem, drag the lower edge of the title bar down on the screen, thus revealing the rest of the window, and the TV picture.

The Program Guide Fails to Download when Switching Channels

If you happen to start WebTV or change channels while the Program Guide is downloading, the download fails. Check your System Tray for the icon that appears when the Program Guide download is happening. If the Guide is in the process of being loaded, wait for it to finish before starting WebTV or changing channels.

Interactive TV

Interactive TV is a new technology that is increasing in popularity very quickly. In fact, interactive television is really where the future of WebTV is. If there were more programs available today on TV with interactive elements built into them, most people would be using WebTV for its interactivity and little else.

Many people have become accustomed lately to using the Internet and all its facets such as the World Wide Web, interactive online chat, and email. People are getting to the point where the interactivity of things such as the Web are taken for granted. You can do custom searches for any kind of information at all, you can talk to your friends, you can meet people from across the world, and you can buy everything from software to automobiles—all interactively, on the Internet.

What interactive television will do for your TV viewing habits is roughly similar to what the Internet did to your PC using habits. It changes the way you watch TV. In fact, where TV viewing used to be a passive activity—you sat and watched while the tube entertained you—it now becomes active—*interactive*. As such, you can be involved to some extent in the very programs you watch. This can be as simple as enabling you to call up instant statistics on your favorite football quarterback or as complex as the viewers having a direct impact on the outcome of a show. Interactive television is a revolution, blending the best parts of TV and the Internet to create, as it were, a new medium—a medium in which you are not merely a passive viewer, but an active participant in the shows you watch.

Alas, interactive TV isn't widely available yet. As this technology grows and becomes more popular, you will notice more and more programs being broadcast with interactive elements embedded in them.

How to Tell If a Program Is Interactive

In WebTV, you can tell if a certain program contains interactive elements by looking for the Interactive icon in the Program Guide and on the TV banner, shown in Figure 3.18. A program displaying this icon contains some sort of interactivity in it.

Figure 3.18

The interactive TV icon button appears on the TV banner.

Interactive icon

Turning Interactive TV On and Off

Interactive TV is enabled by default. To turn it off, click the Interactive TV icon on the TV banner. A small menu drops down, as shown in Figure 3.19. Click Interactive TV to remove the check mark next to it and to turn off interactive features. Click the interactive TV icon again and click Interactive TV to turn it back on.

Figure 3.19

The interactive TV icon button allows you to turn interactive TV off or on.

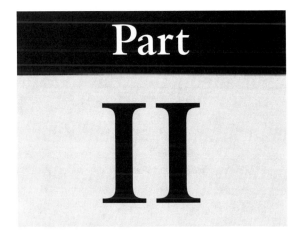

Part

II

Customizing
Windows 98

Chapter

4

Configuring Multimedia

by Adam Vujic

Now that you're familiar with some Windows 98 multimedia basics, it's time to look at how you can change some of your computer's default settings. By making a few adjustments, you can improve the way Web pages look, designate a drive to play audio CDs, and choose an entertaining screen saver.

In this chapter, you'll first learn how you can adjust your Windows 98 display settings. Doing so is a simple right-click away! Then you'll see how to change your sound configuration to choose what program and device you want for sound playback. Next you'll configure a variety of other multimedia components, including installing and removing them.

Adjusting Display Settings

Windows 98 includes a number of display settings that allow you to change the screen area (or *resolution*), colors, and font sizes. You might need to adjust these settings if you have trouble reading onscreen text, or have a game that performs better at a certain resolution and *color depth*.

To access these settings, right-click the desktop and choose Properties (see Figure 4.1). Click the Settings tab to see what's available on your system.

Figure 4.1
When you right-click the desktop, you'll see this drop-down list from which you can access your system's display properties.

Adjusting the Color Depth

You can change your Display Properties by accessing the Control Panel and then choosing the Display icon. Here's a shortcut you can use by right-clicking the desktop.

1. Right-click anywhere on the desktop and choose Properties.

2. The Display Properties dialog box appears. Click the Settings tab to bring up the display settings (see Figure 4.2).

3. Under the heading Colors, select the desired color depth from the drop-down list.

4. Click OK for the changes to take effect. If the Compatibility Warning dialog box appears, choose the second option and click OK (see Figure 4.3).

Figure 4.2

The Settings tab is the place to adjust your screen's resolution, color depth, and video card features.

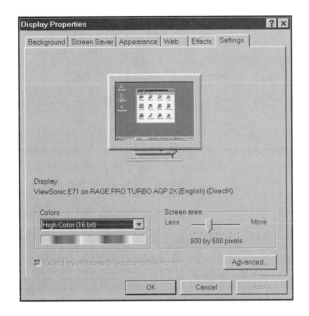

Figure 4.3

The Compatibility Warning dialog box gives you the option of restarting the computer before applying any changes.

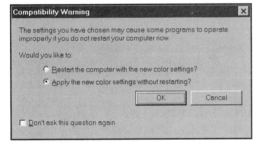

> **NOTE** Another option—32,000 Colors—might appear in the Colors drop-down list. Although you might be tempted to increase performance by selecting this option, the difference is negligible with most video cards. I recommend selecting 16-bit Color to guarantee compatibility with the broadest range of Windows applications and games.

Some, or all, of the following options will be listed, depending on your video card's capabilities:

- 16 Colors—This setting is the minimum number of colors supported by Windows 98. Generally, it is unacceptable for basic multimedia and Internet use and should be used for troubleshooting purposes only. With only 16 colors to choose from, most graphics and videos are hardly recognizable. If there are not enough colors to display a certain image, it might appear in black and white.

Configuring Multimedia

■ 256 Colors—This option is considerably better than the previous one. With 256 colors available to Windows applications, many graphics can be displayed in their original palette of colors. However, images designed for higher color depths appear *pixelated*, detracting from the overall quality. You might also notice a *palette-switching* effect when moving between the desktop and your applications.

■ High Color (16-bit)—Selecting High Color gives Windows plenty of colors to work with—around 65,000. At this color depth, the quality of images is excellent and pixelation is much less apparent. For most users, this option is the best trade-off between image quality and the performance of your display.

■ True Color (24-bit)—True Color is so named because of its capability to display colors exactly as they appear in real life. Incredibly, this option can display up to 16.7 million colors—more than the human eye can detect. True Color is designed for graphics professionals who need precise onscreen colors. With most video cards, the trade-off in performance is not enough to justify the slight improvement in quality.

■ True Color (32-bit)—This option is generally available on high-end video cards only. Although it is capable of displaying a broader range of colors than 24-bit, you pay the price in video performance. I would not recommend selecting 32-bit true color unless you specifically require it.

Applying Color Changes

When you apply a color change on the Settings tab of Display Properties, a Compatibility Warning dialog box might appear. It asks whether you'd like to restart the computer before applying the new color settings.

The following options are available:

■ Restart the computer with the new color settings?—This is the safest option. Restarting the computer ensures that other applications (especially games) are capable of adjusting to the new color settings with no problems. Switching to a lower color depth without restarting the computer might cause a temporary reduction in image quality.

■ Apply the new color settings without restarting?—If you are not running any graphics-intensive applications, or if you are switching to a higher color depth, this option is usually the best one. It applies color changes immediately, without having to restart your computer.

■ Don't ask this question again—Check this box to have Windows automatically use the selected option for subsequent color changes (without displaying the Compatibility Warning dialog box). For example, if you choose Apply the new color settings without restarting? and place a check mark in this box, the changes will take effect immediately every time you select new color settings.

NOTE	Modern games typically require 256 or 16-bit color for optimum performance. If the game runs slower than usual, try experimenting with the color depth. Note that it is not always necessary to manually adjust the color depth—many games do this automatically.

If the Warning dialog box does not appear before applying color changes, you can configure these options via the Advanced button.

You will find the following options under the Compatibility heading:

- Restart the computer before applying the new color settings—This option is identical to the one on the Warning Compatibility dialog box (see the previous list).

- Apply the new color settings without restarting—Also identical to the option in the Warning Compatibility dialog box (see the previous list).

- Ask me before applying the new color settings—Choose this option to have a dialog box appear each time you apply new color settings. You can then specify whether the changes should take effect immediately or after restarting Windows.

Adjusting the Screen Area

The resolution is displayed in the form height×width (measured in pixels). This means that the larger the numbers, the more information you can fit on your monitor. For example, with a screen area of 640×480, Word might be capable of displaying 20 lines of text when maximized. Increasing the resolution to 800×600 might allow you to see 25 lines of Word text at once.

If you performed a *clean install* of Windows 98, the screen area is probably set at 640×480 (the minimum size). For most users, 640×480 is not the best option, especially if you a working with a 15" or larger monitor.

Here are my recommendations for some common monitor sizes:

14"	640×480	
15"	640×480 or	800×600
17"	800×600 or	1024×768
19"	1024×768	
21"	1280×1024	

Configuring Multimedia

Note that these settings are recommended for close-viewing monitors only. For readability purposes, home theatre PCs or those viewed from a distance might need to be set lower than the recommended settings.

> **NOTE**   Pixels are the tiny dots that combine to form an image on your computer screen. The term resolution refers to the number of pixels that can be displayed in a given area (for example, a 15" monitor).

Likewise, on monitors with very clear output, you might decide to increase the screen area above these recommendations. If you find that text is too difficult to read, but are happy with the current desktop size, see the section, "Adjusting Font Sizes," later in this chapter

Adjusting the resolution:

1. Right-click anywhere on the desktop and choose Properties.

2. The Display Properties dialog box appears. Click the Settings tab to bring up the display settings (refer to Figure 4.2).

3. Under the heading Screen Area, drag the slider toward More to increase the size of your desktop. To decrease your desktop size, drag the slider toward Less. Notice that as you drag the slider a preview of the chosen screen dimensions appears in the Preview area of the dialog box.

4. Click OK to apply the changes then click OK in the following dialog box.

5. After switching to the new screen area a dialog box appears to verify that there were no problems (see Figure 4.4). Click Yes to continue, or No to switch back to the previous settings.

Figure 4.4

After applying the new settings, a confirmation dialog box appears to ensure that everything is okay.

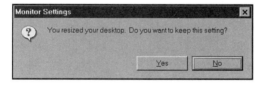

> **NOTE**   If your screen is blank or garbled after clicking OK in step 4, wait 15 seconds and Windows 98 automatically switches back to the previous settings.

Adjusting Font Sizes

There might be times when your screen area is just right but the text in dialog boxes or menus is too small or blurry. This problem is often magnified for far-sighted people or the visually impaired, as well as for monitors that are designed to be viewed at low resolutions.

> **NOTE** Some dialog boxes might appear larger or smaller after adjusting the proportional font size. This behavior is by design. To change font sizes without affecting other Windows elements, use the Appearance tab of Display Properties.

To resolve this problem, Windows 98 allows you to select from two predetermined font sizes: Small or Large. In addition, there is a custom option where you can specify the size that you are most comfortable with.

Adjusting the proportional font size

1. Right-click anywhere on the desktop and choose Properties.

2. The Display Properties dialog box appears. Click the Settings tab to bring up the display settings (refer to Figure 4.2).

3. Click the Advanced button. The Properties box for your video card is displayed (see Figure 4.5 for an example of what this might look like).

Figure 4.5
Here's what the advanced properties look like with an ATI® All-In-Wonder® Pro video card. Your system might have different options.

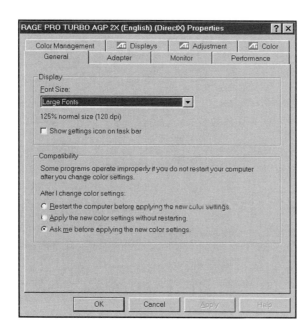

4. Under the heading Display, select Small Fonts, Large Fonts, or Other from the Font Size drop-down list.

5. Click OK to apply the changes. You'll need to restart Windows for the new font size to take effect.

> **NOTE** After applying a custom font size, some applications might have trouble displaying text. The quality of fonts might also be reduced if font smoothing is disabled on the Effects tab of Display Properties. To avoid these problems, choose the Large or Small font size only.

If Other is selected in step 4, a third dialog box appears, prompting you to select a custom font size (refer to Figure 4.5). The font size can be specified by either selecting a value from the drop-down list or by dragging the ruler to the desired length. A preview of the new font size is shown below the ruler. Click OK in both dialog boxes to apply the changes.

Using the Taskbar Display Icon

 For quick access to different resolutions and color depths, a Display icon can be added to the *taskbar tray*. This is not unlike the Speaker icon, which also resides on the taskbar.

> **NOTE** You might remember QuickRes from the collection of utilities called Powertoys. This was an enhancement for Windows 95 only. QuickRes is no longer needed because the new display settings icon matches its features while providing a greater level of integration with Windows 98.

Enabling or disabling the Taskbar Display icon

1. Right-click anywhere on the desktop and choose Properties.

2. The Display Properties dialog box appears. Click the Settings tab to bring up the display settings (refer to Figure 4.2).

3. Click the Advanced button. The Properties box for your video card is displayed.

4. Under the heading Display, place a check mark in the box labeled Show settings icon on task bar to enable this option. Uncheck the box to disable it.

5. Click OK for the changes to take effect.

Now that the Display Settings icon is displayed on your taskbar, it can be used in the following ways:

1. Move the cursor over the Display Settings icon and let it hover there for a second. A *tooltip* appears, describing the current resolution and color depth.

2. Left-click (or right-click) the icon to bring up a list of possible resolutions and color depths (see Figure 4.6). Click an option to switch to it.

Figure 4.6

The range of options available on the Display Settings menu will vary depending on the capabilities of your video card.

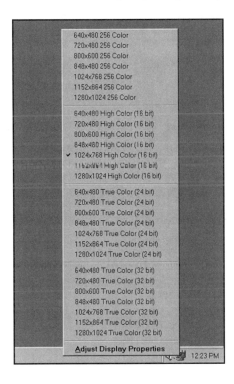

3. Double-click the icon to instantly bring up the Settings tab of Display Properties.

> **NOTE**   The Display Settings icon has a tendency to overestimate your PC's graphics capabilities. While there might be an option for 1280×1024 with 32-bit color, your computer might not support this combination. Refer to your video card and monitor manuals for the upper limits of these components.

Enabling and Disabling the Active Desktop

The *Active Desktop* is one of Windows 98's most touted features, enabling you to personalize your desktop with interactive content. After installing Windows, Active Desktop is enabled by default and the *Channel Bar* is displayed on the right-hand side of your desktop (see Figure 4.7).

Configuring Multimedia

Figure 4.7
The Active Desktop is enabled after installing Windows 98.

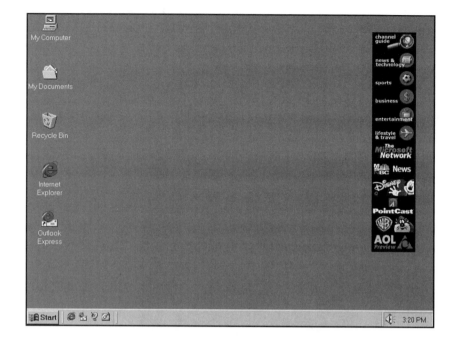

Enabling or Disabling the Active Desktop

1. Right-click anywhere on the desktop and point to Active Desktop.

2. If a check mark appears next to View As Web Page, click this option to disable the Active Desktop. If there is no check mark, clicking it will enable the Active Desktop.

3. The changes take effect immediately.

> **NOTE** The Active Desktop can also be toggled on or off via Display Properties. To access this option, right-click the Desktop and choose Properties. Click the Web tab and place a check mark in View my Active Desktop as a Web page to enable this feature.

Adjusting Sound Settings

If you have multiple sound devices attached to your computer, you can specify which devices Windows should utilize for playback and recording. In this section, I also show you how Windows 98 can take advantage of your computer's speaker setup.

Setting a Playback Device

The playback device is used to play Wave files only. Other sources such as MIDI, CD Audio, and Line-In are handled separately. Windows automatically chooses the best playback device for your computer so you shouldn't need to change this setting.

> **NOTE**   Windows 98 does a lousy job of detecting playback devices—any system component that is vaguely related to sound gets listed in the Playback Devices drop-down list. Take the Game Compatible Device, for example. Although it's just a socket for joysticks, Windows thinks it can play sound because it is attached to your sound card.

Selecting the preferred playback device

1. Click Start, point to Settings and then click Control Panel.

2. Double-click the Multimedia icon. The Multimedia Properties dialog box appears (see Figure 4.8).

Figure 4.8

Select your preferred playback and recording devices in the Multimedia Properties dialog box.

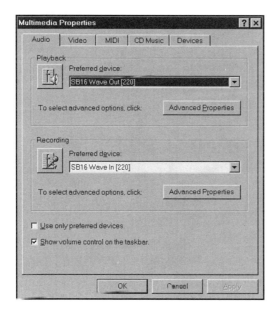

3. Under the heading Playback, select an item from the Preferred device drop-down list. For example, if you'd like your Sound Blaster® 16/AWE32 card to play Wave files, select the SB16 Wave Out entry.

4. Click OK to save changes.

From this point on Windows will attempt to use the selected device to play all Wave files. If this device is already in use, another device (if present) will be used.

Setting a Recording Device

> **NOTE**   If you're in the Multimedia dialog box, you might want to access the volume controls to see which sound sources are available for your devices. Click an icon under the Playback or Recording heading and the appropriate volume controls are displayed.

Unlike the Playback Device, the Recording Device is used to record from all available sources, such as CD Audio, Line-In, and the Microphone. Generally, you should not change this setting unless you want to use a special device for recording purposes.

Selecting the preferred recording device

1. Click Start, point to Settings and then click Control Panel.

2. Double-click the Multimedia icon. The Multimedia Properties dialog box appears (refer to Figure 4.8).

3. Under the heading Recording, select an item from the Preferred device drop-down list. For example, if you'd like your Sound Blaster® 16/ AWE32 card to record sound, select the SB16 Wave In entry.

4. Click OK to save changes.

Windows now uses the selected device to play all Wave files. If the device is not available, an alternative device (if present) is used.

Using Only the Preferred Device

It's possible to tell Windows to ignore all other sound devices in your computer and use only the ones you select (the preferred devices). Note that when this option is selected, sound files might refuse to play if the preferred device is already in use.

> **NOTE**   If you receive audio error messages after choosing to use only the preferred devices, one or both of those devices might not be set up correctly. Another possibility is that they were incorrectly detected by Windows and are not sound devices at all.

Using only the preferred devices for playback and recording

1. Click Start, point to Settings, and then click Control Panel.

2. Double-click the Multimedia icon. The Multimedia Properties dialog box appears (see Figure 4.9).

3. Place a check mark in the box labeled Use only preferred devices. Unchecking the box disables this option.

Figure 4.9

Checking the Use only preferred devices option tells Windows to ignore all other sound devices.

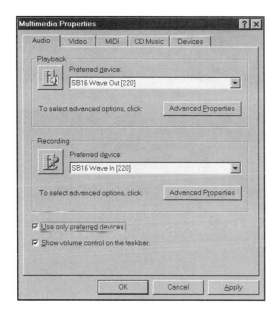

4. Click OK to save changes.

Registering Your Speaker Setup

Windows 98 includes built-in support for a variety of speaker setups, from the monophonic speakers found on some laptops to the five speaker surround sound systems of home theatres.

But before applications and games can take advantage of your speaker system, you'll need to register it in the Control Panel.

> **NOTE** The registration of your speaker setup is a new feature of Windows 98. As a result, there will not be a significant improvement in sound quality until games and applications are designed to take advantage of this feature.

Registering your speaker setup

1. Click Start, point to Settings, and then click Control Panel.

2. Double-click the Multimedia icon. The Multimedia Properties dialog box appears (refer to Figure 4.9).

3. Under the heading Playback, click the Advanced Properties button. The Advanced Audio Properties dialog box is displayed (see Figure 4.10).

Configuring Multimedia

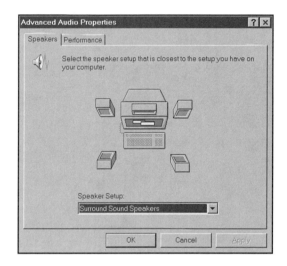

4. Select the closest matching entry from the Speaker Setup drop-down list. A preview of that entry appears in the space above.

5. When you are satisfied with your selection, click OK to save changes.

Setting the Audio CD Drive

If your computer has more than one CD or DVD drive, you can set up one as the default audio CD player.

> **NOTE** To find out which drive is represented by a particular letter name (for example, D:), eject all CDs and insert an audio CD into one of the drives. Next open My Computer and look at the drive labeled Audio CD—the corresponding drive letter appears in parentheses.

Setting the default audio CD drive

1. Click Start, point to Settings, and then click Control Panel.

2. Double-click the Multimedia icon. The Multimedia Properties dialog box appears (refer to Figure 4.8).

3. Click the CD Music tab.

4. Select the desired CD Drive letter from the drop-down list labeled Default CD-ROM drive for playing CD music.

5. Click OK for the changes to take effect.

Configuring Multimedia Components

A large variety of multimedia components is at your disposal in Windows 98. In this section, I'll help you to decide which ones are right for your system, as well as provide instructions for adding and removing individual components.

To find out which components are available, open the Add/Remove Programs icon in Control Panel. The information you're looking for is on the Windows Setup tab (see Figure 4.11).

Figure 4.11

The Windows Setup tab lists all the components bundled with Windows 98.

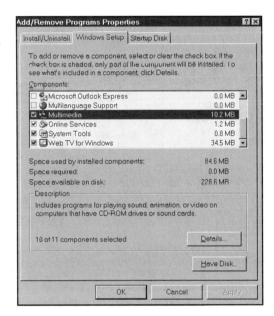

Making Sense of the Multimedia Components

It's a good idea to know what a program does before removing it or installing it on your hard drive. So to take the mystery out of the myriad of multimedia components included with Windows 98, in the next several pages I'll describe each one. (Components are arranged into categories as they appear on the Windows Setup tab. Only those items related to multimedia are shown.)

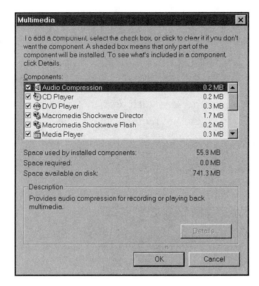

Figure 4.12

As you would expect, most—but not all—of Windows 98's multimedia-related software is listed under the Multimedia category.

Multimedia Category

Here's what the various multimedia category items, shown in Figure 4.12, offer:

- Audio Compression—Includes several audio *codecs* that allow you to play and record sound using a variety of compression formats. Without these codecs, attempting to play certain Wave files might result in an error message. The Audio Compression component is installed by default and should not be removed.

- CD Player—This option is fairly self-explanatory. As you might have guessed, CD Player is an applet for playing music CDs. Uninstall this component if your computer doesn't have a CD or DVD drive, or if you're using Plus! 98's Deluxe CD Player and no longer need the original CD Player.

> **NOTE** Although your computer has a DVD drive, the DVD Player might not appear in the list of multimedia components because your DVD decoder card is not supported. If so, you need use the DVD player that was bundled with your DVD drive.

- DVD Player—A brand new Windows 98 applet, DVD Player enables you to watch and interact with DVD movies on your computer. Unfortunately, this component is not compatible with all DVD decoder cards.

- Macromedia Shockwave Director—A plug-in for Internet Explorer that allows you to view Web sites and play files created with Director. Shockwave is a multimedia format that enhances Web sites with a greater level of interactivity, animation, and sound while maintaining short download times for low-bandwidth connections.

- Macromedia Shockwave Flash—Similar to Shockwave Director, this component is an Internet Explorer plug-in enabling you to view sites created with Flash. The latest versions of Flash and Director can be found at Macromedia's Web site: `http://www.macromedia.com`.

- Media Player—The original version of Media Player that can play a variety of sound and video formats. As explained in Chapter 19, "Common Problems and Their Solutions," this component has now been superceded by Media Player 2. If your player doesn't works as expected, you should investigate downloading the new version.

- Microsoft NetShow Player 2.0—A player for listening to streaming audio over the Internet. NetShow has been superceded by the new all-in-one Windows Media Player, so there's no need to install it.

- Multimedia Sound Schemes—Four theme collections of sounds—Jungle, Musica, Robotz, and Utopia—which you can use to create a unique atmosphere on your computer. Each sound can also be assigned to a particular Windows *event* (for example maximizing a window). These sounds total 6.5MB altogether, so you might want to skip this option if you're low on disk space.

- Samples Sounds—The default Windows sound collection, including: Chimes, Chord, Ding, Logoff, Notify, Recycle, Tada, and the Microsoft Sound. All of these sounds have been updated since Windows 95.

- Sound Recorder—The standard Windows applet for recording sound. You can also use Sound Recorder to perform basic editing functions and to apply a limited number of special effects. For more advanced editing and effects work I suggest using one of the many shareware or commercial sound editing programs on the market.

> **NOTE** Plus! 98 components are not listed on the Windows Setup tab. To add or remove a Plus! 98 component, click the Install/Uninstall programs tab, choose Microsoft Plus! 98 from the list of applications, and click the Add/Remove button.

- Video Compression—Includes several video codecs, enabling you view the most popular compressed video formats. Without these codecs, attempting to play certain video files might result in an error message. As with Audio Compression, this component is installed by default and should not be removed.

Configuring Multimedia

■ Volume Control—This applet is used to control the playback and recording volumes for each of your sound sources (for example MIDI, Wave, CD audio, Line-in). Removing such an essential component as Volume Control is not a good idea unless your sound card includes an alternative mixer that you'd rather use.

Accessories Category

The Accessories category, shown in Figure 4.13, offers a number of components, including desktop wallpaper, games, and the useful Calculator program.

Figure 4.13

Wallpaper, games, and image viewers are available in the Accessories category.

■ Desktop Wallpaper—A collection of pictures and patterns you can use to personalize the desktop background. This component is installed by default.

■ Games—Includes the card games FreeCell, Hearts, and Solitaire, as well as the puzzle game Minesweeper. If none of these interest you, go ahead and remove the Games component to save half a megabyte.

NOTE   For other ways to free up hard disk space, click Start, point to Programs, Accessories, and System Tools, then click Disk Cleanup.

■ Imaging—Two programs for viewing scanned images and documents. Imaging Preview is a simple viewer, whereas Imaging includes basic manipulation and editing tools. *TWAIN* support for scanners is also installed with this component.

■ Mouse Pointers—Several mouse pointer collections, some of which are designed at a larger size for the vision-impaired. One and a half megabytes can be saved by removing this component if it is not required.

■ Paint—The standard Windows applet for viewing BMPs. Paint also functions as a basic drawing and graphics editing program, and can be enhanced to support GIFs and JPGs by installing Office 97. Unless you have another graphics editor that completely replaces the functionality of Paint, I recommend that you keep this component.

■ Quick View—A utility for viewing a variety of popular document and graphics files. Now that Windows 98 has built-in support for previewing files (with Web View), it's hard to justify installing this 4.5MB component.

Double-click the Screen Savers component to bring up a sublist of items, shown in Figure 4.14.

Figure 4.14

Windows 98 some impressive new 3D screen savers, as well as the classic Flying Windows.

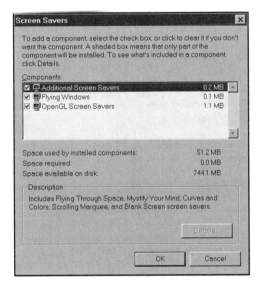

■ Additional Screen Savers—A selection of several two-dimensional screen savers: Blank, Curves and Colors, Flying Through Space, Mystify Your Mind, and Scrolling Marquee (used to leave Out for Lunch messages and so on).

■ Flying Windows—Perhaps the most well-known Windows screen saver, Flying Windows shows a multitude of Windows logos soaring through outer space.

> **NOTE** More than a decade ago, PC monitors were prone to *burn-in*—which caused permanent damages when the same image was displayed for hours at a time. Screen savers were introduced to help prevent burn-in by displaying continuously moving images. However, because modern monitors are virtually immune to this problem, screen savers are merely used for their amusement value.

■ OpenGL Screen Savers—Cool 3D screen savers that take advantage of Windows 98's software *OpenGL* driver, including 3D Flower Box, 3D Flying Objects, 3D Maze, 3D Pipes, and 3D Text. A great way to show off the capabilities of Windows 98 (and your PC's processing power) to your friends!

Communications Category

Windows 98 comes with a plethora of online communication programs, as shown in Figure 4.15, that allow you to dial another computer with your modem, surf the Internet, or chat with other users.

Figure 4.15

Communicate with people across the world with Microsoft's NetMeeting and Chat programs.

■ Microsoft Chat 2.1—A program for chatting with other users via the Internet. Microsoft Chat has a unique comic strip feature where each person is represented by a cartoon character. Chat 2.5 is now available, so you might prefer to skip this option and download the latest version from Microsoft's Web site.

■ Microsoft NetMeeting—Version 2.1 of the video conferencing communication program. With NetMeeting, you can communicate with other people on the Internet or LAN using video and audio. You can even share an application with someone and collaborate in real-time.

Desktop Themes Category

Desktop themes are an entertaining way to customize the appearance of Windows 98. As you can see in Figure 4.16, you can choose wallpaper, sounds, and screen savers grouped around themes such as Dangerous Creatures, Inside Your Computer, and Leonardo da Vinci.

Figure 4.16
Desktop themes can take up a large chunk of disk space, but they are a lot of fun.

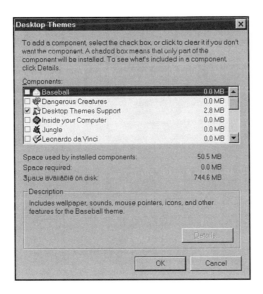

Personalize your desktop with sounds, icons, colors, fonts, mouse pointers, and screen savers. Windows 98 includes all the themes from Plus! 95 as well as four new ones: Baseball, Jungle, Space, and Underwater.

If Desktop Themes don't interest you, you can save a few megabytes of space by removing them. Don't forget to remove the Desktop Themes Support item too.

NOTE Let's say you want to keep the sounds from the Windows 98 theme but are not interested in the pictures, icons or mouse pointers. Using My Computer, locate the `C:\Program Files\Plus!\Themes` folder and delete all files—except for sounds—beginning with Windows 98.

Configuring Multimedia

Internet Tools Category

You can choose to install a variety of Internet tools, as shown in Figure 4.17.

Figure 4.17

Internet tools, including plug-ins that enable you to receive RealAudio content and explore virtual worlds.

- Microsoft VRML 2.0 Viewer—A plug-in for Internet Explorer that allows you to view and wander around 3D virtual reality worlds. As virtual reality is a relatively rare phenomenon on the Internet, you might want to skip this component and save about 4MB in the process.

- Real Audio Player 4.0—An out-dated version of the popular Read Audio Player. Version 5.0 is now available from the RealAudio Web site at `http://www.realaudio.com`. Or you might choose to install Microsoft's Windows Media Player, which is compatible with most Real Audio files.

> **NOTE**   If the Microsoft VRML 2.0 plug-in has captured your interest, check out the new Cult3D® plug-in at `http://www.cult3d.com`.

WebTV for Windows Category

If your computer has WebTV capability, you'll want to ensure the that components shown in Figure 4.18 are installed.

- WaveTop Data Broadcasting—Download Web content via regular analog TV signals using this program. WaveTop requires a TV tuner card to function and is currently available in the U.S. and Canada only.

Figure 4.18

Receive enhanced television broadcasts on your PC with WebTV and WaveTop.

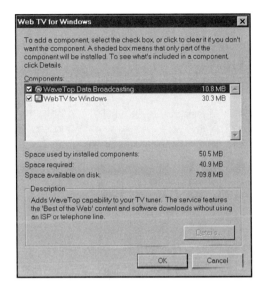

■ WebTV for Windows—If your PC has a TV tuner card, WebTV for Windows turns your computer into a semi-interactive TV. And with or without a tuner card you can download scheduled program listings from the Internet if you live in the U.S, or Canada. WebTV is a hefty 30MB component, so you might want to use an alternative TV viewer if you can't afford the disk space.

Adding and Removing Multimedia Components

Often you'll find that a Windows 98 Multimedia component is not necessary, or not worth the space it claims on your hard drive. One example is CD Player, which becomes redundant after installing the Deluxe CD Player from Plus! 98.

> **NOTE** While the Windows Setup tab is limited to adding or removing components that are included with Windows 98, the Install/Uninstall tab is generally used to uninstall programs not found on your Windows 98 CD-ROM (for example, Microsoft Office).

You might also discover that a component is missing because it was not installed along with Windows 98.

Fortunately, just about every one of these components can be removed or added via the Control Panel. Two notable exceptions are Internet Explorer 4.0 and ActiveMovie, which are now integrated into Windows 98.

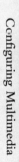

Configuring Multimedia

Adding or removing a multimedia component

1. Click Start, point to Settings, and then click Control Panel.

2. Double-click the Add/Remove Programs icon. The Add/Remove Programs dialog box appears.

3. Click the Windows Setup to bring up a list of customizable components (see Figure 4.19). Wait a few seconds while Windows 98 determines which components are installed on your system.

Figure 4.19

If you're looking to free up some disk space, use the Windows Setup tab to remove any unwanted components.

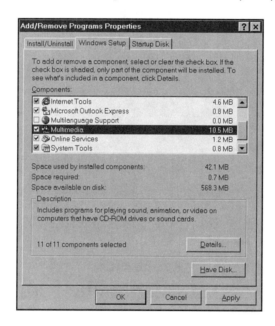

4. Double-click an item (for example Multimedia) to see a list of components belonging to that category. If a component is checked, its size in megabytes is displayed in the right-hand column.

5. Select the item you want to add or remove. Check a box to install the respective component. Uncheck a box to uninstall that component.

6. Click OK in both dialog boxes and insert your Windows 98 CD-ROM if prompted to do so (see Figure 4.20).

7. You might need to restart your computer for the changes to take effect.

> **NOTE**   You can add a category's entire list of components at once by placing a check mark in that category's box (after step 3). Similarly, uncheck a box to remove any installed components belonging to that category.

Figure 4.20
Windows prompts you to insert your Windows 98 CD-ROM if necessary.

Chapter

5

Personaliz-ing Your Desktop

by Adam Vujic

When you move into a house, an apartment, or even a new office, it usually isn't long before you begin personalizing your space. You put a poster of your favorite movie star on the wall of your room. A print by your favorite artist might go above the living room couch. Even your humble cubicle might contain a photo of your family or pet. Windows 98 gives you the same capability to change your environment to reflect your taste and preferences.

In this chapter, you'll learn how to change the appearance of your desktop with new color schemes and even wallpaper that displays a picture or pattern you choose. You'll see how to customize your mouse pointers so they provide information about areas of your screen. You can alter the sounds Windows 98 makes to inform you of system events, even having a humorous sound bite play if a program makes an error or crashes. Then you'll see how to bring all of those elements together in a unified desktop theme. Finally, you'll review the Windows 98 Active Desktop and, for serious system tinkerers, see how to change the screens Windows 98 displays when it launches and shuts down.

Customizing the Appearance of Your Desktop

One of Windows 98's best features is its capability to personalize almost everything you see on your screen. The desktop background, colors, fonts, mouse pointers, and icons can all be customized according to your preference. And if you don't have the time (or patience) to adjust every small detail, there are some predefined appearance *schemes* to make the job a little easier.

> **NOTE**   In Windows 98, a scheme is a collection of elements that are centered around a specific theme. Appearance schemes, mouse pointer schemes, and sound schemes all stem from the same concept. The 3D Pointers scheme is one example—it's a collection of mouse pointers, each with a three-dimensional appearance. You can use a variety of existing schemes or create your own.

Windows 98's desktop settings can be customized via the Display icon in the Control Panel.

Applying an Image to the Desktop

Adding an image to the desktop is one of the easiest and most effective ways to personalize the appearance of your screen. It can even help you to feel more comfortable using your computer.

Windows can display *JPG, GIF, BMP,* and *HTML* files on your desktop background.

Selecting desktop wallpaper

1. Right-click anywhere on the desktop and choose Properties. The Display Properties dialog box appears (see Figure 5.1).

Figure 5.1

Add an image, Web page, or pattern to your desktop background via the Background tab of Display Properties.

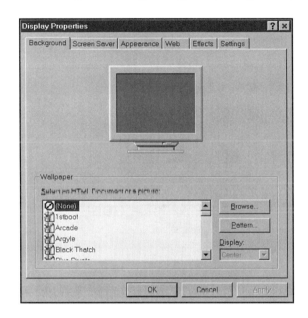

2. In the Wallpaper section, select an item from the list titled Select a HTML Document or Picture, or click Browse to locate a file on your computer. A preview of the selected item appears in the space near the top of the screen.

3. Select how you want the picture to be displayed from the Display drop-down list. The following options are available if you selected a JPG, GIF, or BMP image:

   ■ Center—This option centers the picture on your desktop. If the picture is too small for your screen area, a border appears around the edges of the desktop. However, if the picture is too large, it is cropped to fit your desktop.

   ■ Tile—Choose this option if you'd like the picture to be repeated across your entire desktop. The effect is similar to that of a patterned tiled wall.

   ■ Stretch—With this option enabled, the picture—no matter how big or small—is scaled to fit your desktop exactly. Windows stretches or shrinks the picture to the dimensions of your screen area.

4. Click OK to apply the changes.

> **TIP** Enabling the stretch option might reduce the quality of your wallpaper image. For best results, use an image that matches your screen resolution exactly. HTML files (Web pages) cannot be stretched or tiled.

If the Active Desktop is disabled, a dialog box appears asking if you'd like to activate it (see Figure 5.2). Click Yes to continue or No to choose another wallpaper.

Figure 5.2

This dialog box appears if you apply a GIF, JPG, or HTML file with the Active Desktop disabled.

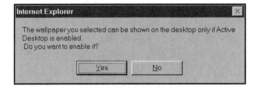

Adding Items to the Wallpaper List

In Display Properties, the Wallpaper section lists all the supported file types (such as, BMP, JPG, GIF, and HTML) found in your Windows folder. To add an item to the list, copy its file across to the Windows folder via My Computer.

If the Display Properties dialog box is already open, click OK and then reopen it to refresh the Wallpaper list.

Applying a Pattern to the Desktop

A potential problem with using wallpaper is the amount of memory it consumes. This can sometimes lead to degraded performance, especially if your computer has a limited amount of RAM.

If you'd like to enhance your desktop without sacrificing performance a simple, patterned wallpaper might suffice.

> **NOTE** A *pattern* consists of two colors—black and the background color. But how do you change the background color? Click the Appearance tab of Display Properties, select Desktop from the Item list, and then choose a color. Click OK for the changes to take effect.

Selecting a wallpaper pattern

1. Right-click anywhere on the desktop and choose Properties. The Display Properties dialog box appears.

2. In the Wallpaper section, select (None) from the list titled Select an HTML Document or Picture.

3. Click the Pattern button to display the Pattern dialog box (see Figure 5.3).

Figure 5.3

Windows 98 includes a variety of patterns to choose from.

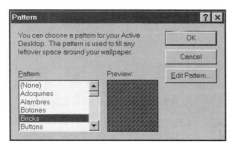

4. Select an item from the Pattern list. A preview of the item is displayed on the right side of the screen.

5. When you are satisfied with your selection, click OK on both dialog boxes.

Editing a Pattern

If you want you can edit a pattern to create your own original work of art. Unless you're familiar with editing images on a small scale, this might take some getting used to.

Creating a new pattern

1. Right-click anywhere on the desktop and choose Properties. The Display Properties dialog box appears.

2. In the Wallpaper section, select (None) from the list titled Select an HTML Document or Picture.

3. Click the Pattern button to display the Pattern dialog box.

4. Select an item from the Pattern list and click the Edit Pattern button. The Pattern Editor appears (see Figure 5.4).

Figure 5.4

Create your own dazzling pattern one pixel at time with Windows 98's Pattern Editor.

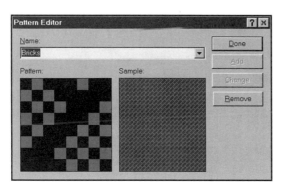

5. An enlarged view of the pattern is displayed in the Pattern box. Click anywhere within this box to change the color of a pixel. The pattern's preview is continually updated in the Sample box.

6. After you are satisfied with how your new pattern looks, type a name for it in the Name box. Click the Add button to save the pattern.

7. Click Done to continue. Then, click OK on both dialog boxes to apply the new pattern to your desktop.

> **NOTE**   For a unique effect use the Pattern Editor to create a pattern with your own initials. Don't forget to add it to the list of patterns when you're finished so all your hard work is saved for later.

To remove a pattern from the list, click the Remove button instead of following step 6. The Change button is used to replace an existing pattern with an edited one.

Applying an Image and Pattern Wallpaper

If you're feeling particularly creative, you might want to combine a regular wallpaper image with a patterned background. The end result is an image centered on the desktop complete with a decorative border (see Figure 5.5).

Applying an image and pattern wallpaper

1. Right-click anywhere on the desktop and choose Properties. The Display Properties dialog box appears.

2. In the Wallpaper section, select an image from the list titled Select an HTML Document or Picture or click the Browse button to locate a file on your computer.

3. Click the Pattern button to display the Pattern dialog box.

4. Select an item from the Pattern list. When you are satisfied with your selection, click OK.

5. Select Center from the Display drop-down list. A preview of the image and pattern combination is shown in the space near the top of the screen.

6. Click OK to apply the changes.

Customizing the Appearance of Folders

Now that Internet Explorer has been integrated into Windows a whole new range of possibilities exist for customizing folders. Most significantly, Windows 98 enables you to add JPG, GIF, or BMP images to a folder's background. The color of icon text is also customizable for each of your folders.

Figure 5.5

A wallpaper-pattern combination can be an effective way to personalize your desktop.

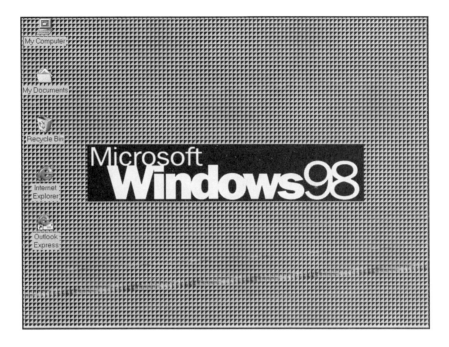

NOTE   When you add a background image or customize the colors of a folder, the changes are stored in a desktop.ini file within that folder. Modifying the contents of this file is not recommended.

Customizing an individual folder

1. Locate the folder you want to customize via My Computer.

2. Click the View menu and choose Customize this Folder. A mini-wizard appears to guide you through the process. The following options are available:

   - Create or edit an HTML document—Select this option if you want to customize the folder like a Web page. Your HTML editor opens the current folder, allowing you to apply a full range of effects using HTML tags. I recommend this option only if you've had experience in designing Web pages.

   - Choose a background picture—The simplest way to customize a folder. This option adds an image or pattern to the folder's background, similar to the desktop wallpaper.

   - Remove customization—You can restore the original appearance of your folder by choosing Remove customization.

3. After selecting Choose a background picture, click Next to continue. You'll see a variety of options to choose from (see Figure 5.6).

Figure 5.6

Any folder can be customized easily in Windows 98.

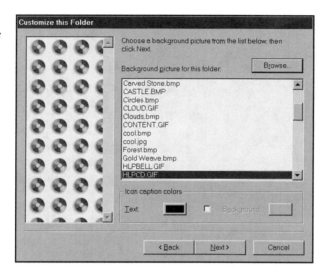

> **TIP**   Try to use a simple, light-colored background image that does not interfere with the icons. Also, keep in mind that a small, repeatable pattern requires less memory than large, complex images.

4. A list of compatible images appears under the heading Background picture for this folder. Just select an image to see a preview of it. Click Browse to locate an image elsewhere on your computer. All folder images are automatically tiled—it is not possible to center or stretch a folder image as with the desktop.

5. Under the heading Icon Caption Colors, select the desired Text and Background colors. Text refers to the captions that appear next to each Folder icon, whereas Background is the area behind an icon's caption. You'll need to place a check mark in the Background box in order to enable this option.

6. Click Next to see a summary of the changes Windows is about to make to the folder.

7. Click Back to revise the changes or click Finish to apply the new settings.

Customizing Colors, Fonts, and Sizes

As you'll soon see, almost any Windows element can be customized, including scrollbars, dialog boxes, menus, and buttons. Not only is this a great way to personalize the appearance of Windows 98, but it can help make things easier if you have trouble reading small fonts or clicking tiny scrollbar arrows.

Windows 98's appearance customization features can be found in Display Properties, on the Appearance tab.

Applying an Appearance Scheme

Windows 98 includes some ready-made schemes to take the hassle out of editing individual screen elements. Each scheme is based on a certain theme or designed with a particular purpose in mind. For example, the Pumpkin scheme is included purely for fun, whereas the High Contrast scheme help to improve the clarity of some laptop computer screens.

> **NOTE** You might notice that (high color) appears next to some schemes on the Appearance tab, as well as in the Desktop Themes applet This indicates that the scheme or theme is designed for 16-bit color depth or higher, and its quality might be unsatisfactory at 8-bit (256) color depth.

Applying an appearance scheme

1. Right-click anywhere on the desktop and choose Properties. The Display Properties dialog box appears.

2. Click the Appearance tab (see Figure 5.7) and select an item from the Scheme list. A preview of the scheme is displayed.

Figure 5.7
Use the Appearance tab to give your computer a dramatically different look and feel.

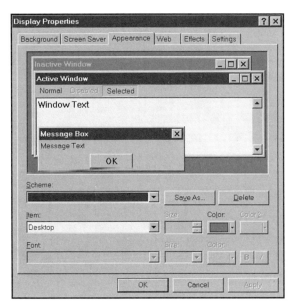

3. When you are satisfied with your selection, click OK to apply the changes.

Customizing Individual Elements

For greater control over the appearance of your screen, you can customize the size, color, and font of individual elements.

Customizing an individual element

1. Right-click anywhere on the desktop and choose Properties. The Display Properties dialog box appears.

2. Click the Appearance tab and select an element from the Item list.

3. Select a new value from the Size, Color, and Color 2 drop-down lists (beside the Item list). The preview area is updated according to your selections.

4. Choose a font from the Font drop-down list then select the desired Size and Color (beside the Font list). You can also click the Bold icon or the Italic icon to apply bold or italic, respectively. The preview area is updated to reflect these changes.

5. Click OK to apply the changes.

> **NOTE**   A new feature of Windows 98 is gradated title bars that change color or shading from left to right across the screen; they give a colorful appearance to the top section of each window. You can apply a gradient using the Color and Color 2 settings on the Appearance tab.

Depending on the item you selected in step 2, some options in steps 3 and 4 might be disabled. For example, it is not possible to change the color of the icon element.

Saving and Deleting Appearance Schemes

After taking the time to customize each individual element, you might want to save the settings for future use. Each saved arrangement is added to the Scheme list.

Saving a new appearance scheme

1. Right-click anywhere on the desktop and choose Properties. The Display Properties dialog box appears.

2. Click the Appearance tab. Set up each element according to your preference.

3. Click the Save As button and then type a name for your scheme and press Enter.

4. Click OK to continue.

To delete a scheme, select it from the Scheme list and click the Delete button.

Adjusting Visual Effects

The term *visual effects* refers to settings that enable you to fine-tune the Windows 98 user interface, including animated menus, font smoothing, and high-color icons.

> **NOTE**   Windows 98 does away with the Plus! tab of Windows 95, but replaces it with a new and improved Effects tab. All the original Plus! features are still there, along with a couple of new options specific to Windows 98.

Windows 98's visual effects can be accessed by right-clicking a space on your desktop, choosing Properties and then clicking the Effects tab. The settings are displayed under the heading Visual Effects (see Figure 5.8).

Figure 5.8

You can fine-tune Windows 98's appearance settings on the Effects tab.

Here's what clicking on the Effects tab elements accomplishes:

- Use large icons—Increases the size of all icons from the regular 32×32 pixels to 64×64 pixels. You might notice that your icons appear in greater detail after enabling this option. This option is best with high screen resolutions, when the icons appear small and difficult to identify. Note that the Start menu, folders in detail, small icons, and list views are not affected by this setting.

■ Show icons using all possible colors—Displays icons in their more colorful version (up to 256 colors). Not all icons support this feature, so some will remain in their original 16-color form. Your display settings must be set to 16-bit color or higher in order for Windows to display icons with 256 colors.

■ Animate windows, menus, and lists—Another of Windows 98's new features relates to the behavior of menus and drop-down lists. Instead of popping up (or down), these elements now slide out when activated. If you're not interested in such animation effects then disable this option. However, keep in mind that windows will no longer shrink or grow when you click the Minimize and Maximize buttons.

■ Smooth edges of screen fonts—Fonts, like everything else on the screen, are made up of pixels. For this reason, onscreen text can sometimes appear rough around the edges. Font smoothing overcomes this problem by using extra colors to blend the edges of the font into the surrounding area. Technically, this effect is known as *anti-aliasing*. It is available in 256-color and higher modes only.

■ Show window contents while dragging—This feature continuously updates the contents of a window as it is resized or dragged around the screen. The end result is a real-time animation effect. Generally it is better to leave this option enabled, but I encourage you to experiment to see which setting you prefer.

> **NOTE**   If you are the kind of person who likes to customize every last detail, then TweakUI is for you. TweakUI is a utility that was created by Microsoft programmers in their spare time. You can find it on your Windows 98 CD-ROM in the tools\reskit\powertoy folder. But be warned: This is an unsupported product and might cause more harm than good if you're not careful.

An additional option on the Effects tab is labeled Hide icons when the desktop is viewed as a Web page. When this option is enabled together with the Active Desktop, your desktop icons are temporarily hidden from view. Hiding your icons can be useful if you'd like to unclutter the desktop—perhaps to view a desktop wallpaper or Web page in its entirety.

Customizing Desktop Icons

Windows 98 enables you to easily customize two types of icons—*shortcuts* and *special desktop* icons.

Shortcut to 3½
Floppy (A)

A shortcut is a link that points to a file on your hard drive; it can be identified by the small arrow at the bottom-left corner of the icon. One example is the Outlook Express icon, which can be found on your desktop (unless you deleted it, of course).

TIP	To create a shortcut, right-click on the desktop or inside a folder and then point to New and choose Shortcut.

Customizing a shortcut icon

1. Use My Computer to locate a shortcut on your hard disk.

2. Right-click the shortcut's icon and choose Properties. The file's properties dialog box is displayed.

3. Click the Change Icon button. Alternative icons for that file are displayed (see Figure 5.9). Select one of these icons or click Browse to locate an icon elsewhere on your computer.

Figure 5.9
Depending on the file, this box displays a variety of icons for you to choose from.

4. Click OK in both dialog boxes to apply the changes.

Special desktop icons include My Computer, Recycle Bin, My Documents, and Network Neighborhood (see Figure 5.10). They are special because they cannot be removed without the use of a utility such as Tweak UI.

Figure 5.10

These special desktop icons can be easily customized but not removed. However, all these icons might not appear on your desktop.

> **NOTE** Although the Network Neighborhood icon appears on the Effects tab, it might not appear on your desktop. This icon is used for networking purposes only, so it won't be available if your computer is not connected to a network or a modem.

Customizing a special desktop icon

1. Right-click anywhere on the desktop and choose Properties. The Display Properties dialog box appears.

2. Click the Effects tab. Under the heading Desktop Icons are the five special icons just mentioned.

3. Select the icon you want to change, and then click the Change Icon button.

4. Select an alternative icon or click Browse to locate an icon elsewhere on your computer.

5. Click OK in both dialog boxes for the changes to take effect.

Customizing Mouse Pointers

Microsoft has gone to great lengths to create top-notch customization features in Windows, and their efforts are apparent even when it comes to mouse pointers. Almost every cursor, arrow, and hourglass can be modified. And if you're feeling adventurous, Windows 98 gives you the option of using colorful, animated pointers too.

Mouse Pointer Schemes

Like the appearance schemes, Windows 98 includes a few sample pointer schemes to whet your appetite.

> **NOTE** What's the difference between pointers, cursors, and arrows? Well, in this book at least, a *pointer* is any onscreen symbol that can be used to manipulate an object—usually with a mouse. A *cursor* is the blinking vertical line (or box) that prompts you to type something. An *arrow* is a typical Windows pointer, which is also known as Normal Select on the Pointer tab of Mouse properties.

The Windows Standard scheme is available in three sizes—normal, large, and extra large—enabling people of all abilities to control the mouse with ease. The 3D Pointers and Animated Hourglasses schemes are for people who like to add some life to standard two-color pointers.

Choosing a mouse pointer scheme

1. From the Control Panel, double-click the Mouse icon.

2. Click the Pointers tab (see Figure 5.11).

Figure 5.11

Liven up your display with some animated or 3D mouse pointers.

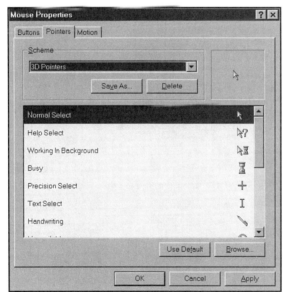

3. Under the heading Scheme, choose a new scheme from the drop-down list. The preview pointers are updated to reflect the selected scheme.

4. Click OK to apply the changes.

Choosing Individual Mouse Pointers

You'll notice that each scheme includes a variety of mouse pointers. Here's a list of the most important ones and what they mean:

- Normal Select—The technical name for the instantly recognizable Windows arrow. When you see this pointer onscreen you know that Windows is waiting for you to click something.

- Help Select—After clicking the Help icon in the upper-right corner of some dialog boxes, your pointer changes to an arrow with a question mark attached. Click a dialog box element to find out what it means.

- Working In Background—When this pointer is displayed Windows is really saying, "there's another program working right now, but go ahead and do your thing anyway." You know the program has done its job when your pointer changes back to Normal Select.

- Busy—Probably the most infamous of all Windows pointers, the Busy pointer is typically displayed as an hourglass. It shows up when Windows or an application is "thinking" and cannot be interrupted.

> **NOTE** If the Busy pointer is displayed while you're working in an application, try moving the pointer to the taskbar or out of the application's window. You might find that the Busy pointer changes back to the Normal Select pointer, enabling you to perform another tasks. This behavior is known as *multitasking*.

- Text Select—This pointer (or cursor) appears in any place where there is text or a space where you can input text. For a quick example, click Start then click Run.

- Unavailable—Whenever you drag an object to the wrong place, this pointer appears as a visual way of saying "Bzzzzt! Please try again." Try dragging the My Computer icon to the Recycle Bin and you'll see what I mean.

- Link Select—This pointer will be familiar to you if you've ever used the Internet or if you use Windows 98's single-click icon interface. It beckons you to click once to open whatever is underneath the pointer.

Now that you understand what each pointer means, we can go ahead and customize each one individually.

Choosing an individual mouse pointer

1. From the Control Panel, double-click the Mouse icon.

2. Click the Pointers tab.

3. Select a pointer from the list in the lower half of the dialog box.

4. Click Use Default to switch back to the default version of that pointer. Otherwise, click Browse to locate a different pointer on your computer (see Figure 5.12). The supported formats have a file extension of ANI (animated) and CUR (static).

Figure 5.12
A preview of the selected pointer appears in the lower-left corner.

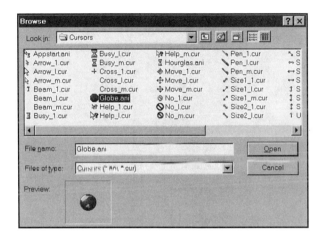

5. Look at the lower-left corner of the dialog box for a preview of the chosen pointer.

6. Click OK to apply the changes.

After customizing each of the individual pointers, you can save the scheme for later. To do so, click the Save As button, type a name for the scheme, and press Enter. Your new scheme then appears in the Scheme drop-down list.

To delete a scheme, select it from the drop-down list and click Delete.

Adjusting Mouse Pointer Settings

Windows 98 includes two options that affect the way your mouse pointer moves onscreen: pointer speed and pointer trails.

You can find these options in the Control Panel by double-clicking the Mouse icon and clicking the Motion tab (see Figure 5.13).

> **NOTE** If special drivers were bundled with your mouse or pointing device (for example, IntelliMouse), you might see some additional options in Mouse properties. Please refer to your product documentation for details on these features.

Figure 5.13

Change the behavior of your mouse pointer on the Motion tab of Mouse Properties.

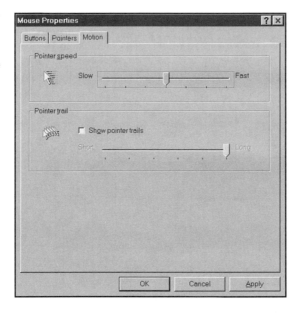

You can customize the following aspects of your mouse pointer:

- Pointer speed—This setting controls the speed of the mouse pointer as it moves across the screen. Dragging the slider all the way toward Slow turns your mouse into a turtle. Although the slowest setting helps to pinpoint an exact spot on the screen, moving from one side to the other can become frustrating. But, if you think setting the speed to Fast is the best choice, think again. Your mouse will become so sensitive that you'll probably need to cut down on your caffeine intake. For most users, the best mouse pointer speed is somewhere in between Slow and Fast. Experiment with each setting to see which one you prefer.

- Pointer trail—A pointer trail is just that—a trail of pointers that follows the original pointer around the screen. Apart from the cool effect that a pointer trail creates, it is designed for one purpose. That is to make the pointer more visible on screens with low refresh rates, such as electronic overhead projectors and some passive-matrix notebook displays. To enable this option, click the box labeled Show pointer trails. Drag the slider toward Long or Short depending on what length you'd like the pointer trail to be.

Modifying Windows Sounds

In Windows 98, sounds can be assigned to *events*, such as starting up your computer, shutting down, or certain error messages.

Windows 98's default sounds (for example, ding, chord, chimes) have been re-recorded in a high-quality, stereo format, which is a welcome change from the outdated Windows 95 and 3.1 sounds. One good example is the new 3D Microsoft sound, which you hear on startup.

> **NOTE** All Windows 98's default sounds are stored in the Windows\Media folder on your hard drive. If Windows is installed on drive C:, click Start then click Run and type `c:\windows\media` in the space provided. Press Enter to open the Media folder.

To see a list of events and their assigned sounds, open the Sounds icon in Control Panel.

As with the appearance and mouse pointer features of Windows 98, a collection of sounds is known as—you guessed it—a scheme. Besides the default Windows sound scheme, you can install four additional schemes via the Add/Remove Programs icon in the Control Panel. They are listed as Jungle, Musica, Robotz, and Utopia.

Choosing a sound scheme

1. From the Control Panel, double-click the Sounds icon. The dialog box in Figure 5.14 appears.

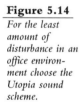

Figure 5.14
For the least amount of disturbance in an office environment choose the Utopia sound scheme.

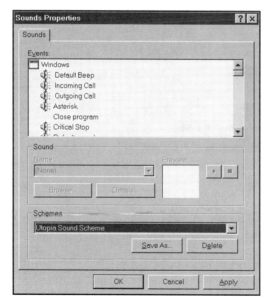

2. Under the Schemes heading, choose a new scheme from the drop-down list.

3. Click OK to apply the changes.

Customizing Individual Sounds

If you're working at an office computer, chances are you (and your colleagues) don't want to hear a rattlesnake shaking its tail every time you click the Start button. Fortunately, Windows 98 enables you to customize or disable every sound you hear.

You'll find many sound events to customize in the Sounds Properties dialog box, but their names are sometimes vague or ambiguous.

| **TIP** | Assign a small (less than 1MB) sound to the Start Windows event to help reduce the startup time. If you decide to use a multi-megabyte sound instead, your computer might temporarily hang while the file is loaded into memory. |

To help you out, the following list provides an explanation for each of these sound events:

- Default Beep—A feature of early versions of Windows; this event is now included for compatibility purposes only. Default Beep appears to have been superceded by the Default Sound event.

- Asterisk—When an application wants to provide you with a tip or other helpful information, this sound event is played. For example, just before you change your screen resolution, the Asterisk event will be played along with an information dialog box.

- Close Program—As you would expect, this event is played when you close a program. However, you might hear this sound even when no applications seem to be running. That's because Windows 98 often calls upon small programs (or *tasks*) to run in the background. You can see a list of these tasks by pressing Ctrl-Alt-Del.

- Critical Stop—This event typically occurs when a device cannot be accessed. For example, double-clicking the Floppy Drive icon when the drive is empty produces a Critical Stop error.

- Default Sound—Probably the most common sound event in Windows 98, the Default Sound is the one that tells you you're doing something wrong. You also hear it when you set the volume level via the Volume Control icon in the taskbar tray.

- Exclamation—The Exclamation event is similar to Asterisk except that it is used to provide more important information to the user. For example, when closing a document in Word without saving changes, a "Save Changes?" dialog box appears along with the exclamation sound.

- Exit Windows—This sound event plays when you shut down, restart, or log off the current Windows session. Windows doesn't actually shut down or restart until this sound has finished playing, so it's best to keep this sound as short as possible.

- Menu Command—The Menu Command event occurs when you click a menu item. For example, clicking Run on the Start menu plays the sound associated with this event.

- Menu Popup—This sound is played when you open any menu or sub-menu. For example, clicking the Start menu or right-clicking the desktop will trigger the Menu Popup event.

- New Mail Notification—When you receive a new message in Outlook Express (or similar email program), you'll hear the New Mail Notification sound.

- Open Program—The Open Program sound event is played when any application or task is opened (see Close program).

- Program Error—When one of the infamous General Protection Fault (or similar) error messages appears, Windows plays the Program Error sound.

- Question—When a program prompts you with a question, you'll hear the Question sound.

- Select—Plays when you select an icon in Explorer.

- Show Toolbar Band—A toolbar band is a row of icons or buttons found on a toolbar. You can trigger the Show Toolbar Band event by double-clicking the vertical line next to a toolbar band.

- Complete Navigation—You'll hear the Complete Navigation sound when a Web page or folder is located and appears onscreen. This event is used in conjunction with Start Navigation.

- Move Menu Item—The Move Menu Item sound is played after you drag a menu item to a new position; this currently works with the Favorites and Start menus only.

- Start Navigation—Clicking a link within Explorer or Internet Explorer triggers this event.

Now let's try customizing an individual sound event.

Assigning a sound to an event

1. From the Control Panel, double-click the Sounds icon.

2. Select the event you want to customize from the Events box.

3. Select a new sound from the Name drop-down list. Choosing None disables or mutes that sound event. Alternatively, you can click Browse to locate a sound somewhere else on your computer (see Figure 5.15).

4. Click the Play button to hear a preview of the sound.

Figure 5.15
Only Wave sounds can be assigned to Windows sound events. MP3, MIDI, and other formats are not supported at this time.

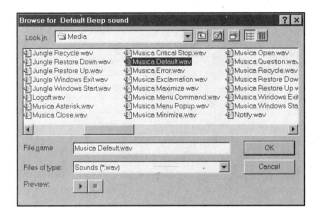

5. When you are satisfied with your selection, click OK to finish.

> **NOTE**   After applying a sound scheme you might hear short sounds play repeatedly when opening and closing applications. If you find this behavior annoying, choose (None) for the Open Program and Close Program events in Sounds properties.

After using the preceding procedure to customize several different sound events, you might find it convenient to save these settings as a new scheme. To do so, click the Save As button, type a name for the scheme, and click OK.

You can also delete a scheme by selecting it from the Schemes list and clicking Delete.

Working with Desktop Themes

If you'd like a complete transformation of your desktop and don't want to waste time fiddling with the individual elements mentioned so far, *desktop themes* are for you. A desktop theme combines wallpaper, mouse pointers, icons, color schemes, screen savers, and more in one convenient package.

Unlike Windows 95, desktop themes are now included as a standard component of Windows 98. All the original Plus! themes are there, as well as four new additions from the Plus! for Kids pack: Jungle, Underwater, Baseball, and Space. Desktop Themes can be configured via the Desktop Themes icon in Control Panel.

Applying a Desktop Theme

Applying a desktop theme is easy. In a few steps you can customize your desktop wallpaper, system colors, mouse pointers, event sounds, and screen saver.

1. From the Control Panel, double-click the Desktop Themes icon.

2. Select a new theme from the Theme drop-down list. A preview of the theme appears at the bottom of the screen (see Figure 5.16). Click the Screen Saver or Pointers, Sounds, buttons and so on to preview those items.

Figure 5.16

Additional themes appear in the Theme list if you have Plus! 98 installed.

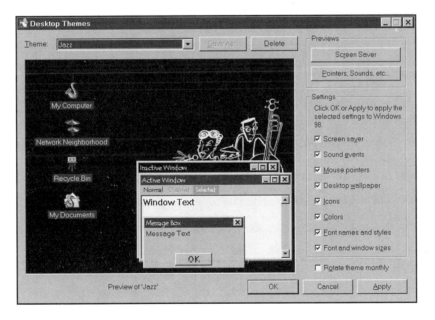

3. Click OK to apply the new settings.

> **NOTE**   If you have Plus! 98 installed, another option is available in the Desktop Themes applet. It is labeled Rotate theme monthly and, when enabled, tells Windows to switch to a different theme on a monthly basis.

Desktop themes are stored in files with the Theme extension. If you download a desktop theme from the Internet, you can apply it to your desktop by right-clicking the Theme file and choosing Apply Settings.

Editing Individual Elements of a Desktop Theme

After browsing through the available desktop themes, you might be interested in a particular theme's wallpaper and icons but none of the other elements (for example, color scheme, fonts, and mouse pointers).

Fortunately, you can tell Windows 98 to use only the elements you want and ignore the rest. You can even mix and match different themes to create your own "hybrid" theme.

Editing an individual element

1. From the Control Panel, double-click the Desktop Themes icon.

2. Select an item from the Theme drop-down list.

3. Under the heading Settings, select only the elements you want to use. For example, if you want to use the theme's wallpaper but have everything else remain the same, uncheck all boxes except Desktop wallpaper.

4. Repeat steps 2 and 3 until you are satisfied with the finished product.

5. Click OK to apply the new settings.

Saving a Desktop Theme

After customizing each element according to your preference, use the following procedure to permanently save the settings to a desktop theme file.

Saving a desktop theme

1. From the Control Panel, double-click the Desktop Themes icon.

2. Select Current Windows settings from the Theme drop-down list.

3. Click the Save As button then type a name for the new theme and press Enter.

4. Click OK to continue.

Permanently removing a theme is accomplished by selecting it from the Theme list and clicking the Delete button.

Activating Your Desktop

When Microsoft said that Internet features would be completely integrated into Windows 98, they weren't kidding. Even the desktop has been overhauled to support Internet content.

> **NOTE** In the past the Active Desktop feature was widely criticized as being unstable and buggy. But now that Internet Explorer (IE) is seamlessly integrated into Windows 98, most of the problems seem to have disappeared. The inclusion of IE Service Pack 1 has probably fixed some major bugs, too.

With the Active Desktop enabled, you can view regularly updated information directly on your desktop, or if you're the creative type you can arrange your favorite images to form a unique wallpaper gallery.

The Active Desktop can be enabled by right clicking a space on the desktop then pointing to Active Desktop and choosing View As Web Page. Follow the same procedure to switch back to the standard desktop.

Note: You can view folders as Web pages even if you've disabled (or never enabled) the Active Desktop feature.

Adding an Item to Your Desktop

Now you can begin personalizing the Active Desktop by adding images and Web content, which are known as *items*.

Add an active desktop item

1. Right-click anywhere on the desktop and choose Properties.

2. Click the Web tab to see a list of available active desktop items (see Figure 5.17).

3. Place a check mark in the box labeled View my Active Desktop as a Web page if it is not checked already.

4. Click the New button then click No on the next dialog box—you'll be visiting Microsoft's Active Gallery later in this book.

5. Click Browse and locate a JPG, GIF, or HTML file on your computer. Double-click the file you want and click OK.

6. Click OK once more to apply the changes.

Your desktop should now look something similar to the one in Figure 5.18. You can add as many items as you like by repeating the preceding steps, but don't overdo it—your system's performance is more important than the appearance of your desktop.

Figure 5.17

All your active desktop items can be configured from the Web tab. Watch the monitor graphic for a preview of your selections.

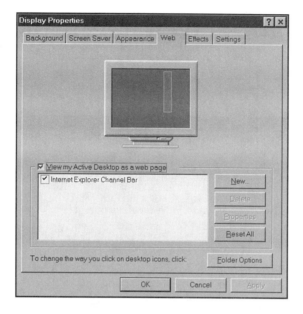

Figure 5.18

An example of what the desktop looks like after adding an active desktop item.

Configuring an Active Desktop Item

Each item on your desktop can be easily repositioned, resized, enabled, or disabled with just a few mouse clicks. You can even overlap items to create a unique wallpaper collage.

> **NOTE** After repositioning or resizing an item, it might disappear from the screen, or you might be unable to configure it again. To fix these problems, return to the normal desktop and switch back again. The item should return to its original size in the center of the screen.

When you're configuring your Active Desktop, you'll see your mouse pointer change frequently. Here's what the various identities of your mouse pointer signify.

- Moving an item—Hover your pointer over the top section of the item until a gray bar appears. Click and drag the gray bar to a new position on your desktop. Active Desktop items always remain behind your desktop icons.

- Resizing an item—Move your pointer over the item so that a thin gray border appears. Then use the border to resize the item, just as you would with a normal window.

- Disabling an item—Hover your pointer over the top section of the item until the gray bar appears. Click the Cross icon to remove the item from your desktop. The item is still displayed on the Web tab of Display Properties.

- Enabling an item—Open Display Properties and click on the Web tab. Under the heading View my Active Desktop as a Web page, check the appropriate item. Click OK for the changes to take effect.

Removing an Item from Your Desktop

If you no longer want an item to appear on your desktop or on the Web tab of Display Properties, you'll need to permanently remove it. The original file will remain on your hard drive after removing an item.

To remove an active desktop item

1. Right-click anywhere on the desktop and choose Properties.

2. Click the Web tab.

3. Under the heading View my Active Desktop as a Web page, place a check mark next to the item you want removed.

4. Click the Delete button and choose Yes when the confirmation dialog box appears.

5. Click OK to continue.

Returning to the Default Settings

At some point the Web tab of Display Properties might be filled with items that you no longer want or use. Don't bother selecting each one in turn and clicking Delete—just hit the Reset All button. The Reset All button returns your Active Desktop to the default settings. In other words, all items are removed except for the Channel Bar.

Creating a Gallery of Images

Let your creative talent show through by taking advantage of the Active Desktop's new customization features.

Here are a couple of things you can do to tweak the performance of your Active Desktop.

- For an unhindered view of your Wallpaper gallery, remove your desktop icons via the Effects tab of Display Properties. If you still want easy access to your icons, right-click the taskbar clock, point to Toolbars, and then choose Desktop.

- Don't forget to adjust your desktop background color to match the color scheme of your Active Desktop items. This can be done via the Appearance tab of Display Properties.

- To complete the Wallpaper gallery effect, remove the Channel Bar from your desktop. Of course, you should keep the Channel Bar if you use it often.

By adding a variety of images to your desktop then positioning and resizing them, you can create a unique collage that reflects your interests and makes you feel at home. See Figure 5.19 for one example of an Active Desktop collage.

Customizing the Startup and Shutdown Screens

The startup and shutdown screens are the ones you see while Windows 98 starts up or shuts down. They might look groovy, but their real purpose is to conceal ugly MS-DOS screens, which are hiding underneath. There are three such screens altogether:

- Startup—This screen appears while Windows 98 loads the necessary files and drivers. It displays the Windows logo with an animated bar along the bottom.

Figure 5.19
Create a gallery of images that reflects your personality and interests.

- Shutdown 1—You'll see this screen when you shut down or restart Windows. It also shows the Windows logo with the words "Windows is shutting down."

- Shutdown 2—The second shutdown screen appears only if your computer cannot power down automatically. The phrase "It's now safe to turn off your computer" prompts you to manually press the Power Off button.

If you're tired of seeing the same screens over and over, I have some good news for you: each one of these screens can be replaced with your own personalized images.

> **NOTE** You might notice that Windows 98's default startup screen contains an animated color-changing bar. This effect is known as *palette cycling*. Producing an animated startup screen is beyond the scope of this book, but you can find instructions on the Internet by searching for animated startup logo.

Creating an Image

When creating an image to replace a startup or shutdown screen, there are some specific guidelines you must follow:

1. The image must be of the dimensions 320×400.

2. The image must be saved as a BMP file, in 256 color (8-bit) format.

3. The image must be saved with the extension SYS. The exact filename depends on which screen you intend to replace.

With this in mind, let's open Paint and create a new startup or shutdown screen. You can use any image editor for the following procedure, although the exact steps might differ somewhat.

Creating a startup or shutdown screen

1. Click Start, point to Programs and Accessories then click Paint.

2. Click the Image menu and choose Attributes.

3. Ensure that the Pixels and Colors options are enabled then type 640 in the Width box and 400 in the Height box (see Figure 5.20). Click OK to continue.

Figure 5.20

Start with dimensions of 640×400 to get the image proportions right.

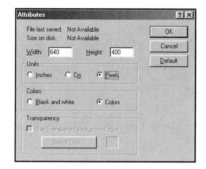

4. Use Paint's drawing and editing tools to create an image.

5. Click the Image menu and choose Stretch/Skew.

6. Type 50 into the Horizontal box and click OK. This step reduces the image to the correct dimensions of 320×400.

7. Choose Desktop from the Save in drop-down list then select 256 Color Bitmap from the Save as type list.

8. Type a name for your image in the Filename box. If this is a Startup image, type logo.sys. Similarly, use logow.sys for Shutdown 1 images, and logos.sys for Shutdown 2 images.

9. Press Enter to save the image.

If you intend to create multiple images, you'll need to save each one in a separate, descriptive folder. That way, you won't keep overwriting the same files on the desktop.

Replacing the Old with the New

The next step is to take your new image and turn it into a startup or shutdown screen. Don't forget to back up the original image by renaming it with the old extension (as shown in step 3 of the following procedure).

Replacing an original startup/shutdown screen with your own

1. Click Start, point to Settings, and then click Folder Options.

2. Click the View tab and select Show all files under the Advanced settings heading (as shown in Figure 5.21). Click OK to continue.

Figure 5.21

SYS files such as logo.sys are hidden until you enable the Show All Files option.

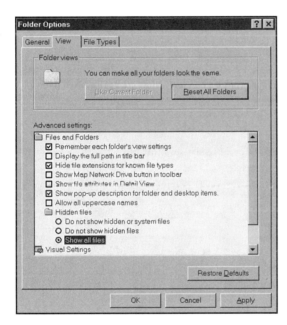

3. Rename the current startup/shutdown image. The exact procedure depends on which screen you are about to replace:

   - Startup screen—Use My Computer to open the hard disk on which Windows 98 is installed. If the logo.sys file exists, right-click it and choose Rename. Type logo.old and press Enter.

   - Shutdown 1 screen—Use My Computer to open the Windows folder on your hard drive. Right-click the logow.sys file and choose Rename. Then, type logow.old and press Enter.

   - Shutdown 2 screen—Use My Computer to open the Windows folder on your hard drive. Right-click the logos.sys file and choose Rename. Type logos.old and press Enter.

4. Locate the new image you want to use (logo.sys, logow.sys, or logos.sys), and then right-click its icon and choose Copy.

5. If you're replacing the startup screen, double-click the Hard Drive icon in My Computer. If you're replacing a shutdown screen, open the Windows folder on your hard drive.

6. Click the Edit menu and choose Paste.

7. Restart your computer to confirm that the new startup or shutdown screen is working as expected.

Restoring the Original Startup/Shutdown Screen

If you're not satisfied with your own startup/shutdown screen, you might want to switch back to the default image. There's no problem with that as long as you backed up the original files as described in the previous section.

Restoring an original startup/shutdown screen

1. Delete the current startup/shutdown image. The exact procedure depends on which screen you are about to restore:

   ■ Startup screen—Use My Computer to open the hard drive on which Windows 98 is installed. Right-click the logo.sys file and choose Delete.

   ■ Shutdown 1 screen—Use My Computer to open the Windows folder on your hard drive. Right-click the logow.sys file and choose Delete.

   ■ Shutdown 2 screen—Use My Computer to open the Windows folder on your hard drive. Right-click the logos.sys file and choose Delete.

2. Click Yes if you are prompted with a confirmation dialog box.

3. Rename the original startup/shutdown image. Again, the next step depends on which screen you are restoring:

   ■ Startup screen—Use My Computer to open the hard drive on which Windows 98 is installed. If the logo.old file exists, right-click it and choose Rename. Type logo.sys and press Enter.

   ■ Shutdown 1 screen—Use My Computer to open the Windows folder on your hard drive. Right-click the logow.old file and choose Rename. Then, type logow.sys and press Enter.

■ Shutdown 2 screen—Use My Computer to open the Windows folder on your hard drive. Right-click the logos.old file and choose Rename. Then, type logos.sys and press Enter.

4. Restart your computer to confirm that the startup or shutdown screen has been restored.

There you have it. At this point you have a big bag of tricks for customizing your Windows 98 interface.

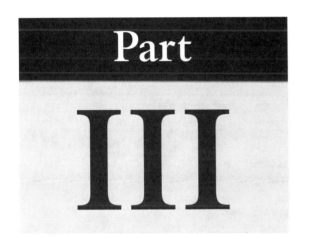

Part

III

Multimedia Devices

Chapter

6

Knowing Your Multimedia Devices

By Adam Vujic and Serdar Yegulalp

In the old days, computers came with relatively few peripheral devices. A desktop PC usually consisted of a central console, a monitor, a keyboard, and a single floppy disk drive—a 5 1/4-inch drive, at that. These days, however, such a simple system has become as obsolete as the 5 1/4-inch floppy drive. Your multimedia PC now boasts at least a CD-ROM drive and a sound card, and perhaps a Digital Video Display (DVD) player and 3D video accelerator card.

In this chapter, you'll explore these hardware concepts to gain an understanding of the physical devices attached to your machine. First you'll come to understand important sound concepts, including bit rate, sampling rate, and MIDI synthesis. Then you'll learn about new sound technologies, such as 3D and environmental audio effects. You'll see how to differentiate between 2D and 3D video acceleration and determine your video card's maximum resolutions and color depths. Finally, you'll learn about exciting CD-ROM and DVD technologies, and find out what's in store for the future.

Sound Concepts

At first glance, you might think that sound is basically the same on all computers. But take a closer look and you'll find that there are many variables that contribute to the quality of your computer's audio output.

These variables can mean the difference between the tinny unrealistic sound, which is the best the computer's built-in speaker can do, and beautiful multi-timbre sound that's difficult to distinguish from the real thing. The major factor is the presence, variety, and setup of a digital sound card.

You'll be pleased to know that Windows 98 takes advantage of the latest digital audio technologies and is capable of transforming your computer (with the right hardware) into a fully-equipped surround sound system.

Bit Rate

One of the properties common to every digital sound is the *bit rate*. The bit rate is the number of bits processed by the computer at a given time. The most common bit rates are 8 and 16, but 4 and 32 bits are also possible.

If more bits are used to describe a sound at any moment, the output of the sound will be closer to the original sound, perhaps undistinguishable or even—after editing—improved. If fewer bits are used for the recording (to save space, for example), the quality of the sound will be reduced. Generally speaking, higher bit rates (16 and 32) and more desirable than lower bit rates (4 and 8).

Having said that, however, 8-bit recordings—in most cases—provide good reproductions of the original sound, while taking up only half the disk space of an equivalent 16-bit recording. I encourage you to experiment with different settings to see which one you prefer.

Although Windows 98 is capable of recording and playing back many different bit rates, the highest bit rate you can use is actually limited by your sound card.

Many early sound cards for the PC—including the original Sound Blaster®—had an upper limit of 8 bits, making it impossible to play the high-quality 16-bit sounds taken for granted today. Recently, 32-bit sound cards have begun to appear on the market, although the disadvantage in disk space consumed by 32-bit sounds probably outweighs any improvement in sound quality.

To find out the bit rate of a particular Wave sound in Windows 98, right-click its icon, choose Properties, and then click the Details tab. You'll see a dialog box similar to the one in Figure 6.1.

Knowing Your Multimedia Devices

Figure 6.1

The Details tab of a WAV file's Properties sheet reveals its sampling rate.

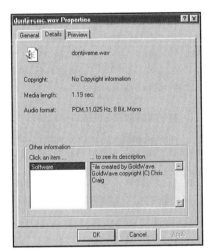

Sampling Rate: 22KHz versus 44KHz

The *sampling rate* is the number of samples taken per second when sound is converted from analog to digital format. For example, 44KHz means there are 44,000 sound samples per second. Sampling rate has a direct effect on the resulting file's size.

> **NOTE**
> A *sample* is a recording of a sound's frequency at any given moment. Likewise, *sampling* is the repeated process of recording a sound's frequency.

As with the bit rate, the sampling rate affects the size and quality of a sound. The lower the sampling rate, the less space it consumes on your hard disk. For instance, converting a 44KHz, 2MB sound to 22KHz reduces the file size to just 1MB.

High sampling rates, such as 44KHz, provide excellent reproduction of the original sound by retaining the highest and lowest audio frequencies. Low sampling rates tend to create a muffled effect, especially at a setting of 11KHz or lower.

In case you're wondering, 44KHz is the approximate upper limit for the human ear. Any higher, and there is no noticeable difference in sound quality. That's why virtually all sound cards have a 44KHz limit for recording and playing back digital sound.

You might have noticed that some newer sound cards support the higher 48KHz sampling rate. But don't be fooled—while true audiophiles might be attracted to such "cutting edge" technology, in reality there is very little difference between the 44KHz and 48KHz sampling rates. This is basically a marketing trick to distinguish a particular sound card from the rest of the market, although it can be useful for professional audio recordings.

When recording audio, keep in mind that the human voice can be compressed to a lower sampling rate while remaining clear and intelligible. However, compressing music to a low sampling rate might have adverse effects, especially if it contains very bassy drums or high-pitched instruments.

> **NOTE** Here are a few everyday examples of sampling rates, which you can use as a guide when recording sound on your PC:
>
> - CD audio—44KHz
> - AM radio—22KHz
> - Telephone—11KHz

MIDI: Electronic Synthesis versus Wavetable

MIDI (Musical Instrument Digital Interface) is a standard that was set up to enable music to be stored in a compact digital form.

 In Windows 98, a MIDI file can be identified by its MID extension or an icon with musical notes. A full-length song, complete with complex orchestration, can be easily stored in a MIDI file less than 50KBs in size. At first glance this looks like a remarkable achievement considering that a Wave file of the same length could take up megabytes of hard disk space.

Let me explain how such a small file size is possible:

In its simplest form, MIDI represents each musical note in terms of its pitch, loudness, and the instrument used. Other factors can also be incorporated, such as stereo positioning, echo, and chorus, but these are not required.

All the instrument sounds are stored outside of the actual MIDI file, which accounts for the small file size. Depending on how Windows 98 is configured, these sounds might be coming from your sound card or generated by software.

Herein lies one of the few drawbacks of MIDI: The output quality of MIDI music depends greatly on your computer's capabilities, resulting in many versions—not all of equal quality—of the same song.

The following list outlines the most popular methods for producing MIDI instruments sounds. Any number of these technologies might be available to you, depending on your sound card and installed software.

- *Electronic synthesis.* Probably the oldest form of MIDI synthesis, this method relies on complex mathematical algorithms to generate the individual sounds of each instrument. While these algorithms have been continually improved and refined, the audio quality still leaves a lot to be desired. Electronic synthesis is included as a standard component of almost all sound cards, mostly for backward-compatibility reasons. The Yamaha® OPL is an example of an electronic synthesis chip.

- *Hardware Wavetable synthesis.* Not satisfied with the tinny unrealistic sound of electronic synthesis, computer users—particularly musicians—demanded better quality MIDI. The result was Wavetable synthesis, which basically stores a whole heap of real instrument sounds in digital format on the sound card. Whenever a MIDI file is played on a computer, the appropriate instruments are retrieved from the sound card's ROM and combined to form a rich orchestration full of depth and emotion. Most people agree that the quality is light-years ahead of the electronic synthesis method.

    - Wavetable synthesis is increasingly becoming the standard for modern sound cards. One example is the popular Creative® Sound Blaster® AWE64 card.

- *Software Wavetable synthesis.* In an attempt to offer a better and more affordable solution than Wavetable synthesis, a new method for generating MIDI instruments was introduced. Software Wavetable synthesis is designed around the same basic concept as standard Wavetable synthesis, except that MIDI instruments are stored in software (for example, files on your hard disk) rather than hardware (your sound card). The idea being that if the instruments are moved to software, the sound card's ROM is no longer necessary, which results in manufacturing savings that can be passed on to you, the consumer.

Knowing Your Multimedia Devices

■ Another advantage is that all your MIDI instruments can be updated simply by downloading files from the Internet or inserting a disk in your computer. A much better alternative than upgrading your sound card, wouldn't you say?

■ Although software Wavetable synthesis looks to become the new standard in MIDI playback, there are a few problems that must be overcome before it is widely adopted.

■ First, because this method does not rely on a sound card to do the processing, it can use up a lot of CPU and RAM resources, causing a noticeable reduction in system performance. This will no doubt become a moot point with the introduction of faster processors and cheaper RAM.

■ Another concern with software Wavetable synthesis is that, generally speaking, the audio quality does not yet match that of traditional hardware Wavetable synthesis. However, judging by the current progress rate of this technology, it won't be long before software synthesis sounds as good as, if not better than, the alternatives.

■ Even Microsoft is jumping on the bandwagon with a piece of software called the Interactive Music Synthesizer (IMS). IMS is an add-on for Internet Explorer, which allows Web designers to include high-quality background music on their Web pages. Interestingly, the music has the capability to transition seamlessly from one tune to another depending on how you interact with onscreen objects. For example, if you're playing an online version of *Wheel of Fortune*, the music tempo might begin at a fast pace as you spin the wheel then gradually slow down in sync with the wheel.

2D versus 3D

Recently, some major advances have been made in computer audio with the goal of creating a more realistic atmosphere for computer games. Three-dimensional audio is one of these technologies, allowing sound to be heard in 3D space. Technically speaking, this means that sounds can be positioned anywhere along the X, Y, and Z axes (horizontal, vertical, and front to back).

Three-dimensional audio represents a true breakthrough for gamers. With 3D audio, you can hear the footsteps of a game monster creeping up behind you, giving you a chance to quickly turn around and fire your weapon. Or, after hearing an enemy load his weapon on your right, you could run for cover in the opposite direction.

Three-dimensional audio not only adds depth to your games, but also brings the quality of sound up to par with graphics, which have been moving in the 3D direction for years.

Amazingly, this technology works with just two external speakers (or stereo headphones), which is the standard setup for most desktop computer systems. The creators of 3D audio technology have developed special algorithms that take advantage of the way the brain determines the origin of a sound.

The first attempts at 3D audio were very crude by today's standards and required that you sit in the middle of your computer's speakers to hear something that kind of sounded three-dimensional. At the time, the technology received lackluster support by the computer industry and wasn't taken seriously by consumers.

However, as with all technologies, 3D audio was continually refined to create a more convincing and user-friendly experience. With the latest 3D software and hardware, you actually feel as though you are part of the virtual world created by the computer.

At the time of this writing, there were a variety of conflicting standards on the market, but the new DirectX software from Microsoft should provide a unified solution for developers and consumers. If you're looking to purchase 3D audio software or hardware, be sure that it conforms to the DirectX standard, which guarantees compatibility with the widest range of games and applications.

One breakthrough technology in terms of 3D audio is Environmental Audio®, which was created by multimedia company Creative Labs®. Environmental Audio not only creates the 3D effect to give depth to computer audio, but it also applies environmental effects such as echo and reverb—in real-time. The result is a much more true-to-life audio experience, putting you in the center of the action.

One great feature of Creative's proprietary technology is that it can be experienced regardless of your position in the room, giving you more freedom to move around.

Environmental Audio works with two speakers, but four or more speakers are recommended for the best effect. This technology is available on the Sound Blaster Live!® sound card, also the brainchild of Creative Labs®. Environmental and 3D effects can be applied to your computer games, MIDI and Wave sounds, audio CDs, and even DVD movies.

Point your browser to `http://www.sblive.com` for more information on these technologies.

The bottom line is this: As with computer graphics, the future of computer sound is definitely headed in the 3D direction. But a single standard has not yet emerged, so you might choose to wait until the smoke clears before purchasing the latest 3D audio gizmo.

Knowing Your Video Card

Video cards can differ in several crucial ways. For example, depending on the model, your card might support more or fewer colors, allow different screen resolutions, or even accelerate processing of 3D graphics. Read on for more details about these differences.

Memory

Your video card's memory (or *RAM*) is a vital component that—along with your monitor—determines the highest possible resolution and color depth of your display. Common video memory configurations are 2MB and 4MB, with 8MB and 12MB becoming standard for the newer 3D acceleration cards.

> **NOTE** There are a few types of RAM in any one computer. While video RAM is found on your video card, system RAM is located on your motherboard and is the primary memory component of your PC. Other types of memory include sound card RAM (for storing MIDI sounds) and CPU cache (which speeds up calculations). RAM on a video or sound card takes an equivalent memory load off your system RAM, resulting in better performance.
>
> Your video card might feature one of several types of RAM, including *DRAM* (Dynamic RAM) and *VRAM* (Video RAM). Of the two, VRAM offers better performance.

If you find that you cannot switch to the highest color depths (most commonly 24-bit True Color) at a certain resolution, your video card probably does not contain sufficient RAM.

Table 6.1 outlines the capabilities of each memory configuration, and you can use it to determine the highest possible resolution and color depth for your video card. I should point out that your monitor also plays a part in the equation, so the actual limits might be lower or higher than what is shown here.

Table 6.1   Highest Video Modes Available for Common Video RAM Configurations

Color Depth	512KB	1MB	2MB	4MB	8MB
16 colors	1024×768	1280×1024	1600×1200	1600×1200	1600×1200
256 colors	800×600	1024×768	1280×1024	1600×1200	1600×1200
16-bit High Color	800×600	1024×768	1600×1200	1600×1200	
24-bit True Color	640×480	800×600	1280×1024	1600×1200	
32-bit True Color	800×600	1024×768	1600×1200		

The available video modes might also be limited when your video card is running in 3D acceleration mode. You'll notice this behavior mostly when you're playing games.

2D and 3D Acceleration

Two-dimensional acceleration is a common feature for almost all video cards and controls most of what you see onscreen, including the Windows 98 user interface and everyday applications such as Word and Excel.

The 2D component of your video card is crucial to the performance of Windows 98's visual features, and a slower graphics chip might result in a delay when opening program windows or choppy animation and video playback.

Three-dimensional acceleration is only a recent phenomenon in the computer industry and has taken the computer gaming industry by storm. A video card with a modern 3D graphics chip allows complex three-dimensional virtual worlds to be displayed in stunning realism and at high frame rates, resulting in smooth, realistic motion.

Games such as Quake® II and Unreal® have been designed to take advantage of 3D accelerators, so if you have a compatible video card, choose the hardware acceleration mode to see a dramatic improvement in quality and performance (frame rate). Figure 6.2 shows the difference between hardware and software acceleration modes.

Knowing Your Multimedia Devices

Figure 6.2
The picture on the left shows a Quake II scene without 3D acceleration mode. The one on the right is the same scene with 3D acceleration enabled (using an ATI RagePro chipset).

Knowing Your CD-ROM or DVD Drive

When the first CD-ROM drives came onto the market, they were regarded as expensive and exotic luxuries. Most CD-ROMs held more information than many conventional hard drives could store, despite their slow transfer rates, proprietary interfaces, and occasional cumbersomeness. Now CD-ROMs are shipped with just about every computer that goes out the factory gates; they plug directly into the same interfaces that hard drives and other mass storage devices use and are intensely fast and reliable.

There is a great deal of similarity between CD-ROMs shipping today, both in terms of speed and compatibility. But it still helps to know the limits of the hardware, and if you wind up dealing with an older CD-ROM for a system that's getting the big upgrade to Windows 98, such knowledge will be useful to help judge if the CD-ROM also needs to be upgraded.

DVD-ROMs are the newest wrinkle in the CD world. DVDs are basically the next step up from CDs—they're double-sided and can store up to two 4.5 gigabyte (GB) layers of information per side, making it possible to store a whopping 18GB on a single disc. That's enough to contain a full-length movie, the soundtrack, trailers and interviews, alternative scenes, and other goodies. On the downside, they are still relatively new, and very few software programs ship on DVD-ROM; most of the DVD-related software is entertainment titles, such as movies. But they are available as an option for just about every system shipped today. You'll learn more about DVD drives in Chapter 8, "Working with CD-ROM and DVD Drives."

Because CD-ROMs are designed to work with massive amounts of data in a cheap, common form factor, there are times when you don't always need the fastest CD-ROM in the universe—just something that can access the data. For instance, a Windows 98 machine that is primarily used casually, or that has a CD-ROM that's not used for anything but installing programs, can get away with having an older 4X or 6X (speed) CD-ROM on it. A machine that's going to be used to do research, play high-end video games, or do other activities that will hit the CD-ROM constantly and demandingly usually require a 12X (speed) or better.

But before you get steeped too far in the alphabet soup that almost always goes with talking about PCs, I have some explanations.

Speed or Transfer Rate

When the specifications for the original audio CD format were created, they dictated that the data would be transferred from the disc at a steady rate of 150 KBs per second—fast enough for a single audio stream and nothing more than that. The first CD-ROMs used that same data transfer speed because many of them were designed from the same basic hardware, and also because no specs existed to make anything faster.

As time and demand progressed, CD-ROMs began to show up in faster and faster implementations. The transfer rate is expressed on CD-ROM drives as a multiple of the original 150 KBs/second transfer rate. For instance, a 4X CD-ROM can transfer data at four times the 150 KB/second speed: 600 KB/second; a 10X: 1,500 KB/second; a 20X: 3,000 KB/second (That's 3MBs a second!) And so on. 20–24X seems to be about the upper limit at which data can be reliably transferred from the disc, because above that the speed of the disc and its mechanical stability become serious problems.

Access Time

Most CD-ROMs that are rated for a given speed often never come close to that speed for a bunch of reasons. First, there is the way data is accessed from the disc. Rarely, if ever, will data be read in a totally linear fashion. When you play a music CD, the data is not designed to be played in anything other than a straight line, beginning to end. CD-ROMs are accessed very much at random, and the time it takes for the laser beam to move from one spot on the disc to another, plus the time it takes for the disc to reach the correct rotational speed, will affect the transfer rate. When your computer accesses the CD-ROM, you can often hear the high-pitched whine of the disc spinning up to speed.

Access time is the combination of the CD-ROM's basic speed and the rate at which it can actually read data. It is generally considered to be the average time it takes for the laser beam to move from one spot on the disc to the other. The computer usually determines this average by forcing a bunch of random reads from different parts of the disc, timing how long the head takes to get there and start returning data, and averaging the results.

Access time is generally measured in milliseconds, and the lower the better. For an example, a recent 20X CD-ROM was clocked as having a 79 millisecond average access time. Don't expect to get hard-disk level access speeds, which are normally in the range of 13–20 milliseconds. One-hundred or less should be considered high quality.

Some manufacturers also list *full stroke* access time. This is the time it takes for the laser to go all the way from the beginning of the disc to the end, or vice versa, and is a good index of the worst-case scenario of speed.

ROM versus RAM

CDs are no longer exclusively a read-only format. The first step toward making CDs a two-way street, as it were, was with the introduction a few years back of CD-R (compact disc-recordable) drives. CD-Rs used a special photochemical technology and specially designed blank discs to allow users to *burn* data onto a CD. The only drawback is that the discs are strictly a one-shot deal: After they're burned, the information cannot be erased or edited, only added to. But both drives and blank media have plummeted in cost, making them an attractive and affordable way to create archival backups of data, or allowing people to author their own CD-ROM or CD audio titles. (CD-R titles do play in conventional CD players.)

The original term used to describe CD-Rs was *WORM*, which was an acronym for *write once, read many* (times). If you come across literature that uses this term, don't be confused—what was once WORM technology has now been absorbed into CD-R. The term WORM itself is obsolete and generally not used anymore.

CD-RW is a format that is readable, writable, and erasable, which allows burned discs to be overwritten and reused freely. Its big drawback is that CD-RW discs do not work in anything except a CD-RW drive; For instance, CD-RWs with audio data will not play in conventional CD players.

Because CD-RW capability is generally available in most CD-R drives brought to market today for little or no extra cost, it should be something you look for if you're planning to buy a CD-R drive in the future.

DVD, originally read-only, is going through a little read-write-erase format war of its own, with DVD-RAM and DVD+RW being the two major contenders. But it'll be at least a year or two before the format war settles down, so it's still safe to invest in a conventional DVD-ROM drive. Some more details on this are available in Chapter 8.

Compatible Standards

If you own a CD or DVD drive already, or plan on buying a new one to replace an antiquated model, chances are you're already wondering which drives are going to be compatible with which kinds of discs, both now and in the future. Table 6.2 illustrates which drives are compatible with which disc formats.

The best buying decision to make will reflect what you really need. If you're going to be doing more reading than writing, a second generation DVD-ROM, which can read CD-Rs safely, is probably the best bet at this point because it handles just about everything out there. If you're planning on burning your own discs in some way, get CD-RW. DVD+RW is included here for the sake of reference, but do not expect to see actual drives until well into next year.

Table 6.2   Compatibility Between Formats and Particular Drive Types

Disc format	CD or audio CD player	CD-R	CD-RW	DVD-ROM	DVD-RAM	DVD+RW
CD	Yes	Yes	Yes	Yes	Yes	Yes
CD-R	Yes	Yes	Yes	No[1]	Yes	Yes
CD-RW	No	No	Yes	Yes	Yes	Yes
DVD-ROM[2]	No	No	No	Yes	Yes	Yes
DVD-RAM	No	No	No	No	Yes	Yes
DVD+RW	No	No	No	No	No	Yes

Knowing Your Multimedia Devices

1. *First-generation DVD-ROM drives cannot handle CD-Rs and might in fact damage them.*
2. *DVD-ROM includes DVD video discs.*

Installing and
Configuring Sound
Drivers

Installing and
Configuring Video
Drivers

Chapter

7

Installing and Configuring Multimedia Devices

by Adam Vujic

Although you might be satisfied that all your multimedia devices (for example, video and sound cards) are functioning and basically getting the job done, there might be times when you want to tweak a certain feature. Or you might come across a problem that cannot be resolved without manually adjusting some driver settings.

In those cases, you can look to this chapter to make sense of the sometimes confusing array of driver settings and dialog boxes found throughout Windows 98. You'll learn how to view and interpret driver information using the Device Manager, and you'll find out how to tweak settings such as the video refresh rate, which helps to reduce onscreen flicker.

This chapter also takes you—step by step—through the process of updating and installing a multimedia driver.

Installing and Configuring Sound Drivers

A *sound driver* is the piece of software that allows Windows 98 to access and control your sound card. If you experience any problems with sound in Windows 98, one of the first places to look is the driver settings.

To make things a little easier, all your driver settings are accessible from one place—a feature known as the Device Manager. You can access the Device Manager by right-clicking My Computer, choosing Properties, and then clicking the Device Manager tab.

Viewing Sound Driver Properties

Before configuring any settings, you'll need to open the sound driver properties in Device Manager.

> **TIP**   If you want, you can access the Device Manager via the Control Panel instead of My Computer. To do so, click Start, point to Settings, click Control Panel, and then double-click the System icon. However, the fastest method is to use the new Windows key—press the Windows and Pause/Break keys simultaneously then click the Device Manager tab.

To view sound driver properties

   1. Right-click My Computer and choose Properties.

   2. Click the Device Manager tab to access the list of devices on your computer.

3. Click the plus sign [+] next to Sound, Video and Game Controllers. A list of multimedia devices appears as shown in Figure 7.1.

Figure 7.1

All of your multimedia drivers are conveniently located on the Device Manager tab of the System Properties dialog box.

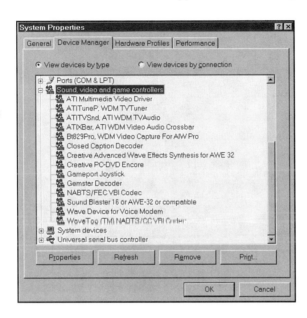

4. Double-click a device to display the Properties for that device's driver. For example, double-clicking Sound Blaster 16 or AWE-32 or compatible summons a dialog box for the Sound Blaster 16 or AWE32 driver.

The General tab contains information about the type and operating status of a driver (see Figure 7.2). If you're having trouble with a multimedia device, check this tab for details about the problem, as well as possible solutions.

Typically, you'll find the following items on the General tab of the properties dialog box:

■ *Device type*—Tells you which category the device belongs to—a sound card belongs in the Sound, Video and Game Controllers category. Windows 98 doesn't always get the device type right, but it's usually on the mark. For example, in the list of hardware devices that appears when registering Windows 98, your voice modem might be incorrectly identified as a sound card.

■ *Manufacturer*—Specifies the company that manufactured your multimedia hardware device.

■ *Hardware version*—Shows the version number of your hardware device, rather than the software driver. It reads Not Available if Windows 98 cannot locate the version number or if that particular device is software-only.

Figure 7.2

Check out the General tab of your device properties for helpful troubleshooting information.

- *Device status*—You'll see a brief description of the driver's operating status under this heading. Most often, the phrase `This item is working properly` is displayed, which is the best possible status. If there's a problem with the driver, it is described here along with a fairly meaningless code number in parenthesis. Possible solutions are also offered. For example, if the device is disabled, Windows 98 suggests you enable the device by clicking the Enable Device button.

> **NOTE**   If you disable a device, the driver for that device will not be loaded the next time you start Windows 98. However, removing a device from the Device Manager list is not permanent—it will be redetected on the next restart.

- *Device Usage*—Up to two options to control how the device driver functions are available in this section. Check the box labeled Disable in this hardware profile if you'd like to temporarily disable the driver—and its respective hardware device—for troubleshooting purposes. Enable the Remove From this Hardware Profile setting to remove the device from the current hardware profile. It can be added again later.

Additional information can be found on the Details tab, including the driver's provider and date of creation. Click the Driver File Details button to see a list of files used by that driver along with their individual version numbers.

Read on to learn about the remaining features of the Properties dialog box.

Configuring Sound Driver Properties

After the driver's properties are onscreen, click the Settings tab to view the available options for your sound card. Some drivers do not have any configurable settings, in which case the Settings tab does not appear. See Figure 7.3 for an example of the Sound Blaster AWE32® card settings.

Figure 7.3

All settings specific to your sound card driver appear on the Settings tab.

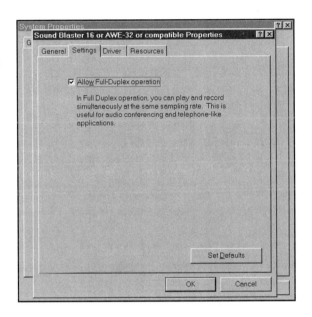

One common option—particularly with recent sound cards—is Full-Duplex mode. *Full-duplex* is a technical term that means you can record a sound (for example, your voice) while another sound is playing (for example, someone else's voice). The concept works in the same way as a telephone conversation.

As a guide, it is generally better to have the Full-Duplex option enabled, especially if you intend to use audio conferencing applications such as Microsoft NetMeeting. Without Full-Duplex mode, holding a conversation over the Internet is like using a two-way radio or walkie-talkie. You'll have to wait until the other person finishes speaking before you can say anything and vice versa.

> **WARNING** In rare cases, enabling Full-Duplex mode might have unwanted side effects on certain Windows applications that use your sound card. You might prefer to disable Full-Duplex mode and reenable it only when using audio conferencing applications.

Installing and Configuring
Multimedia Devices

Configuring Playback and Recording Settings

In addition to the settings in Device Manager, Windows 98 provides some other options to help you troubleshoot sound problems and tweak performance. To access these options, open the Control Panel from either the My Computer window or from the Settings section of the Start menu, double-click the Multimedia icon, and then choose the Audio tab if it isn't selected by default.

With Multimedia Properties displayed, click the Advanced Properties button under the Playback heading. Then, click the Performance tab to display the Audio Playback options as shown in Figure 7.4.

Figure 7.4

Additional options are available on the Performance tab of Advanced Audio Properties.

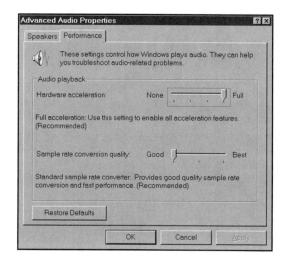

There are two options available on this dialog box—Hardware Acceleration and Sample Rate Conversion Quality. (Sample rate conversion quality is covered in Chapter 6, "Knowing Your Multimedia Devices.")

The Hardware Acceleration option controls how much Windows 98 relies on your sound hardware (sound card) to improve audio performance in games and applications. When the Hardware Acceleration slider is moved all the way to the right (Full), your sound card is used to its full potential and audio performance is maximized. As you move the slider toward the left, Windows 98 relies less on your sound card for acceleration features and more on software emulation, which means a greater burden on your computer's CPU.

The Sample Rate Conversion Quality setting refers to the process of converting a Wave file from one sample rate to another (for example, from 44KHz to 22KHz). The default setting of Good is provides acceptable sound quality after conversion and is also the speediest. While the Best setting might provide the highest conversion quality, your computer takes a noticeable performance hit. The center setting is a compromise between the two.

By all means, experiment with this option if you are after higher quality results when converting between sample rates (and are not particularly concerned about performance).

> **NOTE** There's no real need to adjust these options unless you are experiencing unusual audio problems. Even then, a better solution might be to install a newer sound driver as described in the "Updating a Sound Driver," section later in this chapter.

If you've been trying out different settings and have forgotten where they were to begin with, don't worry. Click the Restore Defaults button and the original settings are restored.

Recording properties can be found by clicking the Advanced Properties button in the Recording section. The options are exactly the same as previously described, except that they affect the way sound is recorded, rather than played back.

Advanced Sound Driver Configuration

There's one tab that you haven't looked at yet—Resources. Here, you can configure advanced settings such as IRQ and DMA, which provide pathways for Windows 98 to access your sound card (see Figure 7.5).

> **NOTE** IRQ stands for *interrupt request* and is a name (or more accurately, a number) assigned to each of your computer's hardware devices. For example, your sound card might be given the name IRQ 5. *DMA* is an acronym for *direct memory access* and is more specific to sound cards. DMA settings inform the operating system as to which channels should be used to access your sound card's 8-bit and 16-bit sound features, respectively.

The Resources tab is also the best place to resolve device conflicts. Device conflicts occur when two or more devices attempt to use the same resources. For example, both the sound card and network card might be assigned to use IRQ 7.

The Plug-and-Play standard mostly resolves this problem by automatically locating and assigning resources to each of your hardware devices. However, the number of resources is limited, so things can get complicated if you put too many devices in the same computer. For Plug-and-Play technology to be truly effective, your motherboard and all hardware devices need to support the standard.

If it is not enabled already, I recommend you check the Use automatic settings box, which tells Windows 98 to assign resources to your sound card automatically on startup. If you have a particularly old sound card, this option might be grayed out.

Figure 7.5

All of the resources currently used by your sound card are listed on the Resources tab.

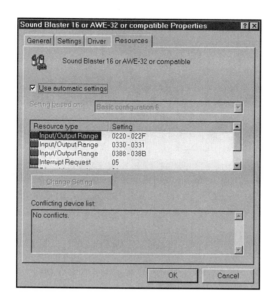

All available resources are listed under the Resource type heading. Their corresponding values are shown in the adjacent column.

> **NOTE**   When attempting to edit a resource, you might receive a message stating that it cannot be modified. This limitation is due to hardware design rather than your software driver. Sound cards that do not support Plug and Play most commonly display this message. The workaround usually involves moving tiny DIP switches on the sound card itself, but please read the manual before even opening your computer's casing.

Here are the most common sound card resources and a description for each:

- *Input/output range*—Generally refers to the MIDI capabilities of your sound device, such as the MIDI I/O port located on the Sound Blaster® card. Each input/output range controls a different MIDI function, depending on the exact capabilities of your sound card. Not all of these I/O ranges can be adjusted manually.

- *Interrupt request (IRQ)*—An interrupt request is a unique resource allocated to each of your hardware devices. The IRQ setting is probably at fault if you are experiencing stuttering audio or if the computer hangs when you try to play a sound. IRQ 5 is probably the most common value for modern sound cards.

- *Direct memory access (DMA)*—Specifies the channels through which Windows 98 accesses the 8-bit and 16-bit playback features of your sound card. Whenever a Wave sound is played in Windows, the appropriate DMA channel is used. The 8-bit DMA channel is usually listed first in the

Resource Type list and can be identified by a default setting of 1. The second DMA channel refers to 16-bit playback and carries a default setting of 5. If you have problems playing back either of these sound types, there might be a DMA conflict that needs to be resolved.

> **NOTE** If you use software that runs under MS-DOS, especially many games, you probably need to configure your computer's sound card settings for the individual program. The setup utility will ask you to supply your computer's I/O port, interrupt setting, and DMA channel. You can use the Resources tab to obtain this information.

Adjusting Sound Card Resources

Before you can adjust resources manually, you'll need to disable the Use automatic settings option on the Resources tab.

Windows 98 provides a quick way to adjust resource settings for your sound card—simply choose a preset configuration from the Settings based on the drop-down list. However, note that you might end up with fewer features or degraded performance after selecting one of these configurations. As a result, this method of assigning resources is not recommended.

> **NOTE** The very first batch of sound cards originally used IRQ 7 to communicate with software. However, it was soon discovered that this setting conflicted with printer port 1 (LPT1), which also used IRQ 7. As a result, the much better setting of IRQ 5 was agreed upon, and this has become the standard for today's generation of sound cards.

The preferred method is to adjust individual resources such as the IRQ or 16-bit DMA, while leaving the other resources intact. Here's how:

To adjust an individual resource

1. Right-click My Computer and choose Properties.

2. Click the Device Manager tab to bring up a list of devices on your computer.

3. Click the plus sign [+] next to Sound, Video and Game Controllers then double-click the name of your sound card.

4. Click the Resources tab then double-click the resource you'd like to change under the Resource Type heading. The Edit Input/Output Range dialog box appears (see Figure 7.6).

Figure 7.6

The Edit Input/ Output Range dialog box is used to adjust resource settings for your sound card and other hardware devices.

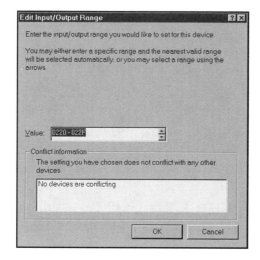

5. Type a new setting into the Value box, or use the up and down arrows to scroll through the available choices. Check the Conflict information section to make sure that no other devices conflict with the settings you have chosen.

6. Click OK on all dialog boxes. You might need to restart your computer for the changes to take effect.

Updating a Sound Driver

It's always good to have the latest version of your drivers installed, and sound drivers are no exception. You might loathe having to update a sound driver every time a new version is released, but there are some logical reasons for doing so.

Sound driver updates serve four main purposes:

1. Ensure compatibility with the widest range of games and applications;

2. Fix bugs that were present in previous versions of the driver;

3. Fine-tune the performance and stability of your sound card driver; and

4. Add new features, such as 3D effects and Full-Duplex capability.

They also ensure that your sound card supports the latest version of Microsoft's DirectX standard, which is used by almost all games designed for Windows 98.

> **NOTE**   *DirectX* is a set of technologies developed by Microsoft to enhance the multimedia experience under Windows. Technically speaking, DirectX gives programmers direct access to your computer's hardware devices, providing a performance boost that is especially noticeable when playing games.

> **NOTE**　For a list of popular software and hardware manufacturers' Web sites, insert the accompanying multimedia CD-ROM into your PC. Click on the Continue button and then the Resource List button.

The ideal place to obtain sound driver updates is the Internet. Visit the manufacturer's Web site (for example, `www.creativelabs.com` for Creative Labs®), and then locate the appropriate driver for your sound card and download it. Be sure to place the driver in a new folder on your hard disk to avoid confusing it with other files. Fortunately, the Save As dialog box you'll see as you begin the download process gives you the option of creating a new folder to store the file.

If your sound card manufacturer does not provide driver updates via the Internet, try contacting them by phone or other means. There might be a charge for sending out an update disk via regular mail.

After you have the driver on your hard disk, the next step is to run the driver's installation program. The update file usually consists of several smaller compressed files, so go ahead and double-click its icon to uncompress them.

If a setup program appears at this point, follow the onscreen instructions to have Windows automatically update your driver, and then skip to the section titled "What to Do After Updating a Sound Driver," later in this chapter.

Some important information relating to the installation and use of the driver might be included in a readme file. Look for a text file named readme (or similar), and then double-click it. Be sure to follow the instructions exactly as described in the document, taking particular note of any known problems with the driver. Skip over to the "What to Do After Updating a Sound Driver," section later in this chapter after updating your driver.

If there's no readme file or specific instructions on how to update your sound driver, you'll need to do it the old-fashioned way—via Device Manager. Here's how:

To update a sound driver

1. Right-click My Computer and choose Properties.

2. Click the Device Manager tab to bring up a list of devices on your computer.

3. Click the plus sign [+] next to Sound, Video and Game Controllers and double-click the name of the sound card, which belongs to the driver you are about to update.

4. Click the Driver tab, and then click the Update Driver button. The Update Device Driver Wizard appears as shown in Figure 7.7).

Figure 7.7

The Update Device Driver Wizard guides you through the complex task of updating a software driver.

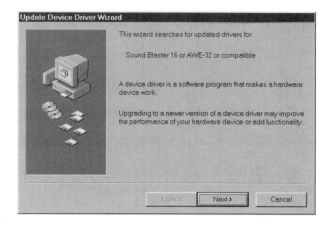

5. Click the Next button to begin.

6. Since you know exactly which driver you want to install (for example the one you downloaded from the Internet), choose the second option and click Next.

7. Click the Have Disk button, followed by the Browse button. Locate and double-click the folder containing the new sound driver, and then click OK.

8. Click OK again to confirm the driver's location.

9. If multiple drivers are available from the Models list, select the one that most closely matches your sound hardware, and then click Next.

10. A final confirmation appears with the name of the driver you are about to update and its location on your computer. Click Next for Windows 98 to replace your current driver files with the new ones. You'll need to insert your Windows 98 CD-ROM as required.

11. After the copying process is complete, click Finish to close the wizard. A restart of your computer might be necessary for the changes to take effect.

What to Do After Updating a Sound Driver

Although it's unlikely that you'll notice any obvious improvements after updating a sound driver, you can be sure that you have the latest version by checking the driver properties in Device Manager. As I mentioned previously, the driver's version and date of creation can be found on the Driver tab.

> **TIP** When you ran the driver's decompression program, it probably created a set of temporary files as it installed the driver on your hard drive. If you check the directory from which you ran the decompression program, you might notice these temporary files still exist, but they aren't necessary. To save space, copy the original file you downloaded and any documentation (readme files) to a safe place, and then delete all remaining extraneous files.

Driver updates often add support for sound card features that were missing from previous versions of the same drivers. There are a few places to look for these new features:

- *Volume Control*—Double-click the Speaker icon on your taskbar, and then click the Advanced button. New settings—such as 3D effects—might appear on this dialog box after you install a new sound driver.

- *Device Manager*—Open the Device Manager and double-click the sound card to bring up its Properties dialog box. Click the Settings tab to see if any new options are available.

- *Multimedia Properties*—Double-click the Multimedia icon in the Control Panel, and then click the MIDI tab. Your updated sound driver might have enabled a higher quality method of playing back MIDI files, which you can select here.

Restoring the Original Sound Driver

If you're experiencing problems with sound and suspect that they are the result of installing a driver update, it might help to revert to the original Windows 98 drivers. The following procedure explains how it's done.

Restoring the Original Sound Driver

1. Right-click My Computer and choose Properties.

2. Click the Device Manager tab to bring up a list of devices on your computer.

3. Click the plus sign [+] next to Sound, Video and Game Controllers, and then double-click the name of the sound card, which belongs to the driver you are about to update.

4. Click the Driver tab, and then click the Update Driver button. The Update Device Driver Wizard appears.

5. Click the Next button to begin.

6. Choose the second option and click Next.

7. Select a driver dated 5-11-98 from the Models list then click Next. If possible, do not choose a driver that contains the letters WDM.

8. A final confirmation dialog box appears. Click Next for Windows 98 to replace your current driver files with the original ones. Insert your Windows 98 CD-ROM as required.

9. After the copying process is complete, click Finish to close the wizard. A restart of your computer might be necessary for the changes to take effect.

Installing and Configuring Video Drivers

A software driver controls your video card in the same way as your sound card. The major difference is that while updating a sound driver might not lead to a noticeable improvement, changing your video driver can mean the difference between painfully slow screen updates and blinding fast 2D and 3D graphics.

Of course, the performance and functionality of your video hardware limits the driver. If your computer has a slow video card, it won't matter what kind of driver you install, because the performance bottleneck—as the techies call it—is in your hardware.

Viewing Video Driver Properties

Windows 98 splits your video driver into two places: Display Properties and Device Manager.

Basic video properties and settings can be accessed via Display Properties in the Control Panel, whereas more advanced options are available in the Device Manager. See the preceding sound driver section for more information on using the Device Manager.

To see an overall summary of your video driver's type, version number, and similar information, I prefer the Display Properties method.

To view video driver properties

1. Right-click a space on the desktop and choose Properties.

2. Click the Settings tab, and then click the Advanced button to display your driver properties.

3. Click the Adapter tab. You should see a dialog box similar to the one shown in Figure 7.8.

Figure 7.8

Driver-specific information and settings are available by clicking the Adapter tab in Display properties.

You'll find the driver information in the Adapter/Driver Information section. The most important pieces of information are the manufacturer, chip type, and software version.

Adjusting the Refresh Rate

The refresh rate determines how often the image on your monitor is refreshed or updated. Your video card and monitor support a limited number of refresh rates and work behind the scenes to have their settings synchronized.

A low refresh rate can cause your screen to flicker and might result in headaches or eye aches after prolonged use of your computer. Setting your video card refresh rate to the highest possible setting is recommended to avoid any discomfort.

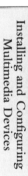

Installing and Configuring Multimedia Devices

> **TIP**   The optimal refresh rate depends on your monitor's capabilities, as well as the resolution of your display. For example, a resolution of 1,024×768 requires a higher refresh rate than 640×480, in order to display a stable, flicker-free image. Video drivers include preset refresh rates for each supported resolution, which helps make things a little easier.

If you are pleased with the onscreen image, and there is no noticeable flicker, I recommend that you leave the current refresh rate setting as it is.

To set the refresh rate

1. Right-click a space on the desktop and choose Properties.

2. Click the Settings tab, and then click the Advanced button to display your driver properties.

3. Click the Adapter tab, and then select a new setting from the Refresh Rate drop-down list.

    Optimal is the recommended choice, and should give the best result for your monitor/video card combination. Adapter default is your video card's default refresh rate for a particular resolution. Leave the remaining settings alone unless you have no luck with the first two options.

Adjusting Video Hardware Acceleration

If you're experiencing unusual display-related problems or your computer hangs for no apparent reason while you're working, it might help to lighten the load on your video card by reducing hardware acceleration.

Click the Performance tab to see the hardware acceleration option (see Figure 7.9). The default setting of Full provides the highest level of performance and utilizes all of your video card's acceleration features. As you move the slider toward None, Windows 98 reduces the dependence on your video card by removing certain graphics features.

Figure 7.9

Windows 98 provides four different hardware acceleration settings, ranging from None to Full.

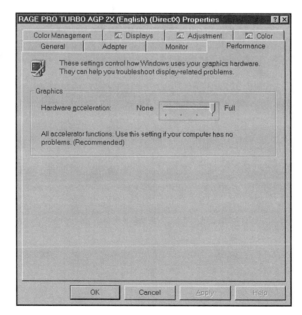

The third setting (just to the left of Full) can be used if you are experiencing trouble with the mouse pointer, such as unwanted pointer trails. For more serious problems—such as unexpected program errors—try the second setting (to the immediate right of None). Finally, use the None setting to help resolve random computer lock-ups.

> **TIP** Don't forget that the Hardware acceleration option is included for troubleshooting purposes only. For best results, I recommend that you enable full hardware acceleration. A better alternative to adjusting this option might be installing a different video driver, as explained in the following section.

Updating a Video Driver

Having the latest video driver installed ensures that you are getting the most out of your video card in terms of performance and features.

Video driver updates are useful because they

1. Ensure compatibility with the widest range of games and applications;

2. Fix bugs that were present in previous versions of the driver;

3. Tweak performance and stability of the video driver; and

4. Add support for new features such as multiple monitors and 3D acceleration.

The Internet is the best place to look for updated video drivers. After downloading the latest driver from the manufacturer's Web site, double-click the program's icon and follow the on-screen instructions. If the program automatically installs your driver, there's no need to read any further (in this section).

You can manually update your video driver via Device Manager or Display Properties. Use the Display Properties method this time because you are already familiar with the Device Manager from updating a sound driver.

To update a video driver

1. Right-click a space on the desktop and choose Properties.

2. Click the Settings tab, and then click the Advanced button to display your driver properties.

3. Click the Adapter tab, and then click the Change button. The Update Device Driver Wizard appears.

4. Click the Next button to begin.

5. Because you know exactly which driver you want to install (for example, the one you downloaded from the Internet), choose the second option and click Next.

Installing and Configuring Multimedia Devices

6. Click the Have Disk button, followed by the Browse button. Locate and double-click the folder containing the video driver, and then click OK.

7. Click OK again to confirm the driver's location.

8. If multiple drivers are available from the Models list, select the one that most closely matches your video hardware, and then click Next.

9. A final confirmation appears with the name of the driver you are about to update and its location on your computer. Click Next for Windows 98 to replace your current driver files with the new ones. You'll need to insert your Windows 98 CD-ROM as required.

10. After the copying process is complete, click Finish to close the wizard. A restart of your computer might be necessary for the changes to take effect.

Restoring the Original Video Driver

If you suspect that a driver update has had adverse side effects on your graphics display, it might be wise to revert to the original Windows 98 drivers.

> **WARNING** Note that by reverting to the original Windows 98 drivers, you might lose some functionality or experience a performance decrease because you are installing an older version of the video driver.

To restore the original video driver

1. Right-click a space on the desktop and choose Properties.

2. Click the Settings tab, and then click the Advanced button to display your driver properties.

3. Click the Adapter tab, and then click the Change button. The Update Device Driver Wizard appears.

4. Click the Next button to begin.

5. Choose the second option and click Next. A list of available drivers appears (see Figure 7.10).

6. Select a driver dated 5-11-98 from the Models list, and click Next.

7. A final confirmation dialog box appears. Click Next for Windows 98 to replace your current driver files with the original ones. You'll need to insert your Windows 98 CD-ROM as required.

8. After the copying process is complete, click Finish to close the wizard. A restart of your computer might be necessary for the changes to take effect.

Figure 7.10

You can tell which drivers are Windows 98 originals by their 5-11-98 date because that was the day Microsoft finalized the device driver programming code.

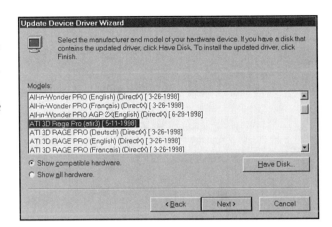

Chapter

8

Working with CD-ROM and DVD Drives

By Serdar Yegulalp

Along with the sound card and video card, CD-ROM and DVD-ROM drives are in many ways the cornerstones of a Windows 98 multimedia system. Every game of any consequence is now shipped on CD-ROM, and the first DVD-ROM games are already popping up in the marketplace as well. These DVDs sport a level of detail in game play and amazingly rich full-motion video that isn't possible on a conventional CD-ROM.

Outside of entertainment titles, of course, there are all the other possible applications: encyclopedic reference works, for instance, plus software libraries for developers, operating systems, and so on.

In this chapter you'll explore the world of CD-ROM and DVD drives. You'll see how to configure these drives and update their device drivers. And, although these drives are quite reliable, you'll also learn how to troubleshoot them when things go wrong.

Working with CD-ROM Drives

CD-ROMss and DVDs tend to be self-configuring, which takes a good deal of the burden of setup out of your hands. However, there are different types of CD-ROM and DVD drives and between them a good deal of differences in the way they're installed and configured.

Both CD-ROM and DVD drives come in two basic implementations: IDE/ATAPI, and SCSI.

- *IDE/ATAPI* drives use the same kind of controller and interface that your PC has on its motherboard. As a matter of fact, an IDE CD or DVD drive generally connects directly to the motherboard as if it were another hard drive.

- *SCSI* drives attach to an SCSI controller, which is designed to handle anywhere from 7–14 mass storage devices at high speed. Some motherboards have SCSI controllers built in, but usually the SCSI controller consists of an add-on card.

Note that motherboards made before 1994 might not properly recognize an IDE CD-ROM or DVD-ROM; have a special setting to designate an attached drive such as a CD-ROM, and therefore might produce an error when booting; or might not let the drive work at all. Sometimes, even though the motherboard can't identify the drive, Windows 98 can talk to the drive directly and still have it work. If your motherboard manufacturer has published an updated version of the BIOS, and you get an error when trying to connect your CD-ROM or DVD drive, this might be a good time to get your hands on it, because it might contain a patch for how IDE drives are identified. For the best results regardless, always set your motherboard to auto-detect the drive rather than trying to hard-assign size or geometry values.

Some manufacturers of SCSI CD-ROM or DVD drives will bundle a low-end SCSI controller with the drive to get it up and running in a computer that doesn't yet have a SCSI controller. These controllers are usually not very good and are not capable of driving more than one device at a time reliably. If you are considering investing in other SCSI devices, such as high-speed hard drives or removable media, also think about getting a controller that can handle the load.

Older CD-ROMs came with their own proprietary controller cards and were usually identified by manufacturer. The first generation of sound cards that also featured CD-ROM controllers on the card usually had three or four different interfaces, each identified by manufacturer: Toshiba, Sony, Creative, and so on. The industry has since consolidated on using either SCSI or ATAPI/IDE controllers for CD-ROMs and done away with proprietary interfaces. Many older CD-ROMs are now almost unusable for this reason, because no controllers are readily available to drive them.

Mounting CD-ROM Drives

Internal CD-ROM drives fit in 5 1/4" bays, and are held in place either with screws or with brackets that mount along the sides of the drive. Most drives are mounted horizontally, but depending on the type of case for your computer, they might be mounted vertically, because many computer cases can be positioned either way.

However, some CD-ROMs cannot be vertically mounted. CD-ROMs that use a tray-loading mechanism are often not usable when mounted vertically, because the CD-ROM cannot sit properly in the tray. However, most tray-style CD-ROMs have an innovation that makes it possible for them to be mounted horizontally or vertically. Look in the tray, around the edges of the depression where the disc is seated, for four plastic flanges, which can be pushed out or snapped in. These flanges help catch the bottom edge of the CD-ROM when it is placed in the tray, allowing the disc to be loaded properly when it's in a vertical position. Always push out the flanges that are toward the bottom; they might vary depending on which way the drive is mounted.

Caddy-style CD-ROMs, which use a case to hold the CD-ROM when it is inserted, can be mounted either horizontally or vertically. Also, some CD-ROMs have the spindle and lens assembly in the tray itself, and the disc mounts directly on the spindle, locked into place with the aid of a few spring-loaded studs. Drives such as this can also be mounted vertically without problems.

Configuring CD-ROM Settings

In addition to the hardware settings for your CD-ROM, which are covered in detail in the following sections, there are also a number of settings in Windows 98 that can affect the performance of your CD-ROM drives.

Configuring Windows 98 Settings for CD-ROMs

The first place to look for CD-ROM drive settings in Windows 98 is in the Device Manager, under the icons for the CD-ROM devices. Open the Device Manager either through the Control Panel, or right-click My Computer and select Properties, and then choose the Device Manager tab. Expand the CD-ROM section of the device tree and double-click your CD-ROM device to bring up its properties sheet.

Keep in mind that with laptops, there are some CD-ROM devices that are not mounted on-board, but they might be attached through a PCMCIA controller card or the parallel port. In these cases, you should still see a CD-ROM drive icon, but keep in mind that the device has to be attached, powered on, and whatever interface the drive is using has to be working properly.

There are several settings in the CD-ROM device's property sheet that deserve attention.

- *Disconnect*—The Disconnect parameter is generally enabled by default and is only really relevant for SCSI CD-ROMS. It allows the controller to handle the device in a more efficient fashion, especially if there are other I/O-intensive devices on the SCSI chain. If this option is checked when you find it, leave it enabled.

- *Synchronous data transfer*—Another SCSI-only option; this is usually enabled for hard disks and disabled for CD-ROMs. Disabling synchronous transfer allows the CD-ROM controller to deal with data from the CD-ROM in conjunction with other devices, so that fetching CD-ROM data doesn't occupy its entire attention. Do not change this option if the CD-ROM drive works by default.

- *Auto insert notification*—When enabled (which it is by default), this allows the CD-ROM to tap the computer on the shoulder and tell it that a new disc has been loaded. Unless you have a specific reason for defeating this function, leave it enabled.

- *Start and End drive letter*—Like removable drives, the drive letter assignments for CD-ROMs in Windows 98 can be adjusted a certain amount. Windows 98 automatically assigns a drive letter somewhere between the Start and End letters. Note that you might not have the full range of drive letters available to you, depending on how many hard drives or partitions you have in your system, because hard drives and drive partitions get priority when it comes to drive letter assignments.

Another set of adjustments for CD-ROM controls exists separate from the device listing itself. To reveal it, open the System Properties sheet, click the Performance tab, click the File System Properties button, and then click the CD-ROM tab.

There are two settings here that are important:

■ *Supplemental cache size*—This slider governs how much live RAM Windows 98 sets aside for transfers from the CD-ROM. A bigger cache uses up more memory, of course, but also reduces the amount of work the CD-ROM has to do to fetch lots of files at once, especially if their size puts them well within the limits of what the cache can handle in one go. If you have more than 16MB of RAM or rely on the CD-ROM consistently, set this slider all the way to the right. Users with less than 16MB of RAM or who do not depend on high performance from the CD-ROM can move the slider to the left to conserve live memory.

■ *Optimize access pattern*—This drop-down list contains descriptions of the various speeds of CD-ROM that Windows 98 can optimize the way it reads for. Unless you are dealing with a very old-model CD-ROM that doesn't read very fast, this should always be set to Quad-Speed or Higher, because the majority of CD-ROMs shipped today run at least at 6X or faster. (For perspective, the *slowest* CD-ROM in my collection of hardware is a 4X.)

Both of these settings are set to the maximum by default. If your CD-ROM seems to be performing poorly, you might want to check these settings to ensure that they have not been tampered with or reset by a third-party program.

Configuring IDE CD-ROM Settings

IDE CD-ROMs can work in one of two ways: Either they attach directly to the IDE controller on the computer's motherboard or they attach to a supplementary IDE controller that is provided by the manufacturer and plugs into either an ISA or PCI expansion slot. In many cases, a multimedia kit, which includes a CD-ROM drive and a sound card, has the IDE connector on the sound card, and the CD-ROM can either be plugged in to that or plugged in to the motherboard.

The IDE controllers on most sound cards are generally cut-rate and not designed to do much more than support a CD-ROM, so, it's best to attach the CD-ROM to the motherboard when possible. Only use an IDE controller mounted on a supplementary card if both IDE channels are occupied with devices, or if the motherboard cannot support a directly attached CD-ROM. Many motherboards made before 1994 cannot do this.

IDE controllers can support up to two devices on each channel. Both devices are attached at different points on the same cable, with one device designated the *master* (usually attached at the end of the cable) and another device designated the *slave*. The master device on the first IDE channel is often designated as the hard-disk boot device unless the computer's BIOS allows another device to be set up for that purpose.

IDE CD-ROMs have jumper settings that designate if the device is a master or a slave device. However, some of the ways the master/slave setups are implemented are not totally consistent, which can be a headache. For instance, some CD-ROMs do not function properly when used on the same IDE chain as some hard drives, or even some other varieties of CD-ROMs. Sometimes the malfunction only happens when the drive is designated as a master; sometimes it happens when it's a slave. Some CD-ROMs need to be designated as a master device if they're the only drive on the chain, but some drives malfunction when you do this!

The best way to work with a new IDE drive is to attach it to an IDE channel as a master—with no other devices present—and see how it behaves. If you need to add other devices to that chain, do so only after you have the CD-ROM running properly, and after you hard-designate other devices on the same chain as slaves. Don't put two devices on the same chain unless you have no other choice.

Configuring SCSI CD-ROM Settings

SCSI CD-ROMs have some of the same pitfalls as IDE CD-ROMs, but in slightly different forms.

Devices are attached to SCSI controllers in a chain, in much the same way IDE devices are, but up to seven devices can be on the chain in pretty much any order. Each device gets a unique SCSI ID number, from 1–6—usually set through a thumbwheel or jumper setting on the device itself. Device 7 is the controller.

There are two cardinal rules for configuring CD-ROM devices.

1. *Make sure each device's ID number is truly unique.* Many controllers will not report an error if two devices have the same device number. Instead, there might be a series of spurious or apparently untraceable errors—devices showing up twice or more in the Device Manager, no devices registering at all, the system hanging on boot-up, and so on. Pay extra attention to the device number assignments for internal devices, which often use jumper settings that are not very obvious at a glance and which might accidentally duplicate other settings.

2. *Terminates the chain correctly.* Two SCSI devices in every chain need to be *terminated*—the devices at the extreme ends of the chain. Terminating a device tells the controller that these devices represent the extreme ends of

the chain and the controller should not try to look beyond them for other devices, or it runs the risk of getting confused. The controller itself also counts as a device to be terminated, but many controllers sold today have the capability to auto-terminate, which is set as an option in the controller's own BIOS.

Terminating a SCSI device is accomplished in one of several ways, depending on the device:

- *By setting a jumper or DIP switch on the device.* Most external SCSI devices come with a jumper or DIP switch setting that turns termination on or off for the device.

- *By adding a termination block to the device.* External devices use this method when they have no termination switch but do have a second port for outgoing SCSI signals. The user places a termination block—a small plastic cap—over the second port.

- *By adding a set of resistors to the device.* This usually only goes for older, internal SCSI devices. Termination for these devices is accomplished by a set of three resistors—stick-like black circuits with several wires protruding from their bottoms, which plug into a row of sockets on the device's circuit board. Sometimes a jumper next to the resistors enables or disables the whole set of them, which prevents the user from having to physically pull them to disable termination.

- *By adding a termination block to the ribbon cable the device is attached to.* This is for internal devices that don't use resistor packs or a jumper. In such cases, these devices are attached to a ribbon cable that has several connectors on it. The device gets attached to the next-to-last connector, and the very last connector on the cable is fitted with a termination block.

Termination blocks and cabling are readily available from just about every computer parts supplier. Be sure to get the correct width of cable as well. Most SCSI devices use 50-pin cables, but newer Ultra SCSI devices use special 68-pin cable. Check with the hardware manufacturer and the printed documentation.

Updating a CD-ROM Driver

Most of the time, when you install a CD-ROM in Windows 98, the default CD-ROM driver supplied with Windows 98 will serve to support the whole gamut of the CD-ROM's functions. CD-ROMs are built to work with a standard specification of functions, so it isn't hard to write a rather global device driver that handles basic CD-ROM operations. This driver is called MSCDROM, which is ostensibly an abbreviation of Microsoft CD-ROM.

Very occasionally, a CD-ROM drive comes from the factory with its own driver. This is usually the case if the drive has some new low-level functionality that's not addressed in the MSCDROM driver, such as the capability to read and write discs. In such cases, the device driver for it is used in place of the conventional MSCDROM driver.

The manufacturers of such drives also publish periodic updates to their drivers, which might improve the efficiency of data transfers or even add functionality. It's considered good computer etiquette to be familiar with the manufacturers of your hardware, and to update the drivers whenever updates become available.

Updating the driver for a CD-ROM tends to follow the same steps as manually updating the driver for any other device. Here's a simple step-by-step recap:

1. Go to the Web site or FTP site where the updated driver is, download it into a folder where you'll be able to find it again later, and unpack it if it's compressed.

2. Open the Device Manager. Expand the subtree for the CD-ROM devices and right-click the CD-ROM you're going to update. Select Properties.

3. Click the Driver tab. If the device in question is using a Microsoft-supplied driver and you're replacing it with a vendor-supplied driver, you might see a message such as `No driver files are required or have been loaded for this device`. This is not exactly true; Windows 98 is merely using the default drivers, and so sees no reason to make mention of what drivers are being used.

4. Click the Update Driver button, which opens the Update Device Driver Wizard, shown in Figure 8.1, and click Next.

Figure 8.1

The Update Device Driver Wizard lets you install new driver software for your CD-ROM drive.

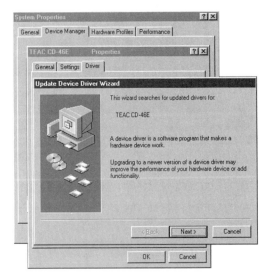

5. Select Search for a Better Driver and click Next.

6. Check the Specify a Location box and in the text box next to it type the location of your newly-downloaded drivers. Or you can click Browse to navigate Explorer-style for the folder with them.

7. Click Next to have Windows 98 search for the drivers. Depending on what it finds, it might either prompt you with a list box of possibilities, or prompt you with the name of the driver it found that matches the hardware in question, as shown in Figure 8.2.

Figure 8.2

If the wizard discovers a driver that matches your hardware, it prompts you with its name.

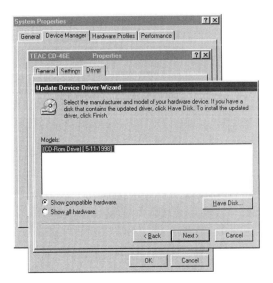

Working with DVD Drives

The good news about DVD and CD-ROM drives is that they are almost functionally identical. If you know how to install a CD-ROM drive in a computer, installing a DVD-ROM drive is fundamentally the same. They are also identical as far as SCSI versus IDE, horizontal versus vertical, and so on, are all concerned.

DVD drives are also backward-compatible to existing CD-ROM drives. With very few exceptions, outlined below, everything that a CD-ROM drive can read, a DVD-ROM can read, and more. All second-generation DVD-ROM drives can handle both music and data CDs, as well as CD-Is, CD-XAs, and just about every other CD format in the alphabet soup.

Second-generation DVD drives *cannot*, however, read CD-R discs. The laser that DVD drives use apparently has problems reading CD-Rs, and might in fact render them unreadable. Do not attempt to put CD-R discs in a DVD drive unless you have confirmed with the manufacturer that they are compatible. The same goes for CD-RW discs, which generally cannot be read on second-generation DVD drives or lower.

As of this writing, third-generation DVD drives have appeared —that is, the third iteration of the DVD standard. Third-generation DVD drives can read CD-R discs, and some models can also read CD-RW discs, although they cannot write to either of them, of course.

A Word About DVD-RAM

You might have heard about another format called "DVD-RAM," or "DVD+RW"—essentially, a rewriteable DVD disc—and you might have wondered whether or not to sell off your new read-only DVD drive. The answer is a qualified no, because there are several, warring rewriteable DVD formats that are not interchangeable, and there needs to be some time before a dominant format is established.

DVD-RAM is the first and what promises to be the most popular of the DVD-compatible formats that can read, write, and be rewritten. However, the format has some limitations: DVD-RAM discs come in a caddy and are not compatible with conventional DVD drives or players. The drives themselves are downward-compatible with DVD-ROM discs, and can also play the broad variety of CD media, including CD-RW.

Another DVD format with read-write-erase capability, called DVD+RW, is in the pipeline from Sony and Philips. DVD+RW is of slightly higher density than DVD-RAM—it packs 3GB per side, as opposed to DVD-RAM's 2.6GB—but cannot be used in existing DVD drives either. To make matters ever more complex, Hitachi has announced its own DVD-RAM format, which is player-compatible with existing DVD-ROM drives and standalone DVD players, but that won't be in the marketplace until at least the middle of 1999.

If you've just bought a DVD-ROM drive—relax—it'll be good for quite some time to come.

Mounting DVD Drives

Most DVD drives are of the drawer type, rather than the caddy type, and can be mounted either horizontally or vertically. A few external models, such as the LaCie DVD-RAM drive, use a unique loading system that involves inserting the disc into a receptacle that catches the edges of the disc.

DVD drives do run faster than conventional CD-ROMs, but they do not throw off a great deal of extra heat, and therefore do not need to be provided with an extraordinary amount of ventilation or a special enclosure.

DVD Disc Care

The most important things to remember about DVD discs is that because they carry several times more information than CD-ROMs, they are also correspondingly more fragile. Because of this, all the stern-sounding rules that applied to CDs when they first came out now go double for DVDs.

DVD discs should be kept in their cases when not in use, should never be placed on a rough surface, and should never be handled except by the center ring and the edges. Also, if possible, do not use DVDs or keep a DVD-equipped system in an area where someone smokes; cigarette smoke and nicotine residue can accumulate on the disc surfaces with far greater speed and with far nastier results than with conventional CDs.

DVD discs also can be double-sided, as compared to single-sided CDs. Most double-sided DVDs can be easily identified by the lack of printing on the surface of either side of the disc; in such cases, the printing is confined to the hub ring. DVDs that contain wide-screen and full-screen editions of the same film use this trick to label each side.

Double-sided DVDs only have one side read at a time. There might be double-sided DVD drives in production by the time this goes to press, but don't count on it: Always ensure that the correct side is inserted facing up when you mount a DVD disc.

Troubleshooting CD-ROM and DVD-ROM Drives

CD-ROM and DVD-ROM drives have a great deal in common operationally. Because of that, there's also a great many problems and attendant solutions that they also share. Here is a quick list of common problems with CD and DVD drives, along with some suggested actions to eliminate the problem.

- *CDs or DVDs refuse to spin up.* After inserting the disc, it sits there in the drive and does not come up to speed, and might even be ejected a moment later. There are several reasons for this:

  1. The most common reason for this problem is that the disc is not properly seated in the tray—some drives are *much* fussier than others about exactly where the drive is seated—and can be fixed by re-centering the disc in the drawer and reloading.

  2. For caddy-style CD-ROMs, check to make sure the door on the caddy—both the spring-loaded shutter that the lens reads through and the hinged door that the CD-ROM loads from—are both

secure in place. Also make sure that the hub assembly inside the caddy, which allows the disc to spin freely, turns and is not stuck or jammed. If any of these is the problem, discard the caddy and get another one.

3. The disc itself might be soiled or of the wrong type (DVDs generally do not spin up properly in a CD drive). If it's soiled, clean the disc carefully, center to edge, with a cleaning cloth and solution specifically designed for CDs.

4. The controller is defective or buggy. Some older models of IDE or SCSI controllers and some late-model CD-ROM or DVD-ROM drives seem to hate each other for no particular good reason. Switch drives, or switch to another controller, if you can.

■ *Data disc spins up, but Explorer cannot read from the disc.* One main reason for this happening can be found to plague earlier CD-ROMs that also had front-end CD player-style controls—for the freestanding playback for CDs without a computer. Sometimes, when a mixed-mode (data and audio) or audio-only CD is inserted, the drive says "Aha! I have to play this disc as an audio CD," and locks out the computer from accessing the disc until it's ejected and a new one is inserted. Often the disc won't even play anyway. If this is the case, you might want to check with the product literature or the manufacturer to see if there's any way to disable this. Also, some SCSI CD-ROMs exhibit this behavior when paired with certain controllers. NEC MultiSpin SCSI CD-ROMs and some Adaptec controllers, for instance, have this problem.

■ *The same drive appears more than once in Explorer.* This problem is most commonly seen in SCSI drives, and is usually due to one of three things:

1. The drive's SCSI device ID is set to that of another device on the chain. Check all the devices on the chain, and make sure there is no duplication of ID numbers, including the number assigned to the controller itself, which is usually 7.

2. The device chain is not properly terminated. Look back over the guidelines for properly terminating a SCSI chain and make sure the first and last devices are the only ones terminated.

3. The device uses a custom device driver, which has not been loaded. The latter might be especially true of CD-R drives. Reread the product literature and make sure the correct device driver has been loaded.

- *Read errors.* Sometimes a disc will read, but will stop and an error message—usually a blue-screen error—pops up. Occasionally this is a transient problem, and will go away after pressing Enter, but if it doesn't, check the following.

    1. Make sure the disc is not dirty. Dust is the most common culprit for read errors.

    2. The data cable for the CD-ROM might be faulty. A broken wire in the cable can create a transient problem, where the drive generates errors all the time during one session and operates perfectly the next session. If the problem is intermittent and does not seem to be because of a particular disc, try changing the data cable.

    3. The controller for the device might be conflicting with another device in the system. This is unlikely, but it does happen, especially for older ISA-based controllers. Check the Device Manager to make sure there are no conflicts with the IRQs used for whatever controller is handling the device.

    4. This disc itself might be defective. This is the most unpleasant of possibilities, but it does happen. If this is an early CD-R disc, it might almost certainly be the case, because many of the early CD-Rs had problems with the dye and the substrates used in the manufacturing process that led to discs having very short shelf lives. Try another drive; some drives are more sensitive to error conditions than others.

- *Disc gets ejected.* A disc might get unceremoniously ejected for many of the same reasons it refuses to spin up or returns data errors.

- *No sound from digital audio cable.* Many internal, and some external, CD-ROMs feature a digital audio connector, which sends audio information from the CD (if it's a music CD or an audio track on a data CD) to the computer's sound card. This allows for the best possible audio playback and is useful for playing CDs and games that use music tracks on the disc. Sometimes these connections will not appear to work, for these possible reasons:

    1. The cable is broken. CD-ROM digital audio cables are cheap enough to replace, but before you do so, try them in another machine to make sure they are defective.

    2. The sound card's drivers are not working properly. Make sure the sound card is functioning in the first place.

Working with CD-ROM and DVD Drives

3. The volume level for digital input from the CD-ROM is too low, or the line-in device from the CD-ROM is not enabled. This is the most common mistake, and also the easiest to fix. Fire up the Volume Control applet either from the taskbar or from Accessories/ Multimedia and check to make sure the volume control for the digital input from the CD-ROM is not set too low. Also, some drivers use the check boxes below the sliders in the Volume Control applet to indicate if something is enabled, not muted. You might also be playing with the wrong slider or it might be mislabeled.

■ *The drive refuses to be recognized by the computer's BIOS.* PC BIOSes made before 1994 might not recognize the CD-ROM or DVD-ROM properly. In a situation like this, the options are limited, but can sometimes yield useful results:

1. Set the type of drive to Auto-detect in BIOS, and ignore all errors that result. Windows 98 can often detect a drive that is connected regardless of what is indicated in BIOS.

2. Upgrade the computer's BIOS, if possible. This might resolve problems with CD-ROM and DVD-ROM drives being identified.

■ *CD-ROM or DVD video playback is jumpy.* If video playback from CD-ROMs (as with MPEG video files) or DVDs suddenly becomes jumpy when it wasn't before, consider the following:

1. The disc might be contaminated with dust; see above for cleaning instructions.

2. Another application might be stealing CPU time and preventing the player application from decompressing the video stream smoothly. Make sure nothing else is running.

3. You might have accidentally launched more than one copy of the player application, and they are basically in competition with each other. Close one copy of the player.

4. Another device might be interfering with the disc controller.

■ *CD-ROM or DVD-ROM "thrashes" constantly. Thrashing* is computer-speak for when the head of a drive slams back and forth repeatedly for no apparent reason, creating a distressing and distinct noise. CD-ROM and DVD drives might thrash for one of the following reasons:

1. A dirty or defective disc.

2. Two programs are running simultaneously, both of which are trying to read from different parts of the CD-ROM. Close one of them.

3. When mastered, the disc was not optimized for data access. This is essentially the same thing as a defective disc, and might be the case with older CD-ROMs or poorly mastered CD-Rs.

Chapter

9

Working with Game Controllers

By Rob Destefano

Most computer programs let you use standard input devices—the keyboard and the mouse—to operate them. From double-clicking a program icon to entering text into a word processor with the keyboard, using these devices has become second nature to most users. But some programs require more sophisticated or specialized kinds of input—specifically, games. Flight simulators such as Microsoft Flight Simulator 98 and Air Warrior III benefit from joysticks that mimic those found in real aircraft. And if you plan to go head to head with evil aliens in games such as Quake II or Duke Nukem 3D, you might decide to invest in a game pad similar to those found on console games such as the Sony PlayStation or Nintendo 64.

In this chapter, you'll see the differences between the various types of game controllers and learn what they have to offer. Then you'll see how to set up your new controller to ensure the most accurate control of your game. At that point, whether you're landing a 747 at Los Angeles International or blowing away mutants and cyborgs, the controller lets you take your skills to the max.

Which Game Controller Is Best for Me?

Choosing a game controller that is best for your needs should be decided by asking yourself a series of questions. For example, what type of games will you be playing? How much do you plan to spend? What kind of quality can you get for the money? And no less important, how does the controller feel when you're using it? Let's examine these questions and see what kind of answers you might come up with.

NOTE   What games do I have or want that I will need a controller for?

In asking yourself this question, keep in mind that most action and adventure games have an options menu for controls (keyboard, game pad, or joystick) allowing you to configure a wide variety of joysticks and game pads. You should know that not all game controllers on the market are compatible with some programs.

For example, in 1997, several games on the market made it extremely difficult to configure the Microsoft SideWinder game pad under Windows 95. Windows 98 has now changed the configuration process making it easier to use joysticks and game pads. Game manufacturers have also simplified configuring controllers in their option menus.

There are several types of controllers to choose from. Examples include basic two-button joysticks, flight sticks—mainly for flight simulator games (these units come with several button controls and are sometimes copied from the control columns of actual fighter aircraft), basic game pads, and ergonomic pads such as the Microsoft SideWinder. When purchasing a game, you need to pay close attention to the system requirements on the box. Some of the manufacturers tell you what types of controllers work in their game.

> **NOTE** Joysticks are fine for flight simulators, but if you want a racing experience that is more realistic, you might want to consider this option. ThrustMaster's NASCAR Pro Racing Wheel, shown in Figure 9.1, has a gas pedal, a brake pedal, and a gearshift. This device is for the true racing enthusiast. ThrustMaster also makes pedal controls and throttles for flight simulation programs.

Figure 9.1
The ThrustMaster NASCAR Pro Racing Wheel has a gas pedal, a brake pedal, and a gearshift for precision control of racing games.

Comfort of the joystick or game pad is very important. You might spend over $100 on a top-rated controller and find that the control is very hard to maneuver (making the games much less enjoyable). And left-handed gamers will discover that not all joysticks are symmetrical, meaning that some are more difficult to adapt to left-hand use.

Prices on controllers can range anywhere from $9 up to $200. Don't always use the old saying "you get what you pay for," because you can find quality controllers in the $30- to $80 price range. Microsoft, Gravis, Logitech and CH Products make some of the top-rated joysticks and game pads on the market today.

To learn more about these controllers, visit the manufacturer Web sites.

```
http://www.logitech.com
http://www.microsoft.com/sidewinder/
http://www.gravis.com/products/
http://www.chproducts.com/
```

Joysticks

A *joystick* is an input device similar to a mouse or keyboard. It is used mostly in games and in some CAD (computer-aided design) programs.

Joysticks have changed how you interact with computers and games. Arcade games such as Space Invaders and Defender were the start of a new era in technology. Since that time, Atari, Commodore, Sega, and several other manufacturers have helped pave the way for more enjoyable game playing on personal computers.

Using the keyboard in some games is very difficult (especially fighting games such as Mortal Kombat) and can be uncomfortable on your hands.

Joysticks are ideal for flight simulator games. Some games require that you use a combination of the joystick and the keyboard (due to limited buttons and multiple game features).

The Microsoft SideWinder Precision Pro, shown in Figure 9.2, is an excellent choice for game playing, comfort, quality, and price range.

Game Pads

A *game pad* is an input device that plugs into the same port on your sound card that the joystick utilizes. If you've ever played one of the popular home video game systems such as Sega or Nintendo, you've used one of these flat multi-button controllers.

The game pad came out shortly after joysticks, redefining the entire gaming experience. Game pads became popular around the time of the ColecoVision system. Later on, Nintendo and Sega came out with entertainment systems that used game pads. Today, the Sega Saturn, Nintendo 64, Sony PlayStation and several others use similar game pad designs. The popularity of the game pad has grown to the personal computer market, making games easier to play.

Game pads are used more for games (such as Mortal Kombat, Descent, Terminal Velocity, and so on) that require many buttons and keys to control the game. Some people use joysticks for these same games but have to rely on the keyboard at the same time.

The Microsoft SideWinder game pad, shown in Figure 9.3, and the SideWinder FreeStyle Pro game pad, shown in Figure 9.4, are excellent choices for game playing.

Figure 9.2

The Microsoft SideWinder Precision Pro usually retails for less than $75.

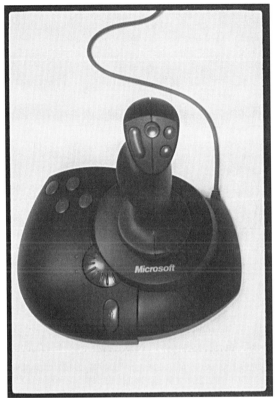

Photo courtesy Microsoft

Figure 9.3

The Microsoft SideWinder game pad lets you control computer games in a fashion similar to console games such as the Sony PlayStation.

Photo courtesy Microsoft

Figure 9.4

Microsoft's Freestyle Pro controller has an internal motion sensor so you can tilt it to control some game functions.

Photo courtesy Microsoft

Setting Up a Game Controller

Depending on the game controller you purchased, installation instructions will vary. Before you get too excited and plug the controller in to expect immediate results, read through the manual that accompanies the device.

The first step to avoid any major headaches is to make sure your sound card is set up properly. Just because you hear CD music, MIDI files, and Wave files, does not mean the game controller portion of the sound card is present or set up correctly.

Configuring Game Controller Settings

The first step toward ensuring your sound card is properly configured is to open the Control Panel. You can do so by selecting the Settings command from the Start menu. You can also double-click the My Computer icon on the desktop and access the Control Panel, or right-click My Computer and choose Properties.

> **NOTE** If you have Active Desktop enabled (with the single-click option enabled that lets you browse your desktop as a Web page), you will not have to double-click to open some items in the following steps.

1. Click on the Start button in the bottom-left corner of the screen.

2. Click the Settings option.

3. Click Control Panel in the resulting pop-up menu.

4. Double-click the System icon.

5. Click the Device Manager tab.

6. Scroll down to Sound, Video, and Game Controllers.

7. Click the plus sign that appears next to Sound, Video, and Game Controllers. You'll see a list similar to the one shown in Figure 9.5.

Figure 9.5

You can check your sound and game controllers in the System Properties dialog box.

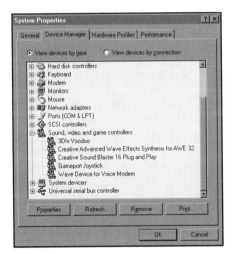

You'll see a device in the submenu Sound, Video and Game Controllers called Gameport Joystick. If not, you need to run the Add New Hardware Wizard to detect the game port. If the wizard fails to detect the hardware, contact the hardware manufacturer for support. If the device is listed, there should not be a red x or a yellow exclamation mark on the device.

> **NOTE**   A red x indicates that the device is disabled.
>
> A yellow exclamation mark indicates that the device is not function-ing properly, has a conflict with another device, or does not have the drivers installed for it to function.
>
> In the event that one of these conditions exist, you need to contact the manufacturer for support, or reinstall the sound card drivers. If you're particularly hardware savvy, you might be able to track down the device that's causing the conflict.

After you have determined the Gameport Joystick device is present and has no conflicts, you can shut down the computer.

Have your computer turned off before plugging in the game controller. Windows 98's Plug-and-Play technology likely finds the controller when you power up again. At this point, it either supports the device with drivers built into Windows 98, or prompts you for a driver disk.

If your device is not listed in the Windows 98 driver library, you must provide it with the appropriate disk(s). If you are prompted for a disk, place the floppy or CD-ROM into the computer and click Next.

Some game controllers might not be found when you start Windows 98. In this scenario, load the software that accompanied the controller first.

When loading the controller software, unload all programs from memory first by closing any open windows. You should also disable any antivirus protection. Doing so prevents another program from interfering with the installation process.

> **NOTE**   Some game controllers do not come with drivers or software. These controllers are usually the less expensive line (two button joystick, basic game pad) that can be configured without software using the Game Controllers setup icon in Windows 98's Control Panel, as shown in Figure 9.6. See the next section, "Updating a Game Controller Driver" for the step-by-step process.

After the software for the controller has been loaded, you need to check under Game Controllers to see if Windows 98 detects it. This setting appears on the General tab of the Game Controllers dialog box that appears when you double-click the Game Controller's icon, as shown in Figure 9.7. If Windows 98 recog-nizes the controller, it is listed in the white box in the General menu. There are two headings under Game Controllers (Controller and Status). The controller heading has your joystick or game pad listed by name. The status heading has either Report OK or Not Detected.

Figure 9.6

You can set up some of the more common joysticks by double-clicking the Game Controllers icon in the Control Panel.

Figure 9.7

If Windows 98 detects your joystick, the Game Controllers dialog box's General tab displays an OK under Status.

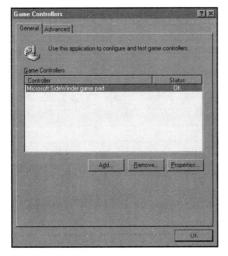

If you see a status report indicating Windows didn't detect your joystick, you should shut down your computer and make sure the controller is plugged in properly. Turn the computer back on and check the status again. If it still reports that the controller is not detected, you might want to unload all software from memory (antivirus, crash monitors, and so on) and check the status once more. In rare cases, you might have a software conflict or configuration problem leaving the controller undetected by Windows 98 (contact your hardware or software manufacturer for support).

After you have determined that your controller is the correct one listed and the status is reporting OK you need to calibrate it. You'll use the Game Controller Properties dialog box, shown in Figure 9.8, to perform the calibration.

Figure 9.8

By calibrating your joystick in this dialog box, you give Windows 98 information about its sensitivity.

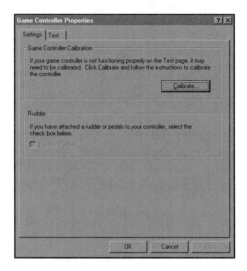

Here's how to calibrate your joystick:

1. Open the Game Controllers dialog box (if it isn't open already).

2. Highlight your controller by left-clicking it once.

3. Click on the Properties button.

4. Click on the Calibrate button under the Settings tab.

5. Follow the step-by-step instructions.

6. Click on the Test tab under the Game Controllers Properties dialog box. You'll see a screen similar to the one shown in Figure 9.9.

7. Test all the buttons and rotate the direction pad or stick, as applicable, to ensure it moves the black crosshair in the square white field.

After the calibration process is complete, you can install and begin playing your favorite games.

> **NOTE**   You might still have to calibrate the controller within the game itself after configuring it in Windows 98.

Figure 9.9

*The Game
Controller
Properties dialog
box's Test screen
lets you ensure
the system
responds to the
input you make
through your
joystick or game
pad.*

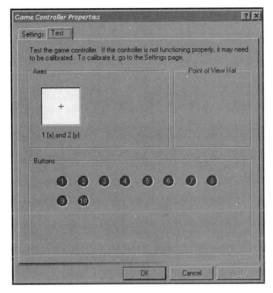

Updating a Game Controller Driver

Updating or changing a game controller driver can be done in a few easy steps. As
before, you'll access the Control Panel's Game Controller dialog box. This time,
I'll show you how to do so by using the My Computer icon on your desktop.

1. Double-click the My Computer icon on the desktop (of course, Active
   Desktop users can single-click).

2. Double-click the Control Panel icon.

3. Double-click the Game Controller icon.

4. Click the Advanced tab at the top of the Game Controller dialog box.

5. Click the Change button.

6. Select a controller from the list provided and click OK.

> **NOTE**   There are several ways of getting to the Game Controller dialog box
> (and many other dialog boxes) in Windows 98. Do not get confused
> by the various routes shown in the step by step processes I have described.

Windows 98 doesn't limit you to a single controller. For example, if you are a
hardcore gamer, you might play driving games, flight simulators, and first-person
shooters such as Doom. In that case, you might want to use a variety of specialized controllers. Fortunately, you can add and remove controllers from the Game
Controllers General menu.

1. Click the Add button on the Game Controllers dialog box.

2. Click the Add other button; you'll see the dialog box shown in Figure 9.10.

3. Insert the CD-ROM or floppy that was packaged with the controller.

4. Click the Have Disk button.

5. Select the drive letter where the disk is located.

6. Left-click the OK button.

7. Select your controller from the list.

Figure 9.10

Installing a new sound or game controller with Windows 98.

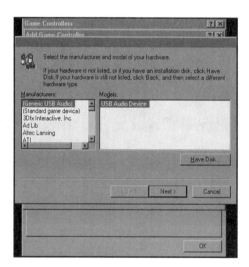

The setup disks that are packaged with the controller might have more than one device listed. Be sure to select the correct one before continuing with the installation.

Chapter

10

Working with USB Devices

By Rob Destefano

One of the enhancements Windows 98 offers is improved support for Plug-and-Play devices. In the days of DOS, adding hardware to your computer was a fairly complicated process. You had to open the case and insert a card into the correct slot. Then you had to run a DOS program that configured the system to use the device, edit your system configuration files, or both.

Plug and Play changes this situation and puts hardware upgrades more within the reach of the average user. All you need to do is plug the device into a port on the back of your computer, run Windows 98, and the system takes care of installing the necessary software. (Of course, it might ask you for a disk or CD-ROM from the manufacturer.) *Universal Serial Bus*, or USB, is the power behind Plug and Play. With USB, you can connect a number of devices to a single port on your computer, and Windows 98 takes care of the rest. In this chapter, you'll learn more about the definition and capabilities of USB. You'll also see some practical examples of working with USB devices such as scanners, digital cameras, and the Microsoft Natural Keyboard Elite.

What Is USB?

USB is a kind of serial port that lets you connect a number of devices, such as mice and modems, to a single port on your computer. These ports allow you to plug in up to 127 devices without using expansion slots, communication ports, or IRQs (interrupt requests). USB is true Plug-and-Play technology. USB connectors are much smaller than a 25-pin parallel printer cable, and provide five volts of power to the attached devices. This compact size eliminates bulky power adapters and cables running across and behind your desk. If words such as jumpers, IRQ, DMA (direct memory address), and I/O (input/output) addresses turn your stomach, USB is the alternative solution for you.

Another advantage of USB comes from the world of PCMCIA devices—namely, that USB devices can be plugged in and unplugged with the computer powered on. Computer mavens call this "*hot-swapping*." What's more, Windows 98 can identify and load the proper device drivers on-the-fly for hardware that's added in this way.

Do I Have USB?

If your PC (personal computer) has an Intel 430 VX chipset or newer (check your motherboard documentation, it should be stated plainly in the specs), you most likely have one or both of the following: USB connectors on the motherboard; USB ports (one or more) on the PC (ready for use). If your motherboard has USB connectors and no ports, there are third-party vendors that manufacture them. If you plan on ordering ports to plug onto your motherboard, you should first refer to the manual that was provided with the motherboard (the pin layout can vary from board to board). Some vendors also carry add-on cards that utilize an available ISA (industry standard architecture) or PCI (peripheral component interconnect) slot.

Another place you can look to learn about your system's USB capacity—if it has it—is in your system's BIOS settings. *BIOS*, which stands for Basic Input/Output System, is the hardware-level program that governs your computer's basic configuration settings, such as interrupts and memory.

Most computers let you access the BIOS settings by pressing a key (usually F1 or the Del key) when the machine is first powered on. There, you can check to see what interrupts, if any, are assigned to the USB controller. If the USB controller isn't showing up in the Device Manager, or no USB devices appear when you plug them in, there's a good chance the USB controller has been disabled.

How do I Install USB drivers?

The Windows 98 operating system versions OSR/2.1 and OSR/2.5 have USB support included (on the CD-ROM). OSR/2 did not have USB included; Windows 98 has built-in USB support. If your PC's operating system is Windows 98, USB is already installed (provided it is enabled in your BIOS). The first thing to do is make sure USB support is enabled in Windows 98's Device Manager.

To access Device Manager to check for USB support, follow these steps:

1. Click the My Computer icon on the desktop.

2. Click the Control Panel icon.

3. Click the System icon.

4. Click Device Manager.

5. Look for Universal Serial Bus Controller.

6. Click the plus symbol (+) next to Universal Serial Bus Controller.

Figure 10.1 shows the Windows 98 Device Manager dialog box.

After you have located the Universal Serial Bus Controller in Device Manager, there will be a plus or minus symbol to the left of the device's name. If there is a plus, click on it to expand a submenu listing various USB devices attached to your system. A minus symbol would indicate the menu is already in expanded view. There should be two devices listed underneath the Universal Serial Bus Controller: Intel PCI to USB Universal Host Controller and USB Root Hub. Make sure there are no red X symbols or yellow exclamation marks on the devices, because these notations indicate trouble with the devices. Without these two devices, the USB ports will not function.

Figure 10.1

The Windows 98 Device Manager lets you control and configure system components such as USB devices.

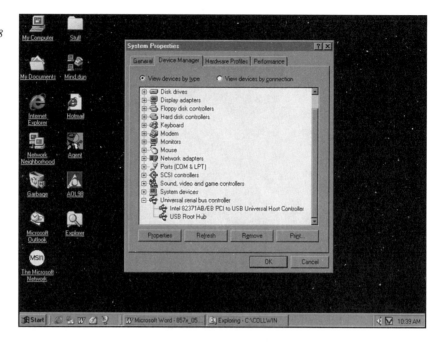

> **NOTE** A red X indicates that the device is disabled. A yellow exclamation mark indicates that the device is not functioning properly, has a conflict with another device, or does not have the drivers installed for it to function.

What Types of USB Devices Are Available?

The USB peripheral (hardware attached directly or indirectly to your computer) market has grown substantially in the past year. Devices such as scanners, digital cameras, printers, joysticks, keyboards, and even speakers are now available in USB design. These USB devices are much easier to set up than the serial, parallel, and SCSI (Small Computer Systems Interface) versions that computer users might have encountered before. USB has redefined the phrase "Plug and Play." Listed below are a few examples of USB devices and how to use them.

Working with Scanners

What specifications should I look for when purchasing a USB scanner?

Several manufacturers have entered the scanner market in the past year. Here are a few companies that manufacture USB scanners.

- Visioneer—www.visioneer.com

- UMAX—www.umax.com (international Web site)

- Acer—www.acerperipherals.com

- Agfa—wwa.agfa.com

All the scanners manufactured by these companies have a one-year limited warranty. The price range for these scanners is from $89 to $190. The scanner that will suit your needs best depends on the types of images you will be scanning, and the software you prefer working with.

Table 10.1 summarizes the features and specifications for some popular USB scanners.

What do Some of These Specifications Mean?

When you're shopping for a scanner, you'll be confronted with a lot of terminology. The following list shows some of the key scanner features you'll need to evaluate.

- DPI (dots per inch)—The resolution of images. The more dots per inch, the higher the resolution.

- Resolution—Sharpness and clarity of an image.

- Bit (Binary Digit)—Graphics are often described by the number of bits used to represent each dot; 24-bit images are higher in resolution or color depth than 8-bit.

- OCR (Optical Character Recognition)—Allows you to scan a page of text into your computer for editing in a text editor or word processor.

The Visioneer Paperport 3100 and the UMAX Astra 1220U have great specifications and user-friendly software. The software bundled with the AcerScan 310U and the Agfa SnapScan might not be as fancy or user-friendly. However, the Acer and the Agfa both offer good quality at a lower price. All the scanners discussed here are easy to install and are very reliable.

Table 10.1 Features and Specifications for Some Popular USB Scanners

Product Name	Resolution	Maximum Scan Size	Color Image Quality	Interface	Software	Dimensions
Visioneer Paperport 3100 Flatbed	Optical resolution: 300 × 600 dpi Interpolated resolution: 2,400 × 2,400 dpi	8.5 × 11.7 inches	30-bit color 10-bit grayscale	USB	Paperport version 5.3 Visioneer OCR Picture Works PhotoEnhancer	17.7 × 11.4 × 3.4
UMAX Astra 1220U Flatbed	Optical resolution: 600 × 1,200 dpi Interpolated resolution: 9,600 × 9,600 dpi	8.5 × 11.7 inches 12-bit grayscale	36-bit color	USB	Adobe PhotoDeluxe NewSoft Presto! PageManager Caere Omnipage LE OCR UMAX Copy Utility	18.4 × 12.2 × 3.9 inches
Acer AcerScan 310U	Optical resolution: 600 × 1,200 dpi Interpolated resolution: 9,600 × 9,600 dpi	8.5 × 11.7 inches 10-bit grayscale	30-bit color	USB	IPhoto Plus Xerox Textbridge	18.1 × 12 × 3.3
Agfa SnapScan 1212U Flatbed	Optical resolution: 600 × 1,200 dpi Interpolated resolution: 9,600 × 9,600 dpi	8.5 × 11.7 inches	36-bit color	USB	FotoLook 3.0 FotoSnap 3.0 IPhotoExpress 3.0 SE	449 × 328 × 103 mm

Scanning an Image

Make sure your computer is off before installing the scanner. Plug the scanner into the USB port and turn on your PC. When Windows 98 boots it finds the scanner and begins the installation, asking you for software disks as necessary. After you have installed all the bundled software, you can begin scanning.

Scanning images with a flatbed scanner is essentially the same as using a photocopy machine. Make sure the scanner is on a flat and level surface. Some scanners have a locking mechanism for shipping and transportation purposes. This mechanism locks the moving parts into place and prevents damage to the scanner. You should remove this device before using the scanner. In some scanners, this is a screw; in others, it's a sliding switch. Check your scanner's instructions.

Most flatbed lids open from the front of the scanner. The glass under the lid should be kept free of oil, dirt, and dust particles. Keeping the glass clean prevents your scans from appearing blurred or distorted. Refer to your scanner manual for the proper cleaning procedure.

All images (pictures or documents) should be placed face down on the glass. The software (in most cases) will have a preview option, which you should select before the final scan is performed. This preview allows you to change software settings (such as cropping a portion of the image to scan) before the image is saved.

Most scanners have an auto lamp shutdown feature, which is designed to keep the scanner cool and lengthen the life of the unit. If your scanner does not have such a feature and will not be used for several hours, it is recommended that you shut it off.

Configuring Scanner Settings

There are several options in the scanner software that will affect the size and appearance of the image being scanned. Here are some of the settings you might find in your software:

- Brightness
- Contrast
- Resolution
- Color mode
- Gray mode
- Line Art mode
- Color filters

- Gamma correction

- Tone control

- Auto color control

I recommend using the automatic or default settings for all categories until you get used to using the software. The auto setting feature of many scan programs adjusts all the options for an optimal scan, resulting in a very clear image. Refer to your software documentation and help files for changing software settings.

The size of the file scanned depends on the format you use to save it. There are several image formats to choose from. Here are the most popular formats used for scanning images.

- JPEG (Joint Photographic Experts Group)—This file format uses compression to reduce the image size. Some detail might be lost using this format, but the gains as far as color depth and compression power more than make up for it. This is best for scanning photos.

- BMP (bit map)—Standard graphics format used in Windows.

- GIF (Graphics Interchange Format)—Format most commonly used by the World Wide Web (WWW). This format includes data compression and is effective for scanning cartoons or images with simple color schemes.

- TIFF (Tagged Image File Format)—One of the most widely supported formats, frequently used for high-end image editing. This format can be any resolution, black and white, grayscale, or color.

After you become comfortable adjusting scanner software settings, you will find which file format best suits your needs for size and quality.

Windows 98 has built-in software that supports most scanners. Imaging For Windows, shown in Figure 10.2, was created for Microsoft by Eastman Software Inc. (a division of Kodak).

Here are some quick and easy steps for using the Imaging program to scan an image in Windows 98.

1. Click the Start menu and scroll up to Programs.

2. Scroll over to the Accessories menu and click Imaging.

3. In the Imaging program, choose Select Scanner from the File menu.

4. Select your scanner from the list.

5. Select New from the File menu.

Figure 10.2

Windows 98 comes with the Imaging program, which you can use with your scanner.

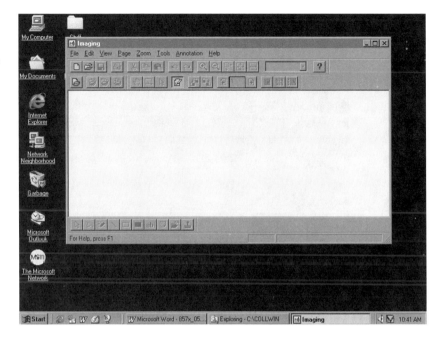

Windows 98's Imaging program then communicates with your installed software and fires up the scanner driver's control panel. From there, preview and scan an image. After the image is scanned, it will export (send the image) to Imaging for Windows. You can add text, highlight areas, rotate, freehand lines, and much more.

Removing a Scanner

When removing a scanner from your computer, you should first engage the locking mechanism (if your scanner has this feature) and unplug the scanner from the wall before moving the unit. After the scanner is removed, the software applications and drivers need to be uninstalled. To do so, click the Start menu, navigate to Settings, and choose the Control Panel. Double-click the Add/ Remove Programs Control Panel to access the dialog box shown in Figure 10.3.

In the dialog box, select your scanner's software and click Add/Remove. When all the bundled software has been removed, reboot your computer to refresh the Registry.

Figure 10.3

You can remove your scanner's software in the Add/Remove programs Control Panel.

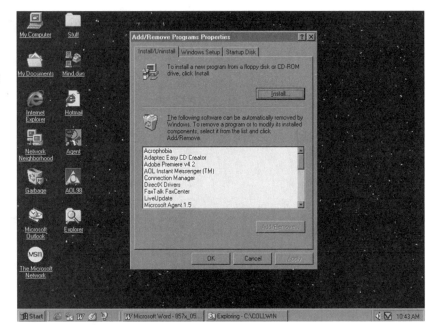

Working with Digital Cameras

Years ago, motion picture cameras were complicated equipment operated only by skilled professionals. These days, anyone can capture the moment by pointing his or her video camera and clicking the camera's button. Digital cameras let you capture images to your computer screen almost instantly.

If the primary use for your camera will be video conferencing, a Connectix QuickCam VC is the perfect choice. The QuickCam VC was designed with video conferencing in mind. This camera can be placed on top of your monitor or on your computer desk (it is not portable). Listed here are some of the features and specifications of the QuickCam VC.

- **Connectix QuickCam VC**

    - USB interface (provided by Lucent Technologies)

    - Frame rates of 15 frames per second (Pentium 166MHz or better required)

    - Adjustable focus lens

    - Six-foot cable

    - Video email

    - Still image editing

- **Minimum System Requirements**

  - Pentium 100MHz processor

  - Windows 95

  - USB port (version 4.00 or later)

  - 16MB RAM

  - 10MB of hard drive space

  - SoundBlaster compatible sound card and speakers (for audio)

  - Microphone

  - 28.8 Kbps modem

If portability is a must, and you don't need to shoot motion video, the Kodak DC220 and DC260 are excellent cameras because of the features they offer. These digital cameras are perfect for taking on trips, shooting family photos, and much more. Here are some of the features and specifications of the Kodak DC220.

- **Kodak DC220 Zoom Camera**

  - Integrated audio support

  - Time lapse and burst capture modes

  - LCD panel

  - 8MB picture card (up to 120 pictures)

  - Self timer

  - Video out

  - Captures one million pixels (1,152 × 864)

  - Crisp picture detail for 5"× 7" printed pictures

  - Optical quality glass lens

  - 2X Zoom (equivalent to 29–59 mm)

  - Digital Zoom for 4X magnification

  - Focus free lens

  - Multi-mode automatic flash

  - Auto exposure and white balance

- **Software**

  - Kodak Digital Science Picture Easy 3.0

  - Adobe PhotoDeluxe

  - Adobe PageMill

The DC260 has the same software as the DC220 but has some extra features. The DC260 is capable of 1.6 million pixels (1,536 × 1,024) in 24-bit color. This camera can produce an 8"× 10" photo-realistic image (depending on printer quality). It also has a 3X zoom lens, an external flash mode, and enhanced album support.

Taking a Picture

Taking pictures with cameras such as the QuickCam VC is done from within the software. These cameras can take still shots, but are best suited to creating full motion videos. You can also create video email (audio and video) with the bundled software. Most of the software packages allow you to compress the video email file down to 675k (less than one megabyte) for approximately 60 seconds of footage. Video email is an excellent alternative for those of you who would like to spend less time typing. It also makes sending and receiving email more fun.

Some businesses use these cameras for video conferencing. This technique allows you to see and hear other users that have the same software and a similar camera. Windows 98 comes with built-in conferencing software called NetMeeting; this program allows users to transfer files, share applications, remote control another computer, and speak to other users anywhere in the world with real-time audio and video.

Taking pictures with a portable digital camera (such as the Kodak) is essentially the same as using a standard camera that uses film. Digital cameras allow you to select the quality level (resolution) of the images before they are taken. Higher resolutions increase the image size (memory size), and lower resolutions decrease the image size. When you take pictures in a low-resolution mode, there will be more memory space available for pictures in the camera.

Video-conferencing cameras work slightly differently, because they can take both single pictures and full-motion videos. Like portable digital cameras, it's possible to adjust the level of quality for individual pictures, but the same thing can also be done for video files. You can shoot a video file with a larger screen size or higher frame rate (the upper limit depends on the camera), but the resulting file size will be larger. It's also possible to compensate for this by increasing the amount of compression on the video. This makes the file take up less space, but the video will be less detailed.

Configuring Digital Camera Settings

Digital camera settings for portable models such as the Kodak can be changed on the camera itself. Settings for cameras such as the QuickCam VC are changed in the software. Most portable digital cameras have a built-in LCD (liquid crystal display) for selecting menu options and viewing the images. After you have the menu opened on the LCD screen, there will be several options to choose from. If you are using the camera for a presentation, the picture should be taken in a high-resolution mode. If you will be taking the camera on a trip, you should set the camera to low-resolution mode, allowing the camera to hold more images. Depending on the variety of camera, this is usually done by pressing a button on the camera that cycles through the various picture qualities. Check the documentation for the exact procedure.

Most of the portable digital cameras have a built-in flash. Some of the flashes are auto-sensing and will activate according to the amount of light detected. The Kodak DC220 and DC260 both have a digital zoom feature, which is perfect for capturing small objects. After you take some pictures and want them transferred to your computer, be sure the camera is set to USB mode. Some of the cameras support more than one type of connectivity (serial, parallel, and infrared). If the camera is set for something other than USB, the computer will not establish communications.

The software for the camera will have an option to retrieve images (pictures). Because the software bundles accompanied with each digital camera differ, you need to refer to the help files for step-by-step instructions. Most of the software packages will display the images as *thumbnails* (tiny pictures) on your computer monitor, which can be clicked for full-screen viewing. These images can be saved on your hard drive, used as wallpaper, printed, and even used as a screensaver.

Removing a Digital Camera

It is best to remove your camera from the computer when everything is powered down. After the camera is unplugged from the USB port, turn the computer on. When the computer has booted into Windows 98, the software can be removed by accessing the Add/Remove Programs Control Panel (refer to Figure 10.3). To do so, open the Control Panel dialog box by choosing the Settings command from the Start menu, or by double-clicking My Computer, and choosing Control Panel. Then double-click the Add/Remove Programs icon.

In the resulting dialog box, find the software you want to remove in the list box and click Add/Remove. When all the bundled software has been removed, reboot your computer to refresh the Registry.

Working with the Microsoft Natural Keyboard Elite

If you've worked with computers for any length of time, you know it can be an uncomfortable experience. Computer mice, keyboards, and even workstations are not always designed for comfort. Mouse manufacturers got the message a while back, and now there are more and more ergonomic mice. And now there's also a keyboard that should prove to be a lot more comfortable—as well as efficient— to use.

The Natural Keyboard Elite, shown in Figure 10.4, was the first ergonomic keyboard designed to work with Windows 95. This keyboard has now been replaced by the Natural Keyboard Elite. The Elite keyboard is based on the original design, but with some major improvements.

Figure 10.4

Microsoft's Natural Keyboard Elite plugs into your computer's USB port.

Photo Courtesy Microsoft

The Elite keyboard is smaller than the prior version, fits into most commercial keyboard trays, and is USB compatible. The split sloped design allows you to type in a more natural position.

To use the USB connector, obviously, you must have Windows 98 and a computer with a USB port. Plug the keyboard into your USB port and turn on your PC. Windows 98 will find the keyboard and install the drivers for you.

The Elite keyboard has shortcut keys, such as the 104- or 105-key. These shortcut keys open Windows 98's Start menu. This is the perfect keyboard for people spending hours typing on the computer.

Chapter

11

Working with MIDI

By Scott Downie

MIDI (Musical Instrument Digital Interface) is a simple and universal way for your computer to make music. Music has been part of the personal computer experience since the days when the only capability they had for making noise was a tinny little speaker. MIDI represents a digital method of recording music using real or simulated digital instruments.

In this chapter, you'll examine the hardware and software prerequisites for making MIDI music, see how to assemble the pieces into a song, and look at generalities of MIDI songs and sounds. You'll learn how to check your Windows 98 MIDI configuration and edit and remove MIDI instruments. After dissecting the anatomy of a MIDI file, you'll explore a very simple multimedia example. Then, you'll go beyond general MIDI into extending Windows 98's MIDI configuration capabilities. This chapter shows you how to make a final check in the Windows 98 Multimedia MIDI Control Panel, and provides some useful MIDI Web links.

In olden days, a roll of perforated paper provided the musical information necessary to drive a vintage player piano into a syncopated symphonic frenzy. MIDI is the electronic descendant of the perforated paper player piano roll. The ones and zeros in a MIDI file are the modern-day reincarnation of perforations in a roll of paper.

A MIDI file is a blueprint that a MIDI application uses to play sound synthesizers, either internally on the sound card or on an external MIDI tone module or keyboard. See Figure 11.1 for a flowchart to help you visualize how MIDI works.

Notice that no durations are specified in these musical instructions. MIDI sends *performance gesture* information within milliseconds of when you do something such as press a MIDI keyboard's key or bang a MIDI drum. So how long will a given note play? It will play until it is told to stop playing. A note can play for one second or one hour, depending on how soon you release the key or when your computer tells it to shut up.

Because MIDI files (also referred to as MIDI *sequences*) are only blueprints and do not contain actual sound information (unlike WAV files), MIDI file sizes are typically very small. MIDI files more than 200KB in size are very rare; typically they range in the tens of kilobytes in size. The small size of MIDI files allows a developer to add another audio dimension to a multimedia presentation or Web page without forcing the file size to mushroom. But there is a downside. The playback quality of a MIDI file depends on the quality of the sound card (or MIDI tone module) that it drives. If you create your MIDI sequences using a state-of-the-art, high-dollar MIDI tone module, it might sound wonderful—on your computer. But if you play that same sequence on a four-year-old sound card, you might be hard pressed to recognize it. If MIDI is important to you, make sure you buy a card that features high-quality built-in sounds. If your MIDI will be distributed, keep in mind the potential audio limitations of your audience's computers.

Figure 11.1
A MIDI setup contains these basic elements.

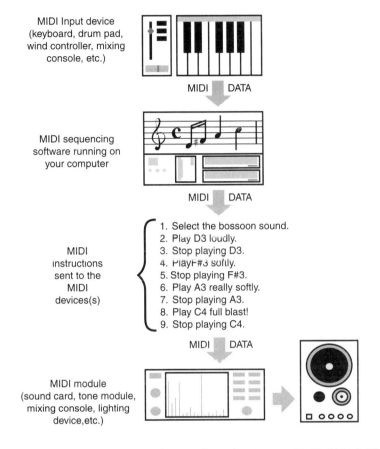

MIDI Input device (keyboard, drum pad, wind controller, mixing console, etc.)

MIDI DATA

MIDI sequencing software running on your computer

MIDI DATA

MIDI instructions sent to the MIDI devices(s)

1. Select the bossoon sound.
2. Play D3 loudly.
3. Stop playing D3.
4. Play F#3 softly.
5. Stop playing F#3.
6. Play A3 really softly.
7. Stop playing A3.
8. Play C4 full blast!
9. Stop playing C4.

MIDI DATA

MIDI module (sound card, tone module, mixing console, lighting device,etc.)

The most common type of MIDI these days is *general MIDI* (GM). The intent behind GM was to create a standard among MIDI playback devices that allowed a file created on one MIDI system to sound "right" on another system. In other words, GM was supposed to solve the problem posed in the previous paragraph. But how can one GM module manufacturer differentiate itself from a competitor if all GM modules are supposed to sound the same? By creating a GM sound set that sounds the same, but is "better" than the others. Unfortunately, it doesn't take much to mess up an orchestral mix that involves 10 MIDI instruments, for example. One sound card's better GM mix becomes another's muddy sonic mess. Adjust your general MIDI expectations accordingly.

Many recent high-end MIDI software applications include the facility to manipulate digital audio as well as MIDI information. A discussion of digital audio is beyond the scope of this chapter; but here's one piece of digital audio advice: If you think that you might ever be tempted to work with digital audio, do not skimp on any of your computer's components. Get a big, fast hard drive, a fast CPU, and as much RAM as you can cram into your motherboard.

Hardware Prerequisites

The MIDI-only card—so painfully common in the DOS days—has become virtually extinct. MIDI is now available as a standard part of the feature set of all but the cheapest sound cards. But beware: Even though some card manufacturers provide a MIDI port (usually a DB-15 connector), they might not provide the MIDI cable itself. A MIDI cable typically costs around $30. If you are buying a sound card, check the box carefully to see whether or not a MIDI cable is included. Of course, if you don't intend to plug in a MIDI instrument such as a guitar or synthesizer, you won't need a cable.

If you are looking to purchase a sound card for your late-model computer, your first choice should probably be a PCI (Peripheral Component Interconnect) sound card. ISA (Industry Standard Architecture) sound cards are cheap, but that's because the ISA standard is on the way out. Of course, if you're a true multimedia maven, all the PCI slots on your new computer might already be spoken for. This fact might force you to go with an ISA card.

If you have external tone modules or keyboards that are equipped with MIDI inputs, you don't have to live with your sound card's audio translation of MIDI files. You can connect external modules or keyboards to your MIDI port and have your computer control the external device or devices. You can also get an external MIDI tone module that plugs into the USB (Universal Serial Bus) port found on most new computers. And eventually you will have the option of connecting your MIDI peripheral via an IEEE 1394 (Institute of Electrical and Electronic Engineers specification 1394) port. *FireWire*—an Apple Computer term—is another well-known name for IEEE 1394. When you decide to build your multimedia computer, remember these expansion options as you plan your system configuration.

Most folks probably associate MIDI input devices with keyboards. But drums, guitars, and even woodwind-like instruments can also be wired in. There are many other techniques to generate MIDI data as well. Gloves, body suits, biofeedback monitors, and motion detectors are a few other sources that MIDI maniacs have used to glean their data.

MIDI doesn't even necessarily have to be associated with audio. One flavor of MIDI—MIDI Show Control—makes it easier for a theater to control and automate its lighting system. MIDI Time Code permits audio and video devices to be synchronized. This chapter discusses only basic musical MIDI issues and avoids the more esoteric tangents. Check the MIDI links listed at the end of this chapter to learn more about the many flavors of MIDI.

Software Prerequisites

Both the Windows 95-vintage Media Player and the newer Windows Media Player play back MIDI files. If you want to edit the files, however, you might have to download or buy a shareware or commercial MIDI application. MIDI applications run the whole spectrum of prices and features, from $20 to $600+. Happily, a MIDI sequencing application is almost always bundled with a sound card, so you might not have to lay out any cash at all.

The MIDI tab in the Multimedia Control Panel allows you to adjust the configuration of your MIDI system. To access this dialog box, click the Start menu and select Settings, or double-click the My Computer icon, and select Control Panel. Then double-click the Multimedia icon and click the MIDI tab, as shown in Figure 11.2.

Figure 11.2

The Multimedia Control Panel's MIDI tab lets you control Windows 98's MIDI settings.

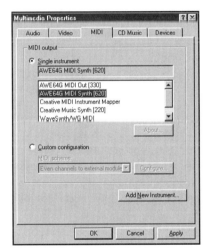

Working with MIDI

Assembling the Pieces

In a best-case scenario, performing a basic GM system setup procedure might be unnecessary—all the necessary elements might already be installed and configured on your computer. If your computer came with built-in sound and you have no external keyboards or other MIDI peripherals to attach, you're probably in business. To get an idea of what MIDI capabilities you might already have, click the Start button and look through your Program listing to find a program group with the name of your sound card (or its manufacturer). MIDI applications are usually bundled together under this heading.

If you are installing a new sound card in your Windows 98 computer, it is almost certainly plug-and-play compliant. With most new sound cards, installation is a painless three-step process: Plug the card into one of your computer's empty slots, start your computer, and install the software from its accompanying CD-ROM. Follow the card's installation instructions and you should be ready to go. Gone are the days when you had to worry about jumper settings and interrupt numbers.

After the card is up and running, you'll want to hook it to a sound system. The sound system could be a cheap set of powered speakers, your stereo system, your Digital Dolby decoder, your USB digital speakers, your…well, you get the picture. There are way too many audio options for this chapter to cover. But there is one suggestion that can be applied to them all: Don't skimp when you go shopping for speakers!

Speakers are the most important element in your multimedia setup. For any serious listening whatsoever, a pair of small, cheap, powered speakers won't cut it. Shoot for at least a pair of satellite speakers and a subwoofer. If you're looking to experience the thrill of three-dimensional sound, seriously consider going to at least four channels. Yes, a number of software companies claim that they require only two speakers to create a "surround sound" illusion, but it's not as convincing as a true four- (or five- or six-) channel setup. And if you want surround sound but are facing a cash crunch, you can take comfort in the fact that the back speakers don't have to be as high in sonic quality as the front speakers.

Enough preaching to the converted! After you get your audio plans squared away, you might be wondering how you could use the MIDI/joystick adapter that came with your sound card. If so, take a look at Figure 11.3. As you can see, hooking up your MIDI computer isn't too much more complicated than connecting your home stereo.

The joystick connectors on the MIDI/joystick cable attach to the back of the sound card and the joystick, if any, like a digital extension cord. Now you not only have more joystick cord slack but you also get two MIDI connections. Most MIDI modules are equipped with three identical-looking MIDI jacks: In, Out, and Thru. A series of MIDI devices can be hooked up in daisy chain fashion and there are only two daisy-chain rules:

1. A MIDI module's input should be piped to the In jack.

2. A MIDI module's output can be taken from either the Out or Thru jacks.

Not too hard, is it? From those two simple guidelines, you can construct MIDI configurations from the totally simple to the hopelessly complex.

Figure 11.3

There are many possible ways to connect external MIDI devices, but they all probably involve plugging in easily distinguishable cables.

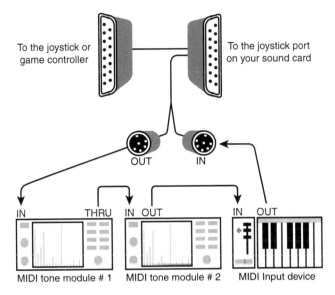

> **NOTE** The difference between Out and Thru is this: A MIDI device's Out transmits *only* the MIDI information generated by that particular device. A MIDI device's Thru transmits *only* the MIDI information that comes in through the In jack. In other words, a MIDI Out jack provides you with information that comes from that particular device. A MIDI Thru jack provides you with information that comes from some other device (or series of devices) in the MIDI chain.

The only other restriction is that the cable that connects one MIDI device to another should not be more than 20 feet long.

Of course, there are exceptions to these rules. For example, most MIDI software allows you to pass MIDI through the computer, from In to Out. If this circumstance was applied to the system just illustrated, it would enable the keyboard to play MIDI tone modules 1 and 2 in real time. Also, a number of MIDI modules allow you to merge the MIDI data that arrives at In with the MIDI data that the modules create internally, broadcasting the combined MIDI data stream on the Out jack.

I wanted to present this whole MIDI chain discussion early, primarily to help you avoid the dreaded MIDI feedback syndrome. Just like a speaker that howls when the microphone that it's broadcasting is too near, MIDI data can also get caught in a vicious circle. If the sequencing software was set to pass MIDI data through the computer (from the computer's In to Out), and both MIDI Tone Module #2 and the MIDI input device were set to send merged MIDI data to their outputs (as in Figure 11.3), you would likely suffer MIDI feedback. This is due to the fact that there would be nothing to stop any bit of data from circling around and around the MIDI loop. This situation is more serious than merely producing an annoying whine. Notes would continue to play when they shouldn't, MIDI data lights that normally blink glow solidly, and your sequencing software might lock up. If you connect external MIDI devices and your system seems sluggish or useless, check the configuration of your MIDI Ins, Outs, and Thrus.

General MIDI Guidelines

A GM-compatible sound generating device must meet the MIDI Manufacturer's Association's (MA's) performance guidelines. Take a look at these guidelines to see what you get with Windows 98 MIDI.

- *Voices*—If a tone module can play more than one note at once, it is *polyphonic*. A GM tone module must offer at least 24 voices for both melodic and percussive polyphony. At least 16 of those voices should be available to play melody parts, with the remaining eight ready to play percussion voices.

  Notice the subtle shift in terminology—voices, not sounds, are specified because one GM sound can require more than one voice to create. For example, a GM tone module might require two voices to generate one honky-tonk piano note. You might think you'd never need more than 24 voices in a GM card or tone module. But if you create a MIDI sequence of any density whatsoever and you begin to notice that some of the parts of your MIDI score disappear when the whole MIDI ensemble kicks in, you'll realize how quickly you can use up 24 voices. If you calculate the polyphony of a 24-voice tone module that relies on two voices to create one honky-tonk piano note, you'll see that the honky-tonk polyphony (in this example) is cut in half! Twenty-four voices can only produce 12 honky-tonk notes.

  All the voices should be *velocity sensitive*—the harder you strike a key, the louder the sound should get.

- *Channels*—A MIDI channel functions just like a channel on a television set. All the channels are accessible to your TV at all times, but you watch only one channel at a time, filtering out the other channels with your TV tuner. Likewise, a series of MIDI commands can be assigned to a particular channel and broadcast throughout your MIDI system. A sound that is tuned to that channel responds to those MIDI commands. A sound that is not tuned to that channel ignores those MIDI commands.

  GM devices offer 16 channels for simultaneous use. Each channel can be polyphonic. The percussion track is always supposed to be located on channel 10. This means that you could have a piano playing a five-note chord on channel 1; a bassoon playing one woody note on channel 2; the drums hitting the cymbal, kick drum, and snare on channel 10; and still (probably) have a fair amount of unused polyphony to spare.

■ *Instruments*—As suggested in the preceding example, each channel can play a different instrument or *timbre* (pronounced TAM-bur). A GM device is, by definition, *multitimbral*—it can play more than one sound at a time. Going hand in hand with the 16 available MIDI channels, a GM device can play a minimum of 16 different timbres simultaneously. The names of the available GM sounds are listed later in this chapter.

■ *Channel Messages*—There is more to MIDI than selecting sounds and turning notes on and off. You can also change the volume of a note while it is playing, bend the pitch of a note (like a guitarist can do with a whammy bar—or tremolo arm, if you please), and otherwise modify the sound in real time. MIDI commands that allow these real-time sound modifications are called *continuous controller* commands (CCs). Here is a list of the GM CCs that every GM manufacturer is required to provide.

Modulation, usually input from a wheel or lever on a keyboard—CC # 1

Main volume—CC # 7

Pan, positioning of the sound in the stereo field—CC # 10

Expression, sort of a sub-volume control—CC # 11

Sustain, designed to work like the damper pedal on a piano—CC # 64

Reset all controllers, sets all controller values on a channel to their defaults—CC # 121

All notes off, turns off all notes on that channel—CC # 123

Most GM devices offer many more continuous controllers. But if you plan to distribute your MIDI files to a wide audience, make sure that you don't depend on a CC that another MIDI device might not support.

There are still more messages that can be sent down a channel: pitch bend and the range of pitches through which you can bend, coarse and fine-tuning options, and *aftertouch* (also known as channel pressure). After you develop an interest in manipulating GM data at this level, it is time to pull out your MIDI device's owner's manual and read.

General MIDI Sounds

The GM sound set is comprised of 16 *families* of sounds. Each family is, in turn, comprised of eight sounds. Table 11.1 lists the GM family tree.

Working with MIDI

Table 11.1 MIDI Sound Families

Sound #	Family	Sound #	Family
1–8	Piano	65–72	Reed
9–16	Chromatic	73–80	Pipe Percussion
17–24	Organ	81–88	Synth Lead
25–32	Guitar	89–96	Synth Pad
33–40	Bass	97–104	Synth Effects
41–48	Strings	105–112	Ethnic
49–56	Ensemble	113–120	Percussive
57–64	Brass	121–128	Sound Effects

NOTE As mentioned in the introduction to this chapter, the GM specification does not provide a hard-and-fast definition for any sound characteristics. The sound names only serve as guides. You can expect particularly wide variations from one GM module to another when you use the vaguely defined synth leads, pads, and sound effects. In other words, it might not be a good idea to make the Goblins sound (#102) the centerpiece of a MIDI sequence if you expect that it will be played back on a wide variety of sound cards and tone modules. Everyone has a general notion of what a piano sounds like. Not everyone agrees, however, on the typical sound a standard Goblin would make.

Expressed in less organized terms, there are 128 GM sounds. Table 11.2 lists all 128 sound categories.

Table 11.2 MIDI Sound Categories

Sound #	Instrument	Sound #	Instrument
1	Acoustic Grand Piano	65	Soprano Sax
2	Bright Acoustic Piano	66	Alto Sax
3	Electric Grand Piano	67	Tenor Sax
4	Honky-tonk Piano	68	Baritone Sax
5	Electric Piano 1	69	Oboe
6	Electric Piano 2	70	English Horn
7	Harpsichord	71	Bassoon

Sound #	Instrument	Sound #	Instrument
8	Clavi	72	Clarinet
9	Celesta	73	Piccolo
10	Glockenspiel	74	Flute
11	Music Box	75	Recorder
12	Vibraphone	76	Pan Flute
13	Marimba	77	Blown Bottle
14	Xylophone	78	Shakuhachi
15	Tubular Bells	79	Whistle
16	Dulcimer	80	Ocarina
17	Drawbar Organ	81	Lead 1 (square)
18	Percussive Organ	82	Lead 2 (sawtooth)
19	Rock Organ	83	Lead 3 (calliope)
20	Church Organ	84	Lead 4 (chiff)
21	Reed Organ	85	Lead 5 (charang)
22	Accordion	86	Lead 6 (voice)
23	Harmonica	87	Lead 7 (fifths)
24	Tango Accordion	88	Lead 8 (bass + lead)
25	Acoustic Guitar (nylon)	89	Pad 1 (new age)
26	Acoustic Guitar (steel)	90	Pad 2 (warm)
27	Electric Guitar (jazz)	91	Pad 3 (polysynth)
28	Electric Guitar (clean)	92	Pad 4 (choir)
29	Electric Guitar (muted)	93	Pad 5 (bowed)
30	Overdriven Guitar	94	Pad 6 (metallic)
31	Distortion Guitar	95	Pad 7 (halo)
32	Guitar harmonics	96	Pad 8 (sweep)
33	Acoustic Bass	97	FX 1 (rain)
34	Electric Bass (finger)	98	FX 2 (soundtrack)

Working with MIDI

continues

Table 11.2   Continued

Sound #	Instrument	Sound #	Instrument
35	Electric Bass (pick)	99	FX 3 (crystal)
36	Fretless Bass	100	FX 4 (atmosphere)
37	Slap Bass 1	101	FX 5 (brightness)
38	Slap Bass 2	102	FX 6 (goblins)
39	Synth Bass 1	103	FX 7 (echoes)
40	Synth Bass 2	104	FX 8 (sci-fi)
41	Violin	105	Sitar
42	Viola	106	Banjo
43	Cello	107	Shamisen
44	Contrabass	108	Koto
45	Tremolo Strings	109	Kalimba
46	Pizzicato Strings	110	Bag pipe
47	Orchestral Harp	111	Fiddle
48	Timpani	112	Shanai
49	String Ensemble 1	113	Tinkle Bell
50	String Ensemble 2	114	Agogo
51	SynthStrings 1	115	Steel Drums
52	SynthStrings 2	116	Woodblock
53	Choir Aahs	117	Taiko Drum
54	Voice Oohs	118	Melodic Tom
55	Synth Voice	119	Synth Drum
56	Orchestra Hit	120	Reverse Cymbal
57	Trumpet	121	Guitar Fret Noise
58	Trombone	122	Breath Noise
59	Tuba	123	Seashore
60	Muted Trumpet	124	Bird Tweet
61	French Horn	125	Telephone Ring

Sound #	Instrument	Sound #	Instrument
62	Brass Section	126	Helicopter
63	SynthBrass 1	127	Applause
64	SynthBrass 2	128	Gunshot

GM Percussion

For reasons that are shrouded in the mists of bygone technology limitations and manufacturing politics, MIDI channel 10 is the place to go for the majority of your GM percussion needs. On channel 10, each MIDI note number (or key number) corresponds to a different drum sound. For example, if your keyboard is broadcasting on channel 10 and you pressed middle C, you will hear a Hi Bongo. If you press the C# above it, you'll hear a Low Bongo. If you press the B flat below middle C, you'll hear the ever-popular Vibraslap. On a non-percussion channel, each note is assigned to a different pitch and all the notes on that channel use the same sound. On the percussion channel, each note is assigned to a different sound. You can check out the MIDI percussion sounds in Table 11.3.

Table 11.3   MIDI Percussion Sounds

Key #	Drum Sound	Key #	Drum Sound
35	Acoustic Bass Drum	59	Ride Cymbal 2
36	Bass Drum 1	60	Hi Bongo
37	Side Stick	61	Low Bongo
38	Acoustic Snare	62	Mute Hi Conga
39	Hand Clap	63	Open Hi Conga
40	Electric Snare	64	Low Conga
41	Low Floor Tom	65	High Timbale
42	Closed Hi-Hat	66	Low Timbale
43	High Floor Tom	67	High Agogo
44	Pedal Hi-Hat	68	Low Agogo
45	Low Tom	69	Cabasa
46	Open Hi-Hat	70	Maracas

Working with MIDI

continues

Table 11.3 Continued

Key #	Drum Sound	Key #	Drum Sound
47	Low–Mid Tom	71	Short Whistle
48	Hi-Mid Tom	72	Long Whistle
49	Crash Cymbal 1	73	Short Guiro
50	High Tom	74	Long Guiro
51	Ride Cymbal 1	75	Claves
52	Chinese Cymbal	76	Hi Wood Block
53	Ride Bell	77	Low Wood Block
54	Tambourine	78	Mute Cuica
55	Splash Cymbal	79	Open Cuica
56	Cowbell	80	Mute Triangle
57	Crash Cymbal 2	81	Open Triangle
58	Vibraslap		

Keep in mind the difference between *pitched* and *non-pitched* percussion. Notice that the timpani—an instrument that you usually find in an orchestra's percussion section—is located in the Strings family of sounds. This is due to the fact that the timpani, unlike the Crash Cymbal, is usually called on to play specific pitches. A timpani sound (or any other percussive instrument such as Woodblock or a Synth Drum) cannot be assigned to channel 10. Likewise, you cannot squeeze a chromatic range out of a Cowbell by somehow attempting to assign it to a channel other than 10. But that still leaves you free to compose the Great American Gunshot Concerto.

Checking Your Windows 98 MIDI Configuration

As I mentioned earlier, the Multimedia Control Panel is the place to check your Windows 98 MIDI configuration. To refresh your memory, refer to the Control Panel in Figure 11.2.

All the MIDI output channels for this particular computer (refer to Figure 11.2) are assigned to AWE64G MIDI Synth 620, the high-quality voices on the internal sound card. The available MIDI options will vary depending on what sound card(s) and what software you have installed.

When a number in brackets (such as 220, 330, or 620) appears, it is a hexadecimal number that indicates the input/output address for that device. If hexadecimal and input/output address don't mean a thing to you, don't worry. You can use these numbers to detect patterns even if you don't want to be aware of your computer's inner workings. When you see 220, that usually means you're connected to a cheesy, old-fashioned FM (frequency modulation) sound source. When you see 330, that usually means your MIDI data is going to be sent to whatever external MIDI device(s) you've connected to your MIDI chain. Other numbers (such as 620) might mean that you're connected to the high-quality sounds on your internal sound card. If there are no numbers at all, that usually indicates that you are connected to a software synthesizer or virtual MIDI device of some kind.

> **NOTE** A hexadecimal (hex) number uses 16 characters (instead of the usual 10) to express a numerical value. The 16 characters consist of the 0 through 9 plus A, B, C, D, E, and F. For example, the decimal number 12 is equal to the hexadecimal symbol C. Decimal 95 is equal to 5F in hex.
>
> Hexadecimal numbers are easier for computers to deal with, so as you dig deeper into the mysteries of the digital world, odds are that you'll run across hexadecimal numbers every once in a while.

Single Instrument Configuration

Referring to the MIDI system loop example used earlier in this chapter, go ahead and assume that MIDI tone module #1 is called SC-55. Also assume that MIDI tone module #2 is called VL70m. If you want to add these two external MIDI modules to your Windows 98 list of multimedia MIDI devices, you have to add them to the correct address. In this example, click the MIDI entry that contains a 330, and then click Add New Instrument. The MIDI Instrument Installation Wizard will appear, as shown in Figure 11.4.

Follow the Wizard's instructions. In this case, the SC-55 is a GM device that is to be attached to AWE64G MIDI Out. The Wizard's last question asks you for the instrument name, as shown in Figure 11.5. Select as descriptive a name as possible—you'll thank yourself if you ever have to do any troubleshooting.

After the second MIDI module, VL70m, is added, the Multimedia Control Panel looks like the one shown in Figure 11.6.

Working with MIDI

Figure 11.4

The MIDI Instrument Installation Wizard lets you add external MIDI modules to Windows 98.

Figure 11.5

The wizard asks you to specify a name for your new MIDI instrument.

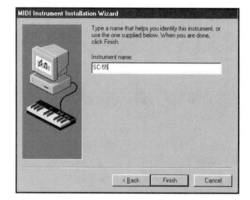

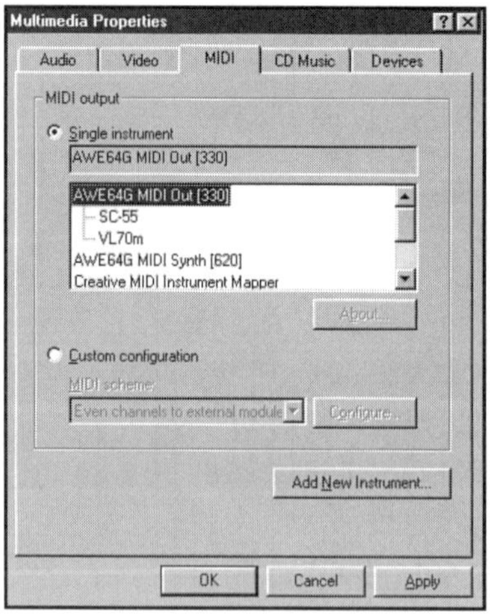

Figure 11.6

The Multimedia Control Panel might look like this after you add two instruments.

Custom Instrument Configuration

To create a more interesting MIDI configuration, you might decide it to assign the even-numbered MIDI channels to the external MIDI device(s) and the odd-numbered MIDI channels to the internal sound card. Because you're talking about multiple instruments, you'll need to take advantage of the Multimedia Control Panel's Custom Configuration option. If you click the Custom Configuration radio button, the lower half of the Multimedia Control Panel comes to life, as shown in Figure 11.7.

Figure 11.7

Setting up a custom MIDI configuration is a click of a radio button away.

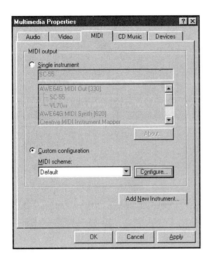

When you click the Configure button, you'll be presented with a blank custom configuration. You need to go through, MIDI channel by MIDI channel, and map the instruments you want to use to the MIDI channels. To do so, click a MIDI channel, click the Change button, select the instrument to use with that channel by clicking the drop-down list, as shown in Figure 11.8, and click OK.

Figure 11.8

Click the instrument drop-down list to assign MIDI instruments to MIDI channels in a custom configuration.

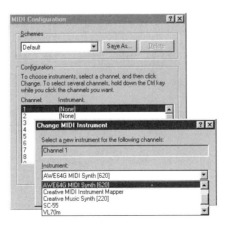

Working with MIDI

Although you aren't required by law to account for every MIDI channel in a custom configuration, it is probably wise to do so. That way you won't be confused later on when the sound associated with a MIDI channel mysteriously disappears. When you've finished creating your custom configuration, rename it and save it. In Figure 11.9, the example's custom configuration is named Even Channels to External Module.

Figure 11.9

Here's the completed custom configuration.

Now you can assign your new custom configuration to your MIDI system. Select the name of the custom configuration from the drop-down list, as shown in Figure 11.10, and click OK to close the Multimedia Control Panel. Your custom configuration is now active.

Figure 11.10

Click the MIDI scheme drop-down list to select your custom configuration.

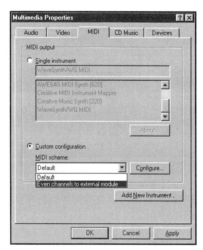

To delete a custom configuration, return to the MIDI Configuration dialog box, select the custom MIDI Scheme in the drop-down list, and click Remove. Notice that doing so only deletes a MIDI configuration. It does *not* delete any MIDI instruments. But what if that's what you want to do? Read on.

Editing and Removing MIDI Instruments

Now that you're a savvy veteran of the Multimedia Control Panel's MIDI tab, you might have noticed that, aside from looking at these new MIDI instruments, there's not a whole lot you can do to edit them. It is not obvious, for example, how to delete an instrument. To edit and delete instruments, you need to click the Multimedia Control Panel's Devices tab. If you click Devices and open the Devices tree all the way down to the external MIDI devices, you'll see something similar to the dialog box shown in Figure 11.11.

Figure 11.11

The Devices tab of the Multimedia Control Panel lets you delete individual instruments.

To see the details of the SC-55's setup, double-click the SC-55 entry and click the Details tab. From this dialog box, shown in Figure 11.12, you can edit the instrument name, change the MIDI port, and change the instrument definition. (Don't worry about the instrument definition for now. It is discussed in the section, "Beyond General MIDI," later in this chapter. Assume that this is a GM instrument for now.)

If you want to remove this instrument, click the General tab, and then click the Remove button, shown in Figure 11.13.

Figure 11.12

Click the Details tab to see an instrument's properties.

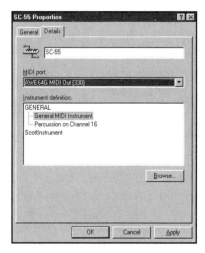

Figure 11.13

The General tab lets you remove a MIDI instrument.

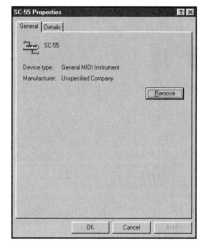

If you have an insatiable curiosity about what is going on behind the multimedia scenes, or if you simply want to kill some time by memorizing the version numbers of your MIDI drivers, the Devices tab of the Multimedia Control Panel is a good place to hang out. You can even add an instrument from within the Devices tab by selecting MIDI Devices and Instruments from the list and clicking the Properties button. But, if you start editing values or deleting devices without a clear understanding of what you are doing, you can seriously mess up your system in short order. Be curious, but be careful!

One more Windows 98 Control Panel deserves a mention: the Add/Remove Programs Control Panel, shown in Figure 11.14. The Add/Remove Programs functionality comes in handy when your software configuration is so loused up that you might as well uninstall what you've got and start over again. Add/

Remove is an all-or-nothing proposition—you can't select the MIDI components that stay and those that go. Using Add/Remove is the proper way to remove software: Deleting individual files by dragging them to the Recycle Bin is, at best, a pain and, at worst, a good way to really confuse Windows 98. Add/Remove finds all the little components that are involved and cleans up the Windows Registry—tasks that even die-hard Windows hackers sometimes hesitate to undertake.

Figure 11.14

As a last resort, use the Add/ Remove Control Panel to remove your MIDI software.

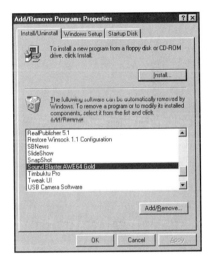

The Anatomy of a General MIDI File

Figure 11.15 illustrates a GM file opened in Cakewalk, one of the many MIDI editing programs you can use to slice and dice MIDI files. Although this display is taken from MIDI software that might differ from yours, the ideas behind the displays are fairly common from software package to software package. The file itself—bsmetana.mid—is included on the CD-ROM that accompanies this book.

Bsmetana.mid is a file that contains the blueprint to B. Smetana's *Dance of the Comedians* from *The Bartered Bride*. It is an orchestral work that plays 12 tracks through 12 MIDI channels. Remember, a *track* is simply a place to organize MIDI data. Multiple tracks can be assigned to the same MIDI channel or one track might contain MIDI data that uses multiple channels. Track functions and limitations depend on the sequencing software you use. Some of the channels (such as #1, Piccolo) are monophonic—only one note at a time is played on that channel. Other channels (such as #11, String) are polyphonic—the strings need to be capable of playing chords. The main Track window displays this fundamental structure, using color to make it easier to differentiate the instruments.

Working with MIDI

Figure 11.15

This is what the GM file bsmetana.mid looks like in a typical MIDI editor.

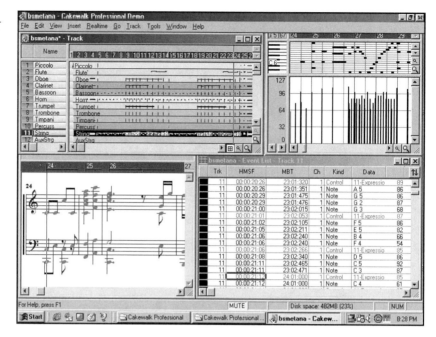

The Piano Roll window, which has two parts, is to the right of the Track window. The top half of the window is true to its name—it displays the MIDI information for the selected channel (#11) in a way that would look right at home on an old-fashioned player piano. The longer the black note bar, the longer the duration of the note. The higher the note bar, the higher the pitch.

The bottom half of the Piano Roll window displays the MIDI Velocities associated with the note bars. The higher a velocity, the louder the note. Velocity values (and most CC data values) range from 0–127. If you assemble these two Piano Roll views in your mind, you can develop a three-dimensional way of looking at the MIDI data as it flows by.

The Event List window is located below the Piano Roll window. If you're into raw number crunching, the Event List window is the place for you. Moving from left to right across one line of information, you see the

- Track number

- Time this MIDI event will be issued (relative to the beginning of the sequence)

- Measure, bar, and tick location of this event within the file

- Channel on which this event will be broadcast

- Kind of event (note, controller, and so on) that it is

- Data for the event itself

- *Note on* velocity (how hard the key was struck)

In this example, the note data for String is displayed in black and the continuous controller #11 (Expression) data is displayed in green.

The Staff window is located to the left of the Event List window. The Staff window tries to civilize the mass of MIDI data by using traditional musical notation for its display. The note heads are colored in this example because all the contents of this track have been selected. Although this might appear to be a user-friendly way to offer up MIDI file info, beware. Depending on the software's capability to translate data into notation and depending on how you have configured your notation display, a notation option can present either an unintelligible mass of squiggles or an oversimplified view of the track, omitting crucial details.

One aspect of the bsmetana.mid file example is not displayed in the screen shot. Although the tracks are arranged in traditional score order (piccolo, flute, oboe ,and so on), that does not mean that the channels to which those tracks are assigned follow the same order. Notice that track 11, String, is assigned to MIDI channel 1. The Horn (or French Horn) track is assigned to channel 11. Why? Because in most MIDI devices, priorities are assigned to the 16 MIDI channels, but not in strict numeric order. In most cases, top priority is given to channel 10 (percussion). Channel 1 is usually next in line, followed by channels 2 through 16. If a GM device is swamped with data, it will start picking and choosing what it can play. Notes on channel 16 will be the first to disappear, followed by the loss of channel 15, and so on. In this example, the intention is to ensure that the string part—the most important information—always gets the highest priority. It is true that MIDI devices and computers are getting more powerful all the time, but if you suspect that your MIDI file might be played back on an older, easily over-whelmed GM device, plan ahead to make sure that the most important elements of your musical presentation survive.

Finally, bsmetana.mid can be used to test the *generality* of GM. This file was created using the first GM tone module: Roland's Sound Canvas SC-55, which appeared in 1991. Since that time, many sound cards, MIDI keyboards, tone modules, software synthesizers, and the like have come and gone. When played back on other GM systems, sometimes there are subtle differences and sometimes the differences are so vast that you'd swear some terrible accident had corrupted the file! Playing this file back on a Sound Blaster AWE 64 Gold sound card is *not* the same as playing it back on the SC-55. There are differences from one GM product to another, even if both products come from the same manufacturer. The oft-repeated moral of this story (and this chapter) is this: Try your GM sequences on multiple GM systems. This gives you the best idea of which GM parameters you should embrace and which GM limitations you should avoid.

A Very Simple Multimedia Example

MIDI files can be embedded in documents, such as Microsoft PowerPoint presentations; integrated into other display engines, such as Macromedia Director or QuickTime for Windows; or distributed in various ways on the Web. Because there are too many situations in which MIDI can be embedded or distributed, this chapter addresses the lowest common denominator: Embedding a MIDI file in an application that you get for free with Windows 98—WordPad.

Figure 11.16 depicts a WordPad document that contains a crude graphic and the bsmetana.mid file. The MIDI file is playing, and the playback controls are visible. (Note the slider in the lower-right corner of the playback controls, indicating the file has played about three-quarters of its length.) A MIDI file can be added to a WordPad document by clicking the Insert menu, selecting the Object command, and locating the MIDI object you want to use. Double-click the MIDI object to play the embedded MIDI.

Figure 11.16

Here's the MIDI file playing from within a WordPad document.

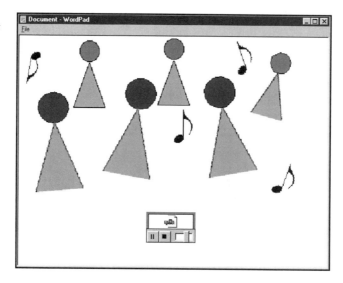

One thing to keep in mind when you add a MIDI file to a document is whether the MIDI data is either embedded in the new document file (as demonstrated) or linked to the new document file. If you embed a MIDI file, you usually don't have to worry about keeping the original MIDI file with the document. But, if you link a document to a MIDI file, the new file needs to refer to the original MIDI file when it is time to play. As a result, when you transport linked files, you will need to send both the new document and the original MIDI files.

Also keep in mind MIDI's minimal but finite playback demands. Given the vast amounts of computational horsepower available on late-model computers, playing a MIDI file by itself—on a sound card that has built-in GM sounds—is a task that the CPU hardly has to think about. But if, for example, you try to play MIDI through a software synthesizer—one that uses the CPU to process the sounds—while you have a number of other large, processor-intensive applications running, your MIDI playback might hiccup now and then. If you do run into a situation in which the playback tempo fluctuates unexpectedly, first look to see what other applications are running in both the foreground and background. If your system is short on resources, your MIDI playback might suffer.

Beyond General MIDI

So far, the majority of this chapter covers basic GM because it provides a low common denominator for MIDI file manipulation. Many of GM's critics consider the GM standard to be too low. Because MIDI appeared about eight years before the GM standard arrived and because new non-GM MIDI developments appear daily, this section only briefly touches on some aspects of MIDI that aren't so general.

Extensions of GM: Roland's GS and Yamaha's XG

The Roland Corporation (`http://www.rolandus.com`) is credited with introducing the first GM tone module—the Sound Canvas SC-55—in 1991. For better or worse, the SC-55 is still the standard against which other GM tone generators are measured. But even the original SC-55 featured one more *standard*: Roland's GS format. Roland claimed that GS provided a significant improvement in the way that the quality of a particular sound could be controlled. For example, GS gives you a way to precisely control *portamento*—the amount of gliding desired when moving from one pitch to another. Yamaha (`http://www.yamaha.com`), Roland's largest and fiercest competitor, introduced the XG standard in 1994. Both Yamaha's XG and Roland's GS systems used GM as a starting point, but after you get past GM, an XG tone module and a GS tone module don't pretend to have much in common.

Both GS and XG were attempts to insulate the MIDI user from the perceived horrors of *system-exclusive* (sysex) MIDI commands. As the name suggests, a system-exclusive MIDI command can be understood by only one system. A sysex command that is intended for an Emu Proteus tone module cannot be understood by a Kurzweil K2500R tone module. This is actually a good thing because a MIDI composer wants to ensure that changes made to one specific sound do not confuse any of the other members of his or her MIDI module ensemble. When

sysex commands are thoughtfully implemented by a particular MIDI manufacturer, sysex greatly enhances a MIDI composer's capability to shape the sounds to
his or her liking. But who has time to learn a new set of sysex commands for
each new MIDI device that comes along? Standards such as GS and XG promised
to eliminate the sysex learning curve. They did to a degree, but now you have to
learn GS and XG to take advantage of the savings.

GS, XG, and just about every non-GM system allow you to break through the
128-sound, one-drum-set barrier. For example, even the original Roland SC-55
contained 289 sounds and seven drum sets. But, if you remain strictly within the
basic GM guidelines, you might never hear what its Car Crash or Electronic
drum set sounds like. With GM, you get a certain degree of sonic predictability
but you lose a considerable amount of sonic flexibility. If you are using GM now,
odds are that your sound card or tone module supports MIDI activity that goes
beyond GM. Check your documentation to see what you have on tap.

Here's a sneak peek into the future. There's a new standard called *DLS*
(Downloadable Sounds). DLS will use GM as a foundation but will then allow
composers to add their own custom sounds to the GM sound set. DLS sounds
will not be limited to musical instruments. A DLS sound could be spoken
dialogue or a special effect. The plan is to have DLS load into your computer's
RAM, rather than hard disk, allowing the downloads to be potentially quite large.
Unfortunately, this also probably means that you will need to have a DLS-
compatible sound card to take full advantage of this new technology. If the DLS
concept appeals to you, keep your eyes open.

> **NOTE**   DLS is a brand new and still emerging technology. For details, see
> www.midi.org or www.pavo.com.

Patch Editors and Patch Librarians

Even though every MIDI tone-generating device comes from the factory with at
least a few preset sounds (at least 128 preset sounds, if the device supports GM),
you might want to change a preset or create a new sound. A *patch editor* is software
that provides a user-friendly way to make such changes. (Patch is another term
that is frequently used instead of sound.) A *patch librarian* is a program that stores
sounds or sound descriptions. An editor almost always comes with some sort of
librarian, but a librarian does not necessarily include an editor.

> **NOTE**   There are actually a bewildering number of synonyms for sound and
> each manufacturer uses different terms. Check your documentation to
> make sure that you are using a vocabulary that fits your MIDI system.

The look, feel, and price of patch editors and librarians is as diverse as the MIDI devices themselves. For example, the powerful but not too polished editor for Yamaha's VL70-M tone generator—a non-GM device that is *monophonic* (it can play only one note at a time)—is provided as freeware from Yamaha. However, you can spend hundreds of dollars on sophisticated editor/librarian software packages that feature built-in databases, allowing you to effortlessly juggle thousands of sounds. It depends on the size of your studio, your desire to experiment, and your willingness to spend.

The Standard MIDI File Format

Before 1988, every MIDI software manufacturer was free to use its own MIDI file format. That meant that files created in one sequencing package might not have been recognized as a MIDI file by another sequencing program, which was a big problem. The creation of the Standard MIDI File (SMF) format was one of the steps that facilitated the (later) development of the GM specification.

There are three SMF formats, the most popular being MIDI Format 0 and MIDI Format 1. Format 1 can store MIDI events in separate tracks, preserving the track assignments that you used when you created the file in a sequencing package. Format 0 places all the MIDI events into one large track. Some crude MIDI sequencers require the MIDI files they accept to be in Format 0. But unless you have a compelling reason to do otherwise, it is best to use Format 1. The sample MIDI file on the CD-ROM—bsmetana.mid—is saved in MIDI Format 1.

Percussion on Channels Other than 10

The Percussion on Channel 16 option in the MIDI Instrument Installation Wizard reminds you that if you aren't worried about GM compatibility, non-pitched percussion does not necessarily have to be located on MIDI channel 10. Long ago, many MIDI musicians put the percussion track on MIDI channel 16—the last of the MIDI channels in those dark, distant days. If you are creating a MIDI sequence that will always run only on your system, you can rearrange the tracks any way you please. You could, for example, send non-pitched percussion information on a number of channels simultaneously To step off the beaten MIDI track, all it takes is a willingness to study your MIDI device's MIDI implementation minutiae.

Using More than 16 MIDI Channels

Yes, it can be done. But it takes more than your sound card MIDI interface to get it. A number of manufacturers, such as Opcode (`http://www.opcode.com`) and Mark of the Unicorn (`http://www.motu.com`), sell sophisticated MIDI interfaces that allow you to easily run your MIDI channel total up to 96, 128, or more. You can use those channels not only for turning notes on and off but also for controlling lighting systems or automating external mixing consoles.

Most of these expanded MIDI interfaces also offer SMTPE (Society of Motion Picture and Television Engineers) synchronization. This feature allows you to precisely synchronize your computer's operation with that of external audio and video recorders. More exotic MIDI interfaces add more and more features. The only thing that can limit your MIDI horizons these days is the size of your bank account.

Extending the Reach of Windows 98's MIDI Configuration Capabilities

Now that you've been alerted to the universe of possibilities beyond GM, it is time to mention one more way to extend the reach of Windows 98's Multimedia MIDI configuration capabilities. For example, you might have a non-GM synthesizer (an Emu Proteus) that you want to fit into your GM world. Sound #1 on your Proteus might be an alto sax while Sound #1 on a GM device is always Acoustic Grand Piano. The Proteus' Grand Piano sound might be #18. If Windows 98 would map the GM sound numbers to the correct Proteus sounds— automatically sending a request for Sound #18 to the Proteus when the GM system is asking for Sound #1—you could use the Proteus easily in a GM environment. This kind of extended Windows 98 capability is enabled by an IDF (Instrument Definition File).

IDFs are generated by Microsoft's IDFEdit program. IDFEdit does not ship with Windows 98, but it is available for free from Microsoft (http:// windows.microsoft.com/directx/pavilion/dsound/midiidfedit.htm). Why doesn't IDFEdit ship with Windows 98? Presumably for the same reason that Microsoft doesn't ship it with Windows 95. According to Microsoft's IDFEdit Web page, "Windows 95 does not include any utilities or Control Panel applets to configure the MIDI Mapper, because these days all new sound cards are GM-compatible and the average user doesn't really need to configure the MIDI Mapper." That's absolutely right. While you download IDFEdit, read the IDFEdit overview; it is informative and short.

After you've installed IDFEdit, take a look at its online help to figure out where the controls are, then dive in. For example, in Figure 11.17, a patch mapping is in progress. Because this Proteus has only one decent acoustic grand sound located in the eighteenth preset, this IDF file will map GM preset numbers 1, 2, and 3 to Proteus preset 18. There does not have to be a one-to-one correspondence between the 128 GM presets and the presets on a non-GM device. Notice also that, by sheer coincidence, the patch numbers for the Rhodes Piano and the Clavinet are the same for GM and for this particular Proteus. But what if your non-GM device has more than 128 presets and the non-GM clarinet you want to map to GM sound #72 is Proteus sound #145? You're out of luck. To make an IDF work in this case, you'd have to rearrange the presets in your Proteus and place its clarinet sound somewhere in the first bunch of 128 presets.

Figure 11.17

Creating an IDF patch map.

IDFEdit's Key Map function allows you to reassign which MIDI note commands are assigned to which pitches. In Figure 11.18, the map is going to transpose the incoming MIDI note data up an octave (12 steps) before sending it out to the Proteus. As with the Patch Map function, your map doesn't have to follow any sort of pattern. You could assign all incoming MIDI note data to middle C (C3), reverse the key order, or create a complete mess; it's your decision.

Figure 11.18

Creating an IDF key map.

IDFEdit's Percussion Map section works just like Key Map, except that you are rearranging percussion sounds (bongos, claves, and cowbells) instead of pitches.

Working with MIDI

IDFEdit's Channels function allows you to stop the transmission of selected MIDI channels to the IDF instrument. This is handy if you are going to use multiple IDFs simultaneously. It also allows you to assign one (and only one) drum channel. In Figure 11.19, I assigned the drums to channel 16. The ever-unlucky channel 13 is muted because the VL70-M tone module will use that channel.

Figure 11.19

Setting IDF channel parameters to mute channel 13.

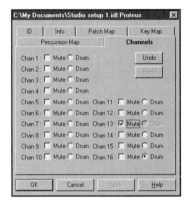

After you name and save your IDF files, you can put them to work by returning to the MIDI section of the Multimedia Control Panel, and clicking the Add New Instrument button to fire up the MIDI Instrument Installation Wizard, shown in Figure 11.20. When you reach the step in which the wizard asks you for instrument definitions, use the Browse function to find and add your new IDF files to the list. You can now mix and match these non-GM instruments with the rest of the devices in your MIDI system.

Figure 11.20

Use the MIDI Installation Wizard to add your new IDF instruments.

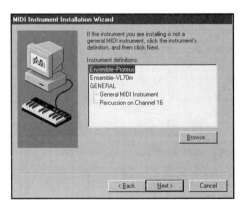

Making an End Run Around the Multimedia MIDI Control Panel

Now that you've waded through the techniques you can use to bend Windows 98 to your MIDI will, here's a sobering observation: You might never need to mess with any of this Windows MIDI stuff at all! Many sequencing packages handle MIDI mapping (GM and otherwise) internally, bypassing the Multimedia Control Panel's MIDI functionality. But hey, this is a Windows 98 book, not an owner's manual for a particular piece of software!

The high-end MIDI sequencing programs handle everything discussed and more. Many make it easy to get around the 128-preset limitation; run 32, 64, 128, or more MIDI channels; and even take some of the sting out of sysex commands. It's rather anachronistic to even call some of them MIDI programs. A number of them handle digital audio and some have the capability to synchronize digital video (such as AVI files) with MIDI data streams. If you have a large MIDI setup or if you think that your MIDI system will grow beyond the basics in the near future, you might be better off buying a MIDI software package that takes over MIDI management duties from the Multimedia Control Panel. But, if you're a frugal combination of Windows geek and MIDI maniac, you've got the tools. Good luck!

Useful MIDI Links

Even though Web sites come and go in the blink of an eye, these sites should provide useful MIDI files and information for some time to come.

- http://www.midi.org—The official home of MIDI. This site is geared toward the MIDI developer, not MIDI neophytes. It is an excellent source for technical information and late-breaking news concerning ever-changing and multiplying MIDI standards.

- http://www.midiweb.com— A reasonably large, well-organized collection of information about MIDI, MIDI files, and MIDI links.

- http://www.midifarm.com—A large, but not terribly well-organized, collection of information about MIDI, MIDI files, and MIDI links.

- http://www.harmony-central.com/MIDI—A very good site that caters to all levels of MIDI enthusiasts.

- http://midiworld.com—Another very good, comprehensive MIDI site.

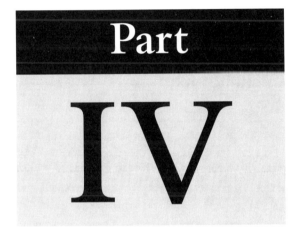

Part

IV

Multimedia Applications

Chapter

12

Working with Multimedia Applications

by Michael Porter

Working with Paint

Paint is the quick-and-easy tool provided with Windows 98 that allows you to create and edit simple graphics, called *bitmaps*. It also allows you to view images in more complex formats, which can be applied to your computer's desktop, inserted into a document or presentation, or printed as a personal work of art. Its emphasis is on freehand drawing. You can start from scratch or modify an existing image with the various tools that Paint provides.

This section discusses the various tools available in Paint, as well as the different types of files Paint supports. You'll learn how to create your own image and modify existing images from making your picture smaller to producing some wild special effects, such as sweeping or skewing. You'll start your journey by opening the program.

To begin working with Paint, go to the Start menu, choose Programs, click Accessories, and then click Paint. The program will open with a blank page. At this point, if you'd like to open an existing file, choose Open from the File menu. Paint only interprets BMP files without a graphics import option loaded onto your system. Office 97 does include a utility that allows Paint to open JPG and GIF file formats, and you might discover Paint supports PCX format images as well. An easy way to find out what type of graphic file can be opened is to choose Open from the File menu, and click the down arrow next to the Files of type dialog box, as shown in Figure 12.1. Any specific file type listed is compatible. You can attempt to load other formats by choosing the All Files option, but if you do Paint will probably crash.

Figure 12.1

By clicking the Files of Type drop-down list, you can see a list of formats that Paint supports.

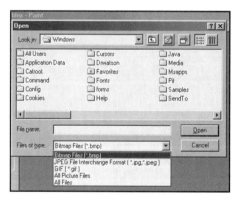

> **NOTE** If you're new to graphics files, the many formats they can assume can be quite confusing. Here's a quick roundup of the major graphics formats Paint can support.
>
> - BMP, or bitmap, files are Paint's native format. They're also the files Windows 98 uses for desktop wallpaper. BMP files never use compression, so large files take up much disk space.
> - PCX files use a format originally developed for the Zsoft Paintbrush program. The PCX format has undergone a number of changes over the years, so you might have trouble opening older graphics.
> - GIF files, which take their name from the Graphics Interchange Format developed by CompuServe, are commonly found on the Internet. Some GIFs can even feature animation, although Paint won't display it.
> - JPG files—another common Internet graphics format—take their name from the Joint Photographic Experts Group that created the format standard. JPG files can incorporate data compression, reducing the file size.

Setting the Image Size

Occasionally you will need to make an image fit into exact specifications for a logo or perhaps a presentation. Paint aides in this process by giving you the option to change the size of your image to a specific height and width.

This option also allows you to reduce the size of the image file by reducing its dimensions. The size of your image file might be a concern if you are planning to distribute the image across a medium, such as a modem line, where the size of the file might inhibit its capability to travel efficiently to its destination.

To set the image size through the Attributes dialog box:

1. Choose Image, Attributes to invoke the Attributes dialog box, shown in Figure 12.2.

2. This window allows you to manually set the width and height of your bitmap by typing in the dimensions you desire. The default size equals the size of your Paint window.

3. You also have a choice of units of measurement, inches, cm, or pixels (which is the standard measure). To change an image from pixels to inches, click the radio button next to Inches. The pixel width and height convert to inches automatically. Now you can enter the desired height and width in inches.

4. After you have chosen your new settings, click OK to return to your Paint window.

Figure 12.2

The Attributes window lets you establish your picture's size and declare the measurement units you want to use.

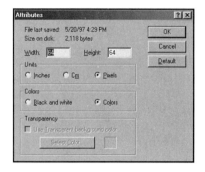

You also have the option of resizing your picture with the mouse. To do this

1. Scroll to the edge of your canvas until you see the dots at the corners and midway sections.

2. Select an area to stretch with the mouse by positioning the mouse over a dot until an arrow appears.

3. Once the arrow is present, you can resize the canvas by holding down the right mouse button and dragging the mouse to the desired size.

Creating a Picture

To create your own BMP picture to use on your desktop or to print

1. Choose New from the File menu to erase any previous image, or select Clear Image from the Image menu.

2. To set the size and color choice for the new image, choose Attributes from the Image menu. Now you must decide what size to set for your new image. If you are creating a picture for a specific purpose, such as a logo for a fax or invoice, you might have a certain height and width in mind. If you aren't sure what size you want, you can always change these settings later on. The default image size will be the size of the canvas as represented in the Paint window.

3. Set the color choice of either color or black and white. Remember, if you are creating or editing a large or complex picture, choosing black and white over color saves memory and disk space.

NOTE A black-and-white photo only takes up one-fourth as much memory and disk space as a simple color photo.

Choosing Background and Foreground Colors

Choosing background and foreground colors is important when you begin to color your image with the various tools in Paint. If you think of your painting as being layers of color on a canvas, the background color will be the color that acts as a base for a drawing, whereas the foreground color will lie on top of that base. Most noticeably, this occurs when the text box is being used with the Draw Opaque option selected. In this case the background color acts as a base upon which the text is displayed. You will learn more about these options later in this section.

As a rule, when using the coloring tools in Paint, the right mouse button invokes the background color and the left mouse button invokes the foreground color. In this way, the classic meaning of the terms can be confusing.

After you set these colors, you are not committed to using them throughout your creation. They can easily be changed at any time. However, changing the background and foreground colors will not affect past coloring; it will only be in effect from that point of change until you are finished (or until you change the colors again). This means that if you want some past coloring to adhere to the new scheme, you must redo the effects with the newly selected colors.

To set the background color

1. Point to the color in the Color Box located at the bottom of the Paint window.

2. Click the right mouse button. The background color you chose appears at the far left side of the Color Box as the lower-right square of color.

To set the foreground color

1. Point to the color in the Color Box, located at the bottom of the Paint window.

2. Click the left mouse button. The background color you chose appears at the far left side of the Color Box as the upper-left square of color.

Now you are ready to begin drawing and coloring your picture.

Paint provides a toolbox at the side of the Paint Application window. (If you don't want to see this toolbox, choose View, and then deselect the toolbox by clicking it.)

To choose a tool, click its icon button. You have 16 tools to choose from. The top two tools are Select options.

■ The dashed Rectangle button allows you to select any area that you can draw a rectangle around with your mouse. To do this

   1. Select the dashed Rectangle on the toolbox.

   2. Position the mouse at the upper-left or lower-right corner and hold down the left mouse button.

   3. Drag the mouse until you have formed a rectangle around the item you want to move or edit.

   4. Release the mouse button to see the selected area and its dashed rectangular frame.

When you have selected the area, it will remain selected until you point and click the mouse outside of your outline.

To move the selected area, click within the selected outline, hold down the left mouse button, and drag the selection to its new location on your Paint canvas.

If you want to copy the selection instead, hold down the Ctrl key and follow the same procedure as you did to move the item. You will see that a copy is placed in the new location while the original selection remains in place.

■ The dashed star is a free form selection tool that allows you to select an irregular area, such as one particular point of interest, without affecting the surrounding picture. It works much like a pen or pencil in the way that it selects an area in free form.

After you have selected your point or area of interest and have released the mouse, an outline appears as a dashed rectangle even though the actual irregular area is all that is really selected.

One neat thing you can do after selecting an area is *sweep* the selected area. This technique results in an interesting effect, as shown in Figure 12.3. To do this, select the area you might copy or move, hold down the Shift key, and then drag your selection. You'll see the selection appears to sweep across the canvas.

The remaining tools are drawing tools. Here's a list of the tools and their functions:

■ Eyedropper—Use this tool as an alternative for selecting colors for the background or foreground, if the color already appears on your canvas. This capability is handy if you need to duplicate a color that doesn't appear on your palette. To do this

   1. Select the Eyedropper from the toolbox.

   2. Place your mouse pointer (which now looks like an eyedropper) over the color in your picture that you want to use as a background

or foreground color. Click the left mouse button to choose this as your foreground color or the right button to make this your background color.

Figure 12.3
You can create a motion effect by sweeping a selected area; all you have to do is hold the Shift key as you drag.

Figure 12.3
You can create a motion effect by sweeping a selected area; all you have to do is hold the Shift key as you drag.

■ Paint Can—This tool allows you to fill any enclosed area with the foreground or background color you have chosen. An enclosed area could be represented as a triangle or square within a canvas, or could be represented as the entire canvas enclosed by its border. Be sure the area you select has no openings or the paint will apply to the entire area until it reaches a full enclosure.

To use this tool, select the Paint Can with your mouse, point the tip of the spilling paint into the area you want to color, and then click the mouse. (Left-click to apply the foreground color, or right click to apply the background color.)

■ Magnifying Glass—Choosing this tool and then clicking over an area of your painting will zoom in on that area. To return to the original view size, you must choose the Magnifying Glass again, and then click a second time on the canvas. Be aware that the view changes according to where you place your mouse after clicking to return to the original size. For example, if you click to the left of the palette, you will view the section to the left of the canvas. You will be required to manually scroll with the bottom and side scrollbars to see the original view.

■ Pencil—This tool works a lot like a real pencil. It paints a free-hand line that is one pixel (dot) wide. Use this tool to sketch quick shapes or when you want to draw straight lines, something the brush does not allow.

To use this tool select the Pencil from your toolbox, click the area of your canvas you want to draw your lines and hold down the left mouse button while you drag the mouse along the canvas.

To make a straight line, hold down the Shift key while you draw your line on the canvas. You will only be able to lengthen the line in the direction you chose to move. Once you start the line, you cannot change direction until you finish the line and start a new one.

- Paintbrush—The Paintbrush is a versatile drawing tool. It can be used as a brush, pen, or marker to create a variety of line styles. The line you draw with this tool depends on what width you select from the box that appears underneath the tools on the toolbox. To use the paintbrush

    1. Choose the type of line you want to emulate with your brush. Each choice simulates a different type of brush stroke. The dots simulate a Pen or ballpoint tool that produces lines with rounded edges, the squares look most like an actual paintbrush stroke, and the lines simulate a marker or calligraphy pen.

    2. Click on your canvas at the desired start point and hold the mouse button to draw, or paint your lines as you drag the mouse along the canvas. Again, to use the foreground color, use the left button; for the background, click the right button.

    3. To stop painting, release the mouse button.

- Airbrush—If you are in a free-form mood, this tool simulates a graffiti-making spray paint can. The mouse button acts as the nozzle; the longer you hold the button, the more densely you apply the color. Depending on which mouse button you hold down, left or right, while dragging the mouse along the canvas, you choose between the foreground or background color. There is also an option in your toolbox for the width of the spray you create: small, medium or large.

- Text tool—The Text tool enables you to add words to your picture. This capability is especially helpful if you are creating a flyer or perhaps adding instructions to a map to give directions. This tool is also useful if you want to add notes to a picture.

    Text can be viewed as opaque or transparent. If you want the text to be presented on its own background, choose Draw Opaque from the Image menu. If the selection is not checked, select it by clicking it. When this option is unchecked, the text is presented on a transparent background, so whatever underlies your text shows through. You can also select which method to use from the two choices that appear at the bottom of the toolbox after you select the Text tool. The top selection represents an opaque background; the bottom selection represents a transparent background.

To insert text into your picture

1. Choose the color that you want for your text by selecting it as the foreground color. If you want an opaque background, choose a background color also.

2. Select the Text tool on the toolbox.

3. Choose whether you want the text to be on an opaque or transparent background.

4. Draw the text box frame with your mouse by starting at a corner; hold down the button while you drag the cursor to the desired size frame. When you finish drawing the frame, release the mouse button. The Text toolbar should appear, which allows you to change the font type, size, and style for your text.

5. Click within the newly created frame to make the cursor appear, and begin typing. Paint wraps the text within the confines of the frame you created. You can also use the standard Windows text-editing commands such as Cut, Copy, and Paste from another location.

6. To resize your text box frame, point the mouse over one of the corners or midway dots—called sizing handles—along the frame until the cursor turns into a double-headed arrow. When it does, drag the frame to the desired size.

7. To move your text box frame, point the mouse along the frame—where there are no sizing handles—until the cursor turns into a single arrow (the standard mouse pointer). Now drag the frame to the desired position.

8. To change the color or background for your text box, select the new text (foreground) color on the color box by clicking it with your left mouse button. If you have already written text and want to change the color, you must highlight the text first, and then change the color in your color box. To change the background from opaque to transparent and vice versa, use the icons at the bottom of the tools on the toolbox.

> **WARNING**   If you want to resize, move, or change the colors for your new text box, you must do so *before* you click outside the frame. Once you have clicked anywhere outside of your text box frame, you finalize your text entry and you may not edit the text attributes any longer. You *can* edit the text as any other element of your picture; for example, you can change the text color with careful application of the Paint Bucket tool.

Working with Multimedia Applications

■ Eraser—If you should make a mistake, you can click and drag with this tool selected to wipe out portions of your drawing. It leaves the area affected completely void, with only the background color remaining. This tool can be used to erase a large section of a picture or to simply touch up lines or stray dots (provided you have a steady hand).

> **TIP** An alternative to erasing is the Undo feature. By choosing Undo from the Edit menu, you might eliminate up to three of your most recent changes. If you change your mind after you choose to undo, you have the option to redo the changes by choosing Repeat from the Edit menu.

Paint also gives you the option to create lines and shapes more easily with six specific tools:

■ Line tool—This tool only draws straight lines. There are six widths to choose from; they appear beneath your toolbox when you choose the Line tool.

■ Curve tool—This tool has a weird twist, pun intended. First, you create a single line, and then you twist it by stretching and bending the line in any direction you choose. To accomplish this twist, click anywhere on the initial line you created, and then drag, bending it in the direction you chose. Use this process to make an S or a ribbon or pretzel shape. You have two chances to bend the line to perfect your creation.

■ Box tool—If you want to draw a quick box or rectangle, use this tool. The Box tool works a lot like the rectangle that selects an object: Place the mouse at the position you want a corner of your box to begin, drag the mouse to the desired size, and release the mouse button. As always, the line is the color of the background or foreground, depending on which mouse button you have pressed during its creation. By the way, holding the Shift key while you draw results in a perfect square.

■ Polygon tool—The Polygon tool allows you to make any enclosed polygon shape. You start by drawing a straight line. Then simply click the mouse at the desired endpoints for your polygon, and a line segment will appear between the last point and the new selected point until you complete the polygon by enclosing it.

■ Ellipse tool—This tool uses the same procedure to draw as the Box tool. To make a perfect circle instead of an oval or ellipse, hold down the Shift key while you drag the mouse.

■ Rounded Box tool—Also works exactly like the Box tool, but instead of 90-degree angles the corners are rounded.

When you are satisfied with your creation, don't forget to save it. (It's a good idea to save a few times when you're working on it, too, especially if you're about to make a change you aren't sure you'll like.) You can save the entire picture or only a specific portion of your picture. To save only a portion of your picture, define an area with a selection tool, and then choose Copy To from the Edit menu. This brings up the Copy To dialog box, which functions exactly like a Save As dialog box. Name the selection, and click Save. When you want to retrieve this selection, open the Edit menu and choose Paste From. The saved selection will be inserted at the upper-left corner of your canvas and can be repositioned by dragging it with the mouse to the desired location.

You can also set your creation as Wallpaper for your desktop. To do this, choose Set as Wallpaper (Tiled) from the File menu to establish a repeating pattern, or choose Set As Wallpaper (Centered) to position the image in the middle of your screen.

Modifying a Picture

After you have created and saved a picture, or if you want to modify an existing BMP or PCX file, choose Open from the File menu. Browse to the picture file you want to edit, and choose Open. The picture appears on your canvas. Now you can use any of the Paint tools to modify the picture. Besides sweeping, there are some other features in Paint (listed here) that modify the appearance of your picture.

- Flipping and rotating—Paint allows you to flip or rotate the entire picture or a selected a portion of the picture. Flipping mirrors the picture in the manner you choose, (horizontal or vertical), whereas rotating turns the picture or selection around a center axis, like a clock. To use this feature, select Flip/Rotate from the Image menu.

- Stretching, shrinking and skewing—This feature allows you to rubber band your picture to look like its being reflected in a carnival fun house mirror. Select Stretch/Skew from the Image menu. You will be able to choose a percentage to shrink or stretch your picture, or a degree to slant, or *skew*, the selection. This feature is fun to use on photographs and can result in some interesting effects, as shown in Figure 12.4.

- Inverting colors—This feature, available from the Image menu, allows you to modify a selection or the entire picture, by changing the colors in the photo to their complementary or opposite color. For example, if the selection is black, inverting changes it to white. A complementary color is defined as the color at the opposite side of the RGB (red, green, blue) color wheel. The resulting image looks like a black-and-white or color photographic negative.

Figure 12.4
You can stretch and skew your image to obtain a number of interesting effects.

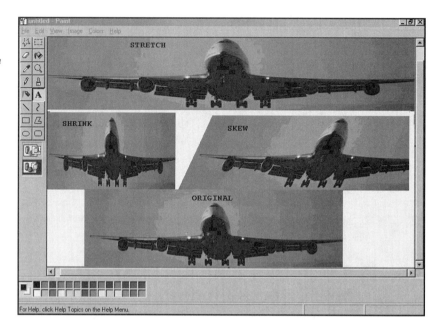

Working with LView Pro

LView Pro is a popular third-party image processing program that manipulates photos and picture formats found in Microsoft Windows. You can use this shareware program in place of or in tandem with Microsoft's default graphic editing applications, such as Paint and Photo Editor. This program is much more sophisticated than Paint, Photo Editor, or Imaging (I'll discuss the latter two later in this chapter). It has complex color and tuning capabilities, plus more ease in fixing mistakes you might make along the way. LView Pro lets you undo up to 32 of the last actions you took in each open image.

> **NOTE** LView Pro is a shareware product that can be downloaded over the Internet from the LView home page (www.lview.com). There are also some third-party sites that are dedicated to imaging software that might have this product available to download. The quickest way to find these alternative locations is to use your favorite Internet search engine, supplying the keywords *LView Pro*.

You can use LView Pro to view, edit, create, and catalog images. It also does image animation, transparency, and interlacing. Most of the editing features can be found under the Retouch selection on the menu bar, whereas positioning and manipulation tools such as Resize and Rotate appear under the Edit menu. You can see LView Pro in Figure 12.5.

Figure 12.5
LView Pro provides an array of sophisticated image manipula- tion and display options.

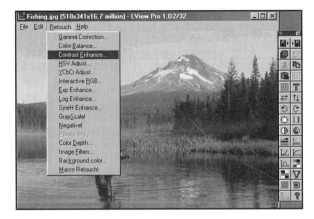

The following is a summary of some of the features in LView Pro. LView allows you to create image catalogs, which facilitates

- Managing large numbers of image files.

- Copying, moving, renaming, and deleting image files.

- Optionally storing thumbnails (miniatures of the original images) and text descriptions.

- Making slide shows with original images, interactive or timed slide advancement. Browsing original images in Full Screen mode.

- Batch converting image files to another format.

Additionally, you can have multiple windows for one image or catalog. This allows you to view the image in its normal size in one window, while editing a zoomed part of it in another window, or you can browse catalog images in one window while viewing the original image files in another window. You also have full animation support, which allows you to

- Create multiframe images for animation.

- Manipulate image frames by cloning and inserting frames from disk files, changing the frame order, and using frame delays.

- Use transparency.

- Create a single, global color palette based on colors in all frames.

- Preview animation without leaving the editor.

Working with Multimedia Applications

Advanced image selection operations are another handy feature. These are similar to Paint's selection utility but with added capability. You can

- Select rectangles, ovals, circles, or squares.

- Use free-hand selection.

- Fill color in conjunction with a selection tool.

- Make selections with paintbrush, giving the capability to select user-defined size and shape.

- Combine selections by adding or subtracting from selected areas.

- Save selections to the disk for later use, copy and paste selections to and from the image or Clipboard, and paste from the Clipboard into new or existing selections.

- Move or clone selected areas.

- Use selections to clip painting operations.

- Drop shadows from selected areas.

- Change the transparency by increasing its feather, or remove transparent pixels.

- Color selected areas.

- Crop your image to a selected area.

With LView Pro, you have more sophisticated color matching to get more exact colors throughout your image. Color matching is used in several operations, such as Color Fill, Selection Fill, and Transparent Pixel removal. You can

- Match colors by red/green/blue components, by hue/saturation/value attributes, or by brightness.

- Utilize the user-defined tolerance factor, which matches similar colors as closely as you want.

- Fill selections with solid colors, patterns, images, or gradients (linear, rectangular, diamond, cross, oval, and radial).

- Separate channels in both RGB and YUV color models. Edit channels individually or combine channels into a single image.

- LView Pro provides support for paint colors. It provides individual support for foreground, background, and transparent colors. By using the Color Selection window, you can select paint colors for palette-based and true color images, sort palette entries, delete unused entries, swap palette entries, change color specifications, and save and open palette specifications to or from disk files. You can also display color attributes in RGB or hue/saturation/luminance, and in a decimal or hexadecimal base. You can even use the Mask feature to quickly match image pixels to respective palette entries.

LView Pro also has much more extensive undo and redo capabilities that allow

- Multiple level Undo and Redo operations, up to the last 32 editing operations per image frame. (This depth is in contrast to Paint's three.)

- It is always nice to be able to zoom in and out and still retain editing functions in the process, and in LView Pro, you get functional zoom scaling from 1:16 to 16:1. You can change the zoom factor with the mouse, menu, or a keyboard shortcut. All editing operations are available in all zoom levels.

- Plus, you have a functional grid that enables user configurable sizes, pixel grid, and snap painting operations to grid.

Another great feature is the variety of brush shapes and sizes. You can choose from square, round, slash, back slash, horizontal, and vertical brushes, sized from 1 to 200 pixels. LView Pro also has a variety of paintbrush options such as

- Normal, Pen, Pencil, Marker, Crayon, Chalk, and Charcoal. All of these can optionally use a paper texture.

- Clone Brush, which paints one image over another image, with user-defined color control, optionally using a paper texture.

- Retouch Brush, which paints localized retouch operations, such as lighten, darken, soften, sharpen, blur, emboss, and smudge, with user-defined color and optionally use a paper texture.

- Color Replacer, which replaces foreground, background, or transparent colors for another color. You can replace colors throughout the entire image or only for a part of it.

In addition to the image selection and painting tools, there are tools to manipulate existing images, which include

- Image transformations that let the you use the mosaic, ellipse, pinch, punch, horizontal/vertical convex/concave cylinder, horizontal/vertical perspective, and horizontal/vertical skew options to create or manipulate an image. LView Pro also supports user-defined transformations.

- Image special effects such as adding borders, creating buttons, using gray palette, motion blur, and seamless patterns options.

- Image filters, which provide edge enhancement, trace contour, blur, soften, sharpen, emboss, despeckle, median, erode, dilate, and noise. User-defined filters are also supported.

- Image color depth, which enable you to change the number of colors on an image, creating adequate palettes or using user-supplied palettes. This also allows optional inclusion of Windows' colors. It applies a user-defined number of palette entries.

- Image color editing including negative, grayscale, contrast, brightness, RGB, gamma correction, HSV, and YUV. User-defined color transformations are supported.

- Common image operations similar to Paint's functions, such as flip horizontal/vertical, rotate left, right, or user-defined angle, and resize. There is also a Resample option for true color images.

- In addition to the common operations, LView Pro has some advanced image operations, which allow you to combine images with add, subtract, multiply, difference, darker, and lighter pixels, with optional divisor and bias parameters.

- As with the other Windows 98 products, you can use LView Pro to insert images into documents with OLE (OLE2).

- You can use LView Pro to interface with your TWAIN compliant device, such as a scanner or frame grabber card. Images are transferred directly into LView Pro to be edited and saved to disk.

As you can see, LView Pro application has extensive tools for complex graphics editing tasks in Windows. It is a great tool to use if you frequently scan and edit photographs to print or distribute to friends and family. You can annotate and manipulate your scanned images before sending them. LView Pro is also a standard tool for Web designers to convert, resize, and add animation to graphics. Another tool that is similar but not quite as extensive in function is the Microsoft Photo Editor, which is covered next.

Working with Photo Editor

Photo Editor, a component of Microsoft Office 97, is a great tool to edit just about any picture file you can imagine. It works with GIFs, bitmaps, JPEG, Kodak Photo CD images, Paint pictures, and various other image formats.

Photo Editor offers you several ways to be creative and artistic with the graphic of your choice. As you're being creative, though, you should bear one important fact in mind: Photo Editor will only undo the last change made to your picture. So, if you make a mistake, press Ctrl-Z, click Undo on the toolbar, or choose Undo from the Edit menu before it's too late!

The Image menu, shown in Figure 12.6, gives you options such as Crop, Rotate, and Resize. Cropping is the process you use to resize an image or selection while eliminating unwanted parts of the picture. For example, in Figure 12.6, you can see the feet of a second cow in the upper-right, and there's a lot of empty space to the left. You can crop the image to eliminate the second cow and some of the grass and wind up with an image that's dominated by a single cow.

Figure 12.6

The Image menu gives you access to some basic picture manipulation tools.

The Image menu also lets you manipulate the color and shade balance of your photo (or a selection of it) for all hues, or specific RBG spectrums. You have the option to balance the brightness, contrast, and gamma correction of your picture. Doing so greatly improves the quality of an image.

Some contrast and color manipulation features can be found under the Effects menu. For example, the Sharpen command gives the image a sharper contrast, while the Soften command results in the opposite effect. The Negative command gives the image the appearance of a photographic negative. The Despeckle command removes clusters or chains of pixels that are inconsistent with the rest of the image to give the overall picture a cleaner look. If you are planning to print a grayscale image, you might want to emphasize color differences by using the Posterize option. Lastly, you can use the Edge option to create a relief of the image that can be presented in horizontal or vertical stroke directions and thin or thick edge widths.

TIP	Softening the contrast tends to blur the image, so use this option sparingly.

The real artistry available to you becomes even stronger in the second group of commands under the Effects menu. Here you will be able to change the photo's texture to give it an entirely new or different look, as you can see in Figure 12.7.

Figure 12.7

The Effects menu lets you make radical and artistic changes to a photographic image, making it appear as a charcoal drawing.

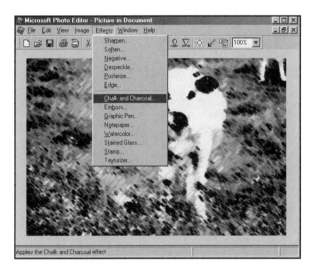

The texture features in the Effects menu include

- Chalk and Charcoal—This feature allows you to recreate the image as if it were a chalk and charcoal drawing (see the result in Figure 12.7). This and the remaining Effect features in Photo Editor are impressive in their artistic interpretations; you get the look of hand-drawn pictures. You will also appreciate the commands' capability to preview the look before accepting any changes.

- Emboss—Another neat artistic look, this feature allows you to emboss the entire photo, or a selection of it, to give it the appearance of a bas-relief or metal stamping.

- Graphic Pen—Just like the Chalk and Charcoal feature, this feature lets you redraw your picture as if you were using graphic pens on art paper. Again, you will be surprised at how realistic an image the effect creates.

- Notepaper—This command gives the effect of working with art paper where wetting and grooving is used to create an image. Like the Emboss feature, the result has a three-dimensional, textured appearance.

■ Watercolor—This selection is a fun way to quickly turn your photo into a painting, as shown in Figure 12.8. You can choose Shadow Intensity, Texture, and Brush Detail options to emulate a variety of artistic styles. Experiment with all the settings to get an idea of how each effects the picture. Be sure to click Preview each time you make a change to refresh the sample image and keep the Undo command handy.

Figure 12.8

Our cow photo is now a bovine painting, thanks to Photo Editor.

■ Stained Glass—Amazing as it sounds, this tool transforms the image to appear as if it were a stained glass panel. Be careful, though—the default cell size tends to be too large to discern the original image and results in an abstract pattern. Experiment with all the settings to get an image that reflects the original without too much distortion. This command also creates fascinating images for Windows wallpaper.

■ Stamp—This tool simulates an ink stamp of your image. If you ever made a linoleum stamp carving in art class, you have a pretty good idea of what this will look like (see Figure 12.9). You might find it a little difficult to get a good stamp image of your photo. Try reducing the Light/dark balance setting and keep the smoothness under ten for the best results.

■ Texturize—Use this tool if you want to change the type of background you are working on. It allows you to change the texture of your picture to appear as if it were created on brick, burlap, canvas or sandstone. You will be amazed at the realistic looks you can create. This is an excellent tool to use for creating Windows wallpaper or Web page backgrounds (see Figure 12.10).

Working with Multimedia
Applications

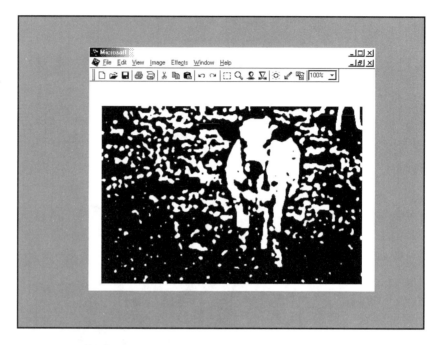

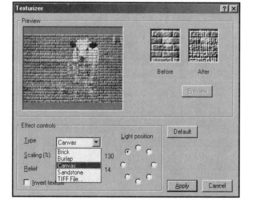

Inserting Multimedia into Documents

A neat feature in Windows is the capability to link and embed objects into a document. You need to decide whether you will link or embed objects into your documents. When making this decision, consider what use you will make of the graphic and the document. By linking the file, there will be only a pointer within the document to the file at another location. Embedding incorporates the file within the document, resulting in a larger file size but easier portability. If you are creating several documents where the same picture is used, consider linking to save disk space and to ease updating the graphic for all documents at a later date. If you are distributing the document, linking is not the best choice; you should embed the file to ensure that it appears on everyone's copy.

> **NOTE**   With Windows 98 OLE function (object linking and embedding), you have the option to either, link or embed an object into a document. Linking and embedding are very different functions and each has its own benefit.
>
> In the case of linking, two separate files exist, such as your document and your image file. The image file can be edited either within the document or from its source application, such as Paint. Any changes done from either setting are reflected in both.
>
> In contrast, when you embed you image into the document, a copy of the image is contained within the document. This image can be edited from within the document, but the changes are not reflected anywhere else. Conversely, if you make changes to the original image in its source application, those changes are not reflected in the image that now remains isolated within your document.

Inserting Pictures

Perhaps you'd like to use your newly created image or BMP file in a document, such as a fax or letter. Incorporating graphics adds pizzazz to your documents and is easy to do.

To insert a picture into a document

1. Open WordPad from the Start menu, choose Programs, choose Accessories, and then choose WordPad. Next, choose Object from the Insert menu.

2. You will see a dialog box listing several object options to choose from, as shown in Figure 12.11. You can also select whether you want to create the object from an existing file or create a new file from within the document.

Figure 12.11

You can embed or link an existing object or create one from scratch.

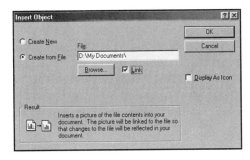

3. If you choose to use an existing file, select the radio button next to Create from File at the upper-left section of the Insert Object dialog box. A Browse dialog box opens, from which you navigate to the file you want to use. At this time, you need to decide whether you will link or embed the picture into your document; you do so by selecting or deselecting the Link check box next to the Browse button.

4. After you have found the file you want to insert, click OK and the picture appears in your document at the point where your cursor is resting. At this time the object is active and can be sized, moved, or edited.

> **NOTE**   After the discussion on the importance of choosing to link or embed an object, you might have noticed that the control for this function is a bit obscure.
>
> It is quite understated as it sits next to the Browse button waiting to be checked. Remember, this is the only chance you have to make this a linked object. Once you make your selection and click OK, you cannot go back and make the now embedded object a linked object. If you change your mind at this point, you must delete the object and reinsert it with the Link box checked.

After you have embedded or linked an image into a document, your options don't end there. You can resize, move, or edit your image the same way you can edit your text documents. The difference is that you edit the image by automatically launching an image editor.

- To size the inserted picture, position the mouse over a sizing handle on the border of the object until the double-sided arrow appears. Click the left mouse button and drag the border to the desired size.

- To move the inserted picture, click within the border of the object frame and hold down the button while you drag the mouse to the desired location. Let go of the mouse button and a small rectangular box appears at the end of your pointer. When the box appears, click the mouse. Your object is now in the new location.

- To edit the picture, double-click the picture and Microsoft Photo Editor or Paint will launch. Now you can edit the document through the appropriate application.

- When you are finished editing the picture, close Microsoft Photo Editor to return to the document, or click outside of the picture to return to the document from the Paint window.

Inserting Sound and Video

To insert your sound or video file you will use a process similar to the one you used to insert a picture. Open WordPad from the Start menu by clicking Programs, Accessories, WordPad. Then choose Object from the Insert menu. To use an existing file, select the radio button next to Create from File at the upper-left section of the Insert Object dialog box. A Browse dialog box opens. Again, you need to decide whether to link or embed the sound or video file into your document by selecting or deselecting the Link check box.

When you have found the file you want to insert, click OK and the first frame of your video, or the Speaker icon for a sound file, appears in your document at the point where your cursor is resting. At this time the object is active and can be sized, moved, edited, or played.

- To play the object, double-click the mouse anywhere within the object's border.

- To size the inserted object, position the mouse over a sizing handle on the border of the object until the double-sided arrow appears. Click the left mouse button and drag the border to the desired size.

- To move the inserted object, click within the border of the object frame and hold down the button while you drag the mouse to the desired location. Let go of the mouse button and a small rectangular box appears at the end of your pointer. When the box appears, click the mouse. Your object is now moved to its new location.

- To edit the object, right click within the object's border. From the resulting pop-up menu, choose Video Clip Object or Wave Sound Object, as appropriate, and then choose Edit, as shown in Figure 12.12. The associated application opens to edit the object. When you are finished editing the object, click outside of the object's border and you return to the document.

Working with Color Management

Images captured from input devices such as scanners and digital cameras are brought together in editing and composition applications, such as Imaging for Windows, Photo Editor or LView Pro. They use a variety of tools and proofing systems to simulate the final output, such as printing on a color printer, inserting graphics into a document, or creating a presentation for the Internet or an intranet. Image color matching ensures the consistent reproduction of the image colors throughout the editing process.

Figure 12.12

Because double-clicking the embedded sound or video plays the file, you right-click its icon to access editing functions.

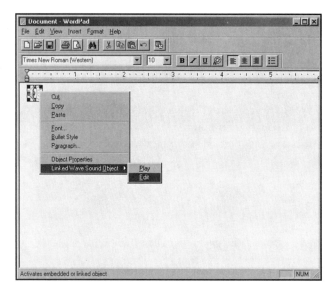

When you scan or acquire an image from an input device, image color matching ensures that the original image colors are accurately interpreted by your monitor or printer, by maintaining the image's original color mapping. To work properly, the input device must either provide an International Color Consortium (ICC) color profile with an acquired image, or output sRGB, using the sRGB profile provided by Windows 98. This provision ensures that display and output devices can properly interpret the color characteristics of the acquired image.

Monitors must also include their own color profile, like printers and other output devices. All components must have an associated color profile so that image color matching can manage the color continuity throughout the entire editing process.

The image color matching capabilities for Windows 98 include

- Support for sRGB as the default color space for images without embedded ICC profiles or specifically tagged color information.

- Support for more color spaces, such as CMYK and CIELAB.

- Support for up to eight color channels for enhanced printing processes, such as hi-fi color.

- A faster, higher quality default Color Management Module (CMM) and support for multiple CMMs.

- Cross-platform compatibility through ICC profiles and the capability to define custom profiles.

> **NOTE** *sRGB* is the Hewlett-Packard standard red, green, blue color scheme. It stores a certain range of color space for each hue used within the RGB spectrum. By using this color profile, you get better color interpretations within the standard parameters. It could be considered the generic color profile.
>
> *CMYK* are the secondary color spectrums. They add more definition than the RGB spectrum and allow an expansion of available color spaces for a greater choice of color representation. CMYK stands for cyan, magenta, yellow and black.
>
> *CIELAB* is an extremely high-end color scheme. CIELAB is used to define perceptual color, or realistic color. It converts color into a three-dimensional spectrum to represent exact, measurable units in space that are translated into the corresponding location of a color. The three-dimensional system is a Cartesian coordinate system. The *LAB* is the lightness value, how light or dark the color is; the position on the red–green axis is *a*; and *b* is the position on the yellow–blue axis.
>
> The LAB position gives an exact measure, which then has a surrounding box of color that is considered the standard acceptance for the color representation.

Associating a Color Profile with Your Monitor

Adding a color profile to your monitor expands Windows 98's capability to accurately display images.

To add a color profile to a monitor

1. Right-click anywhere on the empty desktop and choose Properties. The Display Properties dialog box appears.

2. Choose the Settings tab.

3. Click the Advanced button, and then click the Color Management tab in the Properties dialog box for your video card dialog box. You'll see the dialog box shown in Figure 12.13.

4. Click Add and locate the profile you want in the resulting dialog box. For more information about a profile, right-click the profile in the Add Profile Association dialog box, and then click Properties. You'll see information similar to that shown in Figure 12.14.

> **TIP** If the monitor doesn't have a profile created for it, you can add sRGB color space profile.icm, the default profile for Windows 98.

5. Click the new profile, and then click Add.

You can also access the Color Management tab from the Start menu, choosing Settings, clicking Control Panel, double-clicking Display, clicking the Settings tab, clicking Advanced, and then clicking the Color Management tab.

Working with Multimedia Applications

Figure 12.13

You can assign a color profile to a monitor to ensure accurate onscreen color reproduction.

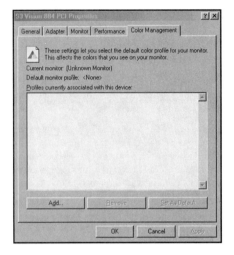

Figure 12.14

Before assigning a color profile, you can view its properties.

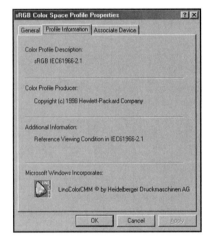

Chapter

13

Working with Multimedia Files

By Michael Porter

One of the advantages of a graphical user interface (GUI) such as Windows 98 is its capability to incorporate images and sounds into its own environment. It encourages you to work with your desktop images, such as desktop themes and wallpaper, and even allows you to place sounds on your desktop or create and apply unique sound themes created entirely on your own for your personal computing experience.

Using sound and images can greatly enhance your ability to express yourself through your unique settings on the computer or through the things you can create with your multimedia system. By using multimedia files, you are able to document and demonstrate concepts that aren't easily expressed through words alone.

You can create a wallpaper image that represents your favorite vacation spot or reminds you of your favorite friends or family. Multimedia options can also employ a sound scheme to set the mood after a long day of work or to help you wake each new day.

Most computers today include the basic equipment to take full advantage of these features, such as sound cards and high speed CD-ROM drives.

If you haven't had the chance to explore these multimedia options yet, you might find yourself surprised at the large scope of options they allow you to undertake. Multimedia today can range anywhere between a simple sound file to alert you of an error to a full-motion video with CD sound accompaniment.

This chapter explores the sound and image files you have available to you in Windows 98 and the different uses and occasions they are best suited for. You'll learn which files you can open in Microsoft Internet Explorer and how to preview them in other image viewers. If you have a file in an image format you don't prefer, you can convert the format or open it in an application other than the default.

Making Sense of Multimedia File Types

The variety of multimedia files available today can seem endless. Files can range anywhere from a Wave file to notify you when you get a new email message to an AVI file, which stores audio, video, and text information in a single file. In fact some companies are making training videos that can be viewed on your personal computer, which often include music, video, or animation and even voice coaching to go along with the traditional text manuals and instructions of the past.

Multimedia files can be stored on a compact disc, a local hard disk drive, a network file server, or a removable storage medium, such as a floppy disk (if the file's small enough) or a ZIP or JAZ drive. The amount of data that the storage medium can continuously relay to the file system for streaming determines the quality of the playback on your computer.

A multimedia data stream (such as an AVI file) generally contains multiple components, such as digital video data, audio data, text, and perhaps other data (such as *hot spot* information and additional audio tracks). As multimedia information is read from a CD-ROM drive, the multimedia subsystem determines what the data stream contains, and then separates and routes the data accordingly. Windows 98 includes the 32-bit CD-ROM file system (CDFS) for reading files from CD-ROM drives quickly and efficiently. This was developed to provide the best possible performance from today's CD-ROM drives.

> **NOTE**   A *hot spot* is a clickable area that can launch a macro or an embedded program.

There are a variety of file types associated with multimedia.

Table 13.1   Some Common Multimedia Files

Format	Corresponding File Extension
Video for Windows	AVI
Waveform audio	WAV
Moving Picture (MPEG)	MPG
QuickTime for Windows animation	MOV
Musical Instrument	
Digital Interface (MIDI)	MID

This chapter concentrates on sound and image files. It gives you a good idea of what file types are available and what their best uses are in Windows 98.

Understanding Sound File Types

Sound files might not be diverse in form (each being essentially digital renditions of sound) but are surely diverse in delivery. Windows 98 multimedia services provide extensive, device-independent audio support with services for sound control for computers that have sound cards and for waveform audio, MIDI, and mixer devices. You can see the variety of sound players Windows 98 provides in Figure 13.1.

Figure 13.1

Windows 98 provides a variety of players for digital sound files.

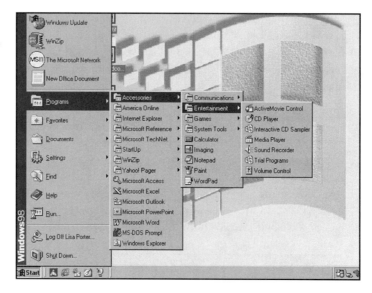

With audio support in Windows 98, users can

- Use Media Player or ActiveMovie Control to play WAV or MIDI files.

- Use applications that take advantage of DirectSound audio acceleration.

- Use the Control Panel's Sound applet to assign sound clips to play each time a specific event occurs.

- Use CD Player to play audio CDs.

- Use Sound Recorder to record sound.

- Use Windows 98 OLE support to copy or link audio clips in other documents.

As I just alluded to, there are two main types of pure sound files, MIDI and Waveform Audio.

MIDI (`MID`) is a serial interface standard that allows for the connection of music synthesizers, musical instruments, and computers.

The MIDI standard is based partly on hardware and partly on a description of the way in which music and sounds are encoded and communicated between MIDI devices.

Windows 98 supports the General MIDI Specification to request specific instruments and sounds. This is an industry standard that defines how MIDI should be used, and it is supported by Microsoft and most MIDI sound card manufacturers.

MIDI devices supported by Windows 98 include FM Synthesis, Hardware Wavetable Synthesis, and Software Wavetable Synthesis.

MIDI is the computer's electronic equivalent of sheet music. Just as if you were playing the music on different instruments with differently skilled musicians, by adjusting the hardware and the software, you can get a different interpretation of that piece of sheet music, some better, some worse. Almost all advanced electronic musical equipment supports MIDI, and MIDI controls provide a useful tool to adjust the equipment accurately.

MIDI Stream is a technology used in advanced sound cards to play very complex MIDI sequences with less processor overhead. This technology allows Windows 98 to receive requests for multiple MIDI instructions at once and process the instructions in the operating system.

As a result, playing MIDI files now requires even less computing power than before, and allows developers to process MIDI instructions, graphics, and other data even more successfully.

To set up a MIDI instrument

1. Plug the instrument into one of your sound card MIDI ports.

2. Go to the Start menu, choose Settings, and then click Control Panel (or open the Control Panel from the My Computer window).

3. Open the Multimedia Properties dialog box and choose the MIDI tab.

4. Click Add New Instrument, and then follow the instructions the resulting wizard displays on your screen.

5. When the Add New Instrument Wizard finishes, click the MIDI tab, click Single Instrument, and then click the device you just installed, as shown in Figure 13.2.

Waveform audio files (WAV) are digital representations of analog sound. They are similar to the digital audio stored on CDs.

When the computer records a WAV file, it converts the sound into a series of bits that represents the shape of the original analog signal. The quality of the WAV file is related to its resolution and frequency.

One advantage that WAV files have over MIDI is that a Waveform file can be similarly reproduced by any multimedia computer system, much like audio CD sound, because it is a direct digital recording and not a musical interpretation of a sound.

Figure 13.2

You activate the MIDI instrument you just installed in this dialog box.

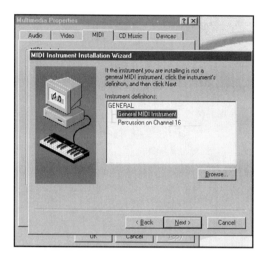

Figure 13.3 shows an example of an WAV audio file's Properties sheet, revealing its compression type, sampling rate, bit depth and channel. To view a sound file's Properties sheet, right-click the file's icon and choose Properties from the resulting pop-up menu.

Figure 13.3

The Properties dialog box for this WAV sound file reveals its compression type, sampling rate, and other data.

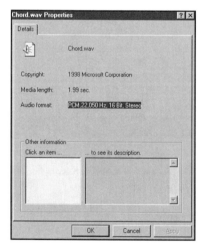

A WAV file has three main components, each of which affect the file's size and sound quality:

■ *Sampling Rate*—This represents the number of times per second that the computer takes an image of the analog audio signal. The sampling rate is measured in Kilohertz (KHz), which represents thousands of samples per second. Audio CDs store sound at 44.1KHz.

- *Bit Depth*—This represents the number of bits that are dedicated to each sample taken. 16-bit audio, used for audio CDs, dedicates two bytes of data to each sample taken. Thus, the higher the bit depth, the higher the quality of sound that can be reproduced.

- *Stereo/Mono*—This determines the number of channels that the audio playback utilizes. Mono playback uses one channel, whereas stereo playback utilizes two channels, which provides spatial quality by enabling the sound to vary between the two different channels.

Sound editing programs such as Sound Recorder let you designate these settings when recording or editing a WAV file. This is described later in this chapter. Be aware, though, that by varying any of these components, you will affect the size and quality of your sound file. The less sound information you store, the less realistic the playback results will be.

For example, limiting the sound to one channel renders playback flat and without spatial cues, such as when instruments or sounds are coming from one speaker over the other. Lowering the bit depth lessens the precision of the playback. Lowering the frequency causes a choppy reproduction.

Space consideration should be balanced carefully with the quality of reproduction you want to create. You should also consider compression utilities if you want to preserve both space and quality.

TIP	Although audio format determines the overall quality of the sound file produced, it is important to consider the quality of hardware in your computer as well.

Understanding Image File Types

Sound files vary primarily in quality, whereas image files offer a wide selection of viewing formats. The format an image file takes can determine the number of colors available for display, reduce file size via a compression algorithm, and even allow for animation. You can view a number of graphics file types by accessing the open dialog box in a graphics editor and clicking the Files of Type drop down list, as shown in Figure 13.4.

As with many other Windows 98 files, image formats are determined by their file extensions. Some formats and their associated extensions include

- Tagged image file format document (TIF, TIFF)—A bitmap file format for describing and storing color and grayscale images in a high-resolution, tag-based image format. TIFF is used for the universal interchange of digital images. This image file format can be compressed.

Figure 13.4

Windows 98 applications support a variety of image formats, even if you never use them all.

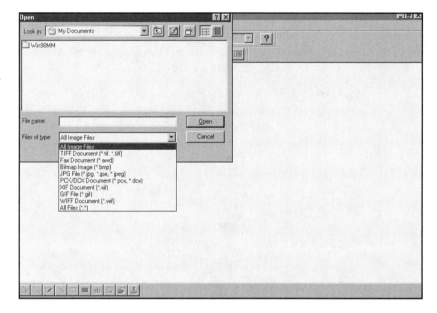

- Fax document (AWD, at work document)—This file type is used by Microsoft Fax. It saves the image in a compressed black-and-white format especially suitable for faxing.

- Bitmap image (BMP)—Images that are created with matrices of pixels or dots. Also called raster graphics. No compression is possible with this file format.

- Joint Photographic Experts Group file (JPG, JPE, JPEG)—A graphical file format used to display high-resolution color images on the Internet. JPEG images use compression that can significantly reduce the large file sizes usually associated with photo-realistic color images. A higher level of compression results in lower image quality, whereas a lower level of compression results in higher image quality.

  This image file type adheres to the proposed universal standard for the digital compression and decompression of still images for use in computer systems as defined by the International Standards Organization (ISO).

- PCX/DCX document (PCX, DCX)—A bitmap format developed originally by ZSoft Corp. for their paint program used by early versions of Windows Paintbrush. PCX can store images up to 64,000 pixels wide and

64,000 pixels high in 24-bit (True color), Red Green Blue (RGB) color scheme only, and its image documents can contain only a single image page.

DCX is similar to PCX as it is also a bitmap format developed by ZSoft. DCX image files are also compressed using PCX compression. However, DCX image documents can contain multiple image pages versus the single image pages available in PCX.

- XIF document (XIF)—XIF is the file type for Xerox image documents. When read by the Microsoft Imaging program, XIF supports the black-and-white page type; its image documents can contain multiple image pages. This format is among the more obscure types that Windows 98 supports.

- Graphics interchange format file (GIF)—A graphical file format commonly used to display indexed-color images on the World Wide Web. GIF is a compressed format, designed to minimize file transfer time over standard phone lines. It supports transparency and animation.

- Wang Image file format (WIFF) document (WIF)—This file type is used by Wang Integrated Image Systems. WIFF supports the black-and-white page type; its image documents can contain multiple image pages. Like the XIF file format, this is a specialized image format many users might never encounter.

Among the differences the various formats allow is the capability to annotate, or add text to, images. Windows 98's Imaging program allows you to annotate bitmaps, TIFFs and Fax documents. All other listed image file types can be opened, viewed, and rotated in Read-Only mode but may not be annotated or otherwise altered without first converting them to an accepted format.

Bitmaps and TIFFs typically retain the original file's appearance. However, a bitmap file cannot be compressed, whereas a TIFF has a variety of color palettes to utilize for editing the image, and the image can be compressed to save disk space.

AWD conversion creates a compressed, faxable black-and-white image, as shown in Figure 13.5, and any annotations added to the image becomes a permanent part of the AWD file you save. The image format you choose should depend on what use you have for your image.

Figure 13.5

You can use Microsoft Imaging to convert an image file to faxable forms and add textual annotations.

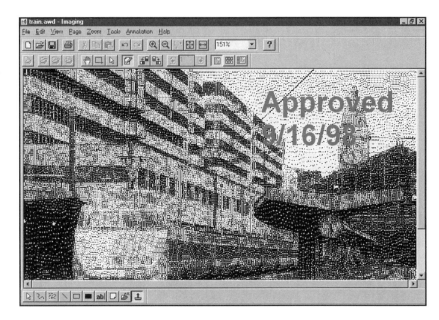

Viewing Images in Internet Explorer

Another strong component of Windows 98 is the Web functionality built into the desktop. Microsoft includes Internet Explorer 4.0 for working on and offline. If you are not connected to the Internet when you open Internet Explorer, you are given the option to work offline. This means that while you can't surf the Internet for files or sites, you can use Internet Explorer to browse through files on your computer. Of course, if you're connected, you are able to browse both your computer's files and those on any accessible Internet site you want to use.

Internet Explorer supports a wide range of viewing formats. The typical formats for viewing images and documents containing images are GIF, JPG, and HTML. You can use Internet Explorer to view any supported file type stored on your computer.

To open an image file in Internet Explorer 4.0

1. Select File on the Internet Explorer menu and choose Open.

2. Type in the path or click the Browse button and navigate to your desired image file.

3. Select the file and choose Open then click OK in the Open dialog box. (Or if you typed the path, choose OK).

The image appears in the Internet Explorer 4.0 window, as shown in Figure 13.6.

Figure 13.6

You can open GIF and JPG files for viewing in Internet Explorer.

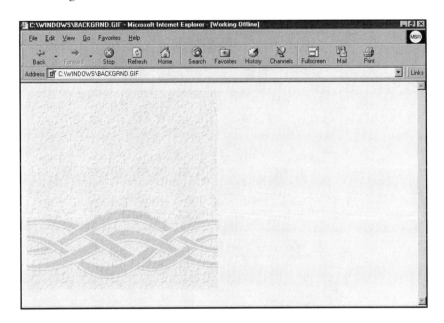

This application is only a viewer and does allow you edit the image in any way. However, you do have the option to apply the image as your desktop wallpaper. Read on to see how.

Applying an Image to the Desktop

Perhaps you have decided that a graphic you have seen on the Web (or even your hard drive or a CD-ROM) would make a nice image for your desktop wallpaper. Windows 98 has made this an easy task.

1. Open (or load) the Web page containing the image (or the image itself, as just discussed) using Internet Explorer.

2. Right-click the image you want to set as wallpaper.

3. Choose Set as Wallpaper from the resulting dialog box, as shown in Figure 13.7.

The image you chose is stored under the filename Internet Explorer Wallpaper in the Display Properties dialog box. If you change the wallpaper to some other image, the current image replaces the old one. Using this method, only the most recent image is saved as the Internet Explorer Wallpaper selection. If you'd like to retain a particular wallpaper graphic, navigate to the Windows folder and copy the file named Internet Explorer Wallpaper.

Figure 13.7
You can apply any image in Internet Explorer as your desktop wallpaper.

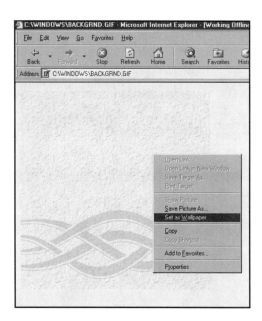

Wallpaper is a fun feature to experiment with using the vast number of images available on any Web page on the World Wide Web.

Previewing Multimedia Files

If you have ever worked with graphics files, you can understand the inspiration behind the thumbnail feature. Opening image files in a catalog viewer is one way to see a picture. But suppose you want to insert an image into your newsletter, fax, or any other document. You might not want to launch a memory-intensive application to get an idea of what is available. Thumbnail views help to solve this problem by allowing you to see a mini-preview version of your available image files, as shown in Figure 13.8.

Figure 13.8

Rather than sort through a confusing list of filenames, thumbnails allow you to preview an image before choosing it.

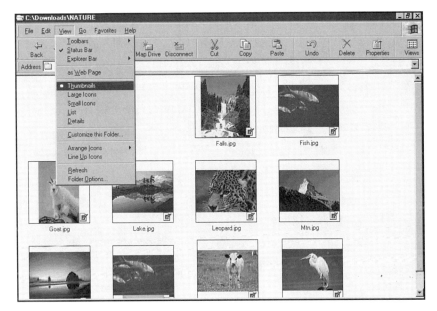

Displaying Thumbnails of Your Images

In order for the thumbnail view option to work, the image files must reside on a write-enabled medium, such as a hard disk. This is because enabling the thumbnail view necessitates the system to create an index file within the folder where the option is selected. (Windows 98 creates a hidden file, Thumbs.db, when you access a folder in this mode.) Therefore, a CD-ROM (which is, of course, read only) full of image files must first be transferred to a write-enabled medium before you can initiate the thumbnail option is initiated.

Another issue to keep in mind is that the option is only valid for an individual folder when you activate the view option. It cannot be set as a universal option in the folder options window.

In fact, even folders within a thumbnail initiated folder must be set individually to utilize the thumbnail option. In other words, contents of other folders do not inherit the thumbnail view property. For example, say you have a folder called Images, which contains subfolders called Animals, People, Buildings, and Trains. If you activate Thumbnail view for the Images folder, you'll see previews of any images in that folder. But if you enter the Animals subfolder, you won't see thumbnails unless you activate thumbnails for it also.

As I mentioned, you must first enable the Thumbnails view for a folder before the option are available under the View selection on the menu bar in Windows Explorer.

To enable the Thumbnail view for a folder

1. Browse to the desired folder containing images you want to use thumbnails to preview.

2. Right-click the folder and choose Properties.

3. Check the box at the bottom of the Properties dialog box labeled Enable Thumbnail View and click OK.

4. Open the folder with the properties you just updated.

5. Select View from the menu and choose Thumbnails.

The compatible image files appear in the Explorer window as miniature versions of the actual image (refer to Figure 13.8).

You can also see a preview version of documents such as an Excel spreadsheet or a Word document by opening the document, choosing Properties from the File menu, checking Save Preview Picture under the Summary tab, and then saving the document.

Any documents with this option checked display a miniature version of the first page of text. The preview is not too informative, as it usually ends up being a collection of blurry black lines (think of Print Preview at about 25 percent zoom). Nonetheless, I am sure there are some fax or letter templates, and certainly spreadsheet documents, where this might be helpful in identifying different formats, especially if there are a variety from which to choose.

> **WARNING**   Be conservative! Each thumbnail-enabled folder creates its own hidden `Thumbs.db` index file. This option could quickly consume more disk space than you intended. Even a folder with only five or six image files could easily create an index file of a megabyte or more.

The thumbnail option is best-suited to preview image files and I recommend that you limit its use to folders holding this type of data.

Default image files formats that permit Thumbnail views in Windows 98 include

- Bitmaps
- GIFS
- JPEG
- HTML

An HTML page displays as a thumbnail version of the Web page it represents, including any graphics contained within the page.

For files that are neither enabled as previews nor image files, Windows Explorer presents a Folder icon or the File icon as the image in the thumbnail border.

Converting File Types

Today's digital images and sounds are getting more and more realistic and detailed. Although this can be a great asset for livening up presentations and documents, it can also cause problems when those creations must be emailed or transferred on a floppy to another user or computer. That is because these great looks and sounds need more and more stored information to make possible the detail and realism they deliver, which in turn means bigger file sizes.

Compression can be your most important feature when transferring with sound and image files in Windows 98. However, some files you work with might arrive in an inefficient format. Options you might find helpful to reduce your file size for ease of transfer and delivery are discussed in the following sections.

Converting Sound File Types

Sound files vary in quality due to their resolution and frequency settings at creation. To view the file's properties, browse to the sound file, right-click the file and choose Properties. In the resulting dialog box, click the Details tab, as shown in Figure 13.9.

Figure 13.9

You can access a sound file's properties in this dialog box.

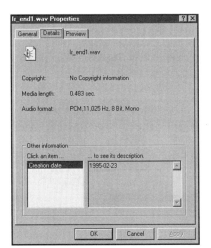

Here you see the file's size and audio format. The audio format includes the compression format, the sampling rate, the bit depth, and the number of channels the sound is recorded in, stereo or mono.

Now that you know the file's current properties, you may decide to change them by using a different type of compression format or by reducing its other sound qualities.

The compression format in your sound file's properties is an audio codec. An audio codec is an algorithm used to compress and decompress sound files. If the codec used to compress a WAV file does not provide the compression ratio or some other feature you want, you can change it.

Windows 98 Sound Recorder offers some default codecs to choose from that compress your sound file. As you can see in Figure 13.10, Sound Recorder provides access to a list of supported codecs (you'll see how to access this dialog box in a moment). Compressing a WAV file makes the file smaller. Because the file is smaller, it takes less time to transfer the file across a network, from a Web page, or between two computers using modems and email.

Figure 13.10

The Properties dialog box you access in Sound Recorder differs from the one you see through Windows Explorer.

Compression files in Windows 98 include

- DSP Group TrueSpeech—Speech specific codec

- Fraunhofer IIS MPEG Layer-3 Codec—Streaming audio compression scheme

- Lernout and Hauspie Codecs—Speech specific codecs

- Microsoft ADPCM

- Microsoft CCITT G.711 A-Law and u-Law

- Microsoft GSM 6.1 audio

- Microsoft IMA ADPCM

- Microsoft PCM Converter

- VivioActive Audio Decompressor

- Voxware Audio Codecs—Speech specific codec for audio conferencing

Not all audio codecs provide the same compression ratio, which makes some audio codecs more useful than others for a particular purpose.

However, many audio codecs that provide higher compression ratios do not provide the additional features that other audio codecs provide (such as higher compression speeds and a greater number of sampling rates). All these factors must be taken into consideration when you are deciding which codec to use in compressing a WAV file.

For example, the Microsoft Adaptive Delta Pulse Code Modulation (ADPCM) and Microsoft Interactive Multimedia Association (IMA) ADPCM codecs can both achieve a 4:1 compression ratio, but the IMA ADPCM codec compresses files faster.

The Microsoft Group Special Mobile (GSM) 6.10 codec can achieve only a 2:1 compression ratio, but offers a greater number of sampling rates.

The Microsoft Consultative Committee for International Telephone and Telegraph (CCITT) G.711 A-Law and u-Law codec can also achieve only a 2:1 compression ratio, but is best when compatibility with current Telephony Application Programming Interface (TAPI) standards are a concern.

The DSP Group Truespeech Software codec achieves the highest compression ratio and is best in voice sampling applications.

GSM is primarily designed for the efficient compression of speech. Using GSM to compress music can result in poor audio quality.

To change the audio codec used to compress a WAV file

1. Click the Start button, choose Programs, and then choose Accessories. From the resulting pop-up menu, choose Entertainment, and then click Sound Recorder.

2. Choose Open from the File menu.

3. Navigate to the WAV file you want to modify, and then click Open.

4. Click the File menu, and choose Properties.

5. Choose the Convert Now button in the Format Conversion section of the dialog box.

6. In the resulting Sound Selection dialog box, click the Format drop-down list and choose an alternative compression format. The default file attributes appear in the Attributes list box below the Format selection, as shown in Figure 13.11.

Figure 13.11

When you change a WAV file's format, its attributes also change.

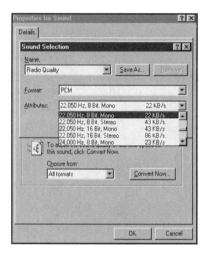

7. If the default attributes are acceptable, click OK; if not, click the Attributes drop-down list and select an alternative attribute setting for that chosen compression format for that file.

8. Click OK, and your changes appear as the file's new properties. Notice the change in the file's data size and file attribute values.

9. Click OK to accept your changes.

If you play the sound now and are not satisfied with the new properties, click the File menu and choose Revert to change the file to its original settings, as shown in Figure 13.12.

Figure 13.12

If you don't like your changes, you can revert to the WAV file's original state.

> **NOTE** An alternative way to change the file's format is to choose Save As. If you want to overwrite the original version of the file with the new version, click Change. If you do not want to overwrite the original version of the file with the new version, type a name for the new version in the File Name box, and then click Change. Adjust to the new settings as described and save the file. *Remember: After you save the file in this manner you will not have the option to revert to the original file format.*

The Sound Selection dialog box offers two other ways to change the size and quality of the sound file, this time without affecting compression. Instead of changing the Format setting, you can change the default Quality Profile or the file's attributes.

Changing either of these settings retains the original format setting but changes the sampling rate, the bit depth, and the number of channels the sound files utilize (stereo or mono). Lowering the KHz and bit depth, and decreasing the channels from two to one greatly reduces the size of any sound file but, of course, also reduces quality.

For example, if you have a 5.2MB audio file recorded at 22KHz in 16-bit stereo, and you reduce the sampling rate to 11KHz, the file size is now be reduced to 2.6MB. Take that same file and adjust it to a bit depth of 8 bits. The new file size is 1.2MB. You reduced the file to almost one-fifth its original size. Change the same file from stereo to mono and you again reduce the file size by half. You could conceivably take a 5.2MB WAV file and reduce it to a 600KB WAV file, nearly a tenth of the original file size, just by changing its attributes—not using compression at all.

Although changing the attributes associated with a WAV file might cause the file to increase or decrease in size, it does not normally make the file sound better. In particular, compressing a WAV file or increasing the compression ratio used on a WAV file does not usually increase sound quality. Neither does reducing the sampling rate, bit depth or output channels—if anything, changing these settings might reduce quality. However, a poor reproduction that is small enough to be practical to send over your chosen medium might be better than not sending the file at all.

Converting Image File Types

Image files typically have even more of an issue of size than does even a complex, high-quality sound file. Using compression is particularly important when you work with grayscale or color images (in other words, everything but strictly black and white), because of their particularly large size. For this reason, image files often have their own compression option and color palette choices to greatly reduce their size and make them more practical to interchange across most media. The imaging program that comes with Windows 98 gives you easy access to these features.

To accomplish this task, you must first be sure that you convert your file to a TIFF format. A TIFF is the only image format that Imaging allows you to compress.

> **NOTE** Remember that you can't apply compression to bitmaps. To enable this function for a bitmap image, you must first open it in Imaging and save it as a TIFF.

After you have your file in the proper format, you can choose to compress it or change its color property.

1. Launch the Imaging program by clicking the Start button, choosing Programs, selecting Accessories, and then clicking Imaging.

2. Choose Open from the File menu.

3. Browse to the file you want to convert, and then click Open.

4. From the File menu, choose Page, and then select Properties. The Page Properties dialog box appears, as shown in Figure 13.13.

Figure 13.13

You can change color depth and other image attributes in the Page Properties dialog box.

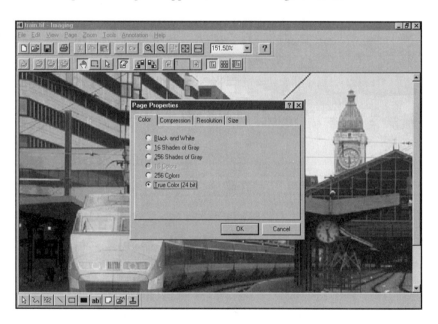

The Page Properties dialog box gives you the option to change the color, compression, resolution, and size of the image you selected.

Compression choices vary depending on which color choice you select. Therefore, you should first decide whether you will use color or black and white. If you are working in color, you need to decide between 256 colors and True color.

True color is the only TIFF color setting that offers JPEG compression. This is your best choice if you need maximum space conservation. JPEG discards some data during compression to get the best reduction in size.

TIP	No compression is recommended if you plan to use your image with other imaging applications that might not support the same compression types as Imaging.

The following is a list of the compression options available in Imaging along with the color conditions necessary to utilize them. You can access these types by clicking the Page Properties dialog box's Compression tab, and then clicking the Compression drop-down list, as shown in Figure 13.14.

Figure 13.14

You can access a variety of compression algorithms.

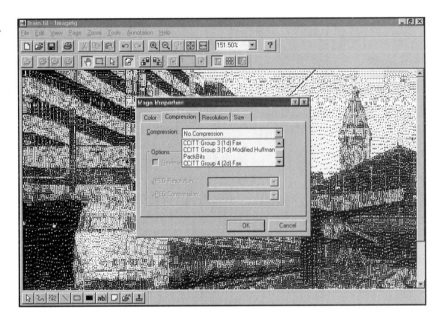

- *CCITT Group3 (1d) Modified Huffman*—This compression type is for black-and-white TIFF image files.

- *CCITT Group3 (1d) Fax*—This compression type is for black-and-white TIFF image files especially designed for fax transmission.

- *CCITT Group4 (2d) Fax*—This compression type is for black-and-white TIFF image files that are sent over reliable data links, such as ISDN or X.25. It provides superior compression for non-dithered images when compared to the Group3 (1d) compression types.

- *PackBits*—Another compression type for black-and-white TIFF image files only.

Figure 13.15 shows the available compression for a 256 grayscale, 256 color, or true color image.

Figure 13.15

A 256-color image offers these compression options.

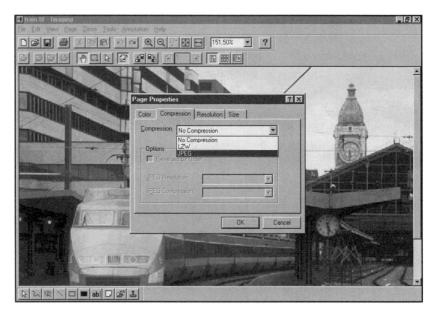

- *LZW (Lempel-Ziv-Welch)* This compression type is one of the two options for true color. It is also available for 256 color and grayscale TIFF image files. LZW does not discard data during compression, and so provides an exact reproduction of the original image. Although the quality of the reproduction is superior, the file will not have a significant size reduction

- *JPEG* This compression type is for true color and 256 shades of gray TIFF image files (but excludes 256 color). JPEG produces a high compression ratio, but discards some image data during compression, which might make the reproduction of the image less exact.

  When compared to LZW compression, JPEG compression produces a significantly smaller file, even using its highest resolution setting and lowest compression setting, without causing a noticeable loss of quality. Thus, JPEG compression, with its highest resolution and lowest compression setting, produces the best overall compression of your TIFF file.

You need to be aware of a few important points about changing the color depth of your image:

1. You can decrease, but not increase, the color depth of your image. After you have reduced an image from true color to 256 colors, you are not able to go back to the original setting.

2. The general rule is that you can take away from the image, but you can't enhance it. You'll notice that the color options go from the bottom up in order of most enhanced color (True color) to least enhanced color (Black and White) in your list of choices.

3. Compression is not available for 16-color images.

4. The Black and White color setting is exactly two colors and offers no variations of gray. This is not a good option if you want to turn a photograph into black and white because you do not have any variation of the shades to give good depth and clarity to the image. For this, choose 256 Shades of Gray and use JPEG compression for your best reproduction in the smallest file.

Now that you have an idea of what color quality you need to use for the compression type you desire, return to the Page Properties dialog box and choose the appropriate color from the color tab, and then click the Compression tab.

If you have chosen to use 256 Shades of Grey or True color in order to utilize JPEG compression, select the JPEG option from the Compression dialog box choices. This selection offers two more adjustments, JPEG Resolution and JPEG Compression, with a choice for each: Low, Medium, or High.

The higher the compression, the smaller the file. The higher the resolution, the larger the file. You might find the best compromise to be a high compression with a high resolution, because lowering the resolution significantly affects the quality of your image.

Other options you have in Page Properties are setting the image's resolution, as shown in Figure 13.16, and changing the image's height, width, or unit of measurement.

Under the Resolution tab, you can choose from a list of available resolutions or enter a custom value. Just as in JPEG, reducing the resolution (measured in dots per inch, or dpi) produces a smaller file, but noticeably affects the quality of your image for the worse.

Lastly, you have the option to reduce the overall height and width of your image. The smaller the image, the smaller the file. Because Imaging does not have a cropping option, this is the only way to achieve a cropped image. This method crops from the lower-right corner only.

Figure 13.16

Microsoft Imaging lets you change your graphic's resolution.

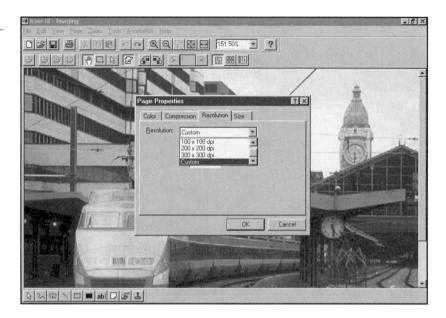

Figure 13.17

You can change your image's size and even the measurement units.

NOTE Reducing image size is a one-way street. Making the height and width larger than the default size of the image only adds white space, as you can see in Figure 13.18. You do have the option to undo your conversion immediately after you change the dimensions (by choosing undo Convert from the Edit menu). However, after you save your changes, you are unable to revert to the original image size.

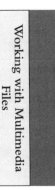

Figure 13.18

Enlarging a previously reduced image merely adds empty white space.

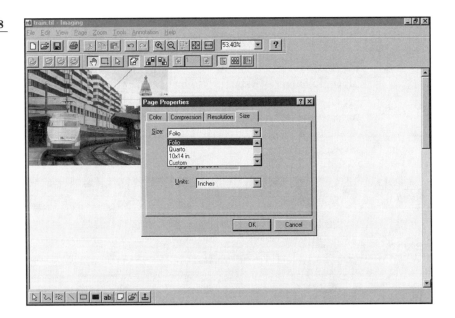

As you can see, there are a number of choices to make your image more practical to share across any medium. In this way, Windows 98 can make it easier to share your creations with co-workers, family, or friends, which makes communicating with your computer a more enjoyable experience in general.

Opening a File with a Different Application

Occasionally, a file is associated with an application that you don't want to launch, even if you want to see the file. For example, you might want to open all text files (TXT) in Write instead of Notebook mode, or maybe one particular bitmap (BMP) in Imaging instead of Paint.

If you want to open a particular file in a different application, you can't access it by double-clicking its icon in Windows Explorer. Doing this launches the associated application. Instead, follow these easy steps.

Bitmap files are, by system default, set to open in Paint. To open the bitmap file in an application it is not associated with, you must do the following:

1. Open the alternative application; in this example, open Imaging.

2. Select Open from the File menu. You see the Open dialog box for Imaging.

3. Browse to the desired BMP file, and click Open. The bitmap image appears in Imaging.

This method works only if the Imaging application can read the file you want to open. To ensure that the file can be opened with your application, click the Files of Type drop-down list in the Open dialog box, as shown in Figure 13.19. This displays the default file types that the application opens. If the file is not capable of being opened by the application selected, an error dialog box appears with a message to that effect.

Figure 13.19

The files of Type drop-down list shows what image formats your program supports.

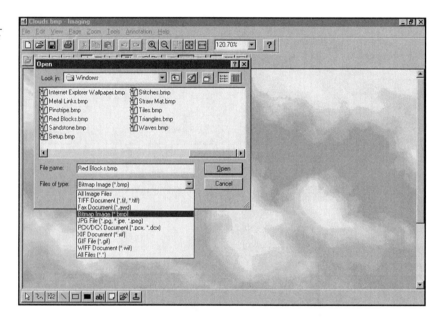

In this example, the bitmap image is opened and can now be saved as a TIFF to be compressed with JPEG of LZW.

This method can be used with any compatible file for any application. For example, you could open text (TXT) files in WordPad instead of Notepad. This option is especially useful when the default Windows 98 application for the file type does not allow or support a function you can utilize in an alternative program.

Associating a File Type with a Different Application

Sometimes, you will want a particular type of file to always be opened by an application other than the Windows 98 default application. Doing so requires changing the file type's association in the computer's system files.

NOTE Remember! Make sure that the file type is supported by the new application with which you have chosen to associate it.

This default application information is actually saved in the Registry files, but Windows 98 makes it safe and painless to change by giving us a graphical alternative to editing the Registry.

To change the default application used to open a file type

1. Open the View menu from the Windows Explorer window, and then choose Folder Options.

2. Choose the File Types tab.

3. Choose a file type from the existing list by clicking on it (or add a new file type by clicking the New Type button and filling out the Add New File Type dialog box).

4. Click on the Edit button to the right of the file type list.

5. Look at the Default Extension for Content Type box and verify that it is displaying the file type extension you want to edit. (Some types have multiple extensions that can be listed by clicking on the down arrow next on this box).

6. In the Edit File Type window there is an Action box with selected actions listed, as shown in Figure 13.20. Highlight Open, and then choose the Edit button.

Figure 13.20

The Actions section of this dialog box describes what happens when you double-click an icon.

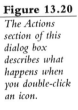
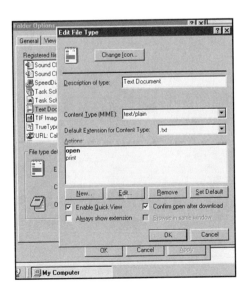

NOTE   The default action for the file type is in bold. Most open by default but you will have the option to change the default action through this dialog box.

7. The Open action appears, grayed out, at the top of the Edit dialog box. You can now change the default application used for this file type, as shown in Figure 13.21, by typing the path, or browsing to the application's executable file in the Application Used to Perform Action dialog box. (If you are using WordPad instead of Notepad, this would change from C:\WINDOWS\NOTEPAD.EXE to C:\Progra~1\Access~1\WORDPAD.EXE "%1")

Figure 13.21

You can change the application associated with a file type.

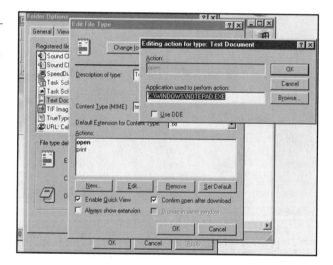

8. Click OK, and then click Close in both the Edit File Type box and Folder Options dialog box.

The new file association appears with the edited file type next to the Opens With label, as shown in Figure 13.22. Now you are able to open the file type through Windows Explorer in the newly chosen application every time without having to open the application first. All you have to do is double-click the file's icon.

Figure 13.22

The file now opens in the newly associated application.

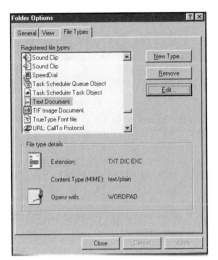

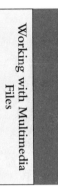

Chapter

14

Using Multimedia on the Internet

By Phil Callihan

A wealth of information is available to Internet users. Much of it takes the form of plain text or graphical Web pages; however, some of the more interesting content includes the wide selection of multimedia files that you can access. Video clips and live audio broadcasts of sporting events are just a few of the many exciting possibilities that can make your computer come alive.

In this chapter, you will learn about *streaming multimedia*—formats that allow you to enjoy the contents of a file while it is downloading to your computer. You will also see how to give your email messages some added emphasis through the use of multimedia. In addition, you will learn how easy it can be to videoconference and share applications with other users on the Internet. Finally, you will explore Internet channels and see how you can use them to customize the content you receive through your browser.

Streaming Audio and Video

Streaming media allows you to enjoy multimedia clips without having to wait for the entire file to download—they can be played while downloading. This is a great feature for users who are connected to the Internet via relatively slow telephone lines, because audio and video files can be quite large, taking a long time to download. Although high speed access to the Internet (cable modems, ADSL, ISDN) is becoming more widespread, a great majority of home users still depend on standard copper phone lines for their Internet access. Web developers who use streaming multimedia file types allow practically all Internet users to enjoy multimedia. Windows 98 has built-in support for the ASF (active streaming format) files that can be played in the Windows Media Player.

> **NOTE**   The ASF file format allows multimedia objects (audio, video, and images) to be synchronized and played in Internet browsers. This format also allows the files to be played while downloading.

Streaming media is sent in a compressed stream which is played as it arrives. The disadvantage of the design is that multimedia files sometimes stutter or freeze depending on the speed of your Internet connection and the load on the streaming server.

Working with the Windows Media Player and ActiveMovie

The Windows Media Player allows you to play a number of different multimedia file types without needing to install a separate player for each one. The Windows Media Player currently supports the following file formats: ASF, Real Video/Real

Audio 4.0, MPEG 1, MPEG 2, WAV, AVI, MIDI, MOV, VOD, AU, MP3, and QuickTime files.

> **NOTE** The ActiveMovie control has been replaced by the Windows Media Player. Like the ActiveMovie control, the Windows Media Player control enables the playback of many popular multimedia types on your computer and on the Internet, including MPEG audio, WAV audio, MPEG video, AVI video, and Apple QuickTime video. You can download the Windows Media Player, at the following URL: `http://www.microsoft.com/windows/mediaplayer/`.

To play a supported file type is easy. Click the file on a Web site from within your Web browser and the Windows Media Player will open and play the file, as shown in Figure 14.1.

> **NOTE** The Windows Media Player has replaced a number of older Microsoft technologies, such as the ActiveMovie control and NetShow player. This was done so users would only have to download one program to play multimedia files from the Internet.

Figure 14.1

The Windows Media Player will open and you will be able to Start, Stop, or Pause the playing of the files using VCR-style control buttons.

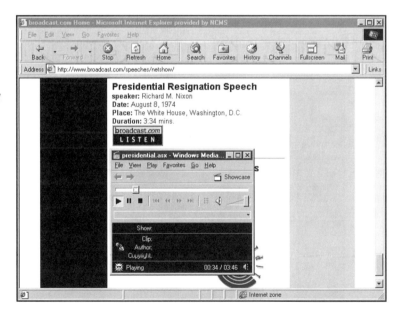

After downloading and installing the Windows Media Player you can connect to the Microsoft Web Events site at `http://webevents.microsoft.com` in order to test your new software. That site, shown in Figure 14.2, contains a variety of files in different streaming formats to confirm that your Media Player is functioning properly.

Figure 14.2

The Microsoft Web Events Web site has a wide variety of streaming multimedia available to test your player.

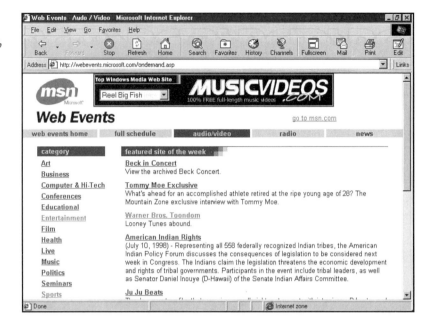

An example of a site that uses the Windows Multimedia Player is `http://www.msnbc.com`, shown in Figure 14.3. From this site, you can view video clips that have aired on the MSNBC cable network.

Figure 14.3

The MSNBC site uses the Windows Media Player to allow you to see latest in breaking news.

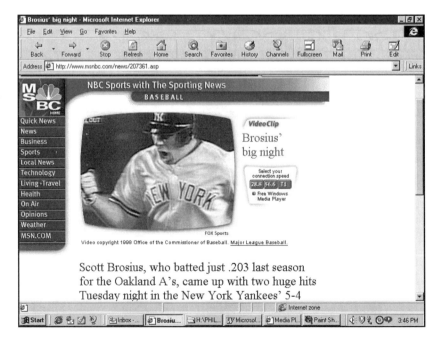

Working with NetShow

NetShow is a Microsoft server product that allows Internet content creators to provide live or prerecorded video and audio content to users on the Internet. The creation of files to be displayed by a NetShow server is more involved than the creation of a standard multimedia file. The media streams must be created by the content provider taking into consideration a number of factors including:

- The Internet access speed of the end user who will be playing the file

- The quality of the video and audio that is desired for the multimedia stream

- Bandwidth and server load considerations for the NetShow server that broadcasts the finished media stream

In order to play content from a NetShow server you will need to install the Windows Media Player. When you access a site that uses NetShow to you will be prompted to install the latest version of player from Microsoft, or you can connect to the Microsoft Web site http:\\www.microsoft.com and download it in advance.

After installing the Windows Media player you will be able to play content from NetShow servers on the Internet, such as the VideoSeeker site shown in Figure 14.4.

Working with RealAudio

RealAudio is a another popular standard of streaming video and audio that is used on the Internet. If you install RealAudio 4.0 support, the Windows Media Player will be able play *ram* (real audio media) files. In order to play Real Audio streaming media, you will need to install support for it during your Windows 98 installation or add it by following these steps:

1. Open the Control Panel by clicking the Start menu, choosing Settings, and selecting the Control Panel.

2. In Control Panel, select the Add/Remove Programs icon.

Using Multimedia on the Internet

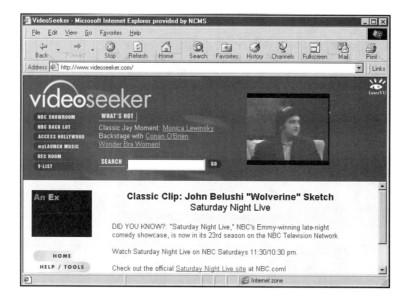

3. In the resulting dialog box, select the Windows Setup tab.

4. Scroll down to Internet Tools in the list box and double-click it.

5. Click the check box next to RealAudio 4.0, as shown in Figure 14.5, and
   then click OK to install the new software.

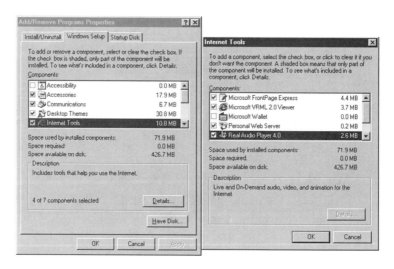

You can now connect to Web sites that use RealAudio file formats and view these
files from within Internet Explorer, as shown in Figure 14.6.

Figure 14.6

You can't hear it, but I'm listening to a baseball game via RealAudio playing in the Windows Media Player.

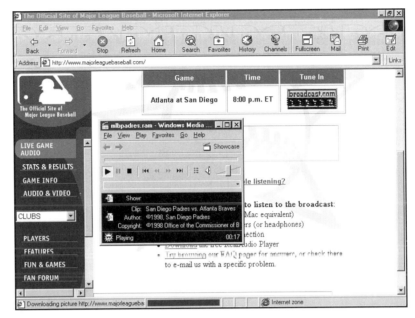

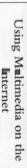

Using Multimedia on the Internet

NOTE   RealNetworks also has a more advanced RealAudio player for purchase from their company Web site (`http://www.realaudio.com/`). The retail RealAudio player supports advanced options such as improved audio and video quality, TV-like picture quality controls, and the capability to record selected content for later playback.

Enhancing Your Email Messages

Sometimes you might want to add some extra emphasis to your email. After reading message after message of plain text, an email message that uses multimedia can really stand out from the crowd. You have the option of adding stationery, pictures, or sound files to spruce up your email messages.

NOTE   Be aware that some features are only available in some email formats. Generally all email users can read view messages sent in plain text. Most users can view messages sent in HTML format, whereas rich text format and Microsoft Word format are supported to a lesser extent. Also, sometimes image files you attach appear in the body of the message, while in other viewers the recipient must open the attached picture separately. Always check with your intended recipients to find out what formatting their mail systems support.

Here are some considerations to keep in mind before you make the decision to enhance your email messages:

- Stationery, pictures, and sound files increase the size of your email messages. Be considerate! It's not a good idea to send a friend a 5MB sound file if he's getting his email over a 14.4Kbps dial-up connection—downloading the file would take a long time.

- Not all recipients will get your enhancements. Things that can interfere are mail server types, security settings, and attachment encoding options. Some companies remove incoming attachments as part of their virus protection policy. Some text-based email systems do not support file attachments.

- Realize that these enhancements will increase the size of your disk usage on your email server. Some providers turn accounts off after they reach a certain size. Be aware of your account limitations. You should also make periodic maintenance checks, deleting files from your sent mail archive as you deem prudent.

Adding Stationery to an Email Message

A nice feature that you can use to give your email a more professional look is to use stationery. Stationery gives your email a professional letterhead appearance by predefining fonts, colors, and even a background image. Note the fonts and the border on the left side of the message shown in Figure 14.7.

Figure 14.7

Email with stationery has a much more impressive and professional appearance.

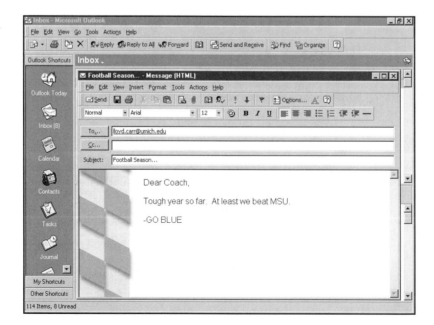

> **NOTE** Outlook 98 is an email client available for purchase from Microsoft that supports stationery. For the latest details on acquiring Outlook 98 check out the following URL `http://www.microsoft.com/outlook/`. Microsoft has been offering free upgrades to Outlook 98 for users of their Web site.
>
> Outlook Express is the free email client that comes with Internet Explorer 4; it too supports stationery. Outlook Express should already be part of the Internet Explorer setup on your machine. You can download Internet Explorer 4 or check for the latest version at `http://www.microsoft.com/ie/ie40/`. Directions on how to use stationery with Outlook Express are discussed a later in this chapter.

If you are using Outlook 98, you can follow these steps to add stationery to your email messages.

1. On the Outlook menu, select Tools, select Options, and then click the Mail Format tab. Select HTML as your message format.

2. Click the Stationery Picker.

3. You'll see a dialog box depicting previews of stationery options, as shown in Figure 14.8. Select a stationery for your email messages, and click OK to continue.

Using Multimedia on the Internet

Figure 14.8

The preview window in the Stationery Picker shows you what your creation will look like.

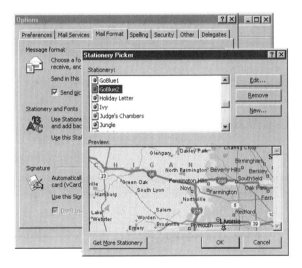

4. Begin a new message by clicking the New Message icon on the Outlook toolbar. Your stationery should appear in the window of your new message.

5. Compose and send your message as normal.

> **WARNING**   Remember to keep in mind that somebody actually has to be able to read a message on top of your stationery. Don't pick stationery that will overwhelm the text of your message, or count alignment to properly place your text on the page of an important message.

After looking at the previews of default stationery, you might decide that none provide the effect you're looking for. Or you might have your own ideas for a stationery that will make your email resemble letters sent on your company letterhead. Fortunately, you can create your own Outlook 98 stationery. If you want to do so, follow these steps:

1. From the Outlook menu, select Tools, Options, and then click the Mail Format tab in the resulting dialog box.

2. Click New to begin creating your own personal stationery.

3. In the resulting dialog box, enter a name for your new stationery.

4. You can then choose to start from a blank stationery, use an existing stationery as a template, or use a file as template. Make your selection and click OK to continue.

5. You can then choose a font that your stationery will use and pick a color or image for its background. Click OK to finish.

6. Your email messages will now use your stationery.

> **NOTE**   Be careful not to use stationery that makes your email text hard to read, such as dark purple text on a black background. Stationery is useless if you cannot read a message written over it.

You don't have to purchase the full commercial version of Outlook to take advantage of stationery. Its junior version, Outlook Express—which is bundled with Internet Explorer 4—also lets you add stationery to your messages. If you are using Outlook Express, follow these steps to add stationery to your email:

1. Open Outlook Express.

2. Click the Compose New Message toolbar button.

3. Select your stationery from the drop-down list. It will appear in the message composition window, as shown in Figure 14.9.

4. Address and compose your email message.

5. Click the Send button to finish.

Figure 14.9
Adding stationery using Outlook Express.

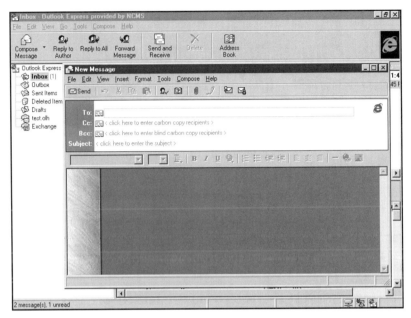

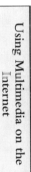

Using Multimedia on the Internet

Of course, Microsoft Outlook doesn't have a monopoly on using stationery. If you are using Netscape 4.06 with Netscape Netcenter, you can also provide stationery to your email. Follow these steps:

1. Open Netscape and select WebMail from the default Netcenter startup page.

2. From the left navigation menu, click Write Mail.

3. Select your stationery from the Use Stationery drop-down menu (see Figure 14.10).

4. Address and compose your message.

5. Click Send to finish.

> **NOTE** Netcenter is Netscape's default start page. It provides lots of information, news, search capability and the WebMail service discussed here. However, you can configure Netscape Navigator to display any page you like when it launches. If you don't see Netcenter when you launch Netscape Navigator, its URL is `http://home.netscape.com`.

Figure 14.10

Composing a message using Netscape Netcenter's mail feature.

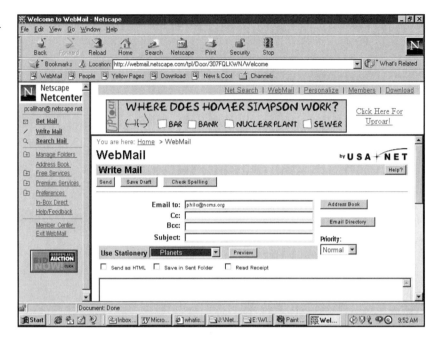

Adding an Image to an Email Message

It is said that a picture can say a thousand words. If you need to show your friends a picture of your new pet or just about anything else, there are two basic ways to go about it: You can attach the image file to your message or insert it directly into the message you're sending.

> **NOTE**   Remember to consider how the recipient of your message will be downloading their email. If it takes a half a minute for you open a message on your corporate network that uses a very fast Internet connection, it might take quite a great deal longer for someone to open a message with an image attachment over a 28.8K modem connection.

Attaching the file means that the recipient must open the file in a separate viewer in order to see it. However, it's a little more efficient, because the user can read the message without waiting for an embedded image to display. You can attach the image files by following these steps:

If you're using Outlook 98 or Outlook Express

1. Open a new message by clicking the New Message toolbar button or pressing Ctrl+N.

2. Address and compose your message as usual.

3. On the Outlook toolbar, click the Paper Clip icon.

4. In the resulting dialog box, navigate to and select the image you want to send, and then click OK.

5. Click the Send button to finish.

Another way to send an image file is to insert it directly into your email message.

If you're using Outlook 98 and Outlook Express, follow these steps:

1. Open a new message.

2. Address and compose your message as usual.

3. From the Outlook menu select the Insert command, and then choose Picture. In the resulting dialog box, navigate to the location of your image. Click OK to insert it and it appears, as shown in Figure 14.11.

4. Click the Send button to finish.

Figure 14.11

This email message has an image file inserted into the body of the message (above) and as a file attachment (below).

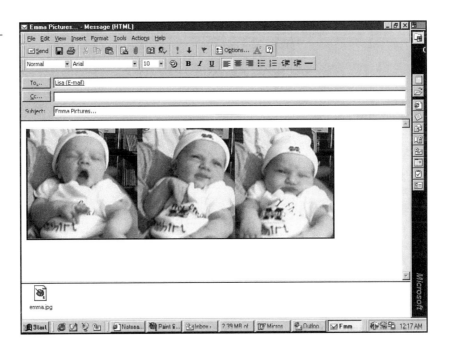

If you are using Netscape 4.06 with Netscape Netcenter email follow these steps:

1. Open Netscape and select WebMail from your startup page.

2. From the left navigation menu, click Write Mail.

3. Scroll down to the bottom of the email screen and click the Add/Remove button next to the Attachments heading.

Using Multimedia on the Internet

4. In the resulting dialog box, shown in Figure 14.12, click the Browse button, navigate to and select the image files that you want to attach, and then click OK.

Figure 14.12

Adding an attachment is easy using Netscape Netcenter email.

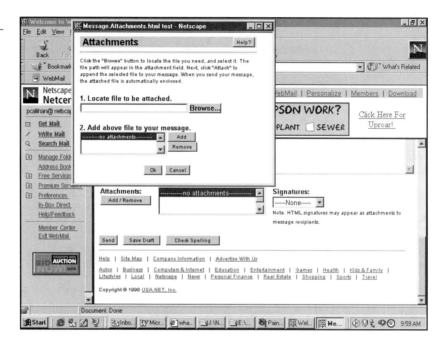

5. Address and compose your message.

6. Click the Send button to finish.

I've described the process of attaching files under several of the more popular email systems. If you don't use one of these methods, the process is nonetheless probably similar for your email client. Look for a Paper Clip icon on the toolbar or an Attach command. And images aren't the only kind of file you can attach, as you'll learn in a moment.

Adding Sound or Music to an Email Message

You can also use other multimedia files to enhance your email. A sound clip or music file is great way to communicate with someone using email. For example, if you're sending a short thank you message, you might jazz it up by finding a similar sound bite from a movie or TV show or recording your own voice.

If you're using Outlook 98 or Outlook Express

1. Open a new message.

2. Address and compose your message.

3. On the Outlook toolbar, click the Paper Clip icon.

4. Navigate to and select the sound or music file you want to send, and then click OK. The embedded sound will appear as an icon at the bottom of the message, as shown in Figure 14.13.

5. Click Send to finish.

Figure 14.13

A sound clip used with stationery can help you get your point across when a plain message just won't carry the same impact.

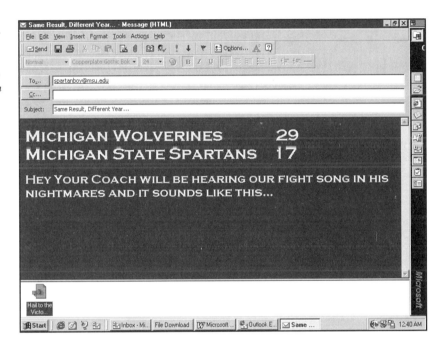

If you're using Netscape Netcenter Mail, follow these steps:

1. Open Netscape and select WebMail from your startup page.

2. From the left navigation menu, click Write Mail.

3. Scroll down to the bottom of the email screen and click the Add/Remove button under the Attachments heading.

4. In the resulting dialog box click Browse, and then navigate to and select the sound files that you want to attach.

5. Click Send to finish.

Again, I've described how to attach sound files under several of the more popular email systems. And as before, the process is probably similar for other email clients such as Eudora. A good clue is a Paper Clip icon on the toolbar. There's also probably an Attach command.

Now you've seen how to send images and sound. Read on to discover how to transmit images and sound over the Internet—in real-time!

Video Conferencing with NetMeeting

NetMeeting is a product from Microsoft that allows you videoconference with other users over the Internet. In addition to being able to see and speak with other users, you can share applications and collaborate on work as well. Even if you don't have a video camera, you can make the equivalent of long-distance telephone calls free of charge with just a microphone and set of speakers. NetMeeting can be installed as a part of Internet Explorer or downloaded as separate application from the Microsoft Web site at the following URL: `http://www.microsoft.com/netmeeting/`. After you've downloaded the setup file, double-click its icon to launch the installation program and follow the program's instructions.

> **NOTE**   Software is constantly being updated. It always a good idea to make sure that you are using the most current version available of software. In the case of NetMeeting, you can check to see if there is a new version available at the following URL: `http://www.microsoft.com/netmeeting/`.

If you are planning to use NetMeeting, your computer should meet the following system requirements:

- A Pentium class computer with 32MB of RAM

- A sound card with speakers and a microphone

- A video conferencing camera (optional)

- An Internet connection (28.8K or faster)

Setting Up a Call

After installing and configuring NetMeeting you are ready to begin. There are two ways to connect with other users. You or the person you are calling can choose to "host" the meeting, or you can choose to connect to a location server that will host the meeting for you. You can also connect to a location server to see who else is connected and initiate a call with someone more or less at random.

> **NOTE** If you are not going to use a location server to host your meeting you will want the hosting party to be the person who has the computer with most resources (processor speed, RAM, and faster modem or Internet connection). A slow computer or modem can create a performance bottleneck that will be worsened by having that computer bear the extra overhead of hosting the meeting.

Microsoft has set up public location servers that you are able to use with NetMeeting; see Figure 14.14 for an example. Unfortunately, these servers are exceptionally busy with many new users who are experimenting with NetMeeting. Many companies that use NetMeeting for business collaborations have their own location servers. If you don't have the luxury of your own location server, you can use one of the public servers provided by Microsoft. Another option is to host a meeting on your computer. If you choose this option you will need to provide your IP address to the person who you want to connect to your meeting.

Using Multimedia on the Internet

Figure 14.14

You can connect to a public location server provided by Microsoft.

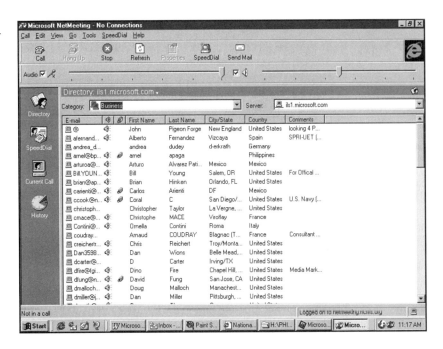

> **WARNING** Only give out your IP address to people that you trust. A hacker could use your IP address to attack your machine over the Internet.

Communicating with the Other Party

To start a meeting with another user, you can follow these steps:

1. Start NetMeeting and connect to a directory server, such as ils.microsoft.com.

2. Double-click the name of the person who you want to communicate with.

3. The person who you are trying to connect to will get a request from you asking them to join your meeting. After they accept your invitation, you will able to begin using NetMeeting to communicate with real-time voice and even video.

After you're in a meeting, you have many options to communicate. NetMeeting supports interactive video, audio, a whiteboard (which lets you draw pictures the other person can see), text-based chat, and file transfer. Sending video allows you to actually see the person you are communicating with, as you can see in Figure 14.15. Unfortunately, it uses a large percentage of your available network bandwidth and the quality can vary greatly depending on your video card and camera type.

Figure 14.15

Your video window appears on the right side of your screen, or you can detach it and change its location.

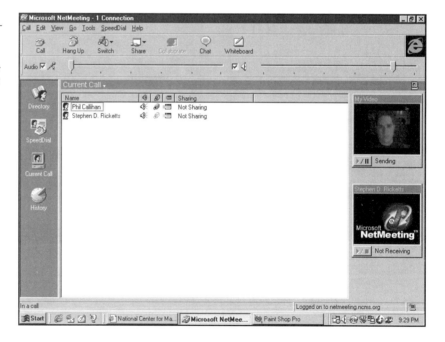

A wide variety of inexpensive ($99 range) video cameras are available that connect to your parallel port. Some newer types use the USB (Universal Serial Bus) connector that is available on the latest personal computers.

> **NOTE** If you are connecting using a modem, it is a good idea to stop sending a video signal after initially connecting. This will free up your available bandwidth for audio and application sharing. If constant updating of video isn't necessary, it's a good idea to pause it.

You can also communicate using audio only with microphones connected to your computer's audio card. Audio has the limitation that only one person can speak at a time unless you are using audio duplexing, which is supported by some state-of-the-art sound cards. Because people are used to being able to speak at the same time it takes some practice to get used to this limitation.

NetMeeting also has a whiteboard application that allows you to share drawings with other users. Each person can take control of the application and make changes, annotations, or additions.

The text-based chat feature, shown in Figure 14.16, is useful for users who don't have audio capability or who want to save the bandwidth that would be used by audio for use in application sharing. If you use chat, you can also copy and paste the contents of the chat session into another application and save it for later reference. This technique is especially useful if you're getting technical help that you might want to refer to later.

Using Multimedia on the Internet

Figure 14.16

The chat feature is a useful option if using audio isn't possible or desirable.

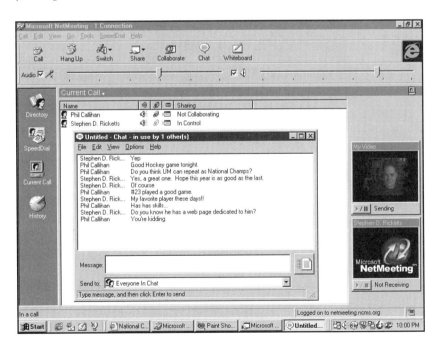

Another great feature is the file transfer option, which allows you to send files to people you are connected to. For example, you might send a photo of yourself, a clever sound bite, some seasonal clip art, a draft contract, or any other file.

> **NOTE** Sending large files can impair the speed and quality of your video and audio reception depending on the speed of your Internet connection.

Sharing an Application

One the best features of NetMeeting is the capability to share applications. By sharing applications, users can collaborate on documents, yielding control of applications to other connected users. This feature works even if one of the users doesn't have the shared application installed on their computer. To share an application, follow these steps:

1. Start NetMeeting and connect to the meeting or individual user that want to share the application with.

2. Click the Share button in NetMeeting's toolbar and navigate to and choose the application you want to share.

3. NetMeeting presents a dialog box warning you that other people will be able see the application but not be able to make changes to it.

At this point you need to decide if you want to let the participants in your meeting see your application or be able to take control and use your application to make changes. If you want to allow your meeting participants to use your application, you need to click the Collaborate button on the NetMeeting toolbar, shown in Figure 14.17. Many companies are concerned that NetMeeting poses a security risk to the network; it is important to realize that depending on what application you share, remote users might have or gain access to your entire hard drive and network resources. As a result, it might make sense to run NetMeeting form a standalone computer with a modem.

> **NOTE** One problem with collaborating is that anyone can take control of the shared application and begin making changes. Anyone in the meeting can click the application and take control, deliberately or accidentally, whether you want them to or not. You might want to establish firm guidelines for who is going to take control and when.

Figure 14.17

*Sharing an
application using
NetMeeting.*

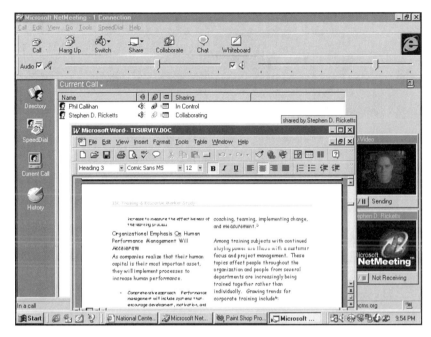

Figure 14.17

*Sharing an
application using
NetMeeting.*

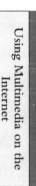

Using Multimedia on the
Internet

Configuring NetMeeting Settings

Depending on the speed of your Internet connection, you might want to change
one or more settings to improve the performance of NetMeeting. By clicking the
Tools menu, selecting Options, clicking the Video tab, and changing the following
video options, you can improve the performance of NetMeeting:

- At the top of the dialog box, deselect the options to automatically send
  and receive video at the beginning of NetMeeting calls.

- Select the Small radio button in the Send Video Size settings.

- In the Video Quality setting, move the slider bar over to Faster Video.

The main way to increase the performance on NetMeeting is to upgrade the
speed of your Internet connection. A new v.90 modem coupled with an Internet
service provider (ISP) that supports 56K dial-up speeds is ideal for regular use of
NetMeeting. An ADSL connection, cable modem, or ISDN connection is also
highly recommended. These high-speed connections allow you to use every
feature of NetMeeting.

Working with Internet Channels

Internet *channels* give you a way to control the content that you receive from the Internet. Channels are usually organized around a similar topic of interest. A channel is a Web site to which you subscribe to be notified of changes; Web sites do this by a process called *netcasting* or *push technology*. Internet channels allow you to program your browser to bring interesting information to you as it becomes available. Internet channels are supported by both the current versions of Internet Explorer and Netscape.

Subscribing to a Channel

To subscribe to an Internet channel with Internet Explorer 4.0, follow these steps:

1. Open Internet Explorer and click the Channels icon on the toolbar.

2. From the resulting Channel pane, select your area of interest.

3. From the list box, choose a specific site that want to subscribe to.

4. The site appears in the right pane so you can preview it, as shown in Figure 14.18. If you want to subscribe, click the Add Active Channel button on the page.

5. Internet Explorer presents a dialog box asking you to choose how you want to subscribe to the channel. You can choose to only be notified of updates, or you can choose to have Internet Explorer actually download a copy of site so that you can view it offline at your convenience.

To subscribe to an Internet channel under Netscape 4.06, you'll use the Netcaster application that comes in your Netscape program group. (The Netscape 4 package provides a number of applications besides the Navigator Web browser; Netcaster is just one of these.) To use Netcaster to select a channel, follow these steps:

1. Open Netscape Netcaster.

2. Select your area of interest from the list, as shown in Figure 14.19.

3. Click the Add Channel button.

4. In the resulting dialog box, click Continue.

5. The first time you subscribe to a channel, you'll probably be asked to supply registration information. Do so and follow the onscreen instructions to complete the process.

Figure 14.18

Subscribing to a channel using Internet Explorer is easy.

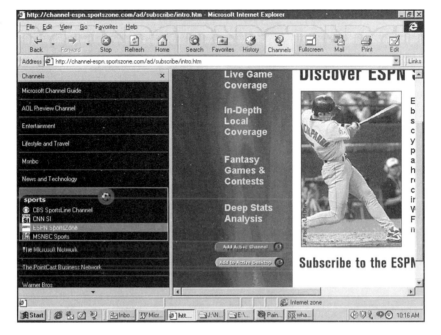

Figure 14.19

Subscribing to a channel using Netscape Netcaster.

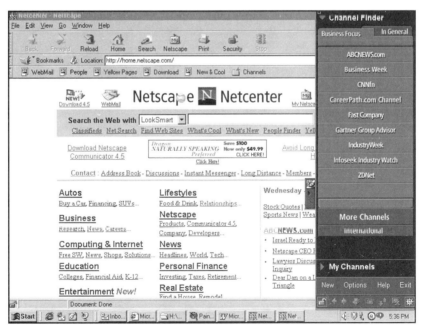

Using Multimedia on the Internet

Configuring a Channel

At some point after you initially subscribe to a channel, you might want to change its configuration. Perhaps you want it to update itself more often, which increases the load on your modem, or not update when you're using your computer, which decreases the load.

To configure a channel in Internet Explorer, follow these steps:

1. Open Internet Explorer and select Favorites from the toolbar.

2. Click the Manage Subscriptions button.

3. A window will appear showing all your channel subscriptions.

4. Right-click the subscription that you want to configure and select Properties from the pop-up menu.

5. In the resulting dialog box, click the Subscription tab, shown in Figure 14.20. The Receiving tab lets you modify your subscription type and indicate whether you want to receive an email notification of the update. From the schedule tab you can modify the conditions for when Internet Explorer updates your subscriptions.

Figure 14.20

To configure a channel in Internet Explorer, use its Properties dialog box.

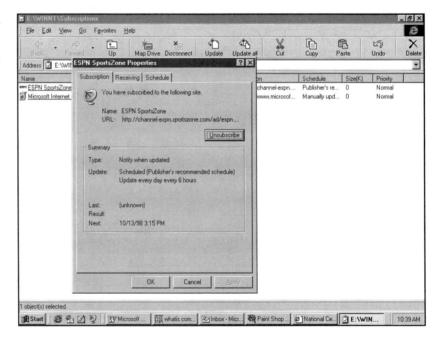

To configure a channel in Netscape Netcaster, follow these steps:

1. Open Netscape Netcaster.

2. Click the Options button on the Channel Finder.

3. Select the Channels tab and click the channel you want to configure.

4. Click Properties.

5. In the resulting dialog box, shown in Figure 14.21, you can customize options such as the channel name and how often it updates.

Figure 14.21

Configuring a channel in Netscape Netcenter.

Unsubscribing to a Channel

If you find that a channel is not delivering the kind of content that you had hoped for, you can choose to unsubscribe from the channel easily.

To unsubscribe from a channel using Internet Explorer, follow these steps:

1. Open Internet Explorer.

2. From the Favorites menu, click Manage Subscriptions.

3. In the resulting window, right-click the subscription you want to delete and select Delete from the resulting pop-up menu.

To unsubscribe from a channel using Netscape Netcaster follow these three steps:

1. From the Netcaster Channel bar, select Options.

2. Select the Channels tab, as shown in Figure 14.22.

3. Click Delete to remove the channel that you don't want to receive.

The availability of multimedia on the Internet increases every day. As more Web sites begin to employ advanced techniques for delivering content, such as active multimedia streaming and channels, you will have a great variety of compelling content to choose from. By using the multimedia components included in Windows 98 and by downloading the free upgrades (Internet Explorer 4.x, Windows Media Player, and NetMeeting) you will be able to enjoy virtually any of the multimedia the Internet has to offer.

Using Multimedia on the Internet

Figure 14.22

Deleting a channel in Netscape Netcaster.

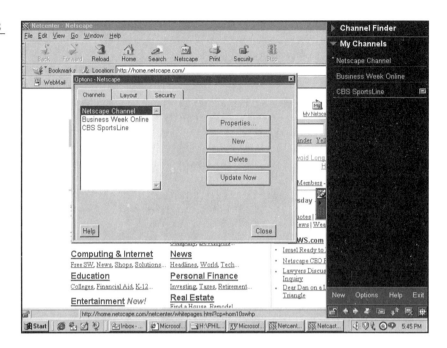

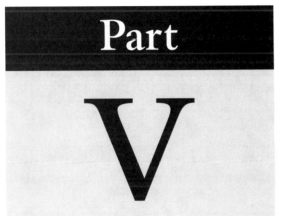

Part V

V

Advanced Multimedia Concepts

Chapter

15

Working with Multiple Monitors

By Dave Adams Saltz

Multiple monitors—you've seen dedicated hackers surrounded by glowing computer screens in the movies and on TV. Maybe you even have friends or coworkers who use more than one monitor on their Macintosh or UNIX workstations. And you, being a PC user, probably felt a little twinge of jealousy at all the benefits enjoyed by using multiple monitors. Well, envy no more—with Windows 98 and the right hardware, you can easily run more than one monitor on your home or business desktop. In this chapter, you'll learn what you need to get you started, a little technical background, how to set the whole thing up, and what to do if things don't work exactly right.

Overview of Multiple Display Support

Like Windows 95, Windows 98 has robust support for many different display settings. However, Windows 98 adds a welcome feature called *Multiple Display Support*, also called *multiple monitors*, or *multi-monitors*.

Essentially, Multiple Display Support enables you to attach additional display adapters and monitors to your systems to reap more desktop space in which to work.

Many people are now used to using an operating system such as Windows 98 that allows us to multitask and use many different programs simultaneously. The big drawback is that until Multiple Display Support, users were forced to constantly switch between all the open programs running in order to use them. Either you had lots of little windows on your screen, or you had to keep clicking the taskbar to bring a new window to the foreground. With Multiple Display Support, you can add an extra monitor (or more than one) and extend your usable desktop space to accommodate many more open applications, and see them all at once.

Your mouse can move back and forth between the multiple monitors with ease, and you can drag windows to any place you like, on any of your monitors, to any point on your virtual desktop. The individual monitors can even be running at different resolutions and color depths.

Imagine that you're looking at your main computer monitor—your *primary monitor*. You're typing a letter in Microsoft Word with the window maximized to take up the whole screen. On your secondary display, to the left of your primary monitor, you have a Web browser opened and are watching the latest stock market ticker come over the wire. You also have your email program open waiting for new mail to arrive. You decide to tile the windows on the second monitor so that you can see both the stock ticker and the email program at the same time.

Now, you've got three open programs, all visible to you, and all accessible without having to click the taskbar. They're all ready and waiting for you to do nothing more than turn your head to check on their status.

Many people have told me that after they've used their systems with Multiple Display Support installed, they don't know how they ever used a single monitor system before. I must agree, it is a great time and effort saver to have more than one monitor attached to the system. Plus it beats the cost of buying one single super-large screen monitor to gain that extra desktop real estate.

System Requirements for Multiple Display Support

In order to use Multiple Display Support in Windows 98, your system must meet some minimum hardware requirements. Not all systems are created equally and the same goes for video cards and their drivers.

> **NOTE** Be sure to check with the manufacturer of your display adapter(s) to see if they have any new drivers available. Video card makers are releasing new drivers almost weekly to enable Multiple Display Support in their cards. Just because a card is listed by Microsoft as not compatible (or isn't listed at all) doesn't mean that the manufacturer will never develop drivers for it to use Multiple Display Support. It simply means that the proper drivers don't ship with Windows 98 and Multiple Display Support will not be available with the default Windows 98 drivers. On the Internet, try the Web sites of some of the bigger display adapter manufacturers:
>
> ATI Technologies
> http://www.atitech.ca
>
> S3, Inc.
> http://www.s3.com
>
> Creative
> http://www.creaf.com
>
> Number Nine Visual Technology
> http://www.nine.com
>
> Microsoft Windows 98
> http://www.microsoft.com/Windows98

What Type of Video Cards Can I Use?

In order to use Multiple Display Support, your display adapters all must be either Peripheral Component Interconnect (PCI) cards or Accelerated Graphics Port (AGP) cards. Plus all PCI or AGP cards must have drivers that enable the Multiple Display Support features of Windows 98. Windows ships with many of these such drivers already, or you can ask the vendor of your video card if newer drivers are available.

You cannot use Industry Standard Architecture/Extended Industry Standard Architecture (ISA/EISA) video adapter cards for multiple monitors. If you have such a card and would like to take advantage of multiple monitors, it's time to think about upgrading.

Unsupported Chipsets

Microsoft does not support the use of certain Permedia video chipsets with Multiple Monitor Support, so it's best to check to make sure that the card you have works. The 3D Labs Web site has information on the Permedia line of chipsets at `http://www.3dlabs.com`, or email them at `support@3dlabs.com` to find out more.

Supported Chipsets

Microsoft also supports a slew of other video cards, and Windows 98 ships with drivers for them contained on the CD-ROM. The list of cards for which Windows 98 has built-in support follows. This list is based on the one at the Microsoft Knowledge Base at `http://support.microsoft.com/support/kb/articles/q182/7/08.asp`. I suggest you check this online article for updates, as Microsoft frequently refreshes its online documentation.

> **NOTE**   If you have a PCI or AGP video card that you'd like to use in a multi-monitor configuration but it isn't listed here, be sure to check with the adapter's manufacturer. There might be new drivers that allow you to use multiple monitors.

ATI Mach 64 GX (GX, GXD,VT)
ATI Graphics Pro Turbo PCI
ATI Graphics Xpression
ATI WinTurbo
ATI Rage I, II, & II+
ATI All-in-Wonder
ATI 3D Xpression+ PC2TV
ATI 3D Xpression
ATI 3D Xpression+
ATI Rage Pro (AGP and PCI)
ATI Xpert@Work, 4 and 8 MB
ATI Xpert@Play, 4 and 8 MB
ATI All-in-Wonder Pro
S3 765 (Trio64V+)
S3 Trio64V2(DX/GX)
Diamond Stealth 64 Video 2001
STB PowerGraph 64V+
STB MVP 64

Miro TwinHead 22SD
Hercules Terminator 64/Video
Number Nine 9FX Reality 332 (S3 Virge)
Number Nine 9FX Reality 334 (S3 Virge GX/2)
Number Nine 9FX Reality 772 (S3 Virge VX)
California Graphics V2/DX
Videologic GraphicsStar 410
Cirrus 5436
Cirrus Alpine
Cirrus 5446
STB Nitro 64V
S3 ViRGE
ViRGE VX
ViRGE DX
ViRGE GX
Diamond Stealth 3D 2000

Diamond Stealth 3D 3000	STB WorkStation (2 and 4 output)
Diamond Stealth 3D 2000 Pro	Miro Crystal VR4000
Number Nine 9FX Reality 332	ET6000
STB Nitro 3D	Hercules Dynamite 128/Video
STB Powergraph 3D	STB Lightspeed 128
STB Velocity 3D	Compaq Armada
STB MVP/64	Trident 9685/9680/9682/9385/9382/9385
STB MVP/64 3D	Jaton Video – 57P

I Have Supported Video Card Adapters, but Will My Motherboard Support Multiple Monitors?

Windows 98 supports up to nine display adapters installed and running for multiple displays. However, only rare systems have nine free PCI or AGP slots available in the motherboard. Typically, if the motherboard has at least two free PCI slots for your video cards, Multiple Display Support works. You can also have a minimum of one free PCI slot and one free AGP slot as well, if your system is so equipped.

Under most circumstances, as long as you have the available slots for the video hardware to be installed into, you'll have no motherboard limitation stopping it from working.

Some Technical Discussion on Multiple Display Support

In order to get a better understanding of how Multiple Display Support works in Windows 98, I want to give you a little insight into what's going on, and some background information on the topic.

The Primary Display Adapter Is Chosen by Hardware Plug and Play

Multiple Display Support basically works on the idea of one *primary display adapter* and one or more *secondary display adapters*. Understanding which display adapter is your primary and why makes using multi-monitors much easier.

When your system first boots up, it finds the hardware attached to it, such as the disk drives, sound card, and of course the display adapters. On most systems, the PCI architecture has multiple PCI slots in the PCI bus chaining off one another. This means that the system finds a card at the beginning of that chain first, before it finds a card at the end. So if you have two PCI display adapters installed in the system, the card that is closest to the beginning of the chain becomes the primary display adapter. Understanding this fact is crucial when you're setting up your video cards.

Also, on systems with an AGP video card installed, you can expect that the AGP card is a secondary display adapter. This is because the PCI bus is configured by the system before the AGP bus. And because the first display adapter found by the system is usually going to be the primary, the AGP card is set as a secondary.

> **NOTE** On some newer systems, the Basic Input/Output System (BIOS) allows you to configure the AGP video adapter to be the primary display adapter in a multiple monitor configuration. Check your system's documentation for more information and to see if this is possible with your hardware.

The Significance of the Primary Display Adapter

For most everyday Windows usage, which adapter is your primary display adapter and which is your secondary has little consequence. However, there are some notable examples of exceptions that you'll want to be aware of.

Your primary display is the one that shows the boot messages from the system BIOS when you first power your system on. It is also the monitor showing the Windows 98 splash screen while Windows is loading.

> **NOTE** Remember that if you are using two PCI adapters, the one closest to the beginning of the PCI chain becomes your primary display adapter. If you power your system on and the wrong adapter is enabled as your primary, shut the system down and swap the two adapters' locations in the PCI slots. When you power back up, the correct adapter should be the primary.

If your primary display adapter happens to be a TV tuner card on which you watch WebTV or some other type of television, you will not be able to drag the TV viewing window onto the secondary monitor. This is due to the way multiple monitors are configured in Windows 98. The secondary adapter only handles basic SVGA functionality.

Items such as 3D acceleration are fully functional on the primary monitor. But if you want to run a full-screen DOS session, you won't be able to do it on the secondary monitor.

> **NOTE** Be sure not to use Windows 95 video drivers in a multiple monitor configuration. If you need to load any new drivers for any of your display adapters, be sure they're specifically built for Windows 98.

So basically you can see that the monitor that is your primary is exactly that: primary. There are some limitations that keep you locked to that primary monitor, but for the most part, things work on the secondary as they do on the primary.

Setting up Multiple Monitors

Setting your system up for multiple monitors is usually a rather painless process as long as you have display adapters that are supported in a multi-monitor configuration. Setup involves actually installing more than one video card into your system then installing the software to run the cards, and finally, configuring the whole thing to your liking.

Remember, you can have up to nine display adapters installed with Windows 98 multi-monitor support. However, through the rest of this chapter, I'll assume you are only using two adapters. The procedure is the same if you have more than two, but if you're like most folks, you'll at least be starting out with only two.

Installation

The first thing you need to do is obtain two video cards that are multi-monitor compliant. Check with Microsoft or the video card manufacturer to ensure that your cards are supported.

> **NOTE** You don't need to have two identical PCI or AGP display adapter cards in order to use Multiple Display Support on Windows 98. You need two cards that are specifically designated as working with multiple monitors. The cards can be different models or different brands; as long as they're supported you can use them.

Insert the first video card into the system, and then the second according to the manufacturer's instructions.

> **NOTE** As always, before opening the computer's case or installing new hardware, be sure to shut the power off on the machine, wait until you hear the hard drive spin down and the fans shut off, and unplug the PC from its power source. It's also a very good idea to place the machine on a static-free surface and to wear a static electricity-dissipating wrist strap while working on the innards of your computer. There are few things more frustrating than forgetting to ground yourself, touching your finger to a component inside the machine and having a static electricity spark jump from you to a metal conductor. In case this has never happened to you, Murphy's Law applies here—it usually happens at night, on a long weekend, and when you absolutely need to use your computer before the stores open up again. Two seconds of forethought can save you days of work.

Working with Multiple Monitors

Boot your system and start Windows 98. Note that the monitor that displays the Windows 98 splash screen is your primary monitor. If you would like the other display adapter to be the primary, power down your computer again and swap the cards in the two slots they are in (assuming both are PCI cards).

Windows finds the new hardware and installs software for the cards. You might be prompted for either the Windows 98 CD-ROM or a driver disk from the card manufacturer; if so, provide the disk requested. When Windows prompts you, restart the computer.

This time, as the system boots up, you again see the Windows 98 splash screen on the primary monitor, but you also see a message appear on the secondary monitor that reads:

```
If you can read this message, Windows has successfully
initialized this display adapter.
To use this adapter as part of your Windows desktop, open the
Display option in the Control Panel and adjust the settings on
the Settings tab.
```

If, by chance, your primary monitor comes up with a resolution of 640×480 and a color depth of only 16 colors, you need to change this setting to at least a 256 color depth before continuing.

To do so, open the Control Panel by either choosing Settings from the Start menu, or double-clicking the My Computer icon and selecting the Control Panel. In the Control Panel window, double-click the Display icon and choose the Settings tab in the resulting dialog box. Click the drop-down list to choose a color depth of at least 256 colors, click OK, and again reboot the system. Having the primary monitor operating at at least 256 colors is necessary to allow multi-monitors to work.

This time, when Windows finishes loading up, go back into the Display applet from the Control Panel and choose the Settings tab again. You'll see a drop-down list under Display that has a list of the installed adapters in the computer. Choose the secondary adapter from this list. Alternatively, you can use the mouse to click on the picture of the second monitor. When you do choose this monitor, Windows gives you a dialog box to let you know that you're about to enable the secondary adapter, as shown in Figure 15.1.

Then click the check box that reads Extend my Windows desktop onto this monitor. You might get a dialog box warning you that some programs don't work correctly with Multiple Display Support, as shown in Figure 15.2.

Click OK to the warning, and then click the Apply button on the Display Properties box. You see the secondary monitor spring to life.

Figure 15.1
Windows makes sure you want to enable the secondary adapter and monitor.

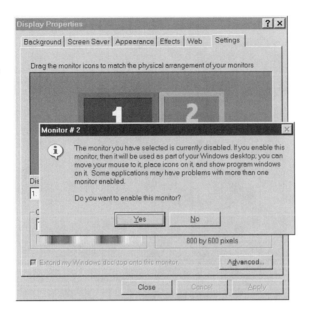

Figure 15.2
Windows lets you know that not all programs work with Multi Monitors.

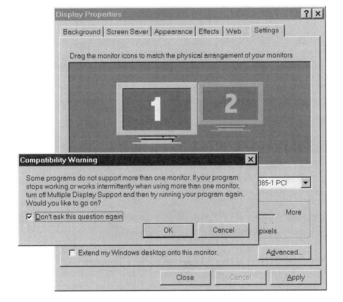

Working with Multiple Monitors

Configuring Display Settings

Now you have the basics of multiple monitors down. You should still have the Display Properties box open on your primary monitor, and your secondary monitor should be on with nothing on it. If the Display Properties box isn't visible, right-click the desktop and choose Properties to bring it back, as shown in Figure 15.3. When you're satisfied that the settings are correct, click OK to accept the settings and dismiss the dialog box.

Figure 15.3

The Display Properties box has a slightly different look when multiple monitors are installed.

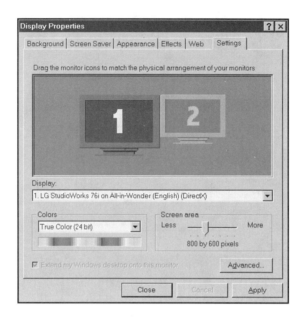

Slide your mouse pointer off the desktop display of your primary monitor and onto the secondary. Get used to the feel of having so much extra space on your desktop.

Customizing Each Monitor

Each monitor you have running can run at its own resolution, color depth and refresh rate. Feel free to change these settings in the Display Properties dialog box to suit your needs. There is no hard and fast rule; the only limitations are those of the video cards you're using.

And You're Off!

With your multiple displays now working, you have added a lot of room to your virtual desktop, as indicated by Figure 15.4. You can move things between monitors as you like, including desktop icons, toolbars, applications, and even the taskbar. What you do from here on out is totally up to you. Experiment a little bit to find what you like best and what's most convenient.

Figure 15.4

Get used to having a whole other monitor to drag your Windows items onto.

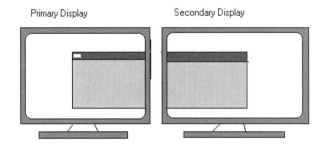

You might find that some programs won't be capable of being dragged onto the secondary monitor, but this limitation is rare and mostly confined to older applications. Be aware, however, that the secondary monitor has only basic SVGA functionality. You won't have the capability to use WebTV or 3D rendering on the secondary monitor. If you have any problems or questions, see the next section, "Troubleshooting Multiple Display Support."

As Microsoft recommends, try using some of the built-in Windows 98 programs to test out Multiple Display Support. Applications such as Paint (included with Windows 98) are perfect for testing. Open Paint by clicking Start, Programs, Accessories, and Paint. With the Paint application not maximized try dragging it from monitor to monitor.

> **NOTE**   You cannot drag any maximized window. When a window is maximized on one of your monitors, it is locked to that monitor. To drag a window to another monitor, restore the program to its normal windowed state then drag it to the monitor you want. After the window is on the proper display, you can again maximize it if you want.

Troubleshooting Multiple Display Support

Here are some of the most common issues people encounter with Multiple Display Support. I'll present the problem and suggest common workarounds, if any. If you have a problem that doesn't appear here, or resists your attempts to correct it, contact the technical support service of your monitor's or display adapter's manufacturer. Also, read the display TXT file in your Windows folder on your PC. This text file contains some valuable information.

Working with Multiple Monitors

Nothing Displayed on the Secondary Monitor

I don't mean to sound condescending, but some of the most common issues people have with regards to multiple monitors involve very simple oversights (I can attest to this—I've done it myself more than a few times). Before you dive in and start troubleshooting, check the simple and obvious things. For instance, is the secondary video card installed properly in the machine? Is the secondary monitor signal cable attached to the adapter? Does the monitor have power? These things are elementary but rather frustrating after you spend two hours trying to find out why it won't work, only to discover that the power cable was unplugged all along.

Is the Adapter Installed in Windows?

To see if Windows sees the adapter, open up the System Properties applet in Control Panel and click the tab for Device Manager. Open the Display Adapters drop-down list and check that all the display adapters you have in your machine appear there. If not, run the Add New Hardware Wizard in the Control Panel to install any missing ones.

Is the Adapter Enabled?

Make sure that you have enabled this display adapter for use in a multiple adapter configuration. Open the Display Properties applet and choose the secondary adapter from the list of installed adapters. Then ensure that the box is checked that reads Extend my Windows desktop onto this monitor. After it's checked, click OK.

Are the Right Drivers Loaded for the Adapter?

If the right drivers aren't loaded for your video card(s), multiple monitor support will not work.

Open the Display Properties dialog box and click the Settings tab. Click the Advanced button, and then the Adapter tab. Here you can tell if the currently installed driver is the proper one for the card that you have in the machine. If you're unsure, check with the manufacturer of the card.

Did Windows Correctly Initialize the Adapter?

After booting the machine, you should have seen the Windows 98 splash screen on your primary monitor, and a message on any secondary monitor you have reading.

```
If you can read this message, Windows has successfully
initialized this display adapter. To use this adapter as part
of your Windows desktop, open the Display option in the
Control Panel and adjust the settings on the Settings tab.
```

If you did not see this message on the secondary monitor, go into Device Manager and check under Display Adapters to see if the adapter is listed. If not, run the Add New Hardware Wizard from the Control Panel to install it.

Is a Supported Video Card Installed?

Make sure that any video display adapters you are trying to use in a multiple monitor configuration are supported. Use the list earlier in this chapter as a guide, as well as the Microsoft Knowledge Base, which you can find on the Internet at `http://support.microsoft.com/support`. Also, you can check with the documentation that came with the card or the manufacturer to see if the adapter is capable of working in a multi-monitor environment.

Unable to Use Multiple Monitors On a Laptop

This is a case of the hardware used in most current laptops not being capable of actually having more than one video card installed. If you have a laptop with a docking station attachment or some kind of cradle that allows you to hook the laptop up to a full-size monitor, mouse and keyboard on your desktop, you might not be able to use multiple monitors.

When a laptop is inserted into a docking station, the function of the display adapter is usually turned over to the docking station itself. The adapter that makes the LCD screen on the laptop work usually redirects its efforts to some extent when in the dock. It can let you view either the full-size monitor alone, the LCD screen alone, or both at the same time (showing the same screen—not multiple screens). Therefore, unless you have a docking station equipped with more than one display adapter, you might not be able to use Windows 98's multi-monitor capabilities in this situation. At this time, there aren't many docks that allow the use of more than one display adapter, but this may change in the future.

Installing and
Configuring Codecs

Configuring
Multimedia Drivers
in MS-DOS

Using WDM Drivers

Chapter

16

Using
Advanced
Multimedia

By Michael Porter

If you have been paying attention to the latest and greatest PC entertainment available, you will notice that 3D imaging and CD and DVD quality sound and graphics are now being deployed for greater realism in the electronic world. Computer games are the most influential medium that spreads this technology to the masses.

While this trend is a great way to bring the realistic images to an otherwise dull desktop, it does present some problems. These delightful sounds and images can take up quite a bit of space on your computer's physical drives (hard drives). Some average length videos (about 15 minutes) can range between 50–100MB in size when uncompressed, not to mention any accompanying files that might need to run at the same time. That might not seem like much in today's market where the average computer has 2GB of disk space, but imagine how quickly that space would be taken up if you had several files of this size and form. Full CD-quality, uncompressed stereo audio contains about 176KB for every second of sound. An entire CD-ROM can contain a little over an hour of music.

Before you panic, Windows has a solution to this dilemma called *codecs*. In this chapter, you'll learn what codecs are and how to install and configure them to improve your computer's multimedia performance. Then you'll take a look at returning to the venerable MS-DOS to configure multimedia drivers—a valuable skill, especially if you play games that run under DOS. Finally, this chapter discusses some advanced concepts regarding 32-bit device drivers that function under Windows 98 and Windows NT.

Installing and Configuring Codecs

As multimedia products have advanced in their capability to provide realistic sound, video, graphics, and CD-ROMs, and the Internet has increased the capability to transfer and transport greater amounts of information, the size of the data files needed to contain more detailed information has also increased. Whereas once you could carry your favorite images and sound bites around on a floppy disk, many files now exceed several megabytes (MBs) in size. So it's no wonder the need exists to compress these complex and often oversized files. To assist this process, Windows 98 (like Windows 95) has audio and video codecs (*compressors/decompressors*), which are algorithms used to compress and decompress files.

Codecs are used to play compressed files by decompressing them, during use, in memory. This process helps to conserve physical disk space on your computer. By using a codec, the system can utilize physical and virtual memory to access the desired file in expanded form, but when it's finished, the file remains unchanged on disk in its original compressed state. This way, you can have several audio/

visual applications on your computer, and plenty of files for each, without using up all your disk space. Adding a specific codec lets you play files compressed in that specific file format, which is discussed later in this chapter.

Codecs are required on the content creation side as well as the destination system to play that content back. If the content creator uses a codec that is not installed on the destination system, the affected multimedia file does not play back.

Installing a Codec

Windows 98 installs a number of default video and audio codecs when it runs its initial setup. You can see a list of these codecs on the Devices tab of the Multimedia Properties dialog box, as shown in Figure 16.1. To access this dialog box, open Control Panel by clicking the Start menu, choosing Settings and clicking Control Panel. In the resulting dialog box choose Multimedia and click the Devices tab. Click the plus next to the Video Compression Codecs label to see which codecs are installed.

Figure 16.1

The Multimedia Properties dialog box contains separate lists for audio and video codecs.

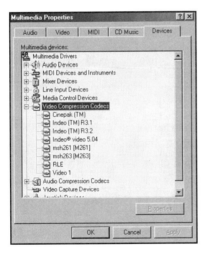

The default codecs, which come in the standard Windows 98 installation, include:

Video compression codecs:

- Cinepak (SuperMatch)

- Indeo R3.1 (Intel)

- Indeo R3.2 (Intel)

- Msh261 (M261)

- Msh263 (M263)

- Microsoft RLE

- Microsoft Video 1

Sound compression codecs can be divided into two groups:

1. Music-oriented codecs, such as IMADPCM, which allow close to CD-quality sound files to be compressed to about one-quarter of their original size.

2. Voice-oriented codecs, such as TrueSpeech, which allow extremely efficient compression of voice data.

You can access a list of sound codecs in the Multimedia Properties dialog box by double-clicking the Audio Compression Codecs category, as shown in Figure 16.2.

Figure 16.2

The Multimedia Properties dialog box lists audio codecs, but does not necessarily differentiate between those dealing with music and speech.

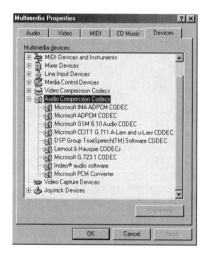

Sound can be played from a compressed sound file, or a sound file can be compressed using the Windows 98 Sound Recorder, which is a built-in sound recording and editing utility. If you have a microphone, you can turn on voice compression when recording so that the file is compressed in real-time. Read on for a list of Windows 98's default audio codecs.

> **NOTE**   To access Sound Recorder, click the Start menu, choose Programs, click Accessories, select the Entertainment category, and click Sound Recorder.

Audio compression codecs:

- Microsoft IMA ADPCM codec

- Microsoft ADPCM codec

- Microsoft GSM 6.10 audio codec

- Microsoft CCITT G.711 A-Law and u-Law codec

- DSP Group TrueSpeech™ software codec

- Lernout & Hauspie codecs

- Microsoft G.723.1 codec

- Indeo audio software

- Microsoft PCM converter

> **NOTE** Microsoft PCM Converter is the default codec for opening and recording WAV files. As a result, WAV files are universally playable in any Windows 98 system, because they all use the same default codec. To facilitate compatibility, this codec cannot be removed.

Don't panic if your list of codecs doesn't include all the ones I've listed as the Windows 98 defaults. To install the Windows 98 default codecs onto your system you'll need the Windows 98 installation CD-ROM.

To add all the default audio and video codecs in Windows

1. Click on Start, choose Settings, and then choose Control Panel.

2. In the Control Panel, choose Add/Remove Programs.

3. Select the Windows Setup tab, and then highlight Multimedia with a single-click.

4. Click the Details button and you'll see the dialog box shown in Figure 16.3.

5. Click the Audio Compression and Video Compression check boxes to select them, and then click OK.

6. Click OK again to add the selection. Windows 98 reads the CD-ROM and installs any missing codecs.

Using Advanced Multimedia

Figure 16.3

The Multimedia dialog box lets you install or remove individual Windows 98 multimedia components, including codecs.

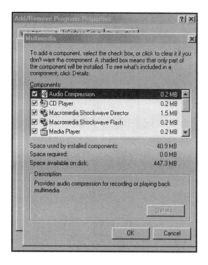

Sometimes you will have a multimedia device that uses a specific codec to compress and decompress files. For example, a 3D video accelerator will typically have a custom codec for a maximum compression with a minimal loss of information. Usually, when the device is installed, the codec is also installed by default. Occasionally, though, you will need to install it manually. The best way to accomplish this task is to reinstall the device with which it is associated. During this process, you will be prompted to install the necessary codec from the Windows default files or from the disk provided by the manufacturer.

To add a specific audio or video codec

1. Click Start, choose Settings, and then choose Control Panel.

2. In the Control Panel, choose Add New Hardware.

3. The Add New Hardware Wizard appears. Click the Next button.

4. Windows presents a dialog box informing you that it will now search for new Plug-and-Play devices, click the Next button.

5. If the device is not found, the Add New Hardware Wizard presents a dialog box asking if you want to search for non–Plug-and-Play devices; choose No.

6. The next dialog box lets you select which type of hardware you want to install. Scroll down and choose Sound, Video and Game Controllers, as shown in Figure 16.4.

Figure 16.4

By reinstalling your sound and video controllers, you'll also reinstall their associated codecs.

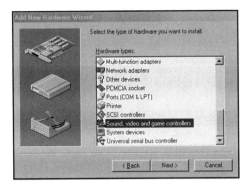

7. Choose the manufacturer in the Manufacturers box and a model in the Models box, and then click the Next button. What happens next might vary, as follows:

   ■ If the codec you want to install is not listed, it is not installed by Windows.

   ■ If the codec was included with another program, you must reinstall the program to reinstall the codec.

   ■ If the codec is located on a manufacturer disk, choose Have Disk and specify the location containing the files.

   ■ If Windows 98 finds a codec, click No to add the device to the list of installed devices.

   Depending on which method you used, follow the wizard's directions until it has loaded the appropriate files.

8. Click the Finish button.

Removing a Codec

By providing compression to multimedia files, codecs can save you a lot of hard drive space. But if you decide codecs are something you don't want to take advantage of, there's no reason to occupy disk space with them. Windows 98 makes this process simple and fairly foolproof.

To remove all default audio and video codecs

1. Click Start, choose Settings, and then choose Control Panel.

2. In the Control Panel, choose Add/Remove Programs.

3. Select the Windows Setup tab, and highlight Multimedia with a single-click.

4. The Details button will become active; click Details.

5. Click the Audio Compression and Video Compression check boxes to clear the checks, and then click OK.

6. Click OK again to remove the codecs.

> **NOTE**   All the default codecs, with the exception of the Microsoft PCM converter, are removable; you cannot remove the Microsoft PCM converter. Some file types, such as WAVs, use this codec to ensure universal compatibility. Also, PCM converter is Windows 98's "if all else fails, try this codec" codec.

Sometimes you won't want to remove all the default Windows 98 codecs. Rather, you might want to get rid of those associated with a device you no longer use. Here's how:

To remove a specific audio or video codec

1. Click Start, choose Settings, and then choose Control Panel.

2. In the Control Panel, choose Multimedia.

3. Choose the Devices tab.

4. You will now see the list of installed multimedia drivers. What you do next depends on what kind of codec you want to remove.

    ■ To remove an audio codec, click the **+** sign to see the installed audio compression codecs, and double-click the codec you want to remove to view its properties. (You can also right-click the installed audio compression codecs and choose Properties.) In the resulting dialog box, shown in Figure 16.5, click the Remove button.

Figure 16.5

You can remove an audio codec in its Properties dialog box.

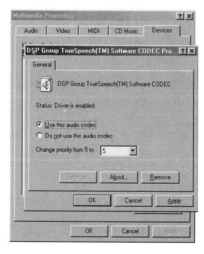

■ To remove a video codec, click the **+** sign to see the installed video compression codecs, and double-click the codec you want to remove to view its properties. (You can also right-click the installed video compression codecs and choose Properties.) In the resulting dialog box, shown in Figure 16.6, click Remove.

Figure 16.6

You can remove a video codec via this dialog box.

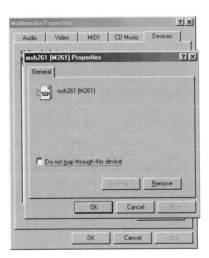

5. Choose OK until all the windows are closed.

Disabling a Codec

You might have an occasion where an application is attempting to use a codec that you don't prefer for a particular file. This might occur if you have a file that can utilize multiple codecs for compression and decompression but the codec it chooses by default does not give the best interpretation of the file in question. On these occasions, you can disable the undesired codec without removing it completely, so that you can enable it after you are finished with the specific file with which it conflicted. The process is similar to removing it, but you can easily reverse your action to restore the codec to function.

To disable an audio or video codec

1. Click Start, choose Settings, and then choose Control Panel.

2. In the Control Panel, choose Multimedia.

3. Choose the Devices tab.

Using Advanced Multimedia

4. You will now see the list of installed multimedia drivers.

■ To disable an audio codec, click the **+** sign to see the installed audio compression codecs, and double-click the codec you want to remove to view its properties. (You can also right-click the installed audio compression codecs and choose Properties.) In the resulting dialog box, shown in Figure 16.7, check the Do Not Use this Audio Codec radio button. The system will not use this device until you repeat this process, but instead choose the Use This Audio codec radio button.

Figure 16.7

Rather than removing a codec, you can temporarily disable it.

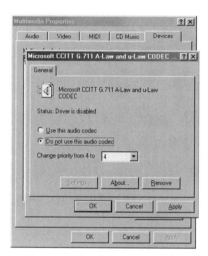

■ You could also change the priority of the audio codec you want to use. When audio codecs are equally capable of compression, the system will use them in the order of the priority assigned to them. By assigning a higher priority to the desired audio codec, you will direct the computer system to choose it over its alternatives.

■ To disable a video codec, click the **+** sign to see the installed video compression codecs, and then double-click the codec you want to remove to view its properties. (You can also right-click the installed video compression codecs and choose Properties.) In the resulting dialog box, shown in Figure 16.8, click the Do Not Map Through this Device check box to select it.

■ The system will not use this device driver until you have reactivated it via the same process or if a program specifically requests it. If the latter occurs and you still want to use an alternative codec, you might want to consider removing the video codec instead.

Figure 16.8

You disable video codecs in a similar manner as audio codecs.

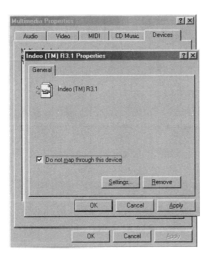

> **NOTE** Again, if you want to disable any multimedia device, you can disable it in its Properties dialog box by the same process as demonstrated earlier for audio and video codecs.

   5. Choose OK until all of the windows are closed.

Configuring Multimedia Drivers in MS-DOS

Windows 98 has a new look for MS-DOS called *DOS 32*. DOS 32 is a 32-bit version of the old 16-bit MS-DOS system. Even though this new version will give your MS-DOS application a faster system response, it has not taken the basic MS-DOS functions away.

Before you attempt to configure a program in MS-DOS, check to see if there is a built-in Windows 98 driver for your multimedia product. The process to install a multimedia device through Windows 98 is much simpler, and most times the driver is more appropriate for use with the operating system overall.

However, if you have tried and failed to use Windows 98's available drivers, you can still use MS-DOS to accomplish this task.

To start the system in MS-DOS, click Start, click Shut Down, and then choose Restart in MS-DOS mode. Insert the manufacturer's multimedia driver disk in your floppy drive and follow the instructions from the manufacturer.

Using Advanced Multimedia

Usually, when you install a driver in MS-DOS you run the Install.exe program. But occasionally the filename might be different, you might have to add a switch, or you might access the install routine through a batch file that calls for input. Again, consult the manufacturer's instructions to be safe.

If you want to load the driver while still in Windows 98, have no fear; most drivers will load in the MS-DOS window (also known as the *command prompt*) from within Windows 98.

To get the command prompt, click Start, click Programs, and then click MS-DOS Prompt.

Again, follow the manufacturer's instructions for installing the specific program or driver. Most MS-DOS driver installation programs will have an install executable (such as `Install.exe`) on the floppy disk, which guides you through the setup process.

Occasionally, the manufacturer will direct you to manually enter instructions in your system configuration files, such as `Config.sys` or `Autoexec.bat`. To do so, open an MS-DOS Command prompt window using the procedure described earlier, and find the `Config.sys` and `Autoexec.bat` files in the root directory. Type `edit Config.sys` or `edit Autoexec.bat` and press Enter.

The MS-DOS editor launches and opens the appropriate system configuration file. You can now edit your files to include the settings recommended by the MS-DOS program's documentation. When you are finished, choose Save from the File menu, choose Exit, and then type `exit` to close the DOS prompt window.

Running an Application in MS-DOS Mode

Windows 98 provides a flexible environment for running MS-DOS applications. Even those applications that must have exclusive access to system resources can be run in Windows 98's MS-DOS mode. MS-DOS mode is the equivalent of Real mode in earlier versions of Windows.

> **NOTE**   For those of you who need a refresher, Real mode was used by Windows 3.x to create an MS-DOS environment. While in Real mode, Windows 3.x gave up all control to the MS-DOS shell and, for all intents and purposes, the machine was running a purely MS-DOS environment.

When an MS-DOS application uses MS-DOS mode, Windows 98 removes itself almost entirely from memory so that the system can provide the application with full access to all the computer's resources.

To accomplish this disappearing act, Windows 98 will end all currently running tasks and programs. Next the system will load an MS-DOS shell. To properly load and run the application in MS-DOS mode, Windows 98 uses its customized versions of `Config.sys` and `Autoexec.bat`—not the ones you edited in the previous section. After you quit MS-DOS, Windows 98 will restart and return to the full Windows 98 user interface.

MS-DOS mode is intended for applications that will not otherwise run in Windows 98. It does not necessarily improve the performance of MS-DOS applications that will run in Windows 98 without using MS-DOS mode. Furthermore, when the system is using MS-DOS mode, you will not have access to any of Windows 98's features, such as multitasking.

Here are some options to consider before you decide to use MS-DOS mode:

■ Use other available property settings to optimize the performance of the application. I'll show you how to access these settings in a moment.

■ The MS-DOS program's Properties dialog box gives you several memory management options, as shown in Figure 16.9, for optimizing the application's performance applications without using MS-DOS mode.

Figure 16.9

The Properties dialog box for MS-DOS programs provides a variety of configuration options.

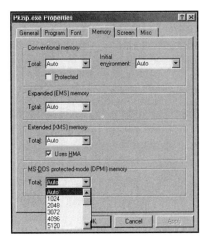

To access the configuration options, click the Memory tab. Here, you can configure the following memory settings:

■ Conventional memory

■ Expanded memory (EMS)

■ Extended memory (XMS)—with or without high memory

■ MS-DOS protected-mode memory (DPMI)

- Check the program's documentation for specific memory requirements or for special drivers that might need to be loaded.

- Open the application's Properties dialog box and click the Screen tab. Click the Full-screen radio button to run the application in Full-screen mode as opposed to an MS-DOS window.

> **NOTE**   In Windows 98, the Properties options replace the PIF Editor, which earlier versions of Windows used to optimize the settings for MS-DOS–based applications.

If you can use these alternative methods of optimization, you will have a much faster and convenient solution. Their main advantage is that you will still have the ability to multitask and to use Windows 98 drivers and settings that would be otherwise unavailable in MS-DOS mode.

Whenever possible, Windows 98 predetermines that an application needs to be run in MS-DOS mode. In such a case, Windows 98 closes down the other applications and automatically switches to this mode when the MS-DOS application is launched. By default, the system warns you when it is about to switch to MS-DOS mode.

Occasionally, you will try to run an application that gives you an error message telling you that you cannot run it in Windows. If this occurs, you have no choice but to configure it to use MS-DOS mode.

To configure an MS-DOS application to run in MS-DOS mode

1. Use Windows Explorer to browse to the application's executable file (its COM or EXE file).

2. Right-click the file's icon and choose Properties.

3. Choose the Program tab and click the Advanced button near the bottom of the dialog box to access the Advanced Programs Settings dialog box shown in Figure 16.10.

4. In the Advanced Program Settings dialog box, select the MS-DOS Mode check box.

5. Click OK twice to return to Windows.

When you've checked the MS-DOS Mode box, you will also have the option to customize the configuration for that particular MS-DOS program during run time. This feature is helpful if the MS-DOS application, such as a game, performs badly because of insufficient memory or a lack of appropriate drivers.

Figure 16.10

The Advanced Program Settings dialog box lets you force a program's execution in MS-DOS mode.

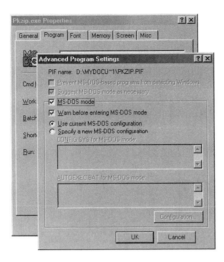

To take advantage of this feature, choose the Specify a New MS-DOS Configuration radio button. The `Config.sys` and `Autoexec.bat` files for that specific application now appear in the dialog box for you to edit, as shown in Figure 16.11. You can type new custom commands in either window.

Figure 16.11

You can specify special configuration settings for programs that run in MS-DOS mode.

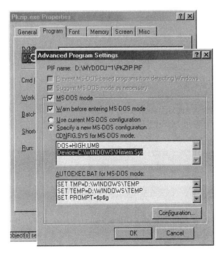

If you want to enable or disable additional options, such as expanded memory specification (EMS) or Direct Disk Access, click the Configuration button in the Advanced Program Settings dialog box. In the resulting dialog box, you can choose from a list of the available configuration options, such as those shown in Figure 16.12, to improve the MS-DOS application's performance.

Using Advanced Multimedia

Figure 16.12

You can designate a number of MS-DOS memory configuration options in this dialog box.

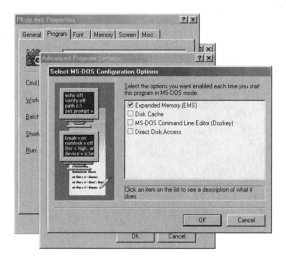

TIP   Here's a tip for users who are familiar with MS-DOS memory configuration:

Windows 98 automatically provides expanded memory for MS-DOS applications that require it to run. Windows cannot provide this memory, however, if you include a statement in `Config.sys` that loads `Emm386.exe` with the noems parameter. If you include `Emm386.exe` in `Config.sys`, use the ram parameter or use the x=*mmmm-nnnn(named range)* statement to allocate enough space in the upper memory area for Windows 98 to create an EMS page frame.

Another option that might affect the performance of your MS-DOS application is having an incorrect or missing path in the `Autoexec.bat` file. After you select a program to run in MS-DOS mode, you can also modify the path in the `Autoexec.bat` file for that specific program.

1. To take advantage of this feature, in the Advanced Program Settings dialog box, choose the Specify a New MS-DOS Configuration radio button.

2. In the Autoexec.bat for MS-DOS mode list box, type in the correct path.

NOTE   A *path* is a list of directories and subdirectories that DOS searches if it can't find a particular file or program in the current directory. You can specify this path in the `Autoexec.bat` file or enter a path from the command prompt (the path stays in memory). By default, MS-DOS searches for programs and files you invoke from the prompt (or that other programs and batch files request) in the current directory. A path statement in memory expands this capability and reduces the chance of returning a bad command or file name error.

For MS-DOS-based applications that do not run in MS-DOS mode, you can only set a working directory. The following options are available in these cases:

■ You can set a global path for all MS-DOS applications by adding or modifying a path statement in the default `Autoexec.bat`.

■ You can write a batch file that sets a path for the specific MS-DOS application by running the path statement immediately before the MS-DOS application is loaded.

  For example, you would write a specific batch file that sets the following path statement for your application: `path=%path%;c:\utils;c:\norton`. Then you would trigger the custom batch file to run its procedure before the MS-DOS application starts. To do so, use setting in the program's Properties dialog box.

To run a batch file before starting an MS-DOS application

1. In the application's (application executable file) Properties dialog box, choose the Programs tab.

2. In the Batch file text box, type the custom batch file's path and name, as shown in Figure 16.13.

Figure 16.13

You can designate a batch file to run in association with your MS-DOS program.

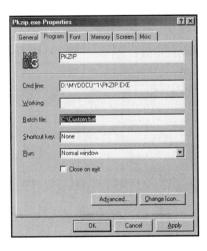

3. If you want the MS-DOS window in which the batch file is running to close after the batch file has finished, select the Close on Exit check box.

In most cases, MS-DOS games run under Windows 98 with no special adjustments. Most popular games are listed in the Windows 98 `Apps.inf` file. (You'll learn more about this file later in this chapter.) You do not need to specify certain PIF settings for these programs because Windows 98 should manage them automatically. These settings include foreground and background priorities, exclusive priority, video memory usage, and video port monitoring.

If you run a game that uses graphics modes and Windows 98 fails to run it in a full screen, hold down the Alt key and press Enter to switch to Full-Screen mode. To direct it to run the game in full-screen every time you open it, right-click its executable file, choose Properties, and then choose the Screen tab. Under the Usage heading, select the Full-Screen option, as shown in Figure 16.14.

Figure 16.14

You can specify that an MS-DOS program always runs in Full-Screen mode.

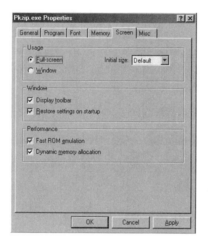

As you might have gathered by now, Windows 98 automates a whole slew of memory management tasks, making it easier for you to run your programs. Of course, when this automation fails, you receive the dreaded critical error message and the program shuts down. Running MS-DOS programs is a little more complicated because of the special configuration requirements some of them have. Here are some other issues that you might encounter using MS-DOS applications in Windows 98:

■ Some Windows and MS-DOS applications might not run well under Windows 98 because they were written to take advantage of characteristics of older operating systems. For example, certain applications use a portion of their title bar to include items other than the title, such as a Quick Help button. Because Windows 98 title bars are not formatted in the same way as Windows 3.x title bars, some information might be overwritten when you run these old applications.

■ Some MS-DOS applications use memory interrupts that are not automatically supported by Windows 98.

■ Some MS-DOS applications do not handle long file names well, or they incorrectly check for the operating system's version number.

■ If you are using an MS-DOS application that was designed for an MS-DOS version other than 7.1 (which is the version that Windows 98 uses), you might receive a message that says you are not using the correct version of MS-DOS. If this is the case, you can add the application to the version table. The *version table* contains a list of executable files, followed by the version number of MS-DOS with which the applications were designed to run. Windows 98 cannot report the correct MS-DOS version to applications unless the version table is loaded into memory.

You can display the version table to verify that it contains the proper notations for your MS-DOS programs.

1. Click Start, choose Programs, and then select MS-DOS Prompt.

2. Type `setver` in a command prompt window.

3. For information about the syntax, parameters, and switches you can use to add an application to the version table, add the question mark (?) switch to the command (that is, type `setver /?` at the command prompt).

   After you've confirmed that the version table is properly configured, you will want to ensure it loads with your DOS program. To load the version table, include a device command in your system's main `Config.sys` file, such as `device=c:\windows\setver.exe`. If you modify the version table or `Config.sys`, the changes will not take effect until the computer has been rebooted.

4. Some applications incorrectly check the version number of Windows 98. Incorrect version-checking techniques sometimes invert the two bytes that record the version number; thus, version 3.10 would be reported as 10.3. Windows 98 tries to accommodate this possible version-checking error by reporting 3.98 as the version. In this way, if an application looks for a version greater than 3.10 or its inverse, 10.3, the new Windows 98 version proves to be greater.

   Windows 98 Setup adds entries to `Win.ini` for many applications that are known to have this problem. Install your application first, and then edit the compiled module name in `Win.ini`.

   If the application looks for an exact match of the version number, such as Windows version 3.10, it might not run under Windows 98.

   To resolve this problem, add the following line to the Compatibility section of `Win.ini`:

   `compiled_module_name=0x00200000`

   If a setup application incorrectly detects the version of Windows 98, you might not be able to install the application. In this case, add an entry to the Compatibility section of `Win.ini` for the setup application (for example, SETUP=0×00200000). Install the application, and then immediately remove the section that you added to `Win.ini`. (Note that this is a generic example intended to give advanced users, familiar with the application they are working with, a place to start.)

5. Some setup applications do not check the version of the system files they are installing and overwrite the newer Windows 98 versions of some dynamic-link libraries (DLLs). Windows 98 restores its original DLLs after every setup application runs and for the first three startups thereafter. If an application stops running or behaves erratically after you install it, you might need to obtain an updated version of the application that does not overwrite Windows 98 system files.

   After you install an application, Windows 98 checks for files that are commonly overwritten by setup applications. If any are found, a dialog box appears enabling you to restore the files from the hidden \Windows\Sysbckup directory.

6. Earlier versions of Windows allowed applications to redistribute parts of the system with no ill effects. For example, an application might overwrite a system file with no adverse consequences until later, when Windows failed to find the file. In Windows 98, multiple system files have been consolidated to expedite the startup process. If an application tries to overwrite a system file that is no longer used, Windows allows the application to copy the file but does not use it. If your application must run with a replacement file, you can add that file to the \Windows\System\Vmm32 directory.

7. Many programming tools not specifically designed to run under Windows 98 might run satisfactorily, but the corresponding debugging tools usually do not. Make sure that both the programming and the debugging tools you use are designed for Windows 98. Some Win16 and MS-DOS disk utilities must be run with special care. In addition, some disk utilities do not perform correctly with long filenames.

8. Some older terminate-and-stay-resident programs (TSRs) rely on MS-DOS interrupts to monitor everything that happens on the system. However, because of its protected-mode file system, Windows 98 does not use MS-DOS interrupts. If Windows 98 detects that a TSR is trying to monitor these interrupts, it accommodates the application and sends all system information through MS-DOS interrupts. In this way, the TSR can monitor system events successfully. However, doing this significantly slows the performance of the operating system.

   Windows 98's `Ios.ini` configuration file includes a list of drivers and applications. If Windows 98 finds the application listed in `Ios.ini`, it will not send system events through MS-DOS interrupts, thus avoiding slowed performance.

Whew! With all these MS-DOS compatibility issues, it's easier to appreciate the uniformity that Windows 98 brings to program execution. Unfortunately, even if you've checked all the configuration pitfalls in the preceding pages, you still might wind up with an older program that stubbornly refuses to run under Windows 98. Fortunately, Windows 98 provides a possible solution.

Windows 98 provides the Make Compatible utility to make an application compatible with Windows 98. You can also use this utility to troubleshoot if you have printing problems, or if an application stalls or has other performance problems.

This utility provides the means to increase stack memory to an application, emulate earlier versions of Windows, and solve other common problems that might cause an application not to run with Windows 98.

To run the Make Compatible utility

1. Click the Start button, choose Run, and then type `mkcompat.exe` in the Run dialog box, as shown in Figure 16.15.

Figure 16.15

You can run Windows 98's Make Compat- ible utility by entering its executable file's name in the Run dialog box.

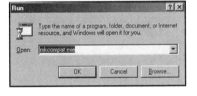

> **NOTE**   The Windows 98 `Apps.inf` file (in the \Windows\Inf directory) contains a section named PIF95 that acts as a master list of settings for MS-DOS applications. Each line in this section corresponds to a subsequent entry in `Apps.inf` that contains information about running that specific application.
>
> Following the PIF95 section are sections for each application listed in PIF95. Each application section includes entries that define any parameters, required memory or other options, and options that can be enabled or disabled for that application. For example, an entry for a DOS version of Microsoft Word might look like the following, which is also shown in Figure 16.16.
>
> ```
> [WORD.EXE]
>
> LowMem=384
>
> Enable=uus
>
> Disable=win,asp
> ```

Figure 16.16

Windows 98's
Apps.ini *file*
saves information
you supply about
MS-DOS
programs.

Windows 98 searches for the application instructions in the following manner:

- First, Windows 98 searches for a PIF file in the directory that contains the executable file you are starting.

- If it cannot find a PIF file there, it searches the default \Windows\PIF directory.

- If there is no PIF file in the \Windows\PIF directory, Windows 98 searches the path specified in **Autoexec.bat** file.

- If still no PIF file is found, it searches the **Apps.inf** file for a match.

- If Windows 98 does not find an entry for an application in **Apps.inf**, it uses default settings for the application.

- If you have replaced Windows 3.1 with Windows 98, a **_default.pif** file remains in the directory. In this case, Windows 98 uses information in the **_default.pif** file to create a PIF file for the application.

- If you do not have a **_default.pif** file and want to create one, you can do so by copying **Dosprmpt.pif** to **_default.pif**.

Regardless of how the settings for an application are initially established, you can always change them by right-clicking the application's executable file and using the various setting options provided in the file's Properties dialog box.

Using WDM Drivers

The following section is a little more advanced and is geared toward those hardware and software gurus who have been using Windows and MS-DOS for a while and understand how the operating systems and hardware interact through system calls and programming specifications. So if you have an interest in understanding what's going on behind the scenes or you simply aren't afraid to find out, read on.

WDM,(Win32 Driver Model), defines a device/driver architecture that provides a common set of I/O services understood by both Windows 98 and Windows NT. With WDM, developers can write a single bus driver or device driver for both operating systems. This allows for a tighter integration of programs between the two separate operating systems.

WDM is based on the concept of layers of driver classes. Each layer isolates portions of the services required of a device driver and allows hardware vendors to contain all hardware-specific functionality into a single file. Before WDM, device drivers had to include commands for each separate operating system, in addition to the particular instructions necessary to interact with a specific piece of hardware for each system.

In order to provide standardized support for a variety of computer devices, Windows 98 provides the following WDM drivers:

- USB—Windows 98 provides a Universal Serial Bus class driver and a PCI enumerator, and supports USB hubs, the Universal Host Controller Interface (UHCI) standard, the Open Host Controller Interface (OpenHCI) standard, and HID-compliant USB devices. The WDM Stream class provides additional infrastructure for most USB-compliant devices (most HID devices and imaging devices). The advantage for the user is that these drivers power the USB capability discussed in Chapter 10, "Working with USB Devices."

- IEEE 1394—Windows 98 provides an IEEE 1394 bus class driver and a minidriver for Texas Instruments Lynx, Adaptec host controllers, and 1394 OpenHCI-compliant host controllers.

One process that takes advantage of this technology is streaming audio and video, which is becoming more and more popular on the Internet. WDM streaming is directly based on the DirectShow model of user mode filters. In essence, this capability allows data streams to be passed through the operating system and move at a faster pace, because CPU cycles are not used to pass the information back and forth between the user mode and kernel levels. The result is better performance when listening to news reports over the Internet or watching a hit movie on DVD.

Using Advanced Multimedia

Additionally, a stream might be produced and consumed entirely in kernel mode, with little interaction elsewhere in the system. If the filters in between reside on the same physical hardware, they might negotiate a faster transfer or interface, which avoids memory copies and might completely eliminate the need to access the system's CPU in their communication. Again, this translates to a much faster and more realistic delivery of an end product.

Typically, the streaming of data involves loading an application responsible for handling large amounts of data in a constant load or stream, over time. The application never loads the data completely into memory; the data file is too large, and the operations on the data file are typically sequential. For example, DVD uses an MPEG-2 video stream. When a computer plays an MPEG-2 file, a program loads and streams the MPEG-2 data across the computer to be decoded and displayed. The data might enter and exit the host processor and bus of the computer several times during this process. In addition, an MPEG-2 stream starts out at approximately 5—10MBps. After the stream is decoded, the data transfer rate can easily exceed 100MBps.

Therefore, a single stream demands a potentially large and constant load on a computer, over what could be considered a long time in computer terms. For DVD, the system must be capable of independently managing and decoding at least four separate streams:

- MPEG-2 video

- AC-3 or MPEG-2 audio

- Subpicture

- Navigation

This management must be done so the streams are totally synchronized when they reach their final destinations, with no dropped frames or degraded video. This goal requires precision in load balancing, synchronization, and processing.

The WDM Stream class driver can deal with these problems because it is optimized to work with any devices that use streamed data. Such devices include those that encode data (for example, video capture devices), and those that decode data (for example, DVD hardware decoders that decode MPEG-2 streams for playing DVD movies).

WDM audio class architecture performs all audio processing in kernel mode. Any number of filters can be connected into the filter graph to manipulate audio/ video streams. WDM also provides a more complete architecture than was possible in earlier versions of Windows operating systems. Code common to all audio hardware on a given bus is now part of the operating system, making for faster development with more consistent results.

WDM audio also supports the following features for games under Windows 98:

- Software emulation of legacy hardware to support MS-DOS–based games. WDM drivers, which run in kernel mode, provide virtual Sound Blaster Pro, MPU 401, and legacy joystick interfaces. As a result, you can continue to enjoy your favorite DOS-based games even after upgrading to Windows 98.

- DirectSound support for software-simulated 3D sound (time delay and volume).

- A Wave table General MIDI synthesizer entirely in kernel-mode software. This provides 32 voices of music synthesis with 22.05KHz output. DirectShow, DirectMusic™, MMSYS, and virtual MPU 401 (via Sound Blaster emulation) can use the synthesizer functions. The architecture supports optimal configuration based on CPU performance and installed hardware. For more information on MIDI, see Chapter 11, "Working with MIDI."

- A high-quality, kernel-mode software sample rate conversion (SRC) capability, which converts data streams, including composite mixes of all 11.025KHz or 22.05KHz sources, to the final audio output mix format, typically 16-bit 44.1KHz (general SRC support includes other rates).

- A kernel-mode, system-wide software mixer that supports DirectSound, DirectShow, and MMSYS clients, as well as kernel-mode WDM filters, including CD-ROM and MIDI drivers. The mixer implements highly optimized pulse code modulation (PCM) mixing at 8-bit or 16-bit 11.025, 22.05, 44.1, and 48KHz. This mixer allows for the highest quality output for the program.

- Flexible control of the output destination. The WDM drivers can send the master 16-bit 44.1KHz or 48KHz or other format output to an Industry Standard Architecture (ISA), Peripheral Component Interconnect (PCI), Universal Serial Bus (USB), or IEEE 1394 audio device. While you'll likely have a relatively new sound card in your Windows 98 machine, WDM drivers ensure compatibility even with older cards such as the Sound Blaster 16.

- Native 32-bit DirectSound support for simultaneous audio input and output, not dependent on 16-bit MMSYS components. This capability is essential for such programs as NetMeeting, which provides real-time voice communications over the Internet.

Using Advanced Multimedia

WDM audio supports the following features for CD and DVD media playback under Windows 98:

- A kernel-mode, system-wide software mixer, which supports DirectSound, DirectShow, and MMSYS clients, as well as kernel-mode WDM filters, including CD-ROM and MIDI drivers. This provides more flexibility for programs that decode DVD audio. It also supports sound mixing at any available sampling rate.

- Flexible control of the output destination. The WDM drivers can send the master 16-bit 44.1KHz or 48KHz or other format output to an ISA, PCI, USB, or IEEE 1394 audio device. Additionally, support is provided for redirection of the PCI-device final-mix output to USB speakers.

- A kernel-mode CD-ROM driver that emulates MSCDEX commands and implements reading, parsing, and streaming of CD digital audio to the kernel-mode WDM system-wide mixer at 16-bit 44.1KHz.

- A Universal Disk Format (UDF) DVD file reader, splitter, and navigator that provides access for DirectShow clients to separate video and audio streams.

Through WDM technology, programmers are given the power to create much more efficient application drivers that can run under both Windows 98 and Windows NT operating systems. They also let Windows 98 use older "legacy" device drivers. By also adding support for new WDM drivers, Windows 98 gives you the best of old and new in one operating system.

What this means to you is less hassle for the setup and installation of the newest video and audio available for your computer with a more realistic playback than ever before.

Chapter

17

Getting the Most Out of Plus! 98

By Bruce Hallberg

When you buy a new house, you usually want to customize it with some personal touches. Maybe you want to paint the trim a different color, or change the window treatments, or maybe you even want to recarpet or put down some new wood floors.

Most people want to customize their computer environment in the same way. Microsoft Plus! 98 is a package of games, customization utilities, and applications that you can put to use immediately, whether you want to play a round of golf with your computer, customize your computer environment, or just enhance the capabilities of Windows 98 in some important ways.

Some of Plus! 98 is just pure fun. For example the three games included, Golf 1998 Lite, Lose Your Marbles, and Spider Solitaire, can provide a temporary retreat from your business day grind or create a pleasant diversion at home. The Organic Art screen saver is downright strange! The Deluxe CD Player will amaze you with its online Internet capabilities. Desktop themes can liven up your PC by creating a personalized multimedia environment with stylish colors, sounds, and pictures. Your PC might only be a computer, but it doesn't have to be dull!

Other parts of Plus! 98 are more serious. Disk Cleanup adds to the capabilities of the Windows 98 Maintenance Wizard. VirusScan helps protect you from computer viruses. If you have a scanner or work with digital images, Picture It! Express will be a great addition to your arsenal of programs. And the Compressed Folders program conveniently compresses (or *zips*) files with only a couple of mouse clicks—very useful when you want to archive files to save hard disk space or to send files via email.

Table 17.1 shows you the various components of Microsoft Plus! 98, the size of each component (so you can decide which components you might want to install), and a brief description of each component.

Table 17.1   Microsoft Plus! 98 Components

Name	Size	Description
Deluxe CD Player	1.6MB	With an Internet connection, your CD Player comes alive with instant updates of CD titles, artists, and songs
Picture It! Express	18MB	Lets you collect, edit, and enhance digital pictures
Desktop Themes	83.6MB	New sets of related wallpaper, sounds, and cursors for Windows 98 (each theme takes from 2–5MB; but you can install just the ones you're interested in)

Name	Size	Description
Golf 1998 Lite	48.5MB	If you're a golf addict, you'll love this realistic game
Lose Your Marbles	10MB	Game of skill from SegaSoft that lets you play marbles in a new way
Spider Solitaire	.6MB	A new version of the age-old Solitaire card game
VirusScan	8.3MB	Network Associates McAfee VirusScan for Windows 98 (with six months of free virus table updates)
Compressed Folders	.5MB	Lets you create folders in which the files are automatically compressed to take up less space
Disk Cleanup Add-ons	1.1MB	Adds the capability for the Disk Cleanup Wizard in Windows 98 to also identify and delete non-critical files for you
Maintenance Wizard	.1MB	Adds Start Menu maintenance and automatic virus scans to the capabilities in Windows 98 Maintenance Wizard
Organic Art Screen Saver	6.2MB	Strange, eerie, morphing artistic screen saver

As you can see, Plus! 98 comes with a wealth of add-on software for Windows 98, ranging from entertainment programs to useful utility programs that can keep your computer running smoothly.

Playing a Music CD (with Style)

Windows 98 comes with a program called CD Player that can play music CDs for you, but it's pretty plain. Sure, it does the job, but it doesn't do it with *style*. The Deluxe CD Player included with Plus! 98, however, is so full of features that you'll never want a different program to manage and play your music CDs.

The real power of the Deluxe CD Player is that it seamlessly interacts with the Internet to help you play and manage your music CDs. When you're connected to the Internet and insert a new CD into your CD-ROM drive, the Deluxe CD Player offers to go out to the Internet in order to update the name of the album and all the tracks automatically. Other, less sophisticated CD players make you type in all of the album and track information, but the Deluxe CD Player does this for you. For example, Figure 17.1 shows what happens when you insert a new music CD into your computer.

Figure 17.1

The Deluxe CD Player offers to get the album information from the Internet for you.

Better yet, after the Deluxe CD Player learns the names of the album and all the tracks, it stores them in a personal music CD database, so the information will be handy when you insert the CD again in the future. More impressively, you can use the Internet button on the Deluxe CD Player to quickly read reviews about the inserted album, find similar music, find other albums by the same artist, or read more about the artist. Figure 17.2 shows the contents of the Internet button with a sample album.

Figure 17.2

Use the Internet button on the Deluxe CD Player to find out more about the music CD you're playing.

Using the Deluxe CD Player

Aside from its nifty Internet features, the Deluxe CD Player works like most CD players. Figure 17.3 shows you the buttons on the Deluxe CD Player and what they do. As you can see, the icons shown on the buttons duplicate the icons that you see on most real CD players.

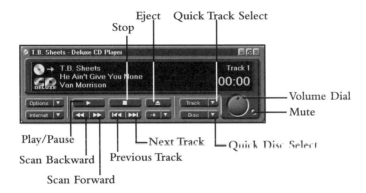

Figure 17.3

The buttons on the Deluxe CD Player.

Editing the Play List

Even on the best albums, there are probably certain songs that you just don't care that much about. One of the nice things about the Deluxe CD Player is that you can edit the playlist for each album, making the player automatically play only the songs you like best, in whatever order you want. To edit the playlist

1. Click the Options button on the player.

2. Choose Playlist from the menu.

3. Select the album in the Playlists tab of the Preferences dialog box (see Figure 17.4).

4. Click the Edit Playlist button.

5. Using the CD Playlist Editor dialog box (see Figure 17.5), you can perform the following functions:

   ■ Remove a track by clicking a track name, and then clicking the Remove button.

   ■ Add a track that was previously removed by choosing the track in the Available Tracks drop-down list box, and then click the Add to Playlist button.

   ■ Change the order of played tracks by dragging them up and down in the Playlist window.

   ■ Return to the default album playlist by clicking the Reset button.

Figure 17.4

Choosing an album in the Preferences dialog box's Playlist tab.

■ Start with a clear playlist from which you can build your desired playlist by clicking the Clear All button.

■ Change the artist name, album name, or track names by editing the names in the appropriate field.

6. Click OK to close the CD Playlist Editor dialog box, and then click OK again to close the Preferences dialog box.

Figure 17.5

Using the CD Playlist Editor dialog box.

Setting the Play Mode

Sometimes you might want to introduce some variety in how your music CDs are played. There are a number of different play modes from which to choose with the Deluxe CD Player. Changing the play mode is easy:

1. Click the Mode button on the player.

2. From the resulting menu, choose one of the following:

   ■ *Standard.*   This option plays all the tracks on the CD, or the playlist if you've set one up.

   ■ *Random.*   This option plays the tracks in a random order.

   ■ *Repeat Track.*   You can choose this option while a track is playing to request that it be played again after it is finished.

   ■ *Repeat All.*   Choosing this option causes the entire CD (or playlist) to be played again.

   ■ *Preview.*   This play mode previews each song for five seconds, or the amount of time you've set in the Preferences dialog box.

Configuring Settings

There are a number of settings you can use with the Deluxe CD Player to further customize its operation. You access these other settings with the player's Preferences dialog box, which you access by clicking the Options button, and then choosing Preferences. There are three tabs in the Preferences dialog box: Playlist, which you've already learned about; Player Options; and Album Options. Figure 17.6 shows the Player Options tab.

The Playback Options section of the Player Options tab lets you choose how the player responds to CD events. You can choose to make the player start automatically when a music CD is inserted, stop automatically when you exit the player, force the player to stay on top of any other open windows, and add a control to the taskbar that can recall the player whenever you like. The Time Display Options section controls what time measurement is displayed in the player while a CD is playing. The Preview Time section lets you choose how long each song should play when you use the Preview play mode.

Clicking the Advanced Audio button displays the Advanced Volume Control dialog box, as shown in Figure 17.7. You can use this dialog box to choose which of several CD players the CD player should use, what installed audio mixer the music CD should be patched through, and how you want to control the volume of the CD player.

Figure 17.6

Use the Player Options tab of the Preferences dialog box to configure general settings.

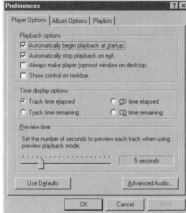

Figure 17.7

The Advanced Volume Control dialog box.

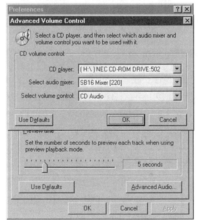

The Album Options tab of the Preferences dialog box (see Figure 17.8) lets you choose how the player interacts with the Internet. There are two important setting areas on this tab. The first lets you choose how album information is downloaded from the Internet. You first choose whether the player should simply download album information automatically and whether you want to be prompted for it to do so. You then choose which Internet music information provider you want to use by default (you can choose either Tunes.com or Music Boulevard). The second important setting concerns whether *Album Download Batching* will be used. This feature remembers times when you inserted a music CD and you weren't connected to the Internet. You can connect to the Internet later, and then use this dialog box's Download Now button to get information on all the CDs you inserted during those times—this is a nifty feature.

Figure 17.8

Use the Album Options tab to set Deluxe CD Player Internet settings.

Working with Picture It! Express

Another useful application included in Plus! 98 is Picture It! Express (PIE). (By the way, doesn't it seem like Microsoft's marketing department has a surplus of exclamation points?) Picture It! Express, also known as PIE, is an entry-level version of the full program, called Picture It! 99. Both levels of Picture It! are used for working with digital pictures and photographs on your computer. Using these programs, you can add special effects, clean up photo problems, such as film scratches or red-eye effects, and you can manage your picture collection.

PIE, while being an entry-level program, still has useful features with which you can be productive, such as the following:

- Crop, flip, and rotate images

- Build collages using multiple pictures (or portions of different pictures)

- Soften edges of photos

- Repair red eye automatically

- Adjust color, tint, and brightness

- Import and work with images in a variety of file formats (such as .JPG, .TIF, .GIF, PhotoCD, and others)

- Export edited photos into most file formats (such as .JPG, .GIF, and so on)

You can also choose to upgrade to the full version of Picture It! 99, which adds quite a few additional features, such as the capability to paint on photos, create cards, use fancy text, and fix dust marks and scratches on photos. You can learn more about Picture It! 99 from Microsoft's Web site at: `http://www.microsoft.com/products/prodref/688_ov.htm`.

Opening an Image

PIE can open images from several different sources. You can open images stored on a disk, CD-ROM, hard disk, digital camera, or scanner, or you can retrieve images from a special photo-processing service on the Internet called PhotoNet, because PIE is a PhotoNet-enabled product. For more details, go to the PhotoNet Web site at: `http://home.photonet.com/partners/enabled_products.html`.

To open an image for editing

1. Click the Get Picture button.

2. Choose from the available choices:

   - *My Picture.*   Use this to open files stored locally, such as on a disk, CD-ROM, or your hard disk.

   - *Scan Picture.*   If you have a TWAIN-compatible scanner installed on your computer, you can use this option to call up the scanner's software to scan a picture.

   - *Digital Camera.*   If you have compatible digital camera software installed, this choice calls up the software for transferring images from the camera.

3. If you chose either Scan Picture or Digital Camera in step 2, use the
   software that appears to select an image for editing. If you chose My
   Picture, you see a folder navigation screen (see next step).

4. Use section 1 of the PIE screen (see Figure 17.9) to select the folder that
   holds the pictures. When you choose the folder, the available pictures
   appear in thumbnail form in the browse area of the screen, as shown in
   Figure 17.9.

5. Double-click one of the available images to open it for editing, type the
   picture's name in the field provided, or drag a picture from the preview
   frame to the Filmstrip.

Figure 17.9
*Browsing for
photos in PIE.*

Saving and Printing Images

When a picture is open and you've worked with it, you'll want to save it and
perhaps print it. You might even want to set it to be your desktop wallpaper—
there's a quick way to do this with PIE.

To save a picture

1. Make sure the picture is selected (double-click it in the Filmstrip if you're
   not sure).

2. Click the Save, Print, & Send button.

3. Choose either Save or Save As.

4. If you choose Save, the picture will be saved using its original name. If you choose Save As, you'll be prompted for the location to which you want to save the picture, the graphic file format to be used, and the filename you want.

To print a picture

1. Make sure the picture is selected (double-click it in the Filmstrip if you're not sure).

2. Click the Save, Print, & Send button.

3. Click the Print This Picture button. You'll see the Print dialog box shown in Figure 17.10.

Figure 17.10

You can send any image to your printer.

4. Set the following options for the printout, and then click the Print button.

    ■ If you have more than one printer, choose the one you want with the Click a Printer button.

    ■ If you want to check your printer's settings, click the Change Printer Settings button.

    ■ Choose the Number of Copies.

    ■ Choose an orientation.

- Choose the print size. You can choose Fit to Page or any other size of printout you want (within the limitations of your printer). If you choose a custom size to print, consider clicking the Maintain Proportions button so that the picture doesn't get distorted.

- Choose a print quality, and select if you want to use color management or not. Some printers support color management that can work with PIE, helping you automatically get the closest printed colors possible for a given image.

Modifying an Image with Picture It! Express

By far the most interesting things you can do with PIE involve correcting and editing photos on the system. The following sets of steps show you how to accomplish the different editing functions available. For example, to modify image size or position

1. Click the image in the Filmstrip and choose Switch To in the dialog box that appears.

2. Handles now appear around your picture, as shown in Figure 17.11. You can use these handles to resize (drag the corner or side handles), rotate (drag the long handle), or move (drag from the center) your picture.

Figure 17.11

Handles let you resize and rotate pictures.

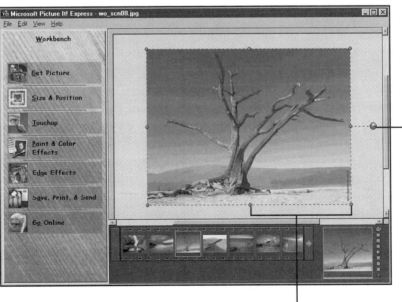

Edge and corner handles

Rotation handle

If you'd like to edit out unwanted portions of a picture, you can crop it. Cropping images is useful for two reasons: first, some pictures look a lot better if they're properly cropped; second, if you're building a collage of different pictures, you can crop out just the portions you want and paste them all together into your final collage. To crop a picture

1. Click the Size & Position button.

2. Click the Crop button. You see the Crop screen, shown in Figure 17.12.

Figure 17.12

You can crop out unwanted portions of your photos.

3. Choose one of the shapes, scrolling through the list as necessary.

> **TIP** Picture It! 99 allows you to do freehand cropping, whereas PIE is limited to cropping with the shapes shown.

4. Use the handles of the visible shape to select an area of the photo, resizing the crop area as necessary. Keep adjusting the crop area until just the area you want is highlighted within the crop marks.

5. Click the Done button to make the crop.

> **TIP** You can also quickly rotate or flip pictures using built-in functions. Click the Size & Position button, and then click either Flip or Rotate. The appearing dialog boxes then give you quick ways to accomplish either of these functions.

Resizing and cropping aren't the only editing tools you have at your disposal. For example, there's another one I find particularly useful. I don't know why it is, but you'd think I had some sort of pact with the devil; pictures of me *always* have my eyes glowing eerily red. And this happens with lots of people when flash photography's involved. However, if you're working with PIE, you can quickly and easily correct such problems. Here's how:

1. Select the photo for editing.

2. Click the Touchup button.

3. Click Fix Red Eye, which brings up the Red Eye correction dialog box shown in Figure 17.13.

4. Zoom in on the picture so that just the two eyes of the person are visible.

5. Click once on the reddest spot of each eye.

6. Click the Smart Task Fix button.

Figure 17.13
Use this dialog box for fixing red eye problems.

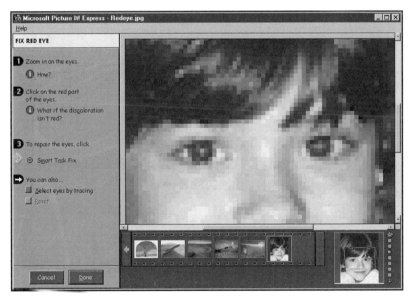

> **TIP** If the preceding steps don't properly resolve the red eyes, or the resolution causes other problems, such as turning their lips brown or something, then you might try clicking the Select Eyes by Tracking button, which lets you choose just the red portions of the eyes for correction.

You can give pictures a softened edge to help highlight the central theme of the picture. You can use this technique with portraits, for example, to produce professional-looking results. To soften the edges of your pictures

1. Select the picture to edit.

2. Click the Edge Effects button, and then the Soft Edges button, which is the only choice.

3. Use the slider to adjust the amount of softness to impart. After releasing the slider, the softening will be previewed for you; click Done to make the change permanent.

If you've been taking pictures for any length of time, you know how hard it is to get the lighting exactly right. Many pictures come out too dim, or with distorted colors. Or sometimes, the negative might be accurate, but when printed its colors seem off, or you might like to brighten it up. Fortunately, you can adjust your image's brightness and contrast by following these steps:

1. With the picture selected, click the Paint & Color Effects button.

2. Click the Brightness & Contrast button

3. In the resulting dialog box (see Figure 7.14), click the Smart Task Fix button to try to automatically adjust the brightness and contrast.

4. If Smart Task Fix doesn't work well, use the brightness/contrast/richness wheel to try different settings, or type different settings into the appropriate fields.

Figure 17.14

Use this dialog box to adjust the picture's brightness and contrast.

Another way you can alter the appearance of colors in your image is to change the tint, not unlike the tint control on your television set. Here's how you use it in Picture It! Express:

1. With the picture selected, click the Paint & Color Effects button, and then the Correct Tint button (see Figure 17.15).

2. Click the picture on as pure a white area as you can find; this causes the Smart Task Fix feature to try to automatically adjust the picture's tint.

3. Alternatively, use the color wheel to select a color, and then use the slider beneath it to increase or decrease that color.

Figure 17.15
Adjusting a picture's tint is easy in PIE.

Customizing Your Desktop with Plus! Themes

The Plus! 98 package includes a large number of new desktop themes that you can choose to customize your Windows 98 environment. These themes span a variety of different interests, and you're sure to find a few that you like to use. Each desktop theme is a collection of professionally choreographed and designed desktop wallpaper, screen savers, mouse pointer cursors, Windows sound events, icons, and fonts.

Selecting a Plus! 98 Theme is easy. Here's what you do:

1. Click the Start button, select the Programs menu, open Microsoft Plus! 98, and then Desktop Themes.

2. You'll see the Desktop Themes dialog box shown in Figure 17.16.

3. Scroll through the Theme drop-down list at the top of the dialog box to choose from the available themes. The theme will be previewed for you.

4. After finding a theme you like, select or deselect the check boxes in the Settings section at the right of the dialog box to choose which aspects of the theme will be applied to your desktop—wallpaper, sounds, fonts, screen savers, and more, in any combination.

5. When you decide on a particular theme, click OK to apply the theme to your PC.

Figure 17.16

Using the Plus! 98 Desktop Themes dialog box.

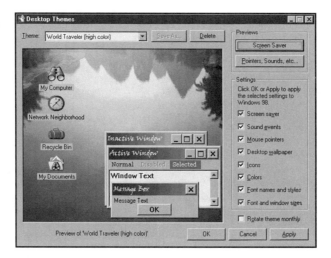

Introducing Plus! Games

There are three games included with Plus! 98. Although these games can't compete with the likes of Quake II, Doom, or Flight Simulator 98, they are well designed and enjoyable nonetheless.

- *Microsoft Golf 98 Lite.* A single-course version of the full Golf 98 game, this is one of the more impressive golf games available for PCs. It features photo-realistic players and golf courses, as you can see in Figure 17.17, instructional videos, and sound and commentary. If you're a golf fan, give it a try!

- *Lose Your Marbles.* In this quickly addictive game, shown in Figure 17.18, you try to line up three marbles of the same type in order to remove them from the board (sort of the way you line up blocks in Tetris). If you can keep from letting the playing field get full before the computer opponent's does, you win!

■   *Spider Solitaire.*   This game puts a different spin on the classic Solitaire game. The player tries to arrange the cards into straight suits within the rules of the game.

Figure 17.17

You can shoot a birdie on a virtual golf course in Microsoft Golf 98 Lite, included with Plus! 98.

Figure 17.18

Don't lose your marbles when playing this colorful logic game.

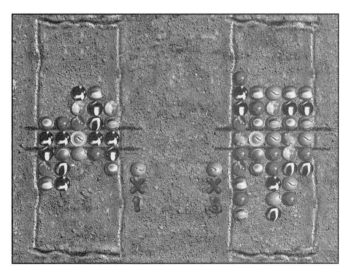

Keeping your Computer Virus-Free with VirusScan

Even if you're not familiar with computer viruses, you've probably heard woeful tales of the damage they can do. In reality, viruses are quite simple—they're small and they covert programs that can get into your computer and cause all sorts of mischief, ranging from causing strange things to appear on your display to locking up your computer, to even malicious actions such as erasing your hard disk and all your files. They are written, generally, by hackers for whatever mischievous reasons they have. Your computer can get infected by a computer virus—there are thousands of different types—by downloading and running programs from the Internet or running programs given to you by other people on disk. Even word-processing documents can contain macro viruses. Because computer viruses tend to hide until some sort of trigger goes off to activate them, they're not obvious and it's easy to get one and not even know you have it.

Fortunately, included with Plus! 98 is a version of McAfee VirusScan from Network Associates. This program, which is a well-respected antivirus program, can do two things to help protect you from viruses:

- Scan your computer regularly, looking for viruses that are known to VirusScan.

- Scan the memory in your computer, watching for any suspicious activity that might indicate the presence of a computer virus.

When viruses are detected, VirusScan can remove most of them safely. Let's look at this program in more detail.

Scanning for Viruses

You can perform a scan of your computer with VirusScan whenever you like. Usually, the scanning process is fast and should take—on most systems—not more than 10–15 minutes.

To scan your computer for viruses

1. Click the Start menu and choose Programs. From the Microsoft Plus! 98 menu, choose the McAfee VirusScan submenu, and then choose VirusScan.

2. After VirusScan does a quick scan of your computer's memory, looking for any active viruses, you see the main VirusScan window shown in Figure 17.19.

3. On the Where & What tab, choose which hard disk (or folder) you want to scan.

4. Click the Scan Now button to start the scan.

Figure 17.19

McAfee VirusScan's simple interface leads to powerful antivirus protection.

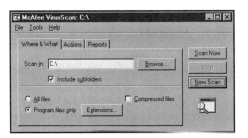

> **NOTE** The best results are usually obtained when you use the Program Files Only scan option in the Where & What tab of VirusScan. This scans all COM, EXE, and DLL files, as well as others that commonly harbor viruses (such as DOC and XLS files).
>
> You usually won't improve VirusScan's capabilities to find viruses if you use the All Files option; your scan times will increase dramatically, and VirusScan will be looking in files that either don't or can't contain viruses.
>
> If you're worried about a particular file type, you can add it to the list of files checked by the Program Files Only scan. Click the Extensions button, and then click the Add button on the resulting dialog box to add a new file type.

The default settings in VirusScan's Action and Report tabs will be fine for almost all users. VirusScan will log any viruses it files into a file shown on the Report tab, will inform you about these viruses, and will ask you what action you prefer to take. You might want to spend a couple of minutes looking at the options on the Action and Report tabs so that you're familiar with these different choices, but you'll probably be happy with the defaults.

> **TIP** If you want to get a sense of how many different viruses VirusScan can search for, pull down the Tools menu and choose Virus List. You can select any of the viruses and click the Info button for more information about that particular program.

Updating VirusScan

A virus scanner is only as good as its list of known viruses. Because new viruses are introduced into the wild almost every day, it's important to keep the list of viruses that your scanner can recognize updated regularly. With the included version of VirusScan, you can update its list of viruses over the Internet for six months from the first update. To do so

1. Connect to the Internet.

2. Open VirusScan.

3. From the File menu, choose Update VirusScan.

4. Your registration information will be confirmed if this is the first time you've updated VirusScan.

5. You'll be offered the choice to either update the virus definition files or to upgrade the entire version of VirusScan. I recommend that you only download the update. Updating the definition table takes about 20 minutes with a 28.8Kbps modem.

Configuring Virus Monitoring

You'll remember from the beginning of this section that there are two ways that VirusScan can help you. I just described the first—the VirusScan program that looks for viruses in memory. The second is with a companion program called VShield. VShield watches your computer *as you use it* and examines files that you open, work with, and save. If there are viruses in these files, VShield detects them. VShield can also watch your disk drives to make sure that you don't inadvertently use a disk that has a virus on it.

To configure VShield

1. From the Microsoft Plus! 98 folder, choose McAfee VirusScan, and then choose VShield Configuration.

2. You'll see the VShield Configuration dialog box shown in Figure 17.20.

3. Use the Scan Files On area to choose which activities will cause VShield to check the contents of files (usually, leave all these selected).

4. Use the Scan Floppies On area to select when disks will be scanned. Choosing Access causes them to be scanned whenever you access a file on them (after insertion). Choosing Shutdown does a scan for a certain kind of virus that can infect a computer if you mistakenly try to boot the computer from the disk.

5. The What to Scan area of the dialog box works just like it does in VirusScan.

6. Finally, you can choose if VShield starts automatically when you start the computer, whether or not it can be disabled (sometimes you might want to improve performance), and whether or not an icon will appear, allowing quick access to VShield on the taskbar.

Figure 17.20

Configure VShield to keep an eye out for viruses.

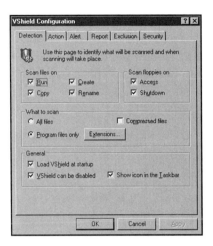

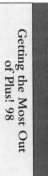

Click the other dialog box tabs—Action, Alert, Report, Exclusion, and Security— to set additional parameters for how VirusScan will provide feedback on viruses detected, what actions to take, reporting methods, and security rules. Generally speaking, these settings can be left at the default values.

Conserving Disk Space with Compressed Folders

If you've been using computers for awhile, you're probably familiar with compressing files using the Zip file format. *Zipping* a file means to use a utility program that can minimize the amount of room the file takes on your computer's disk drives. There are a variety of utility programs available that can do this for you, ranging from the original PKZip (from PKWare, `http://www.pkware.com/`, the designers of the original Zip program), to others such as WinZip, `http://www.winzip.com/`.

Usually you want to zip, or compress, files that you don't frequently access, particularly when you can realize significant space savings by doing so. Most document files, such as Word or Excel documents, can be compressed to about 15 percent of their original size. Other types of files have different amounts of savings, depending on how compressed they are naturally. For example, most graphics files (such as GIF or JPG) are not greatly compressible; those formats already compress the file contents about as much as is possible.

Included in Plus! is a utility that lets you create special folders under Windows 98. Anything placed into those folders is automatically compressed using the Zip format. The neat thing about Compressed folders is that you don't have to do anything special to compress or decompress the files; just copy the files into the folder to compress them, and either open them from within the folder or copy them to another location to decompress them. Nothing could be simpler! Even better, you can give an entire Compressed folder to another user, and they can access its contents using standard Zip archive utilities; they don't need the Compressed Folders utility from the Plus! pack.

To create a compressed folder, follow these simple steps:

1. Open the folder into which you want to create the Compressed folder or you can create the folder on the Windows desktop.

2. Right-click in a blank area of the folder or desktop and choose New from the pop-up menu.

3. Choose Compressed Folder from the available choices.

By default Compressed folders will be created with an extension of ZIP. You can accept that extension, change it, or remove it. However, it's usually a good idea to keep it, because it will identify the compression type if you ever send or give the folder to another user. Remember, by default, folders have no extension at all.

You can see the power of Compressed folders by running this experiment:

1. Create a Compressed folder on your desktop, or in whatever location you would like.

2. Identify another folder of yours that contains documents or other files that you want to compress.

3. Copy the contents of the normal folder into the Compressed folder.

4. For each folder (the normal one and the compressed one), right-click the folder and choose Properties from the pop-up menu. Examine the amount of space being used by each folder's contents.

For example, examine the two Properties dialog boxes shown in Figure 17.21. On the left you can see a sample folder containing a number of documents. The sample folder contains 1.7MB of files, which consume 2.57MB of disk space (the difference is due to inefficiencies in how Windows stores files). On the right you can see the Compressed folder, with identical—but compressed—copies of all the files. The Compressed folder has files taking up only 525KB of space (only 31 percent of the originals), and only consumes 540KB of disk space (only 21 percent of the original).

Compressed folders have another advantage over normal folders: You can also choose to encrypt the contents of a compressed folder. What encryption does is scramble the contents of all the files within the Compressed folder using a password you supply. Without the password, the contents of the folder are unreadable.

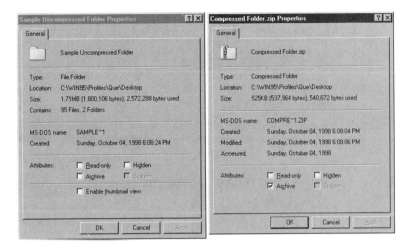

Figure 17.21

Comparing identical contents between a normal and Compressed folder shows substantial disk savings.

To encrypt the contents of a Compressed folder

1. Right-click the Compressed folder.

2. Choose Encrypt from the pop-up menu.

3. In the password dialog box that immediately appears, type in the password you want to use, twice, making sure that you type exactly the same both times.

4. When you click OK, the folder's contents are then encrypted using the supplied password.

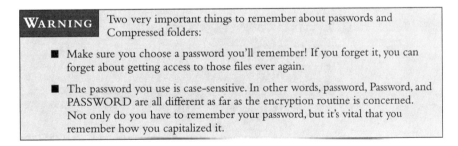

WARNING Two very important things to remember about passwords and Compressed folders:

■ Make sure you choose a password you'll remember! If you forget it, you can forget about getting access to those files ever again.

■ The password you use is case-sensitive. In other words, password, Password, and PASSWORD are all different as far as the encryption routine is concerned. Not only do you have to remember your password, but it's vital that you remember how you capitalized it.

There are two ways to decrypt the contents of an encrypted Compressed folder. First, if you access any of the files within the folder you'll be prompted for the password, and the file will be loaded or copied for you. Second, you can decrypt the entire folder by right-clicking the folder and choosing Decrypt from the pop-up menu. Supply the appropriate password, and the entire folder's contents will be decrypted for you. Also keep in mind that an encrypted compressed folder *can be* deleted so don't develop a false sense of security.

Plus! 98 Improvements to Disk Cleanup

Windows 98 comes with a utility called Disk Cleanup that helps you quickly find files that can be safely discarded when you run short of space. The only problem is that it isn't all that good at finding files that you can dispose of. Fortunately, Plus! 98 comes to the rescue with an important enhancement to Disk Cleanup. Here's how to do it:

1. Click the Start menu and choose Programs.

2. From the Microsoft Plus! 98 menu, choose Disk Cleanup.

3. Select a hard disk to clean up and click OK.

4. Disk Cleanup scans the hard disk looking for files that can be discarded.

5. When the search is finished, you are presented with a dialog box like the one shown in Figure 17.22.

6. To access the new feature of Disk Cleanup, select the check box marked Non-Critical Files, and then click OK.

Figure 17.22

Notice the new Non-Critical Files option in the Disk Cleanup result dialog box.

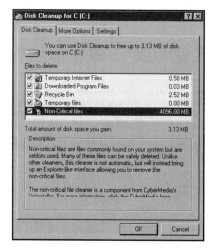

> **NOTE**   If you select other categories of files, such as Temporary Internet Files, Downloaded Program Files (ActiveX controls and Java applets used to view certain Web pages), Recycle Bin, or Temporary Files, these files will be deleted automatically when Disk Cleanup runs without any additional prompting.

Keep in mind that when you select the Non-Critical Files option, those files will *not* be removed automatically; instead a new utility (the CyberMedia Non-Critical File Remover) will appear that will lets you choose which of the non-critical files you want to remove.

You use the Non-Critical File Cleaner, shown in Figure 17.23, to review different types of files. Click each file type, and then in the right pane you will see a list of files on that hard disk that fall into that category. Files in the right pane will have either a green, yellow, or red icon next to them. Green files are safe to delete; you should exercise care in deleting yellow files. You should *never* delete red files, although the File Remover allows you to do so if you want.

Figure 17.23

Use the CyberMedia Non-Critical File Cleaner to selectively delete files.

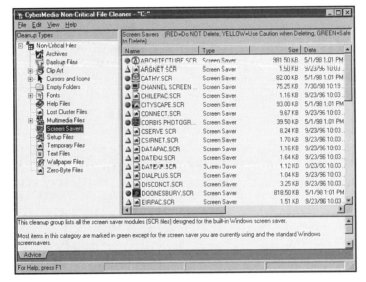

The colored icons are determined by the Non-Critical File Cleaner by analyzing your Windows configuration and all the programs you have installed. This analysis lets the File Remover identify which files are actually being used by other programs, and which are not.

> **WARNING** While the identification capabilities of the Non-Critical File Cleaner are good, there's still no substitute for looking carefully at the files you want to remove.

To remove files, select them in the right pane and right-click them. Choose Delete from the pop-up menu to remove them from the system.

> **TIP** To more easily remove green files, sort the list by the color of the icon. Choose the View menu, choose Arrange Icons, and then choose By Color. You can then select a range of files with Shift-Click and remove them all at once, just like in Windows Explorer.

After removing the files, close the CyberMedia Non-Critical File Cleaner, and you're finished.

Wrapping It Up

In this chapter you learned about making use of the Microsoft Plus! 98 companion to Windows 98. You learned about what is included in the Plus! pack and how to use the utilities included in the Plus! pack. With these useful enhancements to Windows 98, you can play and manage a collection of music CDs easier than ever before, customize your computer, save space on your hard disk, work with and retouch digital photographs, find and remove viruses, and even entertain yourself with some fun Windows 98 games.

Chapter

18

System Requirements

By Dave Adams Saltz

Although the Windows 98 operating system is designed to work on a variety of computers, you can't put the CD-ROM into any machine and expect to get the same performance. Windows 98 requires that your computer conform to a certain minimum set of hardware specifications. In this chapter, you'll explore the general concept of system requirements, review the hardware requirements of Windows 98, and look at other compatible hardware that is not required with Windows 98.

Overview of Windows 98 System Requirements

As you know, Windows 98 is an operating system (OS) for your personal computer. And as PC technology has grown, so too have the hardware requirements for using the latest software. Microsoft has built Windows 98 to take advantage of the new and emerging technologies available to you, and as such, your system must meet some minimum requirements in order to use it. Some of the requirements are suggestions and others are mandatory. Still others depend on other system configuration details.

Keep in mind that although minimum requirements are the bare standards you need to meet to install and use Windows 98, bigger usually means better. In general, minimum standards are exactly that—the barely acceptable minimum. Don't expect to get even decent performance if your computer just barely measures up. The more RAM you have, the better Windows 98 can perform to its potential. Likewise, if you have a large hard drive with plenty of free space for Windows to work in, your overall system performance is commensurately better.

Hardware Requirements

It's a battle people seem to be facing more and more with each passing year— hardware upgrades. It's tough to keep up with the latest and greatest out there when state-of-the-art machines are becoming obsolete in 18 months. But while you do need a somewhat modern machine for Windows 98 to run, chances are you don't need to break the bank to meet these requirements. Here's a quick overview of the major components you should evaluate in relation to Windows 98.

Processor

With the release of Windows 98, there is a new "feature" in the Windows hardware requirements; Microsoft recommends a Pentium-class processor to run Windows 98. However, the minimum requirement is a 486DX running at 66MHz. The *DX* means that the CPU must have a math coprocessor on it.

The interesting part is that the Windows 98 setup program checks for this minimum processor and if your system doesn't meet the requirements, it won't let you install the software.

At first that might sound a bit harsh, but if you ever tried running Windows 98 on an older and slower chip—even among those the installation program considers acceptable—you'd understand why they did this; the performance is decidedly lacking on anything less.

In all reality, a Pentium-class processor is really the way to go. It's not a necessity, but it is recommended with good reason. Anything less results in noticeable performance delays.

Random Access Memory (RAM)

Again, with memory, you have three sides to the story—the minimum, the recommended, and the reality.

Microsoft has implemented a 16MB minimum for systems running Windows 98, but they also recommend that you use 24MB.

I'm here to tell you that the real-world minimum for running Windows 98 is about 32MB of RAM. And the sweet spot, or level at which you get the best performance, is 64MB. With memory prices at a historical low, if you've been waiting for an excuse to buy some more RAM, here's your chance.

You can run Windows 98 on 16MB of memory, but performance is most likely sub-par until you install at least 32MB. And, if you plan on running any kind of modern software on your Windows 98 machine—which of course you do—this is all the more reason to install more memory.

Hard Drive Space

Some say that you can never have too much money or too much RAM. Let's add free hard drive space to that cliché.

There are several reasons why more hard drive space is better. First, obviously, is that you need to have enough room to install Windows. Second is that you want to have enough space so that you can install other programs as well. Third, and often overlooked, is the fact that you want to have enough space for Windows to have what I call *elbow room*.

Ever since Windows 95, Windows has used a *dynamic swap file*. Basically, a swap file is some room set aside on the hard drive for Windows to move things around in when it takes them out of your RAM. The dynamic part is that this swap file grows and shrinks according to its usage. So, if you're doing things that require Windows to do a lot of swapping, the swap file grows. If your machine is sitting idle, the swap file shrinks.

But if your system is running low on hard drive space that swap file has nowhere to grow. It has no elbow room; and when the swap file can't grow, you'll see symptoms ranging from decreased performance to cryptic errors to full-system lockups.

As you can see, ample hard drive space is at a premium. For the Windows 98 installation alone, you will need between 120MB and 360MB of free hard drive space, depending on how many optional components you install.

An upgrade from Windows 95 to Windows 98 most likely requires between 150MB and 300MB of free space to perform. A full installation of Windows 98 onto a blank hard drive likely consumes between 180MB and 360MB of hard disk space.

Video

You need to have at least a VGA or higher video card for Windows 98. If you have a card that's capable of at least 16-bit or 24-bit color, that's great. Windows 98 is a great multimedia platform. It would be a shame to run it with a mere 16-color video card; for one thing, you won't fully appreciate all the great multimedia features described in this book.

> **NOTE**   Microsoft also requires that you have a 3.5" high-density floppy drive installed in your machine for Windows 98. This component is standard in almost every computer these days, so this usually isn't something you have to worry about.

Other Hardware

Although you might satisfy the minimum requirements for installing and using the basic functionality of Windows 98, there are other things most people typically like to do with computers, especially multimedia enthusiasts.

People like to go online and use the Internet, listen to sounds and music, use peripheral devices such as scanners or digital cameras to input pictures into machines, and some people might even watch TV or movies. For all of these things, your system needs additional hardware—some of which you might or might not already have.

For instance, if you're on a local area network (LAN), you'll need a network adapter, sometimes called a network interface card (NIC). This is where you plug the cable from the network into your machine.

If you'll be using a telephone line to connect to the Internet, you'll need a 14.4 Kbps modem at a bare minimum, with a 28.8 recommended; a 33.6K or 56K modem is even better.

> **NOTE** Modems capable of 56Kbps speeds are becoming very common these days. You should note that although in theory the modem can achieve the advertised 56K transfer rate, in practice the fastest download speed you are capable of reaching is about 53Kbps. This is due to FCC rules regarding the allowed voltage on a regular houschold telephone line. Also, 56K modems are limited to upload speeds of 31.2Kbps. Remember, these figures are a best-case scenario, and your actual connect speeds may differ.

One of the most important components of a multimedia PC system is the sound card. Some systems come with sound capability built in, and some require a card to be installed in the machine. In either case, you'll also want speakers to listen to that sound. For many people, the quality of their speakers is of little consequence; but for others, realistic sound reproduction is very important.

Digital cameras are becoming more popular because they allow pictures to be taken, stored in the camera in digital format, and then transferred to the PC at a later time.

Likewise, scanners are appearing on more desktops. Scanners allow you to import anything that appears on a flat surface, such as a photograph or a magazine article. Scanners operate in a similar fashion to photocopy machines, except that the output isn't on a piece of paper, it's in a picture format on your PC.

One other important use of scanners is in the growing field of *optical character recognition (OCR)*. OCR allows you to scan a text document into the PC and have special software translate the picture it takes into an editable form. Basically, you can put a page, such as the one you're reading, on your scanner, scan it into Microsoft Word (for instance) using OCR software, and have a new document ready for you to edit. This technology isn't perfect yet, as the OCR software still makes some mistakes in translating the characters, which results in more work when you edit the file, but it's getting better all the time.

If you want to use WebTV with Windows 98, you'll need a TV-capable card such as the ATI All-in-Wonder or All-in-Wonder Pro video adapter in the system.

And if you want to use multiple monitors, you'll need both a second video adapter and a second monitor.

Universal serial bus (USB) peripherals are catching on, and Windows 98 supports them. If you want to use USB items, you'll have to make sure your system hardware has USB capabilities built in. And the same goes for IEEE 1394 bus technology, better known as *FireWire*. Windows can use it, but your hardware must support it first.

System Requirements

> **NOTE**   IEEE 1394 technology (FireWire) is a high-speed serial bus channel
> for allowing peripheral devices to connect to your system. The
> FireWire bus can carry video, audio, and other kinds of data very quickly (up to
> 400Mbps). Plus it has the added benefit of being hot-swappable, which means you can
> add and remove devices at will, without turning your machine off. You can also daisy-
> chain several devices off of one another, eliminating the need for many slots or ports on
> your machine to handle all your hardware. The technology is catching on as more
> FireWire-capable devices are brought to market. Go to their Web site at `http://`
> `www.FireWire.org`, for more information.

It almost goes without saying that no modern multimedia PC would be complete without a CD-ROM drive. My first real multimedia system had a *2x* CD-ROM drive in it, meaning that the drive spins (and thus, hopefully, reads) the data off the CD-ROM at twice the normal speed. Today, CD-ROM drives of 24x, 32x, and 40x are very common. I even saw a CD-ROM drive at a recent computer show that boasted of being capable of 100x! Although exorbitant CD-ROM speeds are enticing, the truth is that a 32x speed drive is more than capable of keeping up with any tasks you throw at it.

Another new technology appearing on many machines is *digital video disc (DVD)*. This format of compact disc allows most full-length movies to fit onto a disc the size of a normal music or data CD. Plus the movie is in digital format, resulting in super-clear picture and sound. To use DVD, you must have a DVD-capable drive as well as a video adapter that can receive and decode DVD signals.

Summary

All in all, Windows 98 is a very robust operating system and it requires a decent amount of horsepower to make it go. But many modern systems already meet or exceed the minimum requirements for running Windows 98. And, if your system doesn't quite match up, it shouldn't take a whole lot to get you up to speed.

As I've said before, if you can exceed the minimum requirements, definitely do it. Windows 98 only gets happier as you give it more room to run. If Windows is running smoothly, that means your multimedia applications perform better.

Chapter

19

Common Problems and Their Solutions

By Bruce Hallberg

It's an unfortunate fact of using a computer these days: Computers have problems, and often much more frequently than you would like. No matter how carefully you use your computer, how good a computer or its components are, or how little software you use, you're going to have problems from time to time.

The problems that you'll have to solve will fall into two broad categories. First, you might experience basic functionality problems—the computer isn't doing something that it should, or something that it used to do properly no longer works correctly (or at all), or when something is working, but not in the manner in which you think it should. The second broad category concerns problems when you want to get the computer to do something, but don't know how to go about it.

This chapter discusses both of these types of problems, with an emphasis on functional problems. During the course of the chapter, you'll learn about basic troubleshooting skills and about solving specific problems in different multimedia-related areas, including sound, video, CD-ROMs, and DVD.

Basic Troubleshooting Skills and Procedures

Different people have different views of troubleshooting. Some enjoy the challenge of solving a difficult problem, while others consider it a tiresome chore that they wish they didn't have to do. Regardless, problems should be approached in the same way: carefully and methodically. While approaching problems in this way takes more time, you improve your chances greatly of finding and solving the problem, not to mention reducing the chance of worsening the problem.

When attacking a particular problem, make sure that you only change one thing at a time, testing it each time to see if the problem has been resolved, reduced, or worsened. (It's actually good news if you can make a problem worse, because it usually indicates that you're working in the right area.) Moreover, when you make changes step by step, it's easy to reverse the most recent step you took.

It helps to understand how your computer works when troubleshooting, but you don't need to hold a Ph.D. in computer science to do a good job. If you know the basics and—more important—use good sources of information (such as this book!), you should be able to work through most problems.

Knowing When to Get Outside Help

The information in this chapter will help you troubleshoot many different types of problems related to the use of multimedia devices under Windows 98. However, no chapter and no book can resolve all possible problems.

If a problem seems intractable to you, don't hesitate to fall back on the vendors of the hardware and software in question. Because they support thousands of users that have equipment and software similar to yours, they often have already seen and found solutions to many types of problems. You can tap that knowledge with a phone call, a visit to a Web page, or some email, and some patience in describing the problem. For instance, there are many problems that are related only to particular types of add-in cards, from particular manufacturers, and even only affecting certain models or versions. You're simply not going to be in a position to know about all these different permutations and what they do, whereas the vendors will.

Keep in mind that falling back on vendors for support is not a panacea. Many times you'll find that they don't know what the solution to a particular problem is. At a certain point, if the option is open to you, you should consider simply returning the product causing problems and seek a different one that fills the same basic need. For instance, I once had a MediaVision sound and CD-ROM system that worked fine under all versions of DOS and Windows but wouldn't work properly under OS/2 (even though other OS/2 users had no problem at all). Eventually I upgraded the computer and tried the same system on the new computer, and it worked flawlessly with OS/2. Some weird incompatibility between an otherwise perfectly functioning computer and an otherwise perfectly functioning sound and CD-ROM system just didn't work right. In retrospect, it would have been cheaper to have found a way to get a different system earlier, considering all the time I spent trying to track down and solve what was probably an insolvable problem!

Checking Software Versions

There are several types of problems that can impact any of the multimedia trouble areas I described earlier. One of these common problems involves mixed versions of important software programs (and their associated drivers and *dynamic link libraries*) on your system. This mixture can happen when you install a program that has multimedia capabilities and the installation of that program replaces certain Windows 98 files that it shouldn't (this occurrence is especially common with software that was released before Windows 98 was available). Unfortunately, many installation programs behave this way, so you're likely to run across this type of problem sooner or later.

> **NOTE**   A dynamic link library, (DLL), is a programming feature of Windows that allows certain executable *routines* (parts of programs) to be stored separately, as files with DLL extensions. Windows 98 loads these DLLs only when needed by a program, in order to conserve computer memory.

The good news is that Windows 98 includes new tools that help you quickly find and resolve such cases. There are three important programs that can help you with this:

- *System Information.* Shows you the installation history of Windows 98 support programs.

- *System File Checker.* Searches for support programs that have been updated or replaced since Windows 98 was installed.

- *DirectX Information.* Helps you verify version numbers for DirectX software, which supports most multimedia activities.

- *DirectX Driver Tool.* Helps you troubleshoot DirectX by turning off DirectX acceleration features.

In the following steps, you learn how to use these three tools to search for software version incompatibilities.

First, I'll discuss using the System Information tool.

1. Start the System Information tool. Either use the Run command on the Start menu and type `MSINFO32.EXE`, or start it by clicking the Start Menu, choosing Programs, clicking Accessories, choosing System Tools, and clicking System Information. Either way, you'll see the program window shown in Figure 19.1.

Figure 19.1
Windows 98's System Information tool gives you clues about which system component is causing trouble.

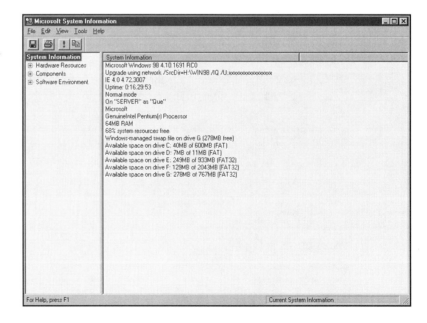

2. Using the left pane, open the Components branch by double-clicking it, and then choose History from the list that drops down beneath it.

3. If the problem started recently, click the Last Seven Days radio button at the top of the display; otherwise, choose Complete History. Figure 19.2 shows a sample history.

Figure 19.2

System Information shows you the history of any driver changes.

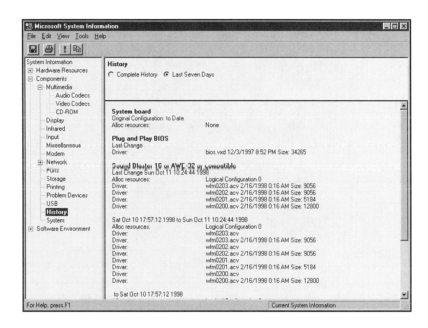

4. Carefully examine the list of changes, paying particular attention to changes that would impact the use of multimedia features in Windows 98. For example, Figure 19.2 shows that there have recently been changes to the SoundBlaster driver. Other areas to examine closely include game port or joystick drivers and video drivers.

5. If you find a driver that was replaced or updated when the problem started, re-install the driver in question (this might be a good opportunity to download and install the latest driver for the resource from the manufacturer's Web site on the Internet).

Another important tool for version troubleshooting is the System File Checker. This program uses a database containing details about all Windows 98's programs and files and can alert you to changes to these files. When a changed file is detected, you are offered the choice to update the database with the new information or reinstall the original Windows 98 file.

Common Problems and Their Solutions

Using the System File Checker is easy. Follow these steps:

1. Start the System Information tool by clicking the Start Menu, choosing Programs, clicking Accessories, choosing System Tools, and clicking System Information.

2. From the Tools menu of the System Information program, choose System File Checker. Figure 19.3 shows the resulting System File Checker dialog box.

Figure 19.3

The System File Checker examines a database of Windows 98 programs and files.

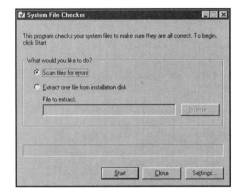

3. Click the Start button.

When System File Checker finds a changed file, it presents a dialog box similar to the one in Figure 19.4. Carefully examine the dates and versions shown. For instance, Figure 19.4 shows that the TWAIN.DLL file (a driver used to support scanners) has been updated since Windows 98 was installed. However, the size of the file and—more important—the version match the original version, so there's nothing to worry about. In cases such as this, choose the Update verification information radio button so that this particular change is not shown again.

> **NOTE** To maximize the effectiveness of the System File Checker, start the System File Checker Program, click Settings, and enable the Check for Changed Files and Check for Deleted Files options.

Of more interest is when System File Checker shows that the size or version of a file has changed, as in Figure 19.5. As you can see, you have several choices:

■ If the date of installation corresponds to when the problem you are experiencing started, consider restoring the file. Choose the Restore File radio button and click OK. You will then be prompted for your Windows 98 CD-ROM so that the original version can be reinstalled.

Figure 19.4

When System File Checker detects a change in a driver, it presents a dialog box like this one.

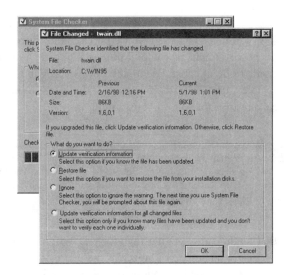

■ If the version number of the file is higher than the original version, it's probably safe to keep the file and update the System File Checker database. For instance, perhaps you've used the Windows Update Web page since Windows 98 was installed and the changed file simply represents a newer version that was installed. Or, perhaps you installed a recently released program that automatically installed an available update from Microsoft. However, again, examine the date of the change; if it corresponds to when your problem started, you might want to restore the original version. Just because a program is newer doesn't mean that it isn't causing problems.

Figure 19.5

When the System File Checker finds a newer file, it presents a dialog box like this one.

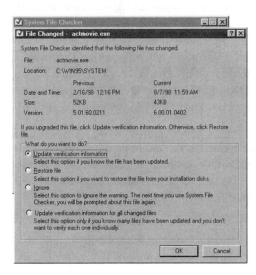

Common Problems and Their Solutions

Continue running the System File Checker until it is finished. If you've never run it before, and you've installed and used your computer a lot since Windows 98 was installed, this process might take a long time to complete and there might be many files that need to be updated. Eventually, however, it will finish; you can then run System File Checker more frequently in the future to keep the database updated with current information on your system.

> **WARNING** While the System File Checker is a welcome addition to Windows 98, it is principally designed to be used by knowledgeable individuals who are familiar with the system's file structure. Unless you are sure that a file replacement is the correct course of action, arbitrarily replacing files with original Windows 98 files might not solve your problem and could make matters worse.

Another item that might cause—rather than solve—version differences in Windows 98 is DirectX technology. DirectX is the name of a set of support programs that provide multimedia services to programs under Windows 98. Made up of a number of programs, the following DirectX services run under Windows 98:

- Direct3D
- DirectDraw
- DirectInput
- DirectPlay
- DirectSound

Different application programs might mistakenly install incorrect versions of DirectX software onto a system, causing problems. Two utilities let you see information about DirectX subsystems. The first of these is called DirectX Information. You run it by using My Computer or Windows Explorer to open the Program Files folder, and the DirectX folder it contains, and then double-click the program DXINFO.EXE. The DirectX Information program window displays information about DirectX, as illustrated in Figure 19.6.

It is unlikely that you would use the information shown in the DirectX Information window yourself. Instead, you might be called on to provide it to third-parties working with you on resolving a multimedia-related problem. Still, it's nice to know about this obscure utility, which provides information about the emerging DirectX technology.

The second utility that you can run to gather DirectX information is called the DirectX Driver tool. It shows you the version numbers of the major DirectX components, and optionally allows you to disable certain acceleration features in DirectX. You run this program by opening My Computer or Windows Explorer to the DirectX folder under Program Files and double-clicking DXTOOL.EXE. You can see its display in Figure 19.7.

Figure 19.6

DirectX Information (DXINFO.EXE) shows you details about DirectX.

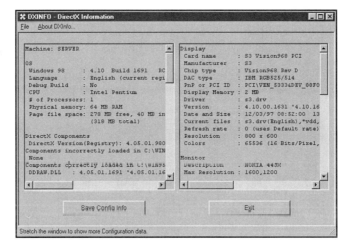

Figure 19.7

The DirectX Driver tool shows a small window with DirectX version information.

Again, you might supply the information provided by the DirectX Driver tool to a help desk or technical support specialist. If you know you're experiencing problems that are display related, however, you can try turning off the Direct3D or DirectDraw hardware acceleration features by deselecting their respective check boxes and clicking OK. It's possible that these acceleration features are not working properly with your combination of hardware and software. While disabling these features might slow program execution, you will have a chance to discover whether or not the DirectX accelerations are actually to blame for whatever display-related problems you might be having.

Preparing and Using an Emergency Boot Disk

So far, you've looked at tools that provide you information about Windows 98 and its drivers. However, you will also read information about updating drivers and about other procedures later in this chapter. While changing certain settings is a sensible approach to Windows 98 troubleshooting, following these procedures might also cause your computer to be unable to start. Because of this, it's important to prepare an emergency boot disk (EBD) from which you can still start your computer. Using this disk, you should be able to repair any errors that might have been made while you've been troubleshooting.

You should prepare a new EBD before you begin any troubleshooting endeavor or at least before you do anything beyond examining information.

NOTE You might have already created an emergency boot disk, also known as a *Windows 98 Startup disk,* when you installed or upgraded to Windows 98.

To prepare an emergency boot disk

1. Open the Control Panel either by clicking the Start menu, choosing Settings, and choosing Control Panel, or by double-clicking the My Computer icon and choosing Control Panel. Then double-click the Add/Remove Programs icon.

2. Select the Startup Disk tab, and then click the Create Disk button, shown in Figure 19.8.

Figure 19.8

To make an emergency boot disk, click the Create Disk button.

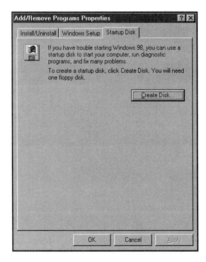

3. You will be prompted for a disk that can be overwritten with startup information for your computer. A single 1.44MB disk should suffice. Be aware that the disk will be erased completely, so it's best to start with a blank disk.

> **WARNING** Test your newly created disk immediately after you create it. Make sure that you can boot with CD-ROM support. Don't wait until you have a boot problem to find that the Windows 98 generic CD-ROM drivers are not compatible with your CD-ROM drive.

If changing your system configuration files prevents your computer from booting, you can still start it (unless there's a really major hardware failure) with the boot disk. The disk boots the system and creates a 2MB RAM disk (a virtual floppy disk in your computer's memory), onto which it places the key utilities you might need to repair a system. When you boot a system with the emergency disk, you'll see a menu with three choices:

- Start the Computer with CD-ROM Support

- Start the Computer without CD-ROM Support

- View the Help File

Generally, you will want to start the system with CD-ROM support. The emergency disk comes with general-purpose CD-ROM drivers that can initialize most IDE- and SCSI-based CD-ROM drives. If you cannot access your CD-ROM drive after booting from the disk in this mode, you'll have to modify the boot disk's CONFIG.SYS and AUTOEXEC.BAT files to use the appropriate drivers for your system's CD-ROM. (You will want CD-ROM support so that you can replace corrupted Windows system files or re-install Windows 98 from the CD-ROM.)

As I mentioned, the emergency disk boots the Windows 98 version of MS-DOS, and then creates a 2MB RAM drive to hold its utilities. It automatically copies the utilities to the RAM drive. The RAM drive will be created using the first drive letter that follows any hard drives defined in the system, and your CD-ROM drive will become the next drive letter available. Note that this CD-ROM drive designation will typically be different than the letter used by Windows 98 when in normal mode.

The boot disk's utilities are stored on the disk in a compressed file called EBD.CAB. During the boot process, Windows 98 automatically decompresses EBD.CAB to the created RAM drive as the emergency disk boots. Table 19.1 details the utilities contained in the EBD.CAB file.

Table 19.1   EBD Utilities

Utility Name	*Purpose*
ATTRIB.EXE	Lets you set file attributes; you might use this to remove a file's hidden or read-only attributes prior to replacement
CHKDSK.EXE	An abbreviated version of SCANDISK that checks a drive's directory structure for errors
DEBUG.EXE	MS-DOS debugger that lets you perform byte-level patching of files
EDIT.EXE	Simple text editing program for making changes to system text files, such as CONFIG.SYS or AUTOEXEC.BAT
EXT.EXE	A new file extraction utility that makes it easy to search the Windows 98 .CAB files on the CD-ROM for individual files and extract those files to a destination of your choosing
FORMAT.COM	Utility to format disks
MSCDEX.EXE	CD-ROM extensions for MS-DOS
SCANDISK.EXE	Comprehensive disk testing tool; checks both directory structures and can perform surface analyses
SCANDISK.INI	Configuration file for SCANDISK.EXE
SYS.COM	Utility that places system boot files onto a disk
UNINSTAL.EXE	Uninstalls Windows 98

After you have booted a system with the emergency disk, you'll want to follow certain steps to resolve most startup problems. First, run SCANDISK on the default boot drive, drive C:. Any errors in the directory structure that are keeping the system from starting should be resolved by SCANDISK. Take careful note of any files that SCANDISK indicates are damaged (ones that contain bad sectors, are cross-linked, or have other problems), because you will want to replace them from the Windows 98 CD-ROM after SCANDISK repairs the problems on the disk.

If SCANDISK indicated a few damaged files, use the EXT utility to extract fresh copies of those files from the Windows 98 CD-ROM. Type EXT at the RAM disk command prompt, and then indicate what file you want to replace. You do so by supplying the location where the Windows 98 .CAB files are located (usually *x:*\WIN98, where *x:* is your CD-ROM drive letter), and where you want the extracted file to be placed (usually the main Windows system folders: C:\WINDOWS, C:\WINDOWS\SYSTEM, or C:\WINDOWS\SYSTEM32). Exercise care in choosing the target folder; if in doubt, search the system folders for the presence of the damaged file or files.

If there appear to be many damaged files, run Windows Setup from the Windows 98 CD-ROM to reinstall all the Windows 98 files. If Setup fails to complete, your only alternative is to reformat your boot drive and install Windows 98 again. Of course, you must follow up with the reinstallation of all your program files and data file backups.

Updating Hardware Drivers

When troubleshooting multimedia problems, you will often be called on to install or reinstall software that lets Windows 98 interact with the hardware installed in your computer system. Such support files are generically referred to as *drivers*, in that they allow Windows 98 to drive (work with) the actual hardware devices. Windows 98 uses a modular design that allows for wide latitude in computer hardware. In order for any computer hardware component to work with all Windows 98, all that is required is the appropriate driver program.

You usually install drivers for the following reasons:

- You have installed a new device or software package into your computer.

- You think that the existing drivers have become damaged in some way and need to be reinstalled.

- A newer version of a driver is available; perhaps it offers better performance or maybe it resolves some problem you are having.

In order to install a driver, you first need to have the collection of files that constitutes the driver. Usually you will have these on a disk or CD-ROM that came with your computer or the device in question, or often you can download those or newer drivers from the manufacturer's Web page. Also check the Microsoft Windows Update Web site. Click Start, Windows Update, and then navigate to the Device Drivers Web page link.

You should always follow the installation instructions that accompany a set of driver files; different manufacturers will use different methods. Sometimes they will provide an installation program that takes care of all the installation details for you. Other times, they might ask that you use the Device Manager to update the driver file. If the latter is the case, follow these steps:

1. Click Start, Settings, Control Panel, and choose the System applet or right-click My Computer and select Properties then select the Device Manager tab.

2. In the resulting dialog box, select the Device Manager tab.

3. In the large window, locate the device that you want to update the drivers for, such as the Network Adapters or Monitor.

4. Select the device, and then click the Properties button.

5. Move to the Driver tab of the device's Properties dialog box, as shown in Figure 19.9.

Figure 19.9

You can use the Driver tab of a device's Properties dialog box to update a driver.

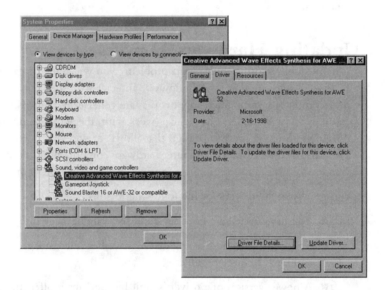

6. Click the Update Driver button.

After you click the Update Driver button, you will be prompted for the location of the driver files you want to install—usually a folder on your hard disk or a floppy disk. You can also choose to let the Update Device Driver Wizard search for a newer driver. If the driver you have is on a disk or CD-ROM provided by the device's manufacturer, you should let the wizard search for the driver. Follow the wizard's prompts and the new driver will be installed. You might be prompted to restart your computer after the driver installs.

Resolving Sound Problems

Although there are many exotic multimedia devices available today, such as video capture devices, DVD-ROM drives, spiffy scanner interfaces, and so on, the most common multimedia device on any computer (besides the monitor) is the sound system. And, because the basic PC design never contemplated sound capabilities, different manufacturers added these features in different ways. Because sound systems for PCs are now ubiquitous, and because they all work a bit differently, you're apt to run into sound problems more often than other types of problems. Check the following problems to see if one of them is occurring to you.

My Computer Keeps Crashing and Indicates a Problem In MMSYSTEM.DLL and RUNDLL32

You will usually see this problem after changing the hardware configuration on your computer. What happened is that a key command was deleted from the SYSTEM.INI file on the computer. Fortunately, fixing the SYSTEM.INI line is easy:

1. Using Notepad, open the file C:\WINDOWS\SYSTEM.INI.

2. Locate the section of the file that begins with the keyword `Boot`.

3. Ensure that the following line is present (if not, add it):

    ```
    drivers=mmsystem.dll
    ```

4. Save the SYSTEM.INI file with the changes.

5. Restart your computer.

The Sound Coming from My Computer Sounds Terrible

Many things can affect the sound quality coming from your computer. If you've always experienced the problem (rather than just noticing it sounded bad one day), it can be tough to know if there's actually a problem or if the sound components just aren't that good. Still, you can try many things to improve sound quality:

- The tiny audio cables that come with most computer audio speakers are pretty poor; you should try moving the cables while sound is playing to see if an intermittent connection is causing the sound problem. If practical, try installing a new set of cables; you should be able to get compatible cables from most electronics stores, including Radio Shack.

■ If the sound is only poor when trying to play audio CDs and not when playing games or using other software that generates its own sound, suspect one of several sources:

1. An audio patch cable that runs from the CD-ROM to the sound card in the computer or to a location on the motherboard might be loose or have a bad connection. Turn off your computer, monitor, and any other peripheral devices. Disconnect all AC power cables. Remove the computer's case. Ideally, you should use a grounded wrist strap to ground yourself to the metal frame. Check the patch cable connections at each end by disconnecting and then reconnecting the cable.

2. Try plugging a set of Walkman-style headphones into the headphone jack on the front of the CD-ROM player and check the sound quality there. If it is poor, the problem is with either the CD-ROM drive or the CD-ROM itself.

3. It sounds simple, but make sure the CD-ROM is perfectly clean with no oily residue, scratches, or fibers on its surface.

4. There are two ways of adjusting the volume coming from an audio CD being played: the sound card's controls and the controls on the speakers. Try turning the volume up with the sound card's controls (usually done with the Volume Control in Windows 98) while turning down the volume on the speakers, and then vice versa. You'll probably find that you're better off raising the volume with one component versus the other, due to differences in the quality of their amplifiers. (My home system, for example, has a really clean amplifier in its speakers, but a crummy amplifier on the sound card, so I always leave the sound card set to relatively low volumes and crank up with the speaker control).

■ There is a rare occurrence where poor sound might be experienced when audio CDs are played while the hard disk is also being accessed (you would see a correlation to hard disk activity and sound problems). Your CD-ROM and hard disk that use the same IDE interface in the computer can cause this problem. Most modern computers support two internal IDE interfaces, each of which can support up to two devices. If possible, try connecting either the CD-ROM or the hard disk to the secondary IDE interface. As an added benefit, you should experience better overall system performance by doing so.

■ Sound quality can be hurt if there are any device conflicts in your system. Use the System Information tool or Device Manager to make sure there aren't any IRQ or DMA conflicts between your sound devices and any other devices in the computer.

- It's always a good idea to use the latest versions of any fixes for Windows 98 and the sound equipment in the system. You can usually download such drivers from the respective vendor's Web site. Sometimes newer drivers will produce better sound due to fixes that have been incorporated.

- If the sound quality worsened after installing some piece of software, such as a game or educational title that uses sound, its installation program might have overwritten an important sound support driver with an older version. Use the procedure described the section, "Checking Software Versions," earlier in this chapter to try to resolve this type of problem.

Media Player Refuses to Play a Sound File

This problem can be caused by two main possibilities. First, the MMSYSTEM.DLL file might not be properly specified in the SYSTEM.INI file. Second, your sound drivers might have become damaged. You should reinstall the sound drivers using Device Manager or the procedure outlined by the manufacturer of your sound hardware.

I'm Having Problems with MIDI Files

MIDI files play sound by using simulated musical instruments that play various notes. Other sounds, such as WAV files, are played when a digital sample of the sound is recorded and played back. Because MIDI files use different sound features to produce their output, there are additional steps you need to take to resolve MIDI problems.

First, you should ascertain that other sounds (non-MIDI) are playing normally. For instance, can you play WAV files? Does the normal Windows 98 startup music play? If you have a sound scheme defined, do you hear what you normally hear?

Many games use MIDI music that plays in the background while you play the game. You might experience normal game sounds, except that the music doesn't work. This is a good indication that you have a MIDI-specific problem. Another indication would be if you can hear WAV sounds but can't play MIDI files through Media Player.

To test Media Player, open it by clicking the Start menu, choose Programs, Accessories, Entertainment, and then choose Media Player. Then choose MIDI Sequencer from the Device menu. You will be prompted to open a MIDI file. Choose one and it should begin playing.

If the MIDI file doesn't begin playing, open the Control Panel, and then double-click the Multimedia icon. Click the MIDI tab, shown in Figure 19.10. Select a different MIDI source, if available.

Common Problems and Their Solutions

Figure 19.10
The MIDI tab of the Multimedia Properties dialog box can help you solve problems playing those files.

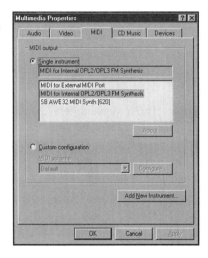

If you still cannot get your MIDI file to play, you should reinstall your sound system drivers, which should include the MIDI-related drivers. After reinstallation of the drivers, you should have properly working MIDI sound.

The Sound File Won't Play

Windows includes an audio mixer that adjusts the volumes of the various sound sources within Windows 98. You might think that a sound file of a particular type (such as MIDI) isn't playing, when in reality the mixer has the volume for that type of file set too low to hear or even muted.

To access the mixer in Windows 98, open the Start menu and then choose Programs, Accessories, Entertainment, and finally Volume Control. You should see the mixer shown in Figure 19.11. You can also right-click the yellow Speaker icon in the System Tray in the lower-right corner of your screen, and select Properties from the resulting menu.

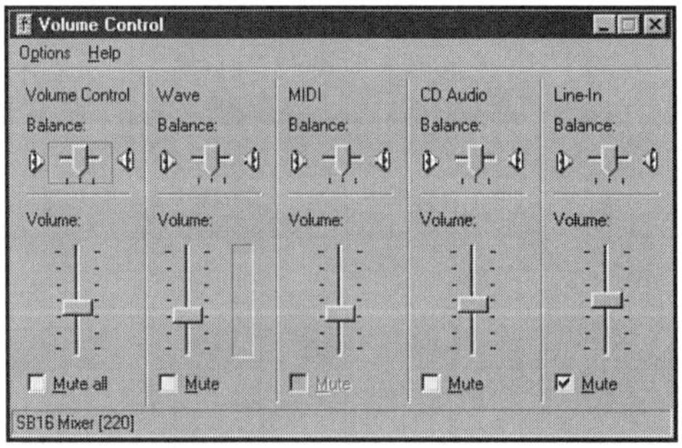

Figure 19.11
The Windows 98 Sound Mixer lets you adjust the relative volume of several sound sources.

For each type of file that you intend to work with, make sure that the volume is set appropriately (some experimentation might be necessary) and make sure that the Mute check box is not selected.

> **NOTE** When developing this chapter, I had my own multimedia trouble-shooting problem to deal with. It turned out that the system wouldn't play MIDI files, although other types of files were playing fine. After spending about 20 minutes examining driver files, reinstalling drivers, trying different MIDI sequencers and what not, I finally checked the mixer settings and, you probably guessed it, found that MIDI volume had been turned all the way down for some unknown reason. I cranked up the volume and it turned out that everything with MIDI was working fine all along.
>
> The moral of the story is this: No matter how much detailed technical information you might have on solving problems, never let all that blind you to looking for simple explanations *first*!

Resolving Video Problems

Video subsystems in today's PCs are extremely complex. Each one supports features that allow it to perform as quickly as possible, working closely with Windows 98 to provide information on the display as quickly as possible. When you consider the number of bits that must be moved through the system in order to display a single screen full of data, you'll quickly realize that your video system moves more data than any other part of your system. Video systems are, therefore, subjected to intense amounts of work, and even the slightest problem in the driver programs can cause obvious and annoying problems.

Video problems can come from a number of sources, including:

- Monitors
- Video card
- Video card drivers
- Video-related problems with Windows 98

There are two levels of severity for video problems you might experience. The first is the worst, where you cannot see anything—or anything recognizable—on your screen. The second involves minor quality problems in the display, where colors might be washed out, miscellaneous pixels might show the wrong color, or fonts could be distorted.

To resolve severe video problems, try the following:

- The first step when having any video-related problem is to try to isolate the problem a bit. For instance, to make sure that the video problem isn't related to the monitor, try using a different monitor with similar capabilities, if available. If the problem still exists, you know that the monitor isn't involved.

- If you can see the normal startup text when your computer initially boots, and perhaps the Windows 98 splash screen that appears before the desktop appears, but then you can't see anything else, your problem is likely related to the resolution and color depth to which Windows 98 is set. (Not all monitors support all possible combinations of resolution and color depth.) Use the following steps:

  1. When Windows 98 is starting, hold down the left-hand Control key to activate the Startup menu. From this menu, choose Safe Mode to start Windows 98, which starts the system using standard VGA resolution (640×480 resolution with 256 colors).

  2. When Windows is finished launching, right-click the desktop and choose Properties. Move to the Settings tab of the Properties dialog box.

  3. Set a resolution and color depth that you know your monitor and video card can support. For instance, most will support 800×600 using thousands of colors.

  4. Restart Windows 98

- If the preceding steps don't work, restart Windows 98 again in Safe Mode and reinstall your video drivers.

- If after taking that step your video still isn't working, you should (using Safe Mode) install standard Super VGA display drivers so you can get up and running, and then you should contact the maker of your computer or video card for additional help.

Minor video quality problems are usually caused by one of two things. First, you might be using a resolution and color depth that simply doesn't work well with your monitor and video card. Try to set a different resolution or number of colors using the Display Properties Control Panel's Settings tab. Second, your video drivers might need to be updated. Try to download a newer version from the computer or video card manufacturer's Web site, and install them using their instructions.

> **NOTE**   If you are sometimes the victim of a "kernel32" system fault while using Internet Explorer or Outlook Express, the problem might be video driver related. This fault is usually remedied by installing an updated video driver.

> **TIP**   Remember to try to use the System File Checker to verify that your existing video drivers aren't damaged.

Reducing the amount of video acceleration that Windows performs might also reduce video quality problems. Right-click the My Computer icon, choose Properties, click the Performance tab, and then click the Graphics button. Normally, the slider you see there is set all the way to the right, providing maximum acceleration. Try moving the slider to the middle or even all the way to the left to disable acceleration. After restarting Windows, see if the problem persists. If not, you can try to gradually adjust the slider to higher levels until you find the level that causes problems. Then contact the maker of the video drivers you're using for permanent resolution of the problem.

> **NOTE** Some monitors can display quality problems due to environmental causes. Line flicker or wavy lines, for instance, is almost always caused by electrical interference, usually by a nearby fluorescent light. Turn off the light to see if this is causing the problem. There also might be other electrical devices sharing an electrical circuit in your house that can cause annoying flickers. Look for motor-based electrical appliances that might be causing problems, such as a space heater.
>
> Color distortion or display distortion can often be caused by nearby magnetic fields. One source of this problem is telephone handsets; make sure there isn't a telephone right next to your monitor. Another source is poorly-shielded computer speakers. While most computer speakers are shielded from causing monitor problems, you might try moving the speakers away from the monitor to see if that makes a difference. Also, sometimes magnetic field color distortion might remain even after you remove the magnetic source. This problem might correct itself after turning your monitor off and back on several times or after using it for several days after removing the source. Some monitors have a built-in function called *degaussing* that can resolve these problems, and sometimes you have to choose to degauss a monitor using a menu built into the monitor (consult your monitor documentation). Finally, a television repair shop can professionally degauss monitors that otherwise don't have a degaussing function built into them.

My Monitor Has Turned Itself Off, but Won't Come Back On

Windows 98, and most modern computers, have power-saving features built into them. The power management software in Windows 98 will turn your computer's monitor off after a specified amount of time when the computer isn't being used. Sometimes, under certain circumstances, your monitor might not come back on when you move the mouse or press a key on the keyboard. Specifically, this can happen when you use the 3D Maze screen saver or when you have your monitor set to a resolution of 800×600.

To resolve this problem

- Try to use a different screen saver besides 3D Maze

- Try to use a different screen resolution besides 800×600

- Turn off the power-saving feature that powers down the monitor using these steps:

    1. Open the Control Panel, and then double-click Power Management.

    2. Set the Turn off Monitor option to Never.

    3. Click OK to close the dialog box.

Movies Won't Play Properly, or at All

Windows 98 lets you choose to install (or not install) video compression, which is responsible for decoding movie files so that they can be played on your computer.

The most likely cause of movie files not playing properly, or playing poorly, comes from not having this component installed. To install the Video Compression component, go to the Control Panel, choose Add/Remove Programs, click the Windows Setup tab, and go to the Multimedia section. If Video Compression is already installed, try uninstalling then reinstalling it.

I Can't Choose a Particular Video Mode

Sometimes your video card or monitor might support a particular video mode, such as 1200×1024, but the option isn't available in the Display Properties dialog box's Settings tab. This can be due to the following reasons:

- Your video card might not have adequate video memory installed to support the desired resolution and color depth.

- Your monitor might not support the desired resolution and color depth, even though the video card does.

- Windows 98 might have incorrect information about which monitor you are using or might have installed a generic monitor information file.

> **WARNING** Choosing a video resolution and color depth that isn't supported by your monitor might cause permanent harm to the monitor. Check carefully before trying to force the system to a higher resolution than it offers.

Assuming you've eliminated the possibility that you don't have enough video memory on your video card, the absence of a video mode option is probably caused by not having your monitor set correctly within Windows 98. To set the monitor type in Windows 98

1. Open the Display Control Panel and click the Settings tab.

2. Click the Advanced button.

3. In the resulting dialog box, click the Monitor tab, as shown in Figure 19.12.

4. Click the Change button.

5. The Update Device Driver Wizard will start. Select the Search for a better driver radio button, and click Next.

6. Complete the wizard's onscreen prompts to locate and install a more compatible monitor driver.

Figure 19.12

Set the monitor type in Windows 98 in this dialog box.

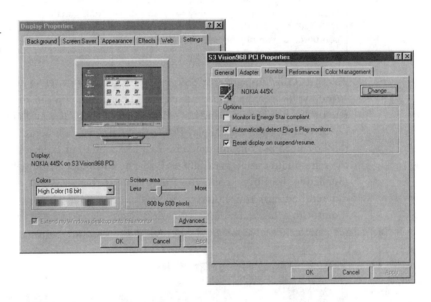

You might have a monitor for which a Windows 98 information file isn't included with the system. In these cases, usually you can download a monitor information file from the monitor manufacturer's Web page and use their installation instructions to install the monitor into Windows 98.

My Monitor Has an Annoying Flicker

The human eye can discern monitor flicker at frequencies up to about 60–65Hz. If you use a computer with a *refresh rate* (the rate at which the display is redrawn, or refreshed) set below 70Hz, you might perceive flicker, particularly if you work under fluorescent lights—which can exacerbate the problem. Perceptible flicker, and even flicker that you might not be able to see, can cause excess eyestrain and vision-related headaches.

Common Problems and Their Solutions

> **TIP**   Always purchase the best quality monitor you can, even if you have to scrimp a little on other components of a computer system. You should purchase color monitors of 17" or more (16" viewable), which are clear to *your* eyes and support any possible video modes you want to use. The slightly higher price you pay for the monitor will be offset by your greater comfort when using your computer; you shouldn't have to squint to look at your monitor!
>
> Also, beware: There are monitors available that have excellent specifications but display poorly when you look at them. You should always view at least an example of a monitor you want to purchase before doing so, or at least make sure that you have the ability to return it and get a different model if you're unhappy with your choice. Also, keep in mind that a high-quality monitor will last longer than the computer system to which it's connected, because you can usually use a good monitor with newer computers as you upgrade.

To correct this problem, first ensure that you have the correct monitor selected in Windows 98 (see the preceding section). Then see if you can adjust the refresh rate of the monitor up using the Adapter tab of the video card's Properties dialog box. To do so, open the Display Properties dialog box, click the Settings tab, click the Advanced button, and then choose the Adapter tab. Figure 19.13 shows how the refresh rate can be manually set with the particular adapter and monitor installed in the sample computer I used for this chapter (yours might offer different settings). You should try to set the highest refresh rate supported by your monitor to achieve the best quality display and the least eyestrain. The goal is to see a perfectly stable image as you look at the monitor, with no discernible flicker.

Figure 19.13

Adjusting a monitor's refresh rate can reduce eyestrain.

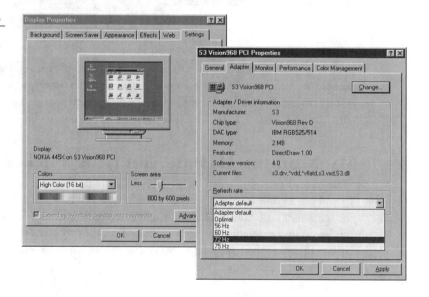

> **NOTE** Different monitors support different refresh rates at different resolutions and color depths. If the refresh rate you want to use isn't available, try reducing the resolution or color depth, and then try to choose a higher rate. Also, make sure to carefully examine the specifications for your monitor, because they usually specify the highest possible refresh rate for different video modes.

Resolving CD-ROM and DVD-ROM Problems

CD-ROM and DVD-ROM drives are relatively similar in that they both use discs that reflect laser light in such a way that the data stored on the disc can be read by the computer. CD-ROM and DVD-ROM drives are connected to some sort of disk interface inside the system (almost always an IDE or SCSI interface) and also have an audio patch cable that runs from the drive to the sound card in the system. The patch cable is for playing music CDs; sound is sent directly from the CD or DVD disc to the sound card, which then amplifies it and sends it to the connected speakers, with no real-time processing required by the computer. DVD drives additionally have a DVD decoder that can help decode video images and other data stored on the DVD. These decoders can either take the form of a specialized DVD decoder card, or they can be emulated by software running on the computer.

The most common problems with CDs and DVD discs (particular CDs) occur when there is dirt, lint, or fine scratches on the disc's surface. While minor scratches won't cause perceptible sound problems for music CDs, they will cause problems for data being served to the computer from the disc. Because of this, always treat data discs with great care, and avoid letting them get dirty or scratched. Use a CD cleaner designed for that purpose to remove dirt or fibers from a CD. Also remember to store discs in jewel cases or other protective cases when not in use. Do not leave discs in drives when not in use.

CD-ROM and DVD-ROM players also rely on drivers installed in Windows 98. These drivers must be configured correctly, there must be no conflicts with other devices, and they obviously need to function correctly. CD-ROM drivers can generally be trusted, as they've been available for a long time and the behavior of CD-ROMs is well understood. DVD players, on the other hand, might suffer from their drivers being fairly new, relatively speaking. For this reason, if you have a DVD-ROM drive, frequently check out your DVD manufacturer's Web site for updated drivers.

Common Problems and Their Solutions

My CD-ROM Drive Is Performing Poorly

A CD-ROM drive might perform more poorly than you expect due to incorrect settings in Windows 98 that affect the CD cache size and how the system seeks for new information. Here's how to optimize the settings for your CD-ROM.

1. Open the Control Panel, and then double-click the System icon, or right-click My Computer, and then click Properties.

2. Click the Performance tab.

3. Click File System.

4. Choose the CD-ROM tab, as shown in Figure 19.14.

5. Drag the Supplemental Cache Size to the far right setting.

6. Set the Optimize Access Pattern For setting to correspond to your CD-ROM drive (usually quad-speed or higher).

Figure 19.14

Use this dialog box to change your CD-ROM performance settings.

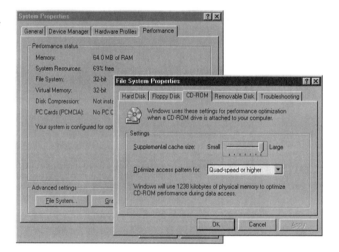

My Computer Won't Automatically Play a Music CD

You can configure Windows 98 to automatically start playing any inserted music CDs or have it require you to start the CD Player program and manually click the Play button. Two things must be done to control this behavior.

1. Launch Windows Explorer, click the View menu, and choose Folder options.

2. Click the File Types tab.

3. Double-click Audio CD in the resulting list of file types. You'll see the Edit File Type dialog box, shown in Figure 19.15.

Figure 19.15

Changing the default action for an audio CD can enable or disable automatic playing.

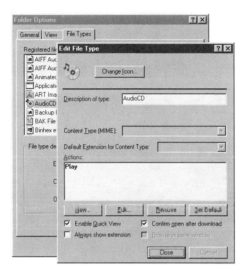

4. If you want audio CDs to play automatically, click once on the Play entry in the Actions window, and then click the Set Default button. The typeface for the word Play will change to bold to confirm your selection.

5. If you do not want audio CDs to play automatically, make sure the Play entry is not selected (click elsewhere in the window), and then click the Set Default button. The type changes from bold to normal typeface to confirm your selection.

6. Close the dialog box.

T IP | You can prevent a music CD from playing automatically by holding down the Shift key while you insert the CD into the drive.

If music CDs aren't playing automatically, perform the following steps:

1. Open the System icon in the Control Panel. and click the Device Manager tab.

2. Double-click the installed CD-ROM device to open its Properties dialog box.

3. Click the Settings tab and ensure that Auto Insert Notification is checked, as shown in Figure 19.16.

Common Problems and Their Solutions

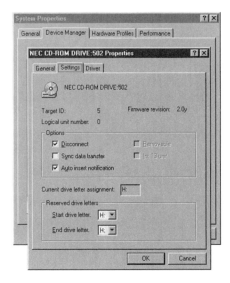

4. Close all dialog boxes and restart the system.

Wrapping It Up

Windows 98 has improved the state of the art in multimedia support to a great
extent over Windows 95 and certainly over Windows 3.x. Not only are more
devices supported, but they are supported more reliably. Windows 98 includes
drivers for most types of devices that you will encounter, and the drivers are
usually of high quality. It used to be that you had to fiddle for hours to get a
sound card and CD-ROM drive to work properly, but now most people find that
it truly is plug and play.

In this chapter, you learned about resolving various Windows 98 multimedia
problems, ranging from the somewhat common problems of having application or
game programs overwrite the correct software with incorrect versions; to testing
the integrity of installed drivers; to resolving some common, specific problems in
different multimedia areas. While solving any type of computer problem can be
frustrating, the information in this chapter should serve to solve the most common problems, or at least put you solidly on the right track to getting them
solved.

Don't forget a point I made early in the chapter: There will be lots of times you
don't have to take on the sole responsibility to troubleshoot and solve a problem.
Most hardware and software vendors are anxious about making your use of their
products as easy and productive as possible. And most have good, solid technical
support staffs that can walk you through problem-solving efficiently and more
quickly than you might be able to accomplish on your own. Remember, they're

the ones with the large technical support databases of problems that other customers have encountered.

The main thing to remember when troubleshooting a problem is to keep your cool, and if you find yourself getting angry at the problem, take some time to do something else so you can approach the problem with a good attitude. Troubleshooting doesn't need to cause you ulcers, and sometimes you might even be delighted when you solve a problem.

Common Problems and Their Solutions

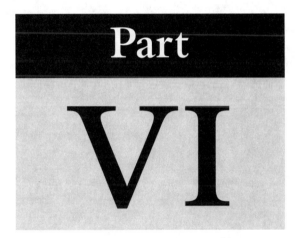

Part

VI

Appendixes

Getting to the
Windows Update
Web Site

Options on the
Windows Update
Web Site

Appendix

A

Windows 98
CD-ROM
Listing

by Serdar Yegulap

No operating system remains immune to change, especially an OS with as much hardware support and as many software components as Windows 98.

When Microsoft saw how troublesome it could be for users to update their Windows 95 systems whenever driver updates or new applets became available, they decided to build in a way to enable the user to get operating system updates automatically. They did this by creating a Web site called Microsoft Windows Update.

I'll cover the Windows Update Web site in this section. Along the way, I'll show you how to find the Web site and examine the various options it offers.

Getting to the Windows Update Web Site

You can access the Windows Update site by going to the URL `http://windowsupdate.microsoft.com`. Rather than making you enter the URL manually in Internet Explorer, however, Microsoft has provided a shortcut. You can get to the Web site in one step by simply clicking on the Windows Update icon on the Start button, as shown in Figure A.1.

Figure A.1

The Windows Update icon, which takes you directly to the Windows Update Web site, can be found on the Start menu.

Note that the Web site is designed to be used with Internet Explorer 4.0. Other Web browsers, such as Netscape Navigator, might not display the page properly or at all. Be sure to have Java support enabled, regardless of what browser you *do* wind up using.

When you open the Web site you'll see the main Windows Update Web page, which gives you several options, as shown in Figure A.2. These options appear on the menu bar on the left-hand side.

As this page loads, the browser might prompt you to allow the system to download and install a few ActiveX controls. This operation is critical for the proper operation of the site, doesn't take more than a couple of minutes, and needs to be done only once.

Figure A.2

The Windows Update Web site has several available options when you connect to it.

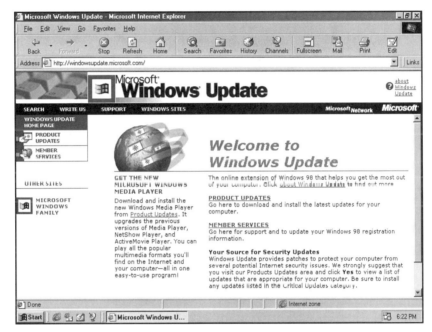

Options on the Windows Update Web Site

When you're connected to the site and have loaded the page, you have several possible places to go:

- *Product Updates.*   This is the main attraction: Click this link to bring up a list of possible component downloads.

- *Member Services.*   Go here if you want to update or make changes to your Windows 98 user registration information.

For starters, click the Product Updates link.

When you've loaded the Product Updates page, which you can see in Figure A.3, a dialog box pops up which reads something like:

    This program can determine what components are installed on
    your computer and whether new components are available. Would
    you like to do this now?

You can see this dialog box in Figure A.4.

Figure A.3

The Product Updates page looks like this in Internet Explorer.

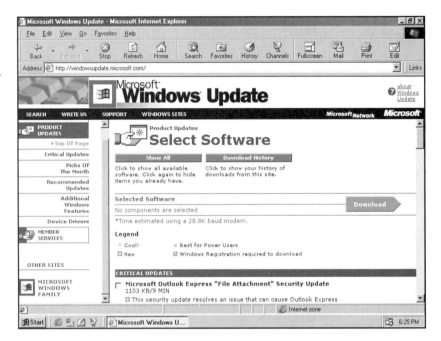

Figure A.4

The Web page launches an automatic component-check query dialog box.

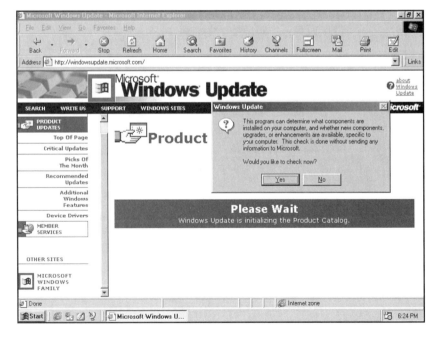

If you want the computer to automatically handle the process of checking your system for new components, click Yes. This is the best choice for novice users, because they will not have to make decisions based on something they don't know. When you click Yes, the computer checks your system to see whether anything needs updating, and then marks everything in the Web page's component list that you should download.

The actual system checkout is done by a downloaded ActiveX applet. Contrary to various ugly rumors, the program does not download any personal information whatsoever—just details on what revisions of components are currently installed.

If you are an experienced user and want to make the choices based on your own judgment and what's available on the menus, click No and go on. If you click No, however, you might see updates that you've already downloaded. Be familiar with the state of your computer before clicking No.

Regardless of whether you have the program check your system, this portion of the update site features a list of possible types of components to download on the left side. Click a category to see a list of possible downloads. Here's a quick overview of the categories:

- *Critical updates.*   These are *the* most important things available right now—bug fixes for severe or system-crippling problems, major updates to key software technologies, and so on. If you see anything new in this section when you connect, get it.

- *Picks of the Month.*   These updates are not absolutely essential, but Microsoft feels that they will provide a major boost in productivity or usability for the majority of users. Download from this category if what you see is appropriate or intriguing.

- *Recommended Updates.*   Here are more updated components that might not be critical to the system, but which are important and represent technological advancements in one area or another. It's a good idea to get these anyway, because they will eventually become useful.

- *Additional Windows Features.*   These add-ons are provided as a way of jazzing up Windows—adding functionality, replacing an existing applet with a fancier one, and so on. Downloads from here are at the user's discretion; many of them might not be relevant or useful to a given user.

- *Device Drivers.*   This section contains, as the name implies, updated device drivers for hardware. Checking this section is pretty much mandatory, because updated device drivers make life easier for anyone who uses the computer—providing improved functionality, fewer bugs, and so on.

Windows 98 CD-ROM Listing

To download the components in a section, scroll through the list and click the check boxes for the components you want to obtain. When you're finished, go either to the top or the bottom of the list and click the blue Download arrow. You'll then get a confirmation list, such as the one shown in Figure A.5, which lets you double-check which components you want to obtain.

Figure A.5

The confirmation list appears letting you ensure you're getting the right components.

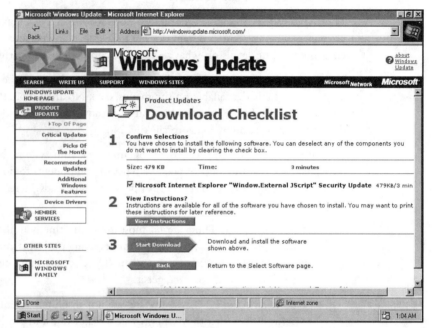

When you've finished double-checking, click the blue Start Download arrow to begin downloading. The download and installation process is automatic. You might be asked to reboot the machine when the downloads and installs are finished.

The one exception to the paradigm described in the previous paragraph is when you click Device Drivers. After you click there, a dialog box appears (shown in Figure A.6) which asks you whether you want to check for automatic device driver updates.

When you click Yes, the computer loads and runs the Update Wizard, such as the one shown in Figure A.7, to download and install your drivers. This process can take a few minutes, depending on the speed of your Internet connection.

To use the wizard, wait until the Loading components text disappears. The wizard searches your computer for available updates, which it lists in the bottom pane. To install those updates, click Install, and the wizard downloads and installs those components automatically. You might be asked to reboot your computer.

Figure A.6

The automatic driver update dialog box.

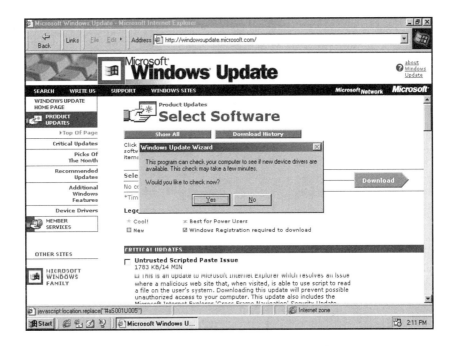

Figure A.7

The Update Wizard for device drivers appears, automating the installation process.

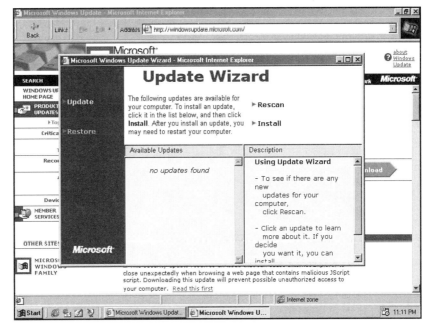

If you use your computer once a day or more, make a habit of checking out the update site at least once every six weeks. Windows 98 will continue to be updated and revised as time goes by, so it only makes sense to reap the benefits of having

Windows 98 CD-ROM Listing

an automatic tool to keep your system up to date. Microsoft might in the future provide a way to have updates optionally provided without user intervention, but until that time, keep checking the site.

Appendix B

Easter Eggs

by Dave Adams Saltz

The lure of the unknown. The search for treasure. The joy of finding what someone thought was hidden very well. We have all these feelings beginning in childhood, yet we sometimes forget how fun it is to find something that we have only a vague knowledge of. And computers are chock-full of hidden goodies that don't really do a lot for your productivity, but sure are a lot of fun to find. Easter eggs are all around your PC in the software and in the hardware, yet you usually never see them. The fun part is finding them! In this appendix, you'll see what Easter eggs are and how to find the ones secreted in Windows 98 and Plus! 98. You'll also learn a few more tidbits about these hidden treasures as you wrap up your multimedia extravaganza.

What Are Easter Eggs?

Easter eggs are hidden applets or pieces of programming code that software developers put into their programs (or even hardware!) as a fun diversion, a place to give credit to themselves, or even for copyright protection. Some Easter eggs even include small games you can play.

The name *Easter egg* comes from the fact that you've got to hunt around in strange places to find them.

Many of today's programs have hidden Easter eggs and programmers have been putting them in for more than a few years. Most eggs aren't really that dazzling, but the fun is in finding them—and that's why people seem to love them so much.

Easter eggs aren't limited to software either. For instance, there is a Hewlett-Packard flatbed scanner that actually has an Easter egg built into it that will play Beethoven's "Ode to Joy"!

> **TIP** To hear your HP ScanJet 5PSE flatbed scanner play you some Beethoven, the steps are simple. First, set the SCSI setting knob in the back of the scanner to 0. Turn the scanner off. Then as you hold in the green scan button on the front of the scanner, turn the power back on. Keep holding the green button until the song starts playing. Then let go and enjoy the serenade. Of course, don't forget to return the SCSI setting knob back to its original setting before putting your scanner back to its intended use.

Some companies even put in hidden Easter eggs to protect their copyright on the software. If anyone else ever claims to have built the program, the company can walk over, fire up the Easter egg, and prove that the claim is bogus.

The Windows 98 Easter Egg

A few people during the Windows 98 beta test tried in vain to find the egg that they only assumed would be there. After all, Easter eggs are never officially announced by any company, but rather leak out from testers, or from internal employees. Alas, the egg was finally revealed, only to prove so hidden that almost no one of sound mind would ever have found it on their own.

Here are the steps to reveal the Windows 98 Easter egg:

1. Double-click the clock in the System Tray. This opens the Date/Time Properties Window.

2. Choose the Time Zone tab to display a map of the world.

3. Hold down the Ctrl key, point to Memphis, Egypt with your mouse, and click and hold your left mouse button.

> **NOTE** When pointing and dragging to Memphis, Egypt, Memphis, Tennessee, and Redmond, Washington, you only need to be in the general vicinity on the map. If you're close enough to the area of these cities, the Easter egg will trigger. If it doesn't, try again.

4. With the Ctrl key still held in and the left mouse button still depressed, drag the cursor from Memphis, Egypt to Memphis, Tennessee (USA). Let go of the mouse button when you're over Memphis, Tennessee.

5. While still holding in the Ctrl key, click the left mouse button again and drag from Memphis, Tennessee to Redmond, Washington (USA).

6. Release the mouse button and watch the show.

If the egg didn't trigger for you, try it again. Your aim over the three cities doesn't have to be perfect, but it does have to be close.

> **NOTE** Where's the picture?
>
> You might be wondering why I haven't included screen images showing the various Easter eggs I mention. The easy answer is I didn't want to ruin the surprise! Don't worry—if you've found the Easter egg, you'll know it without having to refer to a figure in this book.

> **TIP** While you're dragging from city to city, you will see no indication that you're actually dragging anything. This is part of what makes this egg tough to crack. But after you do it once, it will seem much easier next time.

Easter Eggs

> **NOTE** In case you were wondering the significance of the two Memphis cities in the Windows 98 Easter egg, it's because, before Windows 98 was officially named Windows 98. it was known by its code-name, *Memphis*. And of course, the city of Redmond is home to the world headquarters of Microsoft Corporation, the place where Windows 98 was born.

The Plus! 98 Easter Egg

If you've installed the Microsoft Plus! 98 companion CD-ROM for Windows 98, you'll also be able to see a small Easter egg, listing the names of all the folks who worked on the Plus! 98 product.

To reveal the Plus! 98 Easter egg

1. Open the Deluxe CD Player. The egg is hidden in this program. If you don't have it installed, you won't be able to view this Easter egg.

2. Click the Options button on the Deluxe CD Player and select Preferences from the resulting menu.

3. Click the Playlists tab.

4. It's a good idea to put a music CD in the CD-ROM drive at this point so that you can activate the Edit Playlist button.

5. Click one time on either the CD's title or any song in the CD's playlist. This should activate the Edit Playlist button.

6. Click the Edit Playlist button.

7. In the Artist field, type `Microsoft Plus! 98 Product Team` exactly as you see it here.

8. In the Title: field, type `Credits`.

9. Hold in your Ctrl key and click Cancel on this window.

10. There should be a new item in the list of albums, titled "Credits [Microsoft Plus! 98 Product Team]". You can expand this item out to view all the people who worked on Microsoft Plus! 98.

Easter Egg Wrap-Up

There are dozens of different Easter eggs out there, some more entertaining than others. One Microsoft Office product has a rudimentary pinball game in it as an egg, whereas Excel 97 has a very elementary three-dimensional flight simulator—if you can even call it that—embedded as its egg.

I won't tell you all the Easter egg secrets here, because looking for them is most of the fun! Some are really easy to find and others you probably wouldn't find if you were looking with a fine-toothed comb. If you ever get really desperate, try searching on the World Wide Web for "Easter eggs." You'll likely find some that you never would have guessed were there. To get started, try either `http://www.eeggs.com` or `http://www.htsoft.com/easter`, because both are good archives of many different eggs in many different places.

Easter Eggs

Index

C

J

N

O

P

T

W

X -Y -Z

Other Related Titles

Special Edition Using the Internet
By Jerry Honeycutt
0-7897-1403-5
$39.99 USA/
$57.95 CAN

The Big Basics Web Directory
By Mark Cierzniak, Jim Minatel, Jacquie Eley and Henly Wolin
0-7897-1422-1
$14.99 USA/$21.95 CAN

Dan Gookin Teaches Windows 98
By Dan Gookin
0-7897-1688-7
$24.99 USA/$35.95 CAN

Optimizing Windows Performance
By Mark Vanname
0-7897-1752-2
$39.99 USA/$57.95 CAN

Special Edition Using Windows 98
By Ed Bott and Ron Person
0-7897-1488-4
$39.99 USA/$56.95 CAN

Using Microsoft Windows 98
By Kathy Ivens
0-7897-1594-5
$29.99 USA/$42.95 CAN

Windows 98 6-in-1
By Jane Calabria
0-7897-1486-8
$29.99 USA/$42.95 CAN

Windows 98 from A to Z
By Keith Powell
0-7897-1625-9
$16.99 USA/$24.95 CAN

Windows 98 User Manual
By Jim Boyce
0-7897-1657-7
$19.99 USA/$28.95 CAN

Peter Coffee Teaches PCs
By Peter Coffee
0-7897-1703-4
$24.99 USA/$35.95 CAN

Using PCs
By Shelly O'Hara et al
0-7897-1454-X
$19.99 USA/$28.95 CAN

Upgrading PCs Illustrated
By Jim Boyce
0-7897-0986-4
$34.99 USA/$49.95 CAN

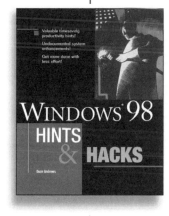

Windows 98 Hints & Hacks
By Dean Andrews
0-7897-1750-6
$19.99 USA/
$28.95 CAN

Upgrading and Repairing PCs 10th Anniversary Edition
By Scott Mueller
0-7897-1636-4
$54.99 USA/
$78.95 CAN

www.quecorp.com

All prices are subject to change.